CASSELL STUDIES IN PASTORAL CARE AND PERSONAL
AND SOCIAL EDUCATION

EDUCATION, SPIRITUALITY AND THE WHOLE CHILD

CASSELL STUDIES IN PASTORAL CARE AND PERSONAL
AND SOCIAL EDUCATION

EDUCATION, SPIRITUALITY AND THE WHOLE CHILD

Edited by
Ron Best

CASSELL

Cassell
Wellington House 215 Park Avenue South
125 Strand New York
London WC2R 0BB NY 10003

First published in 1996

British Library Cataloguing-in-Publication Data
A catalogue record for this book is available from the British Library.

Library of Congress Cataloging-in-Publication Data
Education, spirituality, and the whole child / edited by Ron Best.
   ' p.   cm. — (Cassell studies in pastoral care and personal and social education)
     Includes bibliographical references and index.
     ISBN 0-304-33533-9.—ISBN 0-304-33534-7 (pbk.)
     1. Religious education of children.   2. Children—Great Britain—
  Religious life.   3. Counselling in elementary education—Great Britain.
     I. Best, Ron, 1945– .   II. Series.
     BL42.5.G7E38   1995
     291.7—dc20   95-19814
                                             CIP

ISBN 0-304-33533-9 (hardback)
   0-304-33534-7 (paperback)

Acknowledgements
The editor and publisher wish to thank the following for permission to reprint copyright material. Although every effort has been made to contact the owners of the copyright material reproduced in this book, it has not been possible to trace all of them. If such owners contact the publisher, the appropriate acknowledgements will appear in any future editions.

Wendy Cope, lines from 'New Season', from *Serious Concerns*, published by Faber and Faber, 1992. Reprinted by permission of the publisher.

'maggie and milly and molly and may' is reprinted from *Complete Poems 1904–1962*, by e.e. cummings, edited by George J. Firmage, by permission of W. W. Norton & Company Ltd. © 1956, 1984, 1991 by the Trustees for the E. E. Cummings Trust.

T. S. Eliot, lines from 'Little Gidding', from *Collected Poems 1909–1962*, published by Faber and Faber, 1963. Reprinted by permission of the publisher.

Alistair Reid, lines from 'Growing, Flying, Happening' from *Weathering*, published by Dutton, New York, 1978.

R. S. Thomas, lines from 'One Day', from *Mass for Hard Times*, published by Bloodaxe Books, 1992. Reprinted by permission of the publisher.

R. S. Thomas, lines from 'The Casualty', from *Later Poems 1972–1982*, published by Macmillan General Books. Reprinted by permission of the publisher.

Typeset by Action Typesetting Limited, Gloucester
Printed and bound in Great Britain by Biddles Ltd, Guildford and King's Lynn

Contents

Series Editor's Foreword

Given what has happened to educational policy over the last three or four years, it would be difficult not to describe the publication of any book concerned with the moral and spiritual dimensions of education as timely. In the case of a book as broad in coverage and strong in the quality of thought, analysis and ideas as this one, it is doubly timely.

Although teachers have always recognized their importance (at a subconscious level at least), the sudden prominence given by the National Curriculum Council and OFSTED to the moral and spiritual aspects of education came as a somewhat unnerving surprise to many teachers and some schools. Many are still struggling to respond in coherent and meaningful ways. They have not been helped by the somewhat contradictory discussion paper produced by the National Curriculum Council in 1993, which never quite reconciled the self-created tension between the development of a personal morality and the promotion of over-simplistic moral absolutes. It remains unclear quite how OFSTED will inspect an area so fraught with peril as to lead the authors of the paper cited above to give this warning:

> Schools are strongly advised not to attempt to assess pupils' spiritual and moral development. Such an activity could be regarded as intrusive and any judgements made highly subjective. (National Curriculum Council, *Spiritual and Moral Development: A Discussion Paper.* London, 1993)

There is of course a danger that the combination at a policy level of stress on the importance of moral and spiritual education and lack of clear guidance about how it is to be achieved will encourage some knee-jerk reactions. For those responding in this way this book will be of little value, for it does not offer any easy tips. What it may well do, however, is to act as an antidote to such reactions by offering a basis for action informed by considered reflection. So far, little of specific relevance to this aspect of the curriculum has been published since the advent of the National Curriculum. For those who see the new emphasis on moral and spiritual development in a positive way this book has much to offer. In the first place it provides both a wide resource from which ideas and strategies can be developed. It also offers a number of conceptual maps and specific applications which demonstrate just how broad an area is involved in the full understanding of the moral and spiritual. Of particular importance is the way spiritual and moral development are treated as part of an essentially holistic view of education, arguing that it should be seen as integral to the development of the whole person. It is not a 'bolt-on' extra offering marginal benefits in terms of pupil experience.

The area with which this book is concerned, and which it deals with in such an informative and stimulating way, is of fundamental importance to education and indeed to all sentient human beings. In this regard its focus is very different from those of many of the current policy imperatives, which, if the experience of the last few years is anything to go by, stand a good chance of changing rapidly. Unlike the more transient of educational fashions, the feelings of Hardy's Gabriel Oak on the starlit hilltop in the nineteenth century (see p.31) and of Derek Webster as he viewed a thousand rainbow-hung spiders' webs in the twentieth (see p.245) are a facet of human experience which is unchanging.

Peter Lang

Acknowledgements

I would like to record my thanks to the following members of staff at Roehampton Institute, London:

David Rose and Elaine McCreery for their collaboration and teamwork in planning the conference from which this book originates, and for their helpful comments on drafts of the Introduction and Conclusion.

Carol Jollie, Pauline Lewis and the CEDARR team for the organization of the conference.

Penny Pleece for her participation in the planning and organization of the conference, and for assisting me in many ways throughout the editing of this book. Her patience, skill and personal support were invaluable.

Thanks are also due to David Lambourn for commenting on the drafts for the Introduction and Conclusion. The faults remain mine, of course.

Finally, my thanks to Joan Bagnall for cheerfully preparing the index, and to all the contributors who kept to the deadlines and responded so positively to my editorial suggestions.

Ron Best
January 1996

Notes on Contributors

Gavin Baldwin is a senior lecturer in the School of Education at Middlesex University, with specific responsibility for history. He teaches on primary education courses at undergraduate and postgraduate level. His research interests include the relationship between the historical environment, identity, morality, spirituality and education. He is currently investigating these issues in a museum context.

Marisa Crawford teaches at Our Lady of the Sacred Heart College, Kensington, Sydney, Australia. She has worked as a consultant in religious education and personal development and has conducted in-service programmes throughout Australia and New Zealand, and in Canada, the United States, Hong Kong and the Pacific Islands. With Graham Rossiter, she has co-authored teacher and student texts in religious education, including *Missionaries to a Teenage Culture: Religious Education in a Time of Rapid Change*.

Clive Erricker is a principal lecturer and Head of the School of Religion and Theology at the Chichester Institute of Higher Education. He has published a number of books and articles in the fields of religious studies and religious education. He is a former secretary of the Shap Working Party on World Religions in Education and editor of its journal. He is co-director of the Children and Worldviews Project.

Jane Erricker is a lecturer in Science Education at King Alfred's College, Winchester. She is a researcher with the Children and Worldviews Project and has a particular interest in science and religion. She has published articles on children's spirituality with the Project team and co-authored a book on Buddhist festivals for key stage 2 children.

Peter Gilliat is a history and theology graduate, and currently works as an independent school inspector and an Open University tutor. Until 1993 he was senior inspector for the south-east division of Hampshire, and from 1975 to 1986 humanities adviser for Avon.

David G. Kibble is a deputy headteacher at Huntington School in York. A graduate in theology, he has written extensively in journals on theological, educational and management issues. A naval reservist and former

Commanding Officer of HMS *Ceres* in Leeds, he has also written on defence issues, particularly on the Islamic background to problems in the Middle East and on the ethics of nuclear deterrence.

Jean-Pierre Kirkland is an OFSTED Inspector for primary, secondary and special schools, having been an LEA adviser and former head of the PSE faculty in an inner city high school for many years. He is also a fully trained and qualified counsellor, currently in private practice and serving on the Training and Trauma Care sub-committees of the British Association for Counselling. He is a stress management consultant, combining this with his private advisory and consultancy work with schools nationwide. He is a child protection trainer, and has written numerous articles on this, on stress, residential experiences and other educational issues. He is currently the chair of the Greater Manchester branch of the National Association for Special Educational Needs.

David Lambourn is a research assistant in the Institute of Education at the University of Warwick. Formerly a trainer in youth work and personal-social education, he is now Development Officer for NAPCE.

Brenda Lealman is based at Westhill College of Higher Education, Selly Oak, Birmingham. She is an OFSTED school inspector, a religious educator, and a well-travelled writer, teacher and poet. She has published widely and has a particular interest in the spiritual and moral dimensions of education. She co-directed a research project into spirituality and values.

Terence H. McLaughlin is University Lecturer in Education and Fellow of St Edmund's College, Cambridge. He specializes in Philosophy of Education and was previously a head of year and head of sixth form in two comprehensive schools. He has recently published *Values, Education and Responsibility* (with Elizabeth Pybus), commissioned by the Centre for Philosophy and Public Affairs at the University of St Andrews, and a collection of papers, *Education and the Market Place* (edited with David Bridges), published by the Falmer Press.

Elaine McCreery is a senior lecturer in the Faculty of Education at Roehampton Institute, London. Her main area of interest is primary religious education and she has published in the area of school worship and children's spiritual development.

Kevin Mott-Thornton is joint head of religious education at Mulberry School in Tower Hamlets. He is a research student in the philosophy of education at the University of London Institute of Education. His research into spiritual development and education is currently supported by the St Gabriel's Trust and has benefited from a financial award from the Philosophy of Education Society of Great Britain.

Mike Newby teaches at the School of Education, Kingston University. He is responsible for religious education and philosophy of education and has researched in both areas. He has published a number of journal articles and is at present engaged in an investigation of the place of fiction in personal and social development at the primary school stage.

Rebecca Nye is a research fellow in children's spirituality in the School of Education at Nottingham University. She has a background in developmental psychology research. In addition to articles about children's spiritual development, she has written on a variety of issues in contemporary child psychology including children's theory of mind and children's understanding of representation.

Roger Prentice is founder of the Holistic Education Institute. Anyone interested in holistic education can reach him by telephone at 01403–256790. His e-mail address is 100044.2261@compuserve. com.

Alex Rodger is Development Director for Secondary Education at Northern College, Aberdeen and Dundee, where he directs a Values Education Project and convenes the College's Religious and Moral Education Unit. His current activities include research, lecturing and publication on human spirituality in education and codes of professional conduct for teachers. He is also active in consultancy work with schools seeking to clarify their values and express them in the life of the school community and through the curriculum.

David Rose is principal lecturer in the Faculty of Education at Roehampton Institute, London. He has worked for many years in religious education in the classroom as well as in higher education. He is actively involved in research on SACREs and has published books, articles and visual material on multi-faith RE. He is currently co-ordinating religious education at RIL.

Graham Rossiter is Associate Professor, Head of the Religious Education Department and Co-ordinator of the Moral and Religious Education Research Project at the Australian Catholic University, Sydney. He has specialized in in-service professional development in religious education with colleague Marisa Crawford, and has published mainly on the theory and practice of religious education.

Don Rowe is a director of the Citizenship Foundation. He has directed numerous citizenship curriculum projects for both primary and secondary schools. Within this field his particular interests are law-related education, moral education, human rights education and critical thinking. He edits the journal *Citizenship*.

Louise Rowling is Associate Dean in the Faculty of Education at the University of Sydney, New South Wales, Australia. She has recently completed her doctoral thesis entitled 'Loss and grief in the context of the health promoting school' at the University of Southampton. She is co-author of *Learning to Grieve: Life Skills for Coping with Losses* and currently president of the Australian Health Promoting Schools Association.

Bernard Stuart is head of the religious education department at St George's Roman Catholic High School, Salford, where he is also a member of the senior staff team and a teacher governor. He is currently undertaking research at the Liverpool Institute of Higher Education looking at a particular aspect of spirituality in the high school.

Jasper Ungoed-Thomas is an OFSTED Registered Inspector and educational consultant. He was previously an HMI. He is the author of various books and articles on moral, religious and personal and social education.

M. A. Warner is an independent OFSTED inspector who, as a head, was a primary school's representative on the ILEA Headteachers' Consultative Committee and chairman of the London Diocesan Headteachers' Council. She has also taught in a middle school and held head of department posts in two comprehensive schools and a secondary special school. Her research has been on children's interest in nature; the organization of a primary school; spelling, handwriting and word-processing skills in the first school phase; and provision for the spiritual life of young people throughout their school years. She has supervised students on teaching practice and mentored colleagues at various stages in their careers.

Derek Webster is Senior Lecturer in Educational Studies in the University of Hull and an Anglican priest in the diocese of Lincoln. His research interests are in religious education and Christian spirituality and he has published widely in both areas. His most recent books are *Bread for a Wilderness* (St Paul, 1995) and *Collective Worship in Schools* (Kenelm Press, 1995).

John White was head of the English department in a London school and is now an examiner in speech and drama for the Poetry Society and the Guildhall School of Music and Drama. He is involved in the work of multi-faith bodies concerned with moral and religious education and represents the Humanist tradition on the Religious Education Council and local SACREs. He is secretary of the British Humanist Association Education Committee.

Andrew Wright is Lecturer in Religious and Theological Education at King's College, London University. He has taught extensively in both secondary schools and higher education and has researched and published in the fields of religious and multi-cultural education.

For JB

Introduction

In 1972 I was teaching in a secondary modern school somewhere in the East of England. The school had a vertical system of houses. The pupils in each form consisted of children from the first to the fifth years drawn randomly from one of the houses. As it was a maintained day-school, the 'house' was, of course, no more than a convenient unit for pastoral and administrative purposes. There was no (physical) house and no one lived in. Inter-house competitions were, so far as I can recall, virtually non-existent and there were no visible grounds for the 'house spirit' to which one heard occasional reference. Indeed, there was no reason why the 30 or so children who made up my form should have anything in common beyond living in the same catchment area and attending the same school.

The headteacher, who was something of a 'progressive' for his time, decided to introduce a regular 20-minute form period at the beginning of each day, during which staff were expected to discuss particular topics of social or moral interest. In later years I was to become especially interested in pastoral care, and that part of it (the 'pastoral curriculum') which is most often associated with tutor time, and would now applaud his motives. But at the time I was aghast.

Along with several colleagues I protested vehemently. I hadn't been trained for this! How was I to discuss matters of morality and social responsibility with such a diverse group? How was I to make such a discussion relevant to youngsters of such different ages and levels of maturity? Where would I get information on each topic? Come to that, where was I to find suitable things to talk about in the first place?

The Head's response was simple: *he would ask the RE teacher to prepare a list of topics.*

Since then, things have moved on apace. Pastoral curricula, tutorial programmes and syllabuses in personal, social, moral and health education are features of most, if not all, secondary schools and have their counterparts (though more often taken for granted than explicit) in primary schools (Lang, 1988). Commercially-available programmes such as *Longmans' Tutorial Resources* (Watkins *et al.*, 1989) and *Skills for*

Adolescence (Quest International/TACADE, 1986) provide rich collections of materials and suggestions for their use with tutor groups, in PSE periods or across the curriculum. Books by Blackburn (1978), Adams (1989), Marland (1989) and Griffiths and Sherman (1991) provide a range of theoretical justifications and practical prescriptions for the role of the tutor. Significant issues such as preparation for life in a multi-cultural society, equal opportunities, problem-solving and personal and social skills are included in the cross-curricular dimensions, skills and themes which are required of schools to complement the more subject-based programmes of study of the National Curriculum. (Their status in the revised orders published in January 1995 is less clear, but let that pass.)

Moreover, teachers' awareness of their contribution to personal and social development has been heightened by the activities of such bodies as the National Association for Pastoral Care in Education (NAPCE), by options or specialist courses within in-service degree and diploma programmes offered by universities and colleges of higher education, and in school-based staff-development days. I suspect there are still teachers who are as ill at ease in discussing the dangers of glue-sniffing and unsafe sex with their forms as I was in 'discussing' equivalent topics twenty-odd years ago, but I hope they are rather fewer in number now than they were then.

Not everything has changed, however. In some respects we seem to be as unclear and ill-prepared for this aspect of our roles as ever.

When my headteacher turned to the RE department as the obvious source for a list of issues of personal, social and moral import, he was (I suspect) employing a simple syllogism:

> Issues of personal, social and moral concern are about 'right' and 'wrong';
>
> 'The Church' teaches us what is right and wrong;
>
> Religious Education is about 'the Church';

therefore:

> The RE teacher is the best person to draw up a list of discussion topics for form periods!

In the days where the United Kingdom might reasonably have claimed to be a Christian country, morally led by an established Church, and its faith defended by the monarch, there might have been some truth in this. In the liberal and multi-cultural society of the 1960s and early 1970s it was an anachronism. In the post-modern 1990s, when the Prince of Wales lets it be known that, as king, he will seek to be 'defender of faiths', and when the clergy (at all levels) seem less agreed about what is 'right' and 'wrong' as each day passes, such an equation has no substance. In any case, it is (as it always was) a massive *non sequitur.*

Yet something very like this is being said today, and by people of influence. A good many politicians and a good many newspapers are on record as expecting schools to contribute to raising what are seen as 'the moral standards' of the country. It is part of the 'discourse of derision' (Ball,

1990) directed at the educational establishment, that educationalists are failing in their social duty if they do not promote schooling as a force for conformity to established values and behaviours. In all this, religion is seen to be significant.

Recent calls by the Government of the day – including the immediate past Secretary of State for Education (Patten, 1992) – for due weight to be given to moral and spiritual development in our schools have resounded through staffrooms up and down the country. Ensuing discussions are overshadowed by the fact that, from 1944 to 1988, RE was the *only* curriculum subject required by law to be taught in the maintained sector, and further complicated by concern over the feasibility and appropriateness of acts of collective worship. Many schools fudge the issue or ignore it altogether. In the political arena, a good deal of the discussion seems not even to distinguish between RE lessons and assemblies!

The fact that 'moral and spiritual development' will be one criterion by which the Office for Standards in Education (OFSTED) will judge schools has led to calls for clarification of precisely what 'moral and spiritual development' might mean. Indications are that OFSTED itself is not at all clear, and it seems that this is not a dimension of educational quality which its members relish inspecting.

It would appear that the educational policy-makers are committing schools to the delivery of something which has as yet to be defined in any meaningful way, and which crudely conflates the moral and the spiritual. Here, too, there seems to be a false syllogism:

Religion is about morality;

Religion is about spirituality;

therefore:

Moral and spiritual development must be inseparable.

Whether or not morality is entailed in spirituality – or vice versa for that matter – is an important issue, as is the way morality and spirituality might be developed through the curriculum. Neither question seems to have received much examination by those most powerfully placed to influence what schools do and don't teach. At its worst, the answers derive from dogma rather than rational argument.

Teachers and others committed to education deserve better guidance than this. Yet within the teaching profession there are plenty of instances of similar thinking, of propositions and proclamations which have dogmatic or rhetorical force but are rarely unpacked and examined.

That 'we should be committed to the education of the whole child' is one such proposition. The value of such an education is impossible to dispute. Indeed, if education is the intentional promotion of the development of the individual as an entity, a *partial* development must be less than entirely satisfactory. But unless we can identify the parts which make up the 'whole' that is the child (or the child-as-whole-person), this doesn't get us very far. We shall remain ill-placed to judge the degree to which our educational efforts have contributed to the development of the 'whole' rather than of those 'parts' (principally subject knowledge and subject-specific skills) which are amenable to easy measurement.

With this in mind, the literature of pastoral care and personal-social education records a number of attempts to define the *person* and the *self* as central to the project. Thus, for example, Richard Pring identifies the characteristics of persons as follows:

> First, one characteristic of being a person is the capacity to think, to reflect, to make sense of one's experience, to engage critically with the received values, beliefs and assumptions that one is confronted with – the development, in other words, of the *powers of the mind* ....
>
> A second characteristic of being a person is the capacity to recognise *others* as persons – as centres of consciousness and reason like oneself ....
>
> Third, it is characteristic of being a person that one acts *intentionally*, deliberately, and thus can be held responsible for what one does ...
>
> Finally, what is distinctive of personhood is the consciousness not only of others as persons but of *oneself* – a sense of one's own unity as a person, one's own value and dignity, one's own capacity to think through a problem, to persevere when things get tough, to establish a platform of values and beliefs whereby one can exercise some control over one's own destiny.
>
> (1988, pp. 43–4)

The *cognitive* and *moral* dimensions of personhood are clear enough in this, but there is no reference to the *spiritual*.

Allied to the concept of the person is the concept of 'self'. This concept figures prominently in much that is said and written about pastoral care and PSE: self-esteem, self-discipline, self-awareness, self-evaluation, self-determination and the like are to be found in statements of the aims and objectives of pastoral curricula, and play a major part in the principles and practice of educational counselling. In 1984 one philosopher argued that such concepts have little value unless pastoral care has a clearly worked-out concept of the 'self' (Hibberd, 1984). Over a decade later, it remains doubtful whether it does.

In a paper written in 1985, Chris Watkins of the University of London Institute of Education found the idea of multiple 'selves' helpful in trying to identify the objectives of personal and social education. He argues that we cannot identify such objectives unless we know what 'selves' are being developed. Picking up ideas from W. D. Wall and Douglas Hamblin, Watkins identifies the following selves: bodily self; social self; sexual self; vocational self; moral–political self; self as a learner; and self in the organization (school/college, etc). He suggests that these might form a checklist for those designing a pastoral curriculum, so that they can ask themselves whether they have planned and provided learning experiences which promote the development of each of these selves. If not, he concludes, talk of promoting the development of the *whole* child is rhetoric (Watkins, 1985).

This is a useful contribution to the discussion, but here, too, there is no mention of the *spiritual*.

I am not arguing for a concept of the spiritual as a 'self', separate from the other 'selves' or dimensions of self which Watkins lists, nor that Pring's concept of the person is seriously deficient because he omits the spiritual from his list of characteristics. Rather, I am drawing attention to the fact that the question 'What does spiritual development mean?' has rarely been asked by those who have made the role of the teacher as carer, supporter and developer of persons central to their conception of the mission of the school.

It was against this background that a conference on the topic *Education, Spirituality and the Whole Child* was held in July 1994 at the Froebel Institute College in London. Eighty teachers, lecturers, researchers and others with an interest in this broad area attended. There were keynote presentations from Dr Terry McLaughlin of Cambridge University, Brenda Lealman of Westhill College in Birmingham, HMI David Trainor of OFSTED and John White of the British Humanist Association. Some thirty learned papers and practical workshops were presented by delegates, and there was much reflection and spirited debate.

The range of issues raised demonstrated the breadth of this important topic: What *is* 'spirituality'? What constitutes 'spiritual development'? What is the role of the curriculum in this? What do different faith perspectives have to say about the place of spirituality in personal-social education and in the role of the school as a whole? Can/should spiritual development be integral to Religious Education? What are the dangers if it is not located within a liberal tradition? What are the dangers if it *is*? How do children develop spiritual 'knowledge' and what images do they employ to make sense of 'spiritual' statements and 'spiritual' experience? What are the philosophical and psychological roots and justifications for talking about spiritual and moral education in the way that we do? Must the spiritual be 'religious', or is a fully secular spirituality conceivable? If the conventional school curriculum lacks a spiritual dimension, can it be genuinely educational? In what ways might education be more *holistically* conceived so that the spiritual is given its rightful place while avoiding the pitfalls of indoctrination?

All but two of the papers comprising this book were selected and developed from presentations to the conference. Of the exceptions, one (by David Lambourn) was written as a response to some of the papers presented at the conference, and another (by Derek Webster) was written in response to interest expressed in some of his previously published work. They seemed to me to add some important points to the conference debate so I decided to include them in the collection.

The book is in four sections. The first section, 'Visions and Perspectives', includes three of the four keynote presentations and provides broad-brush statements of the themes and concerns of the conference. The organization of the remainder of the book was not easy, since most papers explore concepts and develop models as well as reporting research and/or exploring the application of analyses of spiritual education in various contexts. The division into three sections – 'Concepts and Models', 'Cases and Contexts' and 'Developments and Applications' – is not entirely arbitrary, however, and the titles are a fair guide to the emphasis to be found in the papers within each section. Some of the papers are concerned with practical matters; others are entirely theoretical. They by no means provide ready answers to the questions which teachers are asking about moral and spiritual development, but they do provide a challenging basis for teachers and others concerned with education to begin to seek their own answers.

Nor is this book a handy guide to preparing for OFSTED inspection under this criterion! What it aims to be is a wide-ranging, critical and thought-provoking discussion of a crucially important and much neglected question: what is the relationship between education, spirituality and the development of the whole child? If it succeeds in this aim it will have made a major contribution to the theory of pastoral care and personal, social and moral education.

REFERENCES

Adams, S. (1989) *A Guide to Creative Tutoring.* London: Kogan Page.

Ball, S. (1990) *Politics and Policy Making in Education.* London: Routledge.

Blackburn, K. (1978) *The Tutor.* London: Heinemann.

Chitty, C. and Simon, B. (1993) *Education Answers Back: Critical Responses to Government Policy.* London: Lawrence and Wishart.

Griffiths, P. and Sherman, K. (1991) *The Form Tutor: New Approaches to Tutoring for the 1990s.* Oxford: Blackwell.

Hibberd, F. (1984) Does pastoral care need a theory of the self? *Pastoral Care in Education,* **2** (3), 174–81.

Lang, P. (ed.) (1988) *Thinking about ... PSE in the Primary School.* Oxford: Blackwell.

Marland, M. (1989) *The Tutor and the Tutor Group.* Harlow: Longman.

Patten, J. (1992) Don't sell pupils short. *The Tablet,* **65**, 10 October.

Pring, R. (1988) Personal and social education in the primary school. In P. Lang (ed.), *Thinking about ... PSE in the Primary School.* Oxford: Blackwell.

Quest International/TACADE (1986) *Skills for Adolescence.* London: Teachers' Advisory Council on Alcohol and Drug Education.

Watkins, C. (1985) Does pastoral care = PSE? *Pastoral Care in Education,* **3**(3), 179–83.

Watkins, C., Marsh, L., Dolezal, A., Leake, A. and Leake, A. (1989) *Longman Tutorial Resources* (six volumes). Harlow: Longman.

Part 1
Visions and Perspectives

CHAPTER 1

Education of the whole child?

Terence H. McLaughlin

The claim that we should 'educate the whole child' is familiar to us from many educational contexts and debates. In common with claims such as 'we should teach children and not subjects' and 'process is more important than content', it sounds intuitively plausible and appealing. Claims of these kinds are often brandished as rhetorical slogans in educational discussion and debate, where they can serve several functions. The important truths the slogans are alleged to contain can make a seemingly decisive contribution to a developing argument, and can sometimes bring discussion to an end by appearing to transcend or resolve matters of dispute. However, since the meaning, let alone the truth, of such slogans is unclear they are better seen as contributing suggestively rather than decisively to educational argument and as opening up educational discussion rather than closing it down.

What is meant by the claim that we should 'educate the whole child' and in what sense is it true? In this essay I shall suggest that, while the claim expresses a number of significant educational truths, it is not unproblematic. In particular, I shall claim that there are important respects in which we should *not* educate 'the whole child'. This conclusion has important implications for education in relation to 'spirituality' and 'spiritual development', and should lead us to approach these matters with caution.

EDUCATION AND WHOLENESS

A critical analysis of the term 'education of the whole child' can usefully begin with attention to what is meant by 'whole' in this context. It is capable of at least two interpretations, which I shall refer to as the 'comprehensiveness' and the 'integration' interpretations respectively.

Wholeness as comprehensiveness
On this first interpretation, 'whole' is opposed to 'narrow' or 'restricted' and can be read as an appeal for education to focus upon a wide range of aspects of the child, and not merely (say) intellectual development or

academic formation. It calls for education to have 'broad', 'rounded' or 'balanced' influence.

In evaluating such claims it is important at the outset to call into question a tendency to see the different 'aspects of the child' as sharply distinct from each other, as in the drawing of crude contrasts between the 'intellectual' and the 'emotional' and between the 'cognitive' and the 'affective'. Such distinctions, including the well-established tripartite categorization of domains of the person into the 'cognitive', 'affective' and 'conative', are untenable in any very rigorous form, and require more nuanced re-statement. All the dimensions of a person are logically as well as psychologically related to each other. A person's beliefs, for example, are logically tied in complex ways to (*inter alia*) his or her attitudes, emotions, virtues and motivations. One way of putting this point is to draw attention to the 'cognitive core' of all aspects of mind and of all human capacities. Emotions, for example, are partly constituted by forms of cognition in which situations are seen under various aspects. To feel fear is to see a situation as threatening, to feel guilt is to see it as involving undischarged obligations and responsibilities, and so on. A proper understanding of a person, therefore, requires a 'holistic' perspective in at least the sense that involves a rejection of the sorts of the sharp distinctions and dichotomies which have been mentioned.

One implication which might be thought to follow from this point is that education is therefore inherently holistic in its effects. To introduce a child to a subject of study is to open up not only possibilities for cognitive or intellectual development but also for the development of new attitudes, emotions, feelings and motivations. Any educational influence, therefore, can transform the whole person. The qualification 'can' is important here, however, because whilst 'holistic' implications are implicit within education, they do not necessarily follow and, if desired, need to be deliberately aimed at. So although there is some substance in the descriptive claim that education *is* as a matter of fact, of the whole child, the prescriptive claim that education *should* be of this kind is not redundant.

What is involved in the claim that education *should* aim at 'wholeness' in the 'comprehensiveness' sense? Whilst we might not accept the early claim of R. S. Peters that 'education is of the whole man' expresses (although imprecisely) a 'conceptual truth' about education (Peters, 1966, p. 32), an aversion to narrowness and restrictedness in educational aims and processes is widely felt. Such narrowness or restrictedness can take many forms, relating to the goals of education, its subject matter and its methods. Educational goals, for example, can be limited to the achievement of basic literacy and numeracy, to narrowly-conceived vocational preparation or to specialized academic training. The 'subject matter' of education may be conceived in a way which excludes or underemphasizes significant elements of knowledge and understanding or kinds of development, and educational methods may concentrate on (say) memorization to the exclusion of critical questioning and other strategies more likely to bring about genuine engagement and understanding.

It is easier to criticize such narrow or restricted conceptions of educational aims and processes than to provide a positive account of an appropriately broad conception. Notions such as 'breadth' and 'balance' in themselves are of limited help here since they are uninformative about the nature and justification of the evaluative judgements they imply (Dearden, 1984, chapter 5). The elements of personhood and learning in relation to which 'breadth' and 'balance' are to be sought, and the criteria which tell us what constitutes 'breadth' and 'balance' all need to be specified and justified. This cannot be done satisfactorily without giving attention to fundamental educational aims, values and purposes.

Without entering in detail into these matters, it is possible to identify a central issue which arises in relation to the claim that education is of persons (Langford, 1985, chapter 7) and that it should exert wide-ranging or 'holistic' influence upon them (on this, see, for example, Bonnett, 1994). Underlying this general claim is the question 'What sort of person does education seek to develop?' The complexity of the judgements of value involved in this question comes readily into focus. In part, this complexity is inherent in questions of this kind, but it is enhanced by the 'value diversity' and 'pluralism' characteristic of liberal democratic societies, which will be discussed in more detail later. In our lack of agreement about what constitutes human good or perfection we are suspicious of claims to wide-ranging educational influence upon the child. This central issue concerning the notion of 'education of the whole child' – the value basis on which we can construct a vision of 'holistic' educational influence – comes still further into focus in relation to the second interpretation of the term.

Wholeness as integration

On this second interpretation, 'whole' is opposed to 'fragmented' and can be read as an appeal for education to ensure that the different aspects of the child be 'integrated' in some way. Education here seeks 'coherence' for the person.

Leaving aside the complex philosophical difficulties which arise in relation to the notion of personal identity (on these see, for example, Parfit, 1984, Part 3), it can be plausibly argued that since the concept of a person is one of a 'complete existent' it brings with it the notion of 'wholeness' in the sense of 'unitariness' (Langford, 1979, pp. 68–70). What is involved in the 'unity' of a person is complex. One aspect of it is the notion of a person having, or striving towards, a unity of 'purpose and outlook' (Langford, 1979, p. 70) in which, through the governing of conflicts by a stable system of priorities, the person's life becomes, or at least aims towards, a harmony and a wholeness in the 'integration' sense. Mary Midgley claims that this desire to integrate is related to some of our most basic wishes, capacities and needs. She writes: 'People have a natural wish and capacity to integrate themselves, a natural horror of being totally fragmented, which makes possible a constant series of bargains and sacrifices to shape their lives' (Midgley, 1980, p. 190). A continuing preoccupation with the significance of 'wholeness' in the 'integratedness' sense is a feature of Midgley's latest book *The Ethical Primate* (1994).

The notion of a person 'integrating' his or her life in this way gives rise in an even sharper way to the value questions mentioned in the last section. What is the nature of the 'coherence' which is aimed at? 'Coherence' in itself merely suggests the notion of elements fitting together according to some principle. But what the principle, or principles, in question should be remains to be settled (Dearden, 1984, chapter 5). Some of the principles which persons might invoke in relation to their achievement of 'coherence' are 'architectonic' in the sense that they relate to the fundamental structuring elements of a person's overall view of life. Examples of such 'architectonic' principles are those relating to religious belief or unbelief. A position on these matters can shape in a basic way individuals' views of themselves and their lives, and provide central principles for 'integration'. Whilst value questions arise in relation to all aspects of 'integration', 'architectonic' principles illustrate sharply the concerns expressed at the end of the last section about the evaluative basis on which we can approach such matters educationally. One of the features of liberal democratic societies, and their associated cultural and philosophical developments, is absence of agreement about 'thick' or substantial views of human good. We lack a shared view of 'the meaning of life' and, therefore, about what 'architectonic' principles are appropriate for the achievement by persons of 'integration' and 'coherence'. Indeed, we lack a shared conception of what, in detail, 'integration' and 'coherence' mean in relation to the human person. What value-basis can education therefore appeal to in relation to these matters, and to 'education of the whole child' generally?

The significance of these questions can be illustrated by reference to the work of an educationalist particularly noted for his preoccupation with the notion of 'wholeness', Friedrich Froebel.

FROEBEL AND EDUCATION OF THE WHOLE CHILD

The educational thought of Friedrich Froebel is particularly interesting for our purposes, because he placed great emphasis not only on 'wholeness' in the aims and methods of education but also on the need for 'the spiritual' to be cultivated in children. Froebel is not much studied these days, and there has been a long-standing tendency to abstract his methodological principles from the wider framework of his thought, together with its religious and metaphysical assumptions. Close attention to Froebel's overall view does, however, illustrate some of the evaluative concerns expressed earlier in relation to the notion of 'holistic' educational influence.

Froebel placed great emphasis on 'unity' in his educational theory, differing in this respect from Pestalozzi (see Bantock, 1984, pp. 80–90). At the heart of Froebel's theory was a teleological (or purpose-directed) conception of the universe and of human beings, involving an 'inner law' binding all into a unity with God. Froebel writes:

> An eternal law pervades and governs all things. The basis of this all-controlling law is an all-pervading, living, self-conscious and therefore eternal Unity. This unity is God. God is the source of all things. Each thing exists only because the divine spirit lives in it and this divine spirit is its essence. The destiny of everything is to reveal its essence, that is, the divine spirit dwelling in it.
>
> (Quoted in Bantock, 1984, p. 81)

For Froebel, the 'wholeness' or 'unity' of the educational process is related to, and characterized in terms of, this particular metaphysical theory which, in its affirmation of the 'wholeness' of reality, has affinities to idealism. (On idealism and its educational significance see Gordon and White, 1979.)

The centrality to Froebel's thought of religious concepts and claims is clear, as is the importance of specifically religious teaching and formation to his theories of educational practice (Hamilton, 1952). Froebel writes: 'By education ... the divine essence of man should be unfolded, brought out, lifted into consciousness, and man himself raised into free, conscious obedience to the divine principle that lives in him, and to a free representation of this principle in his life' (Froebel, 1888, pp. 4–5. See also chapters V and VI, pp. 237–48.) Froebel's account of educational 'wholeness' and 'unity', as incorporated, for example, into the Froebellian 'gifts', is inseparable from his religious views. The aim of instruction, claims Froebel, is 'to bring the scholar to insight into the unity of all things, into the fact that all things have their being and life in God, so that in due time he may be able to act and live in accordance with this insight' (p. 128). Froebel's overall framework of thought also needs to be brought to bear if we are to grasp his distinctive interpretation of the claim that we should attend to the 'universal cultivation of the spiritual' in our children (p. 328). For Froebel, the religious sentiment manifests the unity of all things.

Although Froebel expresses his overall metaphysical theory in an imprecise and somewhat 'mystical' way, its religious elements are sufficiently prominent to give rise to serious doubts about the acceptability of the theory as a basis for 'holistic' educational influence in the common schools of a liberal democratic society. This is because, in such societies, we are confronted by the wide-ranging and deep-seated disagreement about values which was alluded to earlier. Froebel's religious assumptions are now seen as highly controversial. Referring to the key concept in his overall theory, Froebel claims: 'a quietly observant human mind, a thoughtful, clear human intellect, has never failed, and will never fail, to recognize this Unity' (1888, p. 1). Froebel is surely wrong about this, at least as far as his own interpretation of 'unity' is concerned, and his view is now likely to be seen as only one of a number of rival overall views of life as a whole which require critical understanding and assessment. To base 'holistic' educational influence on Froebel's theory in its fullness is to invite accusations of metaphysical, if not religious, indoctrination.

VALUES, PLURALISM AND HOLISTIC EDUCATIONAL INFLUENCE

The central issue which arises in respect to the notion of 'education of the whole child', whether in the 'comprehensiveness' or 'integration' sense, is therefore the difficulty of establishing, especially in the context of the pluralism of a liberal democratic society, an acceptable evaluative basis for 'holistic' educational influence (on this see, for example, Standish, 1995).

This is not to suggest that such societies are completely lacking in value agreement, or that education based on liberal democratic principles is without any value foundation. However, what is distinctive about the 'liberal democratic' approach to values, in its typical articulation in the philosophical theory of liberalism, is the self-conscious attention paid to the scope of influence and validity of particular value judgements. In this approach, the values which can be insisted upon for all are precisely seen as applying to part, not the whole, of life, and imply a principled forbearance of influence on the part of education.

In liberal democratic societies we are confronted by people holding many different, and often incompatible, views of life as a whole. Catholics, Jews and Muslims live alongside atheists and agnostics. Their differing 'holistic perspectives', articulated by contrasting 'architectonic principles', give varying accounts of human nature and flourishing, and of what constitutes 'integration' in the shape of a whole human life. Education based on such 'holistic' views can specify in some detail the sort of person it seeks to produce. Examples of such 'holistic' educational influence include certain forms of religious schooling, which seek to form (say) Christian or Islamic persons in a substantial way. Froebel's educational recommendations, though more general, can be seen as similarly 'holistic'.

From a 'liberal democratic' philosophical perspective, however, there is no objectively conclusive way of determining which, if any, of these 'holistic' views of life – or 'thick' theories of the good – is correct. They are deeply, and perhaps permanently, controversial. The differences of belief and value involved are tenacious and fundamental. Therefore such 'thick' views cannot be permitted to impose their particular vision on all citizens in the public domain through the use of political power. For example, from the point of view of some 'thick' theories of the good, remarriage after divorce is morally unacceptable because, since marriage is morally indissoluble and divorce has only legal and not moral force, the couple in question are living in a state of permanent adultery. Such a view is significantly controversial in the sense that a number of different perspectives on these matters exist 'within the moral pale'. The view cannot, therefore, be imposed on all citizens through the civil law on divorce. On similar grounds, the education offered in the common schools of a liberal democratic society cannot be based on 'thick' theories of the good.

From a liberal democratic perspective, such 'thick' theories, and the patterns of life which they generate, are matters for individual and family assessment, judgement and response. Many such theories are reasonable and morally worthy, but lack the objective grounding to be imposed on all. They should, however, be seen as part of a range of options from which people might construct their lives. Whilst such 'thick' theories cannot form the basis of common schooling, they can underpin forms of distinctive schooling chosen by parents as part of the exercise of their moral rights over their children's upbringing and education (McLaughlin, 1994a).

In contrast to the diversity and pluralism associated with 'holistic' or 'thick' theories of the good, the liberal democratic perspective seeks to establish consensus and unanimity concerning basic or 'public' values. In virtue of their fundamentality or inescapability, such values are seen as binding on all persons. Frequently embodied in law and expressed in terms of rights, they include such matters as basic social morality and a range of fundamental democratic principles such as freedom of speech, justice and personal autonomy. The theory of the good underpinning such values is described in the philosophical theory of liberalism as 'thin' not because of the insubstantiality or unimportance of the values involved, but because of the attempt to articulate them in terms which all people of goodwill can accept regardless of the fuller theory of the good which they hold. 'Public' values do not presuppose some particular metaphysical theory of the self, or of the nature of human destiny. Atheists and Catholics differ profoundly on these wider matters, but can share common ground in condemning cruelty and supporting a democratic way of life, even if their overall frameworks of belief given them distinctive perspectives on them. Such 'public' values do not cover the whole of life, but only its 'political' aspects. They form an important part of the value foundation of common forms of education based on liberal democratic principles.

These principles generate a two-fold educational task for common schools which can be expressed roughly as follows. On the one hand, education must 'transmit' the basic or 'public' values, principles and procedures, and secure appropriate forms of respect for, and allegiance to, them. On these matters, the school seeks to achieve a strong, substantial influence on the beliefs of pupils and their wider development as persons. It is unhesitant, for example, in promoting the values of basic social morality and democratic 'civic virtue' more generally. On the side of values associated with 'thick' theories of the good, on the other hand, the school exercises a principled forbearance of influence. It seeks not to shape either the beliefs or the personal qualities of pupils in the light of such theories. Instead, the school encourages pupils to come to their own reflective decisions about the matters at stake, and promotes appropriate forms of understanding, open-mindedness and tolerance.

Much more needs to be said in relation to the articulation of this general perspective and the many problems associated with it (see McLaughlin, 1995a; 1995b). However, regardless of the various philosophical difficulties to which it gives rise, it is recognizable, at least in outline, as a widely-held view of the value basis of education in a liberal democratic society.

From this perspective, the respects in which we should not 'educate the whole child' come into focus. At least in common schools, no substantial 'holistic' view of life should be transmitted to pupils, nor should they be shaped 'as whole persons' in the light of any such theory. Rather, schools should open up views of this kind for critical assessment and exploration. Schools should therefore be suspicious of aiming at 'wholeness' for pupils in the 'integration' sense unless the character of the 'integration' is seen in terms of the pupils' own fashioning of the shape of their lives. With regard to 'wholeness' in the 'comprehensiveness' sense similar worries arise. A school might argue that it was merely exercising 'open' and non-indoctrinatory influence across a range of aspects of the child's life. One issue which such a claim needs to confront is the question of the rights of parents in relation to those of teachers. It is not clear that, without further argument, teachers have a right to exercise influence of whatever kind across all aspects of a child's life.

SPIRITUAL DEVELOPMENT AND EDUCATION OF THE WHOLE CHILD

In the light of the discussion above, it is clear why talk of promoting the 'spiritual development' of pupils in schools as part of the 'education of the whole child' is problematic.

Central to evaluating the issues here is clarity about what is meant by 'spiritual development'. General questions of value in recent educational debate and policy-making have often not been handled in a clear, systematic and sustained way. As is widely recognized, the structure and implementation of our recent educational reforms have not been governed by any clear and defensible overall vision, and questions of value were not squarely addressed at the outset. The reforms are widely regarded, even by those not wholly opposed to their general thrust, as pragmatic and piecemeal. A lack of clarity and critical attention to fundamental issues has also characterized the emergence of the area of 'spiritual development' and the other areas of development associated with it. The initiative is widely seen as a belated attempt to enrich the educational reforms with an explicit value dimension, in which the immensely complex issues at stake in the meaning, let alone inspection, of spiritual development were ignored or glossed over. The straightforward question, 'What is meant by "spiritual development"?' by itself fully reveals this complexity. In these circumstances, one can only have the greatest sympathy for OFSTED in its attempts to make sense of the area and to fulfil its obligations with respect to it. The extent and openness of the consultation process which OFSTED has engaged in has been refreshing, and its discussion paper issued in February 1994 (Office for Standards in Education, 1994) asks the right sorts of questions about the area, and provides a focus for philosophical debate (J. White, 1994).

It is important that the debate about spiritual development in schools be located within an overall view of educational aims and purposes: a 'vision' of the educational enterprise as a whole. Without this it will be hard to achieve the coherence sought for the area and for education itself (McLaughlin, 1994b). 'Spiritual development' also needs to be considered in close relationship to other areas of the work of the school, such as 'education for citizenship' (P. White, 1994).

The obscurity of what is meant by 'spiritual development' (see Hull, 1996) makes it difficult to assess in relation to the sorts of general principles outlined above. An interpretation of the term which insists upon a close connection with religious development (see, for example, Carr, 1995) gives rise to worries about undue influence arising from the presupposition of a 'thick' view of human good, as do views of educational influence on the matters at stake which are explicitly secular (see, for example, White, 1995). What seems necessary for compatibility with the values outlined earlier is a view of 'spiritual development' which is significantly 'open' in the sense that it leaves room for critical exploration of the relevant issues by pupils and does not presuppose any significantly controversial assumptions of the sort indicated. One major difficulty here concerns a specification of what could be meant by 'development' in relation to these matters.

The fact that 'spiritual development' is now part of the formal inspection criteria for schools makes it difficult to ignore these issues or to employ 'edu-babble' (imprecise and platitudinous rhetoric) in relation to them; two strategies commonly used in the past.

'Spiritual development' focuses attention in a strong way on the 'holistic' aspects of education. As we have seen, the notion that we should 'educate the whole child' is not as straightforward as it appears, and there are important senses in which, in the light of the values discussed earlier, we should not attempt this. However, one outcome of the debate about 'spiritual development' in schools may be to focus renewed critical attention upon these values themselves and the liberal democratic educational principles discussed in the last section.

One of the major lines of criticism in general of the philosophical theory of liberalism which has emerged in recent years from a broadly 'communitarian' direction is that its values, and the political community which it generates, lacks the substantiality needed to enable persons to achieve defensible and necessary forms of affiliation and commitment to a 'larger moral ecology' beyond their own individual, and indeed individualistic, concerns. Such a 'moral ecology' embodies a social ethos, a consensus on the common good and notions of loyalty and responsibility to the community as a whole as well as a framework of wider beliefs and values providing (at least to some extent) a culture of 'narrative coherence' as well as 'freedom' for lives. The liberal view, it is claimed, leads to individualism in its various forms, and a tendency for individual choice and self-definition to be based on arbitrary preference or self-interest, rather than a view of life which is more coherent and other-regarding. In addition, attention is drawn to the corrosive effects of private economic pursuits and consumerism on the notion of a caring public ethos, the negative effects of an undue separation of public and private realms and so on (on these matters see, for example, Mulhall and Swift, 1992).

These critiques, amounting to a call for the recovery of a more 'holistic' perspective, are also applicable to liberal educational principles. Is the attempt to confine the value basis of the common school to values which are in some sense not 'significantly controversial' counter-intuitive and damaging? Is the influence of the common school as a result undesirably thin? Does the attempt to exercise a principled forbearance of influence lead to a weakening of the power and coherence of the value influence of the school? Must not a greater substantiality – a 'holistic' vision of life and of society – be supplied to the common school and to education itself?

The wide-ranging debate needed for a proper evaluation of the claim that 'spiritual development' should be seen as part of the process of 'education of the whole child' in common schools raises questions which touch upon some of the central issues relating to the value basis of education in liberal democratic societies.

REFERENCES

Bantock, G. H. (1984) *Studies in the History of Educational Theory. Volume II. The Minds and the Masses 1760–1980.* London: George Allen & Unwin.

Bonnett, M. (1994) *Children's Thinking. Promoting Understanding in the Primary School.* London: Cassell.

Carr, D. (1995) Towards a distinctive conception of spiritual education. *Oxford Review of Education,* **21** (1), 83–98.

Dearden, R. F. (1984) *Theory and Practice in Education.* London: Routledge and Kegan Paul.

Froebel, F. (1888) *The Education of Man.* Trans. W. N. Hailmann. New York: D. Appleton and Company.

Gordon, P. and White, J. (1979) *Philosophers as Educational Reformers. The Influence of Idealism on British Educational Thought and Practice.* London: Routledge and Kegan Paul.

Hamilton, H. A. (1952) The religious roots of Froebel's philosophy. In E. Lawrence (ed.), *Friedrich Froebel and English Education.* London: University of London Press.

Hull, J. (1996) The ambiguity of spiritual values. In M. Halstead and M. Taylor (eds), *Values in Education and Education in Values.* London: The Falmer Press.

Langford, G. (1979) Education is of the whole man. *Journal of Philosophy of Education,* **13**, 65–72.

Langford, G. (1985) *Education, Persons and Society: A Philosophical Enquiry.* London: Macmillan.

McLaughlin, T. H. (1994a) The scope of parents' educational rights. In J. M. Halstead (ed.), *Parental Choice and Education. Principles, Policy and Practice.* London: Kogan Page.

McLaughlin, T. H. (1994b) Values, coherence and the school. *Cambridge Journal of Education,* **24** (3), 453–70.

McLaughlin, T. H. (1995a) Public values, private values and educational responsibility. In E. Pybus and T. H. McLaughlin (eds), *Values, Education and Responsibility.* Centre for Philosophy and Public Affairs, Department of Moral Philosophy, University of St Andrews.

McLaughlin, T. H. (1995b) Liberalism, education and the common school. In Y. Tamir (ed.), *Democratic Education in a Multicultural State.* Oxford: Blackwell.

Midgley, M. (1980) *Beast and Man: The Roots of Human Nature.* London: Methuen.

Midgley, M. (1994) *The Ethical Primate: Humans, Freedom and Morality.* London: Routledge.

Mulhall, S. and Swift, A. (1992) *Liberals and Communitarians.* Oxford: Blackwell.

OFSTED (1994) *Spiritual, Moral, Social and Cultural Development: An OFSTED Discussion Paper.* London: HMSO.

Parfit, D. (1984) *Reasons and Persons.* Oxford University Press.

Peters, R. S. (1966) *Ethics and Education.* London: George Allen & Unwin.

Standish, P. (1995) Post-modernism and the education of the whole person. *Journal of Philosophy of Education,* **29** (1), 121–35.

White, J. (1994) Instead of OFSTED: a critical discussion of OFSTED on spiritual, moral, social and cultural development. *Cambridge Journal of Education,* **24** (3), 369–77.

White, J. (1995) *Education and Well Being in a Secular Universe.* Institute of Education, University of London.

White, P. (1994) Citizenship and 'spiritual and moral development. *Citizenship,* **3**, 7–8.

CHAPTER 2

The whole vision of the child

Brenda Lealman

INTRODUCTION

Four little girls went to play on the seashore. The world was shining. They shrieked with delight and surprise. They were amazed at what they saw.

> maggie and milly and molly and may
> went down to the beach (to play one day)
>
> and maggie discovered a shell that sang
> so sweetly she couldn't remember her troubles, and
>
> milly befriended a stranded star
> whose rays five languid fingers were;
>
> and molly was chased by a horrible thing
> which raced sideways while blowing bubbles: and
>
> may came home with a smooth round stone
> as small as a world and as large as alone.
>
> (e.e. cummings, 1977, p. 8)

Childhood has its moments of wonderment; it has its moments too when we glance out to sea and glimpse the strangeness and bigness of ourselves, and of ourselves as part of something larger.

There are those moments when we are aware of our socks; we have a fleeting awareness of 'me', of 'my self'.

The poet Elizabeth Jennings describes moments like these in her poem 'An Event'. The young child having a game of marbles in the playground suddenly stops in her tracks, and wonders 'why am I here? ... Who am I?' And continues to roll her marbles. These childhood experiences strike a chord with us, but we must ask what concepts of childhood lie behind our empathy.

Does the current understanding go something like this? (The language is that of Cartesian/Newtonian philosophy and science, and of developmental psychology.)

The child comes along, a piece of solid flesh, matter. Somewhere tucked away inside is her self. This self peers out at a world of solid objects. The job of the child is to grow into an adult. She must develop; she must go through increasingly complex stages of thinking, perception and emotion in what is essentially a process of adjustment to the social, cultural norm. The child learns to live in what has been called the personal or normative category of experience. It is this which is described by Western developmental psychology and which defines the work of teachers. It involves the learning of the rules of the game: the learning skills, competencies and roles which mediate the prevailing view of reality, the mythology of our culture.

It is important that children become comfortable in their culture, and develop their egos and esteem through successful adaptation to the norm. Without socialization they would be even more brutish, selfish and greedy than they already are.

But a pertinent question is: does this contemporary, mainstream view of childhood describe the whole child? Does it provide a model which is adequate for understanding the whole child, for viewing the child's whole range of consciousness? Indeed, is it information language which best enables us to reflect on the nature of childhood? As much as information about childhood, do we need inspiration from it?

Austin Farrer said that the stuff of inspiration is living images (Farrer, 1958) and perhaps it is images which will help us to glimpse childhood in its full richness; which will signify and reveal its mystery.

IMAGES OF CHILDHOOD

What, then is childhood?

The child comes bearing the past: a reminder of the beginnings of things, of the origins of life; of primordial unity before differentiation has taken place, before consciousness has separated out from the unconscious. He comes made of the stuff which exploded into being fifteen billion years ago. Yet, the child is a stranger in a strange land. The child has been pushed out on to the water. Moses was surrendered to the river. Siegfried was put to sea in a glass bottle. Romulus and Remus were set afloat on the River Tiber in a tub. Perseus was thrown into the sea in a box.

The basket is drawn ashore. The glass bottle shatters on the sea-shore; the child is in exile. He is not brought up by his true parents, but grows up in the midst of wild nature and the elements. It is as though he is abandoned to the wildness in life and re-lives cosmological origins. So Paris, son of Priam of Troy, was nursed by a bear; Romulus and Remus were fed by a wolf; Siegfried lived with a doe.

The child in exile has lost his true home and parents, and lives in obscurity. Krishna, an avatar of the Hindu god Vishnu, grows up among cow-herds; Siegfried is brought up by a poor smith; Jesus, by a modest carpenter; Perseus by a fisherman. The examples could go on.

But the child becomes uneasy, restless, increasingly aware of his exile. He has deep wisdom and insight which allow him to perceive what is behind appearances, that from which he has descended. He realizes that he must find the true source of his life, his proper home. So, the youth Siegfried kills his stepfather and a dragon, and discovers from Brünnhilde who his real parents are. Perseus kills his grandfather and becomes king of Argos. Gautama Buddha rejects traditional Hinduism and offers a new way. Moses sets out in search of his true homeland. Jesus as a young man confronts evil, is resurrected from the dead and ascends to his real father.

These potent images are embedded in ancient mythologies. I plead for the re-mythologizing of childhood so that we can renew and expand our idea of the child, see the mystery of childhood, wonder at it and interrogate it.

Myths appear out of the perennial mysteries of our lives; through myths we can recognize and name our depths; we are helped in our appropriation of the human situation. Myths are not the opposite of truth but a recognition of mystery. They are one of the forms in which that recognition is enunciated. Myths cluster around images and symbols and allow space for the working of the imagination. Myths of childhood are necessary in order to acknowledge the mystery of the child; they take us beyond the language of information and psychology.

Mythological perspectives on childhood relate most readily to Thomas Traherne's celebration of childhood in his poem 'Wonder'

> How like an Angel came I down!
> How bright are all things here!
> When first among his Works I did appear.
> O how their Glory did me crown
> The world resembled his Eternity
> In which my Soul did walk;
>
> And ev'ry thing that I did see
> Did with me talk....
>
> Great wonders clothed with glory did appear,
> Amazement was my Bliss.

and to Wordsworth's, in

> Our birth is but a sleep and a forgetting;
> The Soul that rises with us, our life's Star,
> Hath had elsewhere its setting,
> And cometh from afar:
> Not in entire forgetfulness,
> And not in utter nakedness,
> But trailing clouds of Glory do we come
> From God, who is our home:
> Heaven lies about us in our infancy!

Mythological perspectives relate, too, to the kind of religious experiences described in Edward Robinson's studies. Here is just one account of an experience which left a small child with a profound sense of mystery, and yet of belonging to the universe despite its strangeness. It is, of course, recounted by the child as adult and memory has played a part in the account – a part difficult to estimate.

My mother and I were walking on a stretch of land ... known locally as 'the moors'. As the sun declined and the slight chill of evening came on, a pearly mist formed over the ground. My feet, with the favourite black shoes with silver buckles, were gradually hidden from sight until I stood ankle deep in gently swirling vapour. Here and there just the very tallest harebells appeared above the mist....

Suddenly I seemed to see the mist as a shimmering gossamer tissue and the harebells, appearing here and there, seemed to shine with a brilliant fire. Somehow I understood that this was the living tissue of life itself, in which that which we call consciousness was embedded, appearing here and there as a shining focus of energy in the more diffused whole. In that moment I knew that I had my own special place, as had all other things, animate and so-called inanimate, and that we were all part of this universal tissue which was both fragile yet immensely strong.... The vision has never left me. It is as clear today as fifty years ago.

(Robinson, 1977, p. 32)

How, then, are we to present and describe a whole view or vision of the child? Is there a model of childhood consciousness which resonates with the insights of mythologies and poetry, and allows us to acknowledge the mystery of childhood?

One suggestion is that, in order to take account of the whole spectrum of childhood consciousness, it is helpful to approach it through five categories: one is the personal category already referred to, that which supports routine living carried out in a more or less mechanical way. Others are the pre-personal, subpersonal, suprapersonal and transpersonal categories (Armstrong, 1985).

Into the prepersonal category comes the child's submergence in the mother, in the unconscious, in the experience of threatening monsters, witches, wolves. The subpersonal category describes the child's deep bonding with mother, earth, animals, places; intuitions, sensitivities, telepathic experiences; body knowing.

The concern here is with the suprapersonal and more especially, the transpersonal category of consciousness. The suprapersonal category is the dimension of childhood consciousness which includes creative aspirations; spiritual and aesthetic qualities and values; intuitive inspirations; greater critical self-awareness, and more reflective living.

It is the transpersonal dimension that is the area of Wordsworth's experience, of William James's and Edward Robinson's studies of religious experience. This is the area of mystical experience; of wonder, transcendence of self, cosmic awareness, glimpses of something more. It is perhaps the child's glimpse of real self, of higher self, or Self as in Jung; of potential for wholeness.

In summary, the psychological map being offered consists of prepersonal, personal, suprapersonal, and transpersonal domains – and is drawn from transpersonal psychology.[1] Has this map in particular, the concept of transpersonal consciousness,[2] a valid and useful contribution to make to the debate about the whole child and about spirituality?

I should like to argue that it has.

'Transpersonal' means 'across' or 'beyond' the personal or individual ego. It implies an expansion of consciousness beyond the limits of the ego-consciousness; I am suggesting that any map of childhood consciousness is incomplete without this dimension. It takes account, too, of the insights of poetry and mythologies.

This is a model – and only a model – which can sustain a vision of the whole child. But, also, the transpersonal perspective can provide a space, or perhaps a spiralling, insubstantial matrix, in which questions can continue not only about the nature of the whole child but about the related issue of spirituality. The transpersonal perspective offers the possibility of inclusive language which does not seek to impose any particular system of doctrine and avoids the objectifying tendency of phrases such as 'enduring reality'.[3]

Even if we are prepared to talk about transpersonal consciousness, however, there are still enormous questions: should childhood experience be excluded from the transpersonal domain? Is transpersonal experience confined to adulthood? If we speak of childhood transpersonal experience, are we really giving the child's pre-personal experience of physical unity a transpersonal status? Can we, dare we, take seriously the intuitions of myths, of poets, and the work of researchers such as Edward Robinson, and attribute transpersonal experience to childhood?

Can we go further and speculate that transpersonal consciousness provides a context which transcends our ego-life and could therefore pre-date it? Does the exile which finds expression in ancient mythologies, for example in the Judeo-Christian myth of the expulsion from the garden, echo within the experience of the child?

HOW CAN WE SUPPORT THE WHOLE VISION OF THE CHILD?

What can we in education do, then, to support the whole vision of the child? In particular, how can we acknowledge the transpersonal dimension of the child's consciousness?

I should like to suggest that the child possesses the potential for three important directions, or movements, which open on to the transpersonal. These three movements are: creating, healing, transcending. How can we release and empower them?

Creating

Schooling has so often led children to doubt their creativity. Writing in 1936, Maria Montessori describes a child's attendance at school in terms of Christ's final suffering, betrayal and torture. The child's hands are made as motionless as the nails of the cross.

> When the child has gone in, into the class assigned to him, a teacher will shut the door. Henceforth she is mistress, she commands that group of souls, with no witness or control.
>
> She will shut the door.
>
> Henceforth those delicate, trembling limbs are held to the wood for more than three hours of anguish, three and three for many days, and months and years.

The child's hands and feet are fastened to the desk by stern looks, which hold them motionless as the nails of the Cross in the feet of Christ. The two little feet still and together; the two little hands joined and still, resting on the desk.

The little hearts so full of love will be pierced by the incomprehension of the world as by a sword. The culture offered to quench that thirst for knowledge will seem very bitter.

The tomb of the soul that was not able to live is already prepared, with all its camouflages, and when that soul is laid there, guards as though in mockery will be set round to see that it does not rise again.

(Montessori, 1936)

One's heart goes out to all those generations of children – including, perhaps, ourselves – whose creativity died in the schoolroom; who, especially last century and early this century, froze with sheer terror and inadequacy.

Consider this rather different situation. A primary school starts the day with creative activities. Parents who have brought their children to school are invited to join in. It is a relaxed, non-threatening environment. All efforts are enjoyed and valued, not classified as good or poor.[4]

But why do we need to have opportunities for being creative?[5]

First, artistic creativity can be a way of affirming the child's experience, be it pre-personal, personal or transpersonal.

Second, it is a way of communicating not a quantity of factual information but living, dynamic experience.

Third, artistic activity means that the child encounters symbols, and symbols are part of the transpersonal realm.

Fourth, artistic creativity involves those aspects of consciousness which formal education and our society in general tend to neglect, and which are marks of the transpersonal dimension: for example, intuition, reverence, awe, seeing, acceptance of tentativeness and ambiguity.

Fifth, creativity is not confined to artistic activity, of course. But artistic activity can help to make possible a generally more open approach to life; the sort of approach which defies cynicism because it trusts in ever fresh possibilities.

Creativity, epitomized in artistic activity, can help to centre the whole child. Here is an image from the making of a pot. The potter, by moving the lump of clay upwards into a cone and outwards into a plane, creates a condition of balance between the outside and inside, so that at whatever single point the clay is touched the whole mass is affected. Making a pot has to do with bringing the lump of clay into an unwobbling pivot and distributing the equilibrium throughout. Only violent spinning round, of course, produces that equilibrium. What sort of learning experiences does this image suggest we should be giving to children?

Healing

Most of us have experienced the healing power of a child's smile or cuddle; of the way he meets us, as one teacher[6] put it, 'full face'; of his gentle interested enquiry – 'Have you had a good weekend, Miss?'

Healing is to do with putting together, fitting parts into a larger context, having an integrating vision. It is about 'wholing', in other words; 'haelan' in Old English is 'to heal' or 'to whole'.

Healing comes from a sense of relatedness and participation. As we have seen, one of the primary experiences of childhood is that of relatedness: to the mother, to nature, to animals, to places. Primarily, perhaps, it is a mark of the pre-personal consciousness, but also of the transpersonal consciousness. How can such experience be revitalized, re-membered, extended and relived within the context of formal education?

I want to give examples of how this is happening from a country outside the United Kingdom. Looking from outside in can help us to see ourselves more clearly.

Sister Mary John Mananzan OSB is Dean of St Scholastica's College, Manila. The curriculum of the college (a secondary school for girls) has been completely revised. It was realized that learning in the school, through its lack of engagement with real and current issues, was in effect supporting oppression by the current government. It was helping to preserve state repression, dehumanization, economic exploitation, militarization. It was allowing the persistence in the Philippines of job discrimination, exposure to health hazards in factories, institutional prostitution due to sex-tourism, torture and rape in military interrogations. So the curriculum was given 'relatedness'. Pressing contemporary issues are now addressed. Students' dissertations relate to urgent questions such as the links between tourism and prostitution, and violence against women.[7]

But surely the context in which educators work within the United Kingdom is quite different: is not our society less violent, the need for change less urgent? Possibly so, but the need for healing is deep. Consider Northern Ireland, and the prevalence of bullying, abuse of many kinds, injustice; greed and consumerism, the negative side of shopping. Consider pollution, cruelty to creatures, plant-life, land. Consider the mentality which seeks to control all things, and which finds a focus in the economics of material progress to the exclusion of almost all else. Consider children who come to hate and who express their hatred through violence; perhaps, as some suggest, because so few parents now dream over their infants, croon nursery rhymes over them and so help children to tune into their feelings and contain them.

> Tom tied a kettle to the tail of a cat,
> Jill put a stone in the blind man's hat,
> Bob threw his grandmother down the stairs;
> And they all grew up ugly and nobody cares.
> (Higgins, 1993)

Consider the power of television, and the millions of people who live, as Jerry Mander put it, 'inside television'. 'Television has become the physical universe that people now relate to, and the mental universe as well' (*Resurgence*, 1994). Millions live off the same television images. Their internal environment is shaped by these images and brought into line with the environment we shape. This environment sustains the culture of market economy in which pupils can be in danger of becoming commodities or the raw material in the production of measurable business advantage and 'profit' of whatever sort.

In short, are we not a society which is geared to exploitation and to fracturing, rather than to healing or wholing, and to the reverie which healing requires?

What sort of learning experiences can help children and young people to have a healing rather than an exploitative approach to life? What sort of learning experiences can give them a sense of belonging which encourages compassion, gentleness and trust?

First, as I have already suggested, participatory methods are important, making sure that issues we deal with have a livingness about them; that their relevance to life today is made clear. Relevance does not preclude academic rigour. Indeed, enhanced rigour is required together with highly-practised critical, investigative and empathetic skills. Nor does relevance amount to skill in adaptation to market opportunities or the equivalent. Rather, it is a matter of pushing all learning into critical questions: questions of purpose and of asking why.

Second, we should always present modules of work whole before going on to study their various parts. We need to present, with passion and excitement, broad overviews and contexts, making links with other 'subjects', integrating various pieces of knowledge and experience.

Third, if we are to contextualize in this way we need a curriculum which is equal to the task. So much of what we do in religious education reinforces tribal consciousness and presents the tribalisms of the various religious communities. How can we encourage something approaching global – even cosmic – vision?

In short, how can we acknowledge the transpersonal?

An initial stage is to allow children to participate in their immediate environment by touching and stroking it. But we should make clear that the context of this is a larger community: a community of town, nation, world, seas, forests, mountains, animals, planets, sun, moon, stars, galaxies; also of stars and species which came to an end in order that new life could emerge. Now we need to share the possibility of new forms emerging from old religions, from old tribalisms and nationhoods.

The healing/wholing approach is integrative: it recognizes the whole as greater than the parts; it reaches out to a greater whole and relates diverse parts to each other within the whole.

Perhaps such awareness shows through the following piece of written work.

> I am adder. I was slithering through the grass. I saw the humans bashing the animals houses. Dont do that I sssssssssed. The humans didnt listen. They squashed me. I was ded.[8]

Transcending
This leads to the third movement we can help to release: transcending.

The child has enormous potential for growth, for moving on, for changing shape. We should encourage children and young people to have a sense of their becoming and of the world's becoming. We hope to give children a focus beyond themselves, a transcendent instead of an immanent point of reference. This does not mean that the individual ego is denied and surrendered. On the contrary it must be affirmed as a vital part of a larger whole: of the planet, the universe, the vast mystery we live in.

What learning experiences are appropriate here?

Simply learning to be still. We must make it possible for children to have times of silent absorption, of amazement and wonder. We go to a Christian church or a Hindu temple not simply to observe but to touch and smell the building. We go to an oak tree to touch it, listen to it and hug it. And these approaches should continue through the secondary school; they should not be confined to the primary phase of education.

We have to wait on those moments when the classroom becomes wide and it is as if a music comes alive for us, as it did for the poet Elizabeth Jennings. In her poem 'A Classroom' she tells how one afternoon she 'stared into verse', and was called back by the teacher's kind inquiry about her age. Then something 'caught me up excited ...' Perhaps, too, the way will be opened up for the working through and transcending of some of that which is expressed in the name of religion: literalism, bigotry, dogmatism, paternalism, sexism, repression.

TOWARDS A WHOLE VISION

To summarize, then:

We have to maintain our vision of the whole child
To do that we have to see that our categories are sufficiently comprehensive to describe the whole experience of the child. In the terminology used here, we must not concentrate on the personal category and overlook or deny the integrating awareness and the intimations of mystery of the transpersonal consciousness.

We have to enable the child to maintain his or her whole vision
By encouraging and empowering the three movements which I describe as supporting the transpersonal consciousness – creating, healing and transcending – we can help to nourish the inner life of the child.

Through reflection on images drawn from myths and poetry, we can recognize the mystery of childhood. We can begin to appreciate the importance of the child motif for the adult. In this way, we are reminded that the adult cannot be whole without the child. It is for adults – teachers – to allow children to teach us something of what wholeness is.

It is the task of the teacher to re-awaken and keep alive the whole vision of the child. By legitimizing and nurturing all aspects of childhood consciousness we can liberate the child's spirituality. By allowing the child to remain within the adult we liberate the adult's – our – spirituality. So the child as adult can go on discovering shells that sing and looking out to sea with anticipation: of the whole that is not yet, but is still to be.

NOTES

1   Transpersonal psychology came into being as a professional field in the 1960s.
2   The word 'transpersonal' (*überpersonliche*) was first used by Jung to refer to contents and processes in the psyche outside the ego or conscious personality.
3   This phrase was used in the 1993 Framework for the Inspection of Schools in *The Handbook for the Inspection of Schools*. (HMSO) 5.1.
4   The work of Margaret Travers, head of Crosby Road North Primary School, Sefton.
5   For more about creativity see Brenda Lealman, 'Drum, whalebone and dominant X: A model for creativity', in Dennis Starkings (ed.), *Religion and the Arts in Education* (Hodder & Stoughton, 1993).
6   Words are those of Margaret Travers.
7   From a conversation which I had with Sister Mary John at Selly Oak Colleges.
8   Written by Thomas King of Crosby Road North Primary School.

REFERENCES

Armstrong, T. (1985) *The Radiant Child*. Wheaton, IL: Theological Publishing House.
cummings, e.e. (1977) *Complete Poems, 1904–1962*, edited by George J. Firmage. New York: W. W. Norton.
Farrer, A. (1958) *The Glass of Vision*. Dacre.
Higgins, R. (1993) Hate in nursery rhymes. In V. Varma (ed.), *How and Why Children Hate: A Study of Conscious and Unconscious Sources*. London: Jessica Kingsley.
Mander, J. (1994) The tyranny of television. In *Resurgence*, **165**.
Montessori, M. (1936) *The Secret of Childhood*. Orient Longmans.
Robinson, E. (1977) *The Original Vision*. Religious Experience Research Unit.

CHAPTER 3

Education, spirituality and the whole child: a humanist perspective

John White

This chapter is in two sections, each with a title taken from familiar writers – Lewis Carroll and Jane Austen. The first is *impenetrability*: the second, *sensibility*.

IMPENETRABILITY

'Impenetrability' was a word much favoured by Humpty Dumpty – a character who would surely have had a brilliant career in the world of politics today with his firmly-expressed belief that 'When I use a word, it means just what I choose it to mean – neither more nor less.' The difficulties of defining words have meant that the highly sensitive area of spiritual education, which deals with inner experiences and with personal beliefs and values, continues to be bedevilled by semantic wrangles.

'Spirituality' – what is it?

What do we mean when we talk of 'spirituality'? Does 'spirituality' refer only to the *Holy* Spirit – and thus remain lodged in the supernatural realm, the province solely of the religious? This, in turn, raises the question of defining who is 'religious' and who is not. Or can 'spiritual' apply with equal effect to the highest aspirations and achievements of the *human* spirit in a naturalistic world?

To illustrate these ambiguities, here are four short passages which express the kind of experiences with which this book is concerned.

We human beings need to look up from the living creatures in the tide-pools on the shore up to the stars – and then back to the tide-pools again. What we value as the most precious aspect of our lives, the *religious* impulse, is simply our realisation that we are part of the universe, that our lives are linked to all creation.

It was not until I had left school that this identity with Nature became a religion to me. Strangely, it was at that cathedral of materialism, Blackpool, that this spiritual experience came. One evening I stood, looking over the green ocean towards the red sunset. As I did so, a great calm came over me. I became lost in the beauty of the scene. I seemed to become part of it.

Gradually my spirit reached out and became one with what seemed the spirit of the sea and sky. I was at one with the universe beyond. I seemed to become one with all life, from the beginning of time, in the present, stretching out into the future.

This experience had a profound effect on me. It came to me often when I was alone with Nature. It swept over me as I looked out to the stars at night. It was a continuous inspiration. I have said it became my religion. It did. I felt now that I was more than an individual. The life of all time was within and about me. I must serve it.

To persons standing alone on a hill during a clear midnight such as this, the roll of the world eastward is almost a palpable movement. The sensation may be caused by the panoramic glide of the stars past earthly objects, which is perceptible in a few minutes of stillness – or by the better outlook upon space that a hill affords – or by the wind – or by the solitude; but, whatever be its origin, the impression of riding along is vivid and abiding.

'The poetry of motion' is a phrase much in use, and to enjoy the epic form of that gratification it is necessary to stand on a hill at that small hour of the night, and having first expanded with a sense of difference from the mass of civilized mankind, who are dreamwrapt and disregardful of all such proceedings at this time, long and quietly watch your stately progress through the stars.

After such a nocturnal reconnoitre, it is hard to get back to earth, and to believe that the consciousness of such majestic speeding is derived from a tiny human frame.

I remember one evening standing by the sea. The sun was setting: the tide was going out, leaving little pools and streams of water, and wet sand. There was a marvellous feeling of light and peace all around me. I felt great joy, and also a strong desire to find a meaning and purpose in life.

A little later I remember feeling the same when I was sitting on a hillside and looking out over the spreading green countryside. It was beautiful, and also strange: you feel you are somehow part of a mysterious whole.

The first passage, with its thoughts on 'the religious impulse' being 'our realisation of our links to all creation', was an entry in the notebook of a famous writer in the Humanist tradition, John Steinbeck, when he was living at Monterey on the Pacific coast of the USA.

The observer of the sunset at Blackpool in the second passage was Lord Fenner Brockway. Right up to his death recently at the age of 99, he was still stumping the country speaking on the twin passions of his life: world peace and freedom for all colonial peoples. Here are a few more lines from that passage in his autobiography, *98 Not Out*:

I have said that this experience is my religion, yet it leaves me an agnostic. I suppose some might describe it as communion with God, yet I have no sense of a personal God. My philosophy is founded on the experience I described. I cannot be other than a world citizen, identifying with all peoples.

(Brockway, 1986, pp. 127–9).

The third passage describes the experience of Gabriel Oak, the shepherd in *Far from the Madding Crowd* by Thomas Hardy, a writer who described himself as 'a reluctant agnostic' (Hardy, 1957, pp. 9–10).

The reason for the choice of these excerpts is doubtless now clear. These three passages describing experiences which would be generally accepted as being of a 'spiritual' nature all come from people in the Humanist tradition.

The fourth passage was specially composed by staff at the Alistair Hardy Research Centre at Manchester College, Oxford, as part of their survey on religious and spiritual awareness in young people. They devised various questionnaires and the passage quoted (an experience at sunset on the coast and on a hillside) was part of one of the four scales they used: the Mystical Experience Scale. The ambiguities of usage mentioned earlier are nicely demonstrated in the explanatory note to this scale:

This Table includes questions about experience which was to be regarded as religious – but of a non-theistic kind. To call such experience MYSTICAL is to invite controversy, but we could find no other suitable term.

(Robinson, 1986)

Those with a background in multi-faith education will not be surprised to hear phrases such as 'religious but of a non-theistic kind'. They may know that Sir Julian Huxley, a former President of the British Humanist Association (BHA), wrote a book explaining his Humanism under the title of *Religion without Revelation* and that the *Chambers' Encyclopedia* definition of Humanism says that it is often described as 'The Religion of Humanity', a phrase much used by that sensitive agnostic, Marian Evans (George Eliot).

Harmonizers and polarizers

My 25 years' experience in the multi-faith world started in 1969 when the BHA approached leaders of the principal faiths to form the Social Morality Council (now the Norham Foundation and very active under the chairmanship of the BHA President, Sir Hermann Bondi). It has continued through 23 years of membership locally on SACREs and ASCs and, nationally, on the Religious Education Council. It also included participation in a Working Party of Christians and Humanists on Spiritual Growth in Young People, pioneered by Brenda Lealman. That was over ten years ago and it is gratifying to see that this dimension of education is now being given such prominence by bodies such as OFSTED who, like our Working Party, conceive it as encompassing both the theistic and non-theistic positions.

One of the multi-faith bodies in which I have worked is the Standing Conference on Inter-Faith Dialogue in Education (SCIFDE). This has had a wide influence in creating mutual respect and understanding, largely thanks to the untiring efforts of its Secretary, Angela Wood, and its Chairman, Rabbi Hugo Gryn. At a SCIFDE conference, I heard Rabbi Gryn make this perceptive comment:

> The longer I live the more it seems to me that the conventional divisions that separate people – such as their political views, their nationality or class, their age or gender – are increasingly meaningless. The world is divided between people who are natural harmonizers – and those who are polarizers.

Humanists try to be among the ranks of the harmonizers. We hope that the titles of our leaflets for teachers and parents, *Standing Together* and *Shared Values*, indicate this. Unhappily, many of us in the profession are aware that the polarizers have much influence in this area of education, despite the fact that they are (as Professor John Hull has argued) 'an unrepresentative minority' (letter to *Education Guardian*, 15 February 1994). 'Unrepresentative' they may be but the extent to which they have the ear of government may be seen in two depressing recent instances. The first was the appearance of Circular 1/94 with its disastrous paragraphs on Collective Worship (Department for Education, 1994). Then came the SCAA RE Model Syllabuses which revealed that the words 'knowledge and understanding of ethical traditions' (of which Humanism is the prime example) had been deleted from *The Aims of RE* (School Curriculum and Assessment Authority Model Syllabuses, 1994). In taking this action, they flouted the wishes of the advisory conferences who wrote the syllabuses, the National Association of SACREs, the RE Council and the teacher unions.

The logic of the polarizers is clear: 'religious' education must be concerned solely with 'religions'. The British legal system says 'religion' rests on a belief in God; ergo, those who hold a non-theistic position have no place on advisory bodies. As that arch-polarizer Lord St John of Fawsley put it in the Lords when speaking on the 1988 Act: 'No religion: no morality' (Hansard, 1988).

However, this discrimination against non-theistic traditions has not been directed at the Buddhist and Jain traditions; presumably nobody at the DfE has realized that, like Humanists, their ways of life do not rest on belief in an omnipotent deity and thus do not fall within the category of 'religions' as the DfE understands it.

Some definitions

It is appropriate here to review some of the many definitions of spirituality that have appeared. The first is that drawn up by the Working Party of Christians and Humanists referred to earlier. Its wording was carefully chosen to respect the integrity of all participants. It read: 'Education in spiritual growth is that which promotes apprehension of ultimate reality through fostering higher forms of human consciousness' (Lealman, 1985, p. 68). It should be noted that the group did not attempt to find agreement on the controversial question of what constitutes ultimate reality, but it *did* agree on the need to foster the higher forms of consciousness through which each individual can approach his or her own concept of the ultimate.

That was ten years ago. Humanists were delighted to see that the Working Party's breadth of view was promoted by David Pascall (then chairman of the National Curriculum Council) in a series of speeches in 1992, and again, when his words were used in the discussion document published by the NCC, *Spiritual and Moral Development*.

> The term 'spiritual' applies to all pupils. The potential for spiritual development is open to everyone and is not confined to the development of religious beliefs or conversion to a particular faith. To limit spiritual development in this way would be to exclude from its scope the majority of pupils in our schools who do not come from overtly religious backgrounds. The term needs to be seen as applying to something fundamental in the human condition ... it has to do with the universal search for human identity ... with the search for meaning and purpose in life and for values by which to live.
>
> (National Curriculum Council, 1993, p. 2.)

The Glossary of Terms published by the Secondary Examinations Council and RE Council is widely used by teachers with their GCSE Religious Studies students and others. The entry for 'spiritual' acknowledges the breadth of the concept by first defining it as: 'The highest expression and activity of the human person deriving from whatever source', and then going on to note that it is 'sometimes used more selectively to refer only to what relates explicitly to God' (Secondary Examination Council and Religious Education Council, 1986, p. 37).

A new RE Syllabus for independent schools had a well-publicized launch at the House of Lords in May 1994. This looks broadly at RE and follows the RE Council's view that reference should be made to Humanism as a non-theistic interpretation of life. Its view on spirituality corresponds closely with that of the National Curriculum Council (Independent Schools Joint Council, 1994, p. 6).

The passages noted above have been taken from a variety of educational sources. The similarity of these with some words taken from Humanist sources should be noted. The introduction to a leaflet produced by the BHA entitled *The Human Spirit* reads:

> Religious believers and Humanists, theists on the one hand, agnostics and atheists on the other, agree on the importance of spirituality, but they interpret it differently. Despite these different interpretations, however, all can agree that the 'spiritual' dimension comes from our deepest humanity. It finds expression in aspirations, moral sensibility, creativity, love and friendship, response to natural and human beauty, scientific and artistic endeavour, appreciation and wonder at the natural world, intellectual achievement and physical activity, surmounting suffering and persecution, selfless love, the quest for meaning and for values by which to live.
>
> (British Humanist Association, 1993)

The organization known as 'The Sea of Faith' was set up after Don Cupitt broadcast the television series of that name with the aim of exploring further the ideas put forward by him. Its magazine printed the text of *The Human Spirit* leaflet, adding the comment: 'To all of which SEA OF FAITH members would surely say a heartfelt 'Hear hear!' (*Sea of Faith*, 1993).

The interest of Humanists in a spiritual dimension, and a naturalistic interpretation of it, is not sudden or recent. Sir Julian Huxley, a President of the Ethical Union and then of the BHA, wrote in 1927:

> I prefer to say that the spiritual elements which are usually styled divine are part and parcel of human nature.
>
> (Huxley, 1927, p. 25)

The essence of the Humanist perspective is contained in some lines from the book, *Individual Morality*, by my colleague, Dr James Hemming. To support his own views he quoted Professor Maslow (who wrote much on 'peak experiences'):

> The spiritual life is part of our biological life. It is the 'highest' part of it – but yet part of it. The spiritual life is part of the human essence. It is a defining-characteristic of human nature, without which human nature is not *full* human nature. It is part of the real self, of one's identity, of one's inner core, of one's specieshood, of full humanness.
>
> (Hemming, 1970, p. 164)

That concept is further developed by Dr Pat Duffy Hutcheson, a sociologist and Professor of Education in Canada. She quotes Lucretius, a writer who is honoured in the humanistic tradition:

> Our lives we borrow from each other
> And we, like runners, pass along the torch of life.

She continues:

> Spirituality represents the potential of those evolved capacities which mark us off from other animals – all the humanly-created aspects of life that we pass along to the next generation. Like our genes, it is a natural product of evolution and it is what defines our species as human.
>
> Being spiritual means that humans tend to look for some sort of reassurance of being part of something beyond the mere individual life span. Even an unsought awareness of this can produce a spiritual 'high,' as when – in the midst of an expanse of mountains or ocean – an understanding of the essential connectedness ... of one's own self in nature's scheme can strike like a sledgehammer.
>
> We are engaged in a spiritual undertaking whenever we yearn for an integrated view of self and human destiny within some larger picture, a picture that orders and makes sense of our daily experience.
>
> (Hutcheson, 1994), pp. 5–8)

This, surely, is a definition which will speak to both the religious believer who will see a theistic reference in that 'larger picture,' and to the Humanist who will relate it to a naturalistic view of the universe and our evolutionary heritage.

SENSIBILITY

Having considered the *what* of spirituality, I want now to move to practical considerations of the *how* we go about stimulating, encouraging and nurturing its development. A helpful concept here is 'sensibility.'

Sensibility is a word not much in use today, but this was not always the case. One recalls that Jane Austen's *Sense and Sensibility* explored the difference between 'sensibility' and intellectual thought, and that one of T. S. Eliot's essays commented on the intense sensibility of John Donne – 'To Donne a thought was an experience; it modified his sensibility' (Eliot, 1953, p. 117). One recalls also *The Critics* programmes on the radio some years ago when the term 'sensibility' was used as a touchstone in their discussion of the arts. It is a pity if the word is declining in use for it is surely a valuable word for educationists in defining what we are trying to do in the area of spiritual development.

The *Concise Oxford Dictionary* defines 'sensibility' as 'a delicacy of feeling'; *Chambers* as 'a capacity of feeling: an acuteness of feeling'. 'Capacity', 'delicacy' and 'acuteness' surely preserve early definitions (from 1735) of 'feeling the misery of others' and 'a responsiveness to beauty.' *Chambers* also gives 'mental receptivity', which adds a further dimension to the concept in line with the way it is used by Eliot.

So the term is offered here in the hope that it may serve as a portmanteau title for the enterprise in which, whether they are aware of it or not, all in education are concerned: the nurture of the spiritual dimension. In the task of trying to identify some of the things we all hope to foster, it is hoped that these items listed in the BHA's leaflet, *The Human Spirit*, will find general acceptance: 'moral sensibility: response to natural and human beauty: appreciation and wonder at the natural world: the quest for meaning and values by which to live' (British Humanist Association, 1993).

In promoting such developments, teachers might usefully think of their task as trying to *sensitize* young people, helping to make them more *open* and increasing their *receptivity*.

It goes without saying that this is a task that demands an overview *across* the curriculum. Humanists share the widespread concern that we often lose sight of the education of the whole child. In his book, *The Betrayal of Youth*, James Hemming devotes a chapter to 'Curriculum Conflict' which is concerned with the problems caused by our rigid compartmentalization of subjects. In it he says:

> If we are to advance from the confused present to a clearer future, we have to switch over from teaching *subjects* to teaching *people*. After all, what is a subject? It is an abstraction from the universal spectrum of human experience.... A subject is a door opening on to a fuller life and the real test is what the learner can find of himself and life by advancing through that door. Of every subject we should ask what experiences, competencies and insights can be provided through it.
>
> (Hemming, 1980, pp. 69–70)

THE PLACE OF RELIGIOUS EDUCATION

RE is the area usually most closely associated with the spiritual, so it is logical to consider it first when looking across the curriculum at places where the 'experiences' and 'insights' referred to above may be gained. However, there is a significant proviso to be made first. I have argued above that the consensus view of spiritual development is that it is open to everyone and not confined to those who hold religious beliefs. The success of RE in developing the sensibility of our children will, therefore, rest upon the view of RE that is taken, and the *aims* on which RE teaching is based. RE that does not aim to help *all* young people to find a framework of belief and values will not be a suitable vehicle. Many young people do not base their values on belief in a deity. They will join the millions of adults (at least one-third of the population of the UK) who do not accept a supernatural dimension to their world-view. They have an equal entitlement to opportunities for spiritual growth and respect for their view of life.

So when we are considering which approach in RE is most conducive to our aims of sensitizing young people, it is necessary to state that it must be an *inclusive* approach. That was the view 24 years ago of the Church of England's Durham Report. It is the recently stated view of the RE Council: 'Humanism and other non-theistic beliefs ought to be part of every child's RE' (RE Council, 1991, p. 42). It is the view that informs many modern RE syllabuses.

This approach is aptly illustrated in the aims of two syllabuses that are worthy of note. Hampshire's RE syllabus, which became the most popular in the country in the 1980s, includes in its aims that:

> RE should foster an attitude of fair-minded enquiry towards the whole range of religious and non-religious convictions. It should encourage a willingness to stand imaginatively in other people's shoes.
>
> (Hampshire, 1970, p. 19)

More recently, the Hounslow syllabus has interested many other LEAs. It identifies the principal aim of RE as 'to learn about and learn from religious and spiritual insights, beliefs and practices' (Hounslow, 1992, p. 2). Another stated aim is 'to help children develop a spiritual awareness and contribute to their search for meaning and understanding in life' (p. 2). The syllabus makes clear that this search should include the Humanist tradition which is listed as one of the seven 'Core Areas of Study' (p. 16).

ASSEMBLIES AND COLLECTIVE WORSHIP

The time when the school community assembles together should be an occasion when significant experiences may occur and insights be gained. That is happening in many schools – despite the infamous Circular 1/94 and the narrow, legalistic, theological straitjacket it is trying to impose (Department for Education, 1994).

Recent comments by headteachers, and resolutions passed at the conferences of the National Association of Head Teachers (June 1994) and the Secondary Heads Association (September 1994), make clear that schools wish to continue with assemblies that contribute to spiritual development by celebrating the *worth-ship* of the values shared by the diverse *collection* of individuals that makes up a school community.

The Humanist approach is shown in the BHA booklet on Assemblies. *Wider Horizons*. In it, James Hemming writes:

> The themes of assembly are the great human themes – courage, achievement, love, compassion, wonder, imagination, joy, tragedy, hope, responsibility, humanitarian endeavour, and the mystery of existence.
>
> (British Humanist Association, 1973, p. 14)

However, the implications of the Circular go beyond the question of content. It is also a matter of how this 'content' is presented. For those in the schools who are involved in OFSTED inspections, whether as teachers or inspectors, there is a simple way of deciding whether an assembly involves *corporate* or *collective* worship. If the officiant says, 'Let us pray, hands together, eyes closed' and then starts a prayer, it is *corporate* worship: an assumption has been made that the assembly is a body of believers, all sharing the belief that a deity exists who can be petitioned or praised. However, in many schools the form of words used is: 'I am going to read a prayer, or a thought, from the Christian (or Hindu or Humanist) tradition. When I have finished we shall have a quiet minute during which you can make the prayer your own, or respond to it in your own way by reflection or meditation.' A procedure of that kind allows for the individual responses of the diverse group a school *collects* together and is thus genuinely *collective*.

Is it not possible for this concept of 'the quiet minute' to be extended across the curriculum? What do we do in that moment *immediately after* a poem has been read? Student activity has been planned – group discussion, perhaps – but the teacher does not want to rush into this before there has been time for the emotions expressed in the poem, or the insights it offers, to make their full impact. The students' response will be deepened if the reading is prefaced with the same kind of invitation: 'Let's all have a quiet minute when we finish it to see what the poem says to each of us.'

In thinking about how we provide opportunities for spiritual growth, is it too fanciful to suggest that 'a quiet minute' should happen as a structured component of many school activities and learning experiences? Many schools now have their own wildlife area: how about sitting down under a tree after a nature walk round it? Or trying to take in what a hundred million years means when looking at Pre-Cambrian rocks on a geography field trip? What about a quiet minute to wonder at the beauty and intricacy of crystal structures examined through a microscope? And on a visit to an art gallery, might not the occasional quiet time to absorb the power and beauty of art (as well as resting the feet!) provide a time for reflection and refreshment of the spirit?

Only a handful of subject areas has been mentioned, but it is clear that an approach of this kind can reveal opportunities for spiritual enrichment over the whole range of school activities, curricular and extra-curricular.

THE PLACE OF LITERATURE

It can be argued that literature lessons offer as many opportunities for 'spiritual development' (in the sense of 'sensitizing' pupils) as do RE lessons.

Earlier, I quoted an aim from the Hampshire RE Syllabus: 'to stand imaginatively in other people's shoes'. That idea is the central motif of Harper Lee's *To Kill a Mockingbird*. The main character is a small girl, nicknamed 'Scout'. After an unhappy clash with her teacher during her first day at school, her wise father says to her: 'If you can learn a simple trick, Scout, you'll get along better with all kinds of folks. You never really understand a person until you consider things from his point of view – until you climb into his skin and walk around in it' (Lee, 1963, p. 35).

It will be recalled that the book is about the evils of segregation and discrimination in the southern states of the USA. When, as the head of an English department, I used this book with secondary school pupils, it produced classroom discussions of a quality and depth encountered only rarely. It must be placed high on the list of books that dramatically increase the sensibility of students who encounter them, especially in the 1735 definition of 'feeling the misery of others'.

There is so much to draw on in literature. However, as this chapter is concerned with a Humanist perspective, the examples that follow are confined to some of the many writers whose humanistic stance is made manifest in their work.

It has been interesting to see the long run being enjoyed by the National Theatre's production of J. B. Priestley's *An Inspector Calls*. This is another work which has been highly successful in stimulating pupils' responses in the classroom with thoughtful discussions evoked by the Inspector's words to the uncaring, selfish Birling family:

> Just remember this. One Eva Smith has died – but there are millions and millions and millions of Eva Smiths and John Smiths still left with us, with their lives, their hopes and fears, their suffering and chance of happiness, all intertwined with our lives, with what we think and say and do. We don't live alone. We are members of one body. We are responsible for each other.
>
> (Priestley, 1947, p. 56)

What better way of stimulating our young people to 'the sense of injustice: developing a sense of community: valuing the worth of each individual', which are all aspects of spiritual development set out in the National Curriculum Document referred to above.

John Steinbeck's words were quoted earlier. He is another writer who has the ability to increase students' sensibility – for instance, to the imprisoning effect of illiteracy in *The Pearl*; and to compassion for the mentally retarded in *Of Mice and Men*.

Sensibility is surely about the ability to 'stand in other people's shoes'. This was a feature of the novels of H. G. Wells. Pupils' eyes can be opened to the limitations placed on the lives of ordinary people earlier this century by a reading of *The History of Mr Polly* and on the lives of women at that time in *Ann Veronica*. Then there is the work of E. M. Forster. The eyes of A-level students are similarly opened to British colonial attitudes in 1920s India in their study of *A Passage to India*.

To conclude this brief tour of the contribution that agnostics can make to spiritual growth, mention must be made of Marian Evans (George Eliot). The attention focused on her by the television adaptations of her novels is welcome. Legouis and Cazamian's *History of English Literature* talks of 'the deep spiritual quality of her thought', an aspect that is particularly well illustrated in the character of Dorothea in *Middlemarch* (Legouis and Cazamian, 1947, p. 1213).

I have left the subject of *poetry* till last. It is sharply relevant to the concerns of this book as it is possibly the most apposite place in the curriculum for the development of sensibility. There is space only to deal with it briefly.

Let me begin by drawing attention to the television interview that Dennis Potter gave only a few weeks before he died. The Bishop of St Andrew's described it as 'a deeply religious, moving experience' (*Guardian*, 7 April 1994). It was for many who watched it one of those moving, revealing, deeply significant events that happen to us rarely – and which can be truly said to be spiritual. Dennis Potter said:

> We're the one animal that knows it's going to die, and yet we carry on, paying our mortgages, doing our jobs, behaving as though there's eternity – and we forget that life can only be defined in the present tense: it *is* and it is *now*.
>
> Below my window in Ross when I'm working the blossom is out in full. It's a plum tree ... it's the whitest, frothiest blossom that there ever could be.
>
> And things are more trivial than they ever were, and more important than they ever were – and the difference doesn't seem to matter. The *nowness* of everything is absolutely wondrous.
>
> (Banks-Smith, 1994)

One might think of many examples of poems that bring students to a realization of both the 'nowness' of beauty and the transience of life that Dennis Potter spoke about so powerfully. One is Gerard Manley Hopkins's poem about the hovering kestrel, 'The Windhover'. It not only captures the beauty and intricacies of the bird's flight but it also brings alive the intensity of the poet's religious commitment. It is surely a 'spiritual' poem (Hopkins, 1953, p. 30).

The same can also be said for Thomas Hardy's calm, thoughtful agnostic statement of what he envisaged 'life after death' to be. In 'Afterwards' he reviews the beauties of the natural world that have delighted him and hopes that he will live on in the minds of people who will remember that 'he was a man who used to notice such things' (Hardy, 1960, p. 159).

These two poems exemplify the point emphasized in this chapter: that 'the spirit' in 'spiritual' can refer equally well to the spirit of God or to the human spirit. Hopkins and Hardy held different views of ultimate reality, but shared the same sensibility, the same openness to experience.

CONCLUSION: EINSTEIN – WONDER AND MYSTERY

The passage that follows is from the autobiography of a man who not only had a giant intellect but was also a fine human being, Albert Einstein. His words encapsulate the kind of sensibility for which this chapter argues: a sensibility in which, whatever area of knowledge and experience we may be dealing with, we are trying to build in opportunities for responses to beauty, to mystery and to wonder:

> The fairest thing we can encounter is the mysterious. It is the fundamental emotion which stands at the cradle of true art and true science. He who knows it not and can no longer wonder, no longer feel amazement, is as good as dead, a snuffed-out candle.
>
> (Knight, 1961, p. 152)

Too many 'snuffed-out candles' are to be seen today in our classrooms. There is an old hymn that runs 'Jesus bids us shine with a bright, clear light'. Some people conceive that illumination to emanate from a religious source: others will see it, as Julian Huxley and Albert Einstein did, as the highest form of experience derived from our evolutionary heritage.

What unites all of us who are concerned with spiritual development in education is surely our desire to liberate and nurture that inner light which dwells, however dormant it might sometimes appear, in every one of the girls and boys entrusted to us.

REFERENCES

Banks-Smith, Nancy (1994) Angels at his table. *Guardian*, 6 April.
British Humanist Association (1973) *Wider Horizons*. London: BHA.
British Humanist Association (1993) *Shared Values*. London: BHA.
British Humanist Association (1993) *The Human Spirit*. London: BHA.
Brockway, Fenner (1986) *98 Not Out*. London: Quartet.
Department for Education (1994) *Religious Education and Collective Worship*. Circular 1/94. London: DFE.
Eliot, T. S. (1953) *Selected Prose*. Harmondsworth: Penguin.
Hampshire County Council (1978) *Religious Education in Hampshire Schools*.
Hansard, Vol. 496, No. 120, 47.
Hardy, Thomas (1957) *Far from the Madding Crowd*. London: Macmillan. (first published 1875)
Hardy, Thomas (1960) *Selected Poems*. Harmondsworth: Penguin.
Hemming, James (1970) *Individual Morality*. London: Panther.
Hemming, James (1980) *The Betrayal of Youth*. London: Marion Boyars.
Hopkins, Gerard Manley (1953) *Selected Poems and Prose*. Harmondsworth: Penguin.
Hounslow, London Borough of (1992) *RE Syllabus*.
Hutcheson, Pat Duffy (1994) A humanist perspective on spirituality. *Humanist in Canada*, Spring.
Huxley, Julian (1927) *Religion without Revelation*. London: Watts.

Independent Schools Joint Council (1994) *A Religious Education Syllabus 5–18 Years.*

Knight, Margaret (compiler) (1961) *Humanist Anthology*. London: Pemberton.

Lealman, Brenda (1985) Grottos, ghettos and city of glass. Conversations about spirituality. *British Journal of Religious Education,* Summer.

Lee, Harper (1963) *To Kill a Mockingbird.* Harmondsworth: Penguin.

Legouis, Émile and Cazamian, Louis (1947) *A History of English Literature.* London: Dent.

National Curriculum Council (1993) *Spiritual and Moral Development: A Discussion Paper.* York: NCC.

Priestley, J. B. (1947) *An Inspector Calls.* London: Heinemann.

RE Council (1991) *RE, Attainment and National Curriculum.* St Martin's College: Religious Education Council of England and Wales.

Robinson, Edward (1986) *Religion and Spiritual Awareness Survey.* Oxford: Manchester College.

Sea of Faith Magazine (1993), **3**.

Secondary Examinations Council/Religious Education Council (1986) *Religious Studies – A Glossary of Terms.* London: SEAC/REC.

Part 2
Concepts and Models

CHAPTER 4

Human spirituality: towards an educational rationale

Alex Rodger

INTRODUCTION

Our spiritual questioning as human beings stems from the fact that we are mysterious to ourselves. Try as we will, humankind finds it impossible to relinquish the insistent search for meaning, value and purpose in life.

The recent resurgence of interest in human spirituality as an appropriate focus for attention within schools coincides with the rediscovery that spirituality is a fundamentally *human* characteristic which, though it may most often take a religious form, is not synonymous with religion.

In June 1993 Professor Stewart Sutherland, the then vice-chancellor of London University and head of the Office for Standards in Education, made some characteristically illuminating remarks in *The Times* on schools' responsibility in this area. He emphasized the fact that spiritual development is to be provided for 'across the school day and week, and alongside rather than absorbed by provision for religious education'. In approving of this, he cited our society's commitment 'to the importance of religion within a religiously free and diverse society'. He then affirmed the 'fundamental need for a common language in which as citizens we can reflect upon the profound questions addressed by religions'.

Professor Sutherland rightly recognized that, though these are powerful reasons for the *attempt* 'to make "non-sectarian" provision for the development of the spirit', we have yet to reach a clear and agreed articulation of what that might mean. He suggested that we can pursue that clarification by developing Kant's remarks about 'the wonder and awe induced in him by reflection upon "the moral law within" and "the starry heavens above" '; and concluded 'that this is a shorthand for making central to education the task of self-understanding, and the capacity to stand in awe and wonder at the world'.

Finding this to be a helpful suggestion, I would like to suggest a possible development. Professor Sutherland might not disagree that his argument – and his quotation from Kant – which is for *spiritual* development in fact embraces both *spiritual* and *moral* development.

Significant in Professor Sutherland's comments is the explicit recognition that this is no safely 'objective' study of the world and human beings, but only one in which we are involved in a process of self-understanding within the context of our relationships to other people and to the cosmos. The very phrases 'self-understanding', 'moral consciousness' and 'awe and wonder at the world' are redolent of the learner's engagement with a world that is to be *lived* in rather than merely *understood*; and understood *for the sake of* being able to live more fully within it.

We might, then, suggest that this approach to spiritual development in education sees spirituality as concerned with the person's sense of

- the kind of universe we live in;
- the nature and relationships of human beings within this universe; and
- how human life ought to be lived.

Two important points should be noted. First, the spiritual development of our young people will entail the provision of a humanly rich and rounded context of experience. Secondly, to be effective, this will have to be encountered by these young people in a *self-involving* way. Something *within* them will have to be invited to engage with what is offered. Therefore what is offered will need to be of such a kind that it is capable of reaching the inner lives of young people. Challenging issues are raised by this recognition.

It should bring some pleasure to those of liberating and expansive faith to know of such developments, since Carl Rogers's vision of a 'fully functioning human being' must have much in common with the view expressed by Jesus that *his* goal was that human beings 'might have life to the full': a thought which was beautifully captured by Irenaeus in his statement that, 'The glory of God is a human being fully alive.' Similar views can be found in the teachings of other faiths, religious or otherwise.

SPEAKING OF SPIRITUALITY

A major difficulty in pursuing spiritual development effectively and providing sensitively for it in education is that human spirituality is, to a large extent, a forgotten language in the Western world. Thus we find a burgeoning interest in recent years in various spiritualities – religious and other – mainly from the East.

It is to be regretted that so many, even among religious people, have no awareness of the treasury of Western spirituality – in Christian and other forms.

We are like people trying to speak in a foreign language about experiences we have ignored or lost touch with. Even the language (and, for some, *particularly* the language) in which our culture was once able to speak of spiritual aspects of experience is a barrier to understanding for so many.

It may, then, be necessary at this stage that those who are concerned to foster and educate interest in spirituality should seek a shared language in which such speaking can begin. This language, which may have to be formed in the dialogue between searchers, will be useful to the extent that it emerges from common human experiences. Shared awareness of what is recognizably the same experience can lead to the emergence of a language which communicates because it is understood from inside the experiences in which it is rooted. This is more likely to foster the kind of progress we need than attempts to see where a traditional language fits our non-traditional experience – or, rather, to ensure that contemporary experience is conceptualized within traditional forms in the manner of the Procrustean bed.

In practice, of course, the bridge has to be built from both sides. Those who are finding ways of articulating their experience will become progressively more receptive to the meanings conveyed by the traditional language, in which things which are (we may reasonably assume, at least as a working hypothesis) fundamentally the same were spoken of in times past. The custodians of the traditional wisdom will, on the other hand, to the extent that theirs is a *living* tradition, become less trapped in traditional words and, perhaps, discover what St Paul meant when he referred to his determination to 'become all things to all men'. Something of this sort of thinking lies behind Polanyi's comment that:

> If the intellectual and moral tasks of society rest in the last resort on the free consciences of every generation, and these are continually making essentially new additions to our spiritual heritage, we may well assume that they are in continuous communication with the same source which first gave men their society-forming knowledge of abiding things.
>
> (Polanyi, 1964, p. 83)

Put in educational terms, this is simply to say that the teacher – even the teacher who believes that he or she knows where the learner must get to – has to start from where the learner *is*! Answers will not be perceived *as* answers unless they can be seen to match questions which are being asked.

There is no suggestion here that 'ancient wisdoms' should be disregarded, and that traditional articulations of spiritual insights may be ignored. It is suggested, rather, that (a) an effort is required if such traditions are to be understood in a way which sheds light on one's own experience and (b) that effort is more likely to be forthcoming in those whose experience defies articulation in the language which is most familiar in their own culture. Hence the use by some spiritual teachers of 'shock tactics' by which the seeker is jolted out of the comfortable, taken for granted way of knowing (and seeing) the world of experience, and so becomes puzzled by things which he or she 'knows' very well. Spirituality, therefore, has an important connection with ecstasy (*ek-stasis* – a standing outside of oneself) in which the formed self is 'left behind' and one is more immediately present to the thing-as-it-is-in-itself than is the case in 'normal' perception or conception.

WHAT DO WE MEAN BY 'SPIRITUALITY'?

So, perhaps we can look at some recent suggestions as to how we may speak of spirituality with a view to discovering some of the terms – and what they refer to – which will enable us to learn how to find our way about in an educated way within this profoundly important aspect of our living as human beings. One writer, dealing with the meaning of 'spirituality', says,

> Suppose that I ask myself, 'When I offered my seat to the old man on the subway train did I do this *in the right spirit*?' Such a question is an invitation to examine my motivation: 'Was I being genuinely altruistic or was I showing off to my companion, or even to myself?'
>
> (Evans, 1993, p. 1)

If we reflect on this, we realize that a motive is, literally, something that we are *moved by*, in action as well as in feeling. The kinds of things we can be moved by, then – our values, attachments, the things which are important to us – indicate what kind of spirit we have. Thus we talk of a loving spirit; a peaceable spirit; an envious spirit; a spirit of competition; a generous spirit; and so on.

Our spirit, then, whatever else it has to do with, relates to the basic orientation or disposition of our life: *the way we are in the world*, in terms of those things to which we are sensitive; of which we are aware; by which we are attracted; which we value; by which we can be moved to act; which shape and guide our lives.

A not dissimilar notion is set forth by Plato when he refers to 'the spirited soul' as that element in the person from which comes the dynamism for living. A person 'with spirit', a 'spirited' person, is one who is 'alive': a person who is 'spiritless' is lacking in vital qualities and not fully alive.

This may help us to understand the widespread sense that our spirituality is important for the quality of our life and living, even before it is shaped within any particular form or tradition.

Spirituality is a very broad and vague concept. There are many definitions of human spirituality and it is not my intention to try to propose one 'correct' one. Nonetheless, a fair degree of consensus exists as to what is meant by educated people in the field when they refer to spirituality. Consider, for example, the following attempts to analyse the concept of spirituality and provide some description of what it means in human lives.

Clive Beck provides a list of what he holds to be key spiritual characteristics, independent of their embeddedness and expression within any particular religion or way of life, believing that 'there is a spiritual dimension to life whch is largely the same for everyone, and this list applies to spiritual people who follow either religious or non-religious "paths"!'

> Spiritual people are characterized, to a greater or lesser extent, by all or most of the following:
>
> a. *Awareness*. In various religions, the spiritual person is described as 'awake', 'enlightened', open to 'the light'....
>
> b. *Breadth of outlook*. Spiritual people see things in perspective ... they are aware of and take account of the wide range of considerations that bear on their daily life.
>
> c. *A holistic outlook*. A spiritual person is aware of the interconnectedness of things, the unity within the diversity, patterns within the whole.
>
> d. *Integration*. Spiritual people are integrated in body, mind and

spirit; and in the various dimensions and commitments of their life, including societal ones.

e. *Wonder.* The spiritual person has a due sense of awe, of mystery, of the transcendent in life....

f. *Gratitude.* Sometimes ... implies the existence of a divine 'person' to whom we are grateful. However, such a belief is not essential....

g. *Hope.* Even without belief in 'providence', a certain degree of hopefulness or optimism would seem to be justified, and indeed necessary for every day living.

h. *Courage.* Plato in 'The Republic' spoke of the need for a courageous, spirited approach to life. Courage is as basic and important as hope.

i. *Energy.* Spiritual people ... their awareness provides a basis for motivation and their integrated life leads to synergy of body, mind and spirit such that they in fact have a high degree of energy.

j. *Detachment.* The approach of 'going with the flow' does not imply lack of concern but rather a skilful working with the currents of life in order to achieve spiritual goals...

k. *Acceptance.* Even in popular, non-religious parlance one is encouraged to accept the inevitable 'with good humour' and 'in good grace'...

l. *Love.* To many, love is the paramount characteristic of the spiritual person...

m. *Gentleness.* ... involves a sensitive, thoughtful, caring approach to other people, to one's own needs and to the cosmos in general ... does not imply weakness or indecisiveness ...

(Beck, 1991, pp. 63–4)

A comparison of Beck's list with the following one offered by Donald Evans (1979 and 1993) provokes a strong sense of congruence – a sense that *generally they seem to be referring to the same thing*, even though there are differences of detail and emphasis. Evans is more deliberately concerned to outline a coherent set of 'attitude-virtues' which provide a comprehensive sketch of the maturely spiritual human being. His list and his explication of these attitude-virtues is as follows:

Basic trust is an inner stance which one brings to each situation, whether this is an ideal community or a concentration camp. It is an initial openness to whatever is life-affirming in nature and other people and oneself ... an expression of an assurance that our human life has significance in a cosmos which is fundamentally for us rather than against us.

Humility is a realistic, unashamed acceptance and exercise of the limited powers and the finite freedom which I have as a human being. One opposite is pride ...

Self-acceptance. The issue here is whether my energies are released for creative involvement in the world as I accept someone's acceptance of me, or whether my energies are directed inwards in destructive self-punishment.

Responsibility is the stance of a person who can be counted on to do a good job of tasks assigned to him or undertaken by him, including the overall task of living as an effective and worthwhile human being. A responsible person is conscientious and competent.

Self-commitment is a stance which integrates my personality and gives me a sense of personal identity. I commit myself to a reliable vision of nature and human history and human community and of my place in relation to them, trying to be true to myself and to my experience of the world.

Friendliness is a stance of readiness and willingness to enter intimate 'I-Thou' relations of love, giving and receiving at a deep personal level. It includes confirmation, confrontation, celebration, devotion, respect, and affection towards other persons.

Concern is a stance of readiness and willingness to help others in response to their needs, especially those who cannot reciprocate in the same way: infants and children, the sick and the helpless, the underprivileged and the oppressed.

Contemplation is the stance of a person who profoundly appreciates the reality and uniqueness of each particular in the universe, including himself. It is fostered by various forms of meditation which discipline his attention, cleanse his vision, and open his heart. Gradually he is liberated from the self-preoccupation and self-consciousness which distort and subjectivize our usual perception of reality.

The eight attitude-virtues are connected in various ways. Friendliness and concern are each species of love, and together they create a context for contemplation, which is also a species of love. The combination of all three is the supreme goal in human life, though the emphasis in this combination differs from person to person. The other five attitude-virtues are prerequisites for these three. Only in so far as we have a firm grasp on ourselves can we let go of ourselves in love.

(Evans, 1979, 1993)

These 'taxonomies' are each recognized by their authors to be *preliminary* attempts to delineate the area of spirituality, and open to development and correction in the light of further reflection and – more particularly – the test of their adequacy to encapsulate what spirituality is, in a way which will be recognized by human beings because it corresponds to their experience.

Such an attempt is fraught with difficulties and dangers. Any adequate definition is required to include every instance of what is defined and to exclude every non-instance: a tall order! What is needed is a *general* statement which is capable of accommodating all the *specific* forms of spirituality so that those whose spirituality it intends to include may be able to say, 'Yes, that does fit, or at least allow room for, what I refer to when talking of my experience of spirituality.'

We are a long way from any perfect definition, but the process of moving towards an adequate – or at least a working – definition is now begun.

TOWARDS A FRAMEWORK

Are we able to find some way of understanding the rich variety of spirituality as it occurs in the experience of people, a framework capable of embracing the most tentative and incidental explorations and also the lives of the mystics? Only some connection between these two can offer a scaffolding for the development of spirituality in our children – or in ourselves. Evans' approach may prove useful here, since it is rooted in a view of human nature – what we are and what we may become – and it starts from human nature *as such*, rather than any particular kind of human living. It is interesting to note that Evans sees his schema as a development of the ideas of Erik Erikson; and that it has, in general terms, strong resonances with the thought of Abraham Maslow. Interesting, that is, that – despite the wide divergences in world-view and, therefore, in the terms in which they express themselves – there is a strong sense that they are providing different descriptions of what are fundamentally the same types of human experience: and that these types of experiencing are conducive to human flourishing or 'actualization'.

This point is reinforced by John Macquarrie:

> Fundamentally spirituality has to do with becoming a person in the fullest sense ... [and] ... this dynamic form ... can be described as a capacity for going out of oneself and beyond oneself; or again, as the capacity for transcending oneself ... It is this openness, freedom, creativity, this capacity for going beyond any given state in which he finds himself, tht makes possible self-consciousness and self-criticism, understanding, responsibility, the pursuit of knowledge, the sense of beauty, the quest of the good, the formation of community, the outreach of love and whatever else belongs to the amazing richness of what we call 'the life of the spirit'.
>
> (Macquarrie, 1972, pp. 40, 44)

This succinct, yet wide-ranging description encompasses diverse human activities in which spirituality is variously expressed. Yet there is a more fundamental aspect of spirituality than the forms in which it is expressed. It can be located by asking, '*What* is expressed in these expressions of spirituality?'

I would suggest that in all of them human beings are giving expression to their *awareness* of features of the world of experience.

This is a particular kind of awareness, different from the awareness which characterizes the knowledge which is most respected in our culture. It is not the awareness of an external observer who, in seeking to be objective, is also separated from what he observes; nor the narcissistic subjective awareness of the person whose sole interest in the other lies in its effects upon himself; but the awareness of a participant whose responsiveness emerges from the fact that he is both respectfully attentive to and subjectively engaged with what is being encountered. It is an awareness in which something of personal engagement with, and a sense of the personal significance of, what is in awareness, is present; together with a recognition of the real otherness of what is known in this way. It is an awareness in which fact and value merge. The reality which is encountered is perceived in a way which engages both cognition and affect, both thought and feeling. In fact, the person is *involved* with what is experienced. The person may sense that he or she is *addressed* by it in a new way; or *recognizes* something he or she knew before in a different way. The person, who may have been familiar with this object or this experience, suddenly *realizes* it. This sort of experience often lies behind phrases like, 'I never saw things in that way before'; or, 'My God, I knew that all the time. I never realized it before.' Some ordinary, commonplace experience strikes us with a new force or depth or intensity – though such experiences need not be dramatic, so much as significant – and we are provoked to wonder.

Spirituality, I believe, is rooted in *awareness*. I want to suggest that, unless it is smothered at birth, it can give rise to *spirituality as response/action* and that, for some, it leads to *spirituality as way of life*.

In the quotation from John Macquarrie above, there is clear recognition that the kind of awareness in which spirituality arises is not self-contained. It has implications for action, inviting us to respond, so that what we have recognized is made available in some form for the enhancement of human lives (though it need not stop there). Kenneth Clark writes,

> A curious episode took place. I had a religious experience. It took place in the church of San Lorenzo, but did not seem to me to be connected with the harmonious beauty of the architecture. I can only say that for a few minutes my whole being was irradiated by a kind of heavenly joy, far more intense than anything I had known before. This state of mind lasted for several months, and, wonderful though it was, it posed an awkward problem, in terms of action. My life was far from blameless: I would have to reform. My family would think I was going mad, and perhaps after all it *was* a delusion, for I was in every way unworthy of receiving such a flow of grace. Gradually the effect wore off and I made no effort to retain it. I think I was right; I was too deeply embedded in the world to change course. But that I had 'felt the finger of God' I am quite sure and, although the memory of this experience has faded, it still helps me to understand the joy of the saints.
>
> (Clark, 1986, p. 108)

This experience of intense awareness was *commanding*, in the sense that he felt under obligation to do something about it. But he was free to choose not to. There is a clear sense of his being addressed by the reality encountered, of being put under obligation to it and of its claim on him. It is significant that, though a response was called for, it was not compelled; and that the refusal to respond in action was followed by a loss of the awareness. This is the kind of thing which Augustine, centuries before, described as 'the return journey to habitual self'. Spirituality is rooted in awareness and calls for expression in action.

We ought not to think that the matter is always as dramatic as this. It can be as mundane as feeling deeply the needs of another person or persons, the inner urging to visit a lonely person, to forgive someone or to risk oneself in an activity where success is not guaranteed. The essentials are the same, as are the consequences of moving forward or holding back.

Such experiences of awareness can lead to specific, short-term responses. Sometimes, however, they initiate a long-term commitment to action of a particular kind. Less often, but not infrequently, an experience of this kind can usher the person into an embracing and permanent commitment, in fact to *a way of life*. This is the implicit end-point of what begins in spirituality as *awareness*. The fullest flowering of the life of the spirit is rooted in such mundane soil and springs from such apparently inconsiderable seeds.

Macquarrie's remark that, 'Fundamentally spirituality has to do with becoming a person in the fullest sense' does not allow us to consider isolated activities as fully adequate expressions of human spirituality. It leads to the recognition that what is in view here is an inclusive (and perhaps, in another sense, an exclusive) *commitment* to the patient and persistent pursuit of the goal of human fulfilment. It is, therefore, a *life work* that is envisaged; the following of a path to its progressively more clearly discerned goal. Such a way of life is pervasive of all aspects of the person's living and unifies the life around one centre. It provides *direction, purpose, values* and a sense of *meaning* for the person whose life is shaped by it. It entails a process of *transformation* of the person in the direction of whatever is conceived as human fulfilment. In spiritual writings this invariably entails a costly transcendence of the narcissistic ego-self. And the progressive recognition of the way is dependent on active following of what it is already seen, at any stage, to call for. The capacity of discernment is linked with the process of transformation. (All these things seem to have been recognized and refused by Kenneth Clark in the incident he describes.)

These spiritual ways normally entail, with greater or lesser degrees of explicitness, some conception of human nature, some associated view of the place of human beings within the cosmos and a resulting conviction as to how they should relate to the total environment of human life, so that they can move towards life's goal, which is normally understood as becoming fully human. That always entails transcending the ego in order to discover the true self, though this is expressed in many different ways and forms. In other words, a spiritual way of life is a way of transformation of the person affecting the whole life and all the person's relationships.

This brief exploration of human spirituality indicates that (a) spirituality is a characteristic dimension of human life; (b) it can take many forms; (c) it can be conscious or not, explicit or implicit in people's lives; (d) it has different degrees of purchase on people's lives. For some, awareness is all; for others, response is made in action; for others again, it may be the pivotal centre of the whole life. These facts have a bearing on any intention to foster the spiritual development of children. However, the notion of development in relation to spirituality will bear some scrutiny.

SPIRITUAL DEVELOPMENT

It seems unlikely that we shall soon (if ever) have any assured picture of the stages of spiritual development. It might be a very bad thing if we did! This is not to say that we need despair and conclude that we know nothing. The 'faith development' theory of James Fowler (1981) is interesting but lacks, as yet, the kind of field-testing that can permit us to use it with confidence. Work continues on it. The list of spiritual characteristics offered by Beck (see pp. 48–9 above) could be used as indicating the sorts of goals educators of spirituality might have in view for their pupils. Evans' list (see pp. 49–50 above) offers more help in identifying aspects of the journey to spiritual maturity and conditions which may foster progress in that direction. The world's spiritual ways, including its religions, provide us with the best available chartings of the journey. Work remains to be done, however, before we can expect the kind of maps, compasses and guidebooks on which we can confidently rely for guidance and which will be directly applicable to living at the end of the twentieth century. It will always be true that spirituality will be understood, not by those who regard it only as a subject for study, but by those who go beyond that and know it as a discipline to follow.

Our task in schools can scarcely be that of being spiritual directors guiding our pupils along a given path to a determinate goal. Fortunately for us and for our pupils, the school's responsibility is a much more humble one!

There is no shortage of schemes of development, intellectual, moral and so on. Some of these seem to be more helpful than others, and the more complicated they are the less helpful they are likely to be in practice. The approaches which are less ambitious in attempting to document and fix the development in terms of particular ages are more realistic. It is a mark of life – and particularly spiritual life – to resist that kind of arbitrary confinement.

A fuller treatment would require examination of some of these schemata of human spiritual development. I simply register here my view that, while there may be broad generalizations which apply to people in general, we ought to be cautious, for at least the following reasons.

- It is not an aspect of human life that has been much studied with our sort of question in mind. We are at a *very* early stage of systematic understanding of human spirituality.
- There is something vaguely incongruous, perhaps even self-contradictory, in the intention to 'measure' spirituality.
- It is reasonable to expect that the ability to discern what is true in this area will require a sensitivity and discrimination which can only be developed through reflective experience of it.

Those who would generally be recognized as having most experience of and insight into this area warn against the view that spiritual growth is either automatic or subject to direct influence by our decision or action. More important is the sort of receptive openness in which the 'otherness' of the spiritual reality is recognized and its agency taken into account.

My sense that such schemes of spiritual development as we have are (a) few, (b) tentative, and (c) not likely to be safe guides by which to build plans for the spiritual development of our young people is, I think, realistic rather than pessimistic. Nor need it leave us stranded with a sense of helplessness before a task we are unable to address.

My suggestion is that we identify in a heuristic way a number of generally accepted characteristics of mature human spirituality. Then, as in other aspects of education, we can try to provide for our pupils a context which supports their spiritual development and strivings (because it is itself open to things spiritual); learning experiences which seem likely to foster their own spiritual growth and insight and understanding; access to patterns of spirituality which are now widely available in forms designed to communicate understanding; and, if possible, the kind of encounter with (various) role models of lived spirituality which will provide a touchstone *in the thing itself* for all their other explorations of it. Needless to say, this touchstone will be of use only for those who are open to the movement *within themselves* of what they hope to understand through this kind of contact with others.

Our tentative list of 'spiritual characteristics' could be taken from any of a number of sources. A list which, because of its eclectic nature and because it is committed to no single 'view of human nature', may be better fitted to our purposes is one such offered by Clive Beck.

In terms of the view developed here, however, more important than specific characteristics of spirituality or 'spiritual people' is the presence of a certain kind of cognition, corresponding to a particular way of relating to – or being within – the world. This can be indicated by distinguishing between two levels, or types, of 'formal operational thinking'. One is characterized by the ability to think symbolically – that is, to recognize and be able to manipulate symbols mentally in a formal and logical way. The other, while it goes beyond this first, has aspects also of a return to an earlier – pre-operational – mode of cognizing. This appears to be connected with a relationship to symbols which makes them permeable, or in which they operate as means of encountering or interacting with the symbolized reality. It entails an intuitive immediacy of cognition, in which the person encounters the thing symbolized through the symbol. The symbol does not merely convey information about, it effects participation in, what is symbolized.

The interesting aspect of this, from our point of view, is the similarity and difference between this 'highest' kind of knowing, and the kind of knowing which *precedes* any kind of operational thinking. There is a recovery of the immediacy – the unmediatedness – of knowing: the kind of knowing by acquaintance which has the character of encounter. The knower is one with, a part of, the same reality that he or she knows – is aware of – in this immediate way. Yet he or she is also capable of cognizing it, of recognizing its relationships with other aspects of experience, of locating it in relationship to other areas of knowledge. It is the sort of thing which T. S. Eliot seems to have had in mind when he wrote, in 'Little Gidding',

> We shall not cease from exploration
> And the end of all our exploring
> Will be to arrive where we started
> And know the place for the first time.

It accounts for the sense of yearning, while also offering more hope than the lament, which is expressed in Edwin Muir's words,

A child has a picture of human existence peculiar to himself, which he probably never remembers after he has lost it: the original vision of the world – certain dreams convince me that a child has this vision, in which there is a completer harmony of all things with each other than he will ever know again.

(Muir, 1983, p. 33)

A ROOT OF THE TRADITION TO WHICH WE ARE HEIRS

A recurrent strand in the intellectual traditions of the world focuses on the complex issues of what we really know; how we come to authentic knowledge; the human condition as being, somehow, alienated from this direct contact with reality; and the question of how we can recover this personal, first-hand knowledge of the world as it is in itself. In different ways these traditions point us to the necessity to make the journey for ourselves from pre-packaged 'knowledge' to the knowledge which comes from personal acquaintance with the world as it is. This, it is insisted, is no merely intellectual pursuit: it involves the whole person and will entail activities of many kinds, all of them directed to establishing contact with what is ultimately real.

Eliot and Muir are among the modern contributors to that tradition which can be recognized by the shared conviction – however differently expressed – that there is a knowing we have lost touch with, which it would be to our great benefit to recover.

It is this dual relationship – to the external reality and to our deep inner selves – that we have to re-establish and which, I am arguing, is a prime focus for education if it is to contribute as it can to the spiritual development and human flourishing of our young people. We must help them (and ourselves) to be able to perceive the world around us; to perceive it, so far as possible, as it is when undistorted by our own needs or conditioning; and to tolerate and face the questions raised thereby about the nature of the cosmos we inhabit. As an essential condition of that possibility being fulfilled, we must be helped to become aware of our own selves, to regain contact with our own experience, unconstrained – so far as possible – by the interpretative frameworks transmitted to us by others or imported by our own fears.

The current interest in the school's contribution to pupils' spiritual development ought, therefore, to occasion no surprise. It is continuous with the above-mentioned tradition in our culture. It does, however, present a considerable challenge to educators.

HOW DOES SPIRITUALITY RELATE TO THE CURRICULUM?

To recognize that spirituality is a fundamentally human phenomenon and that it is crucial to human fulfilment is one thing. To establish that it ought to be a part of the school curriculum and to show that it may be so in an educationally sound way is quite another.

This case can be developed with reference to the attitude-virtues which Evans considers to be constitutive of human spirituality. He recalls a discovery he made while writing his 1979 book *Struggle and Fulfilment*:

As I became convinced that matters of belief are secondary in both religion and morality I began to study the attitudes on which the beliefs depend. These attitudes are pervasive stances of the whole personality which shape our responses to the universe as a whole and to each particular in it ... they are both religious and moral. They are religious in that they are stances towards whatever unifying reality pervades our total environment. They are moral in that they are virtues which radically influence the way we deal with other people ... they are constituents of human fulfilment. So it became clear that religion and morality and therapy can converge in stances which are central in human life as such.

(Evans, 1993, pp. 19, 20)

In that earlier book he had written,

The theoretical structures of religion and morality ... need to be understood in relation to certain life-affirming stances such as trust which are the core of both authentic religious faith and genuine moral character. And since our fulfilment as human beings depends on the extent to which these life affirming stances prevail over their opposites, religion and morality and human fulfilment have a common core.

(Evans, 1979, pp. 1, 2)

Evans thus provides a way of conceiving human development which enables us to see the integral nature of religious faith, moral character and personal fulfilment and to recognize them as distinguishable – though not separable – aspects of a person's spirituality.

It is worth noting that Evans also provides a basis for a pedagogical rationale in which moral education, religious education and personal and social development can likewise be held together in one synoptic vision of their overlapping contributions to the development of the pupil. Attention to this point might provide practical guidance to those responsible for ensuring that pupils receive a coherent educational experience in this, as in other areas of the curriculum. A more radical grasping of the point might even suggest different ways of arranging curriculum provision.

It is not difficult to see that, although Religious Education, Moral Education and Personal and Social Development have a direct contribution to make to pupils' spiritual development (whether, in fact, they do so or not), other areas of the curriculum are no less importantly involved. This follows from the fact that each of these can contribute to the development of specific human capacities of the learner which enhance the quality of personal life. For example, imagination underlies the empathy which is essential to caring in a morally competent way. Similarly, sensitivity to people, art, nature underlies spiritual awareness in a thousand ways. Again, the commitment to truth more than to one's beliefs about what is true – a key spiritual characteristic – is the stock-in-trade of such apparently 'cold' subjects as science and mathematics. There is no subject which is properly regarded as devoid of contribution to the spiritual development of learners of all ages – whatever may in fact be true of the manner in which they are sometimes taught.

We need to recover a sense of the spirituality of learning, of knowing, of relating to the world in its manifold forms of presence.

This sort of approach to learning – and to the world – was classically expressed by Simone Weil in *Waiting on God*. Her insight was taken up by W. H. Auden who, writing about attention, relates it directly to the kind of attitude which *all* education ought to foster.

> To pray is to pay attention to something or someone other than oneself. Whenever a man so concentrates his attention on a landscape, a poem, a geometrical problem, an idol or the true God, that he completely forgets his own ego and desires, he is praying. The choice of attention, to pay attention to this and ignore that, is to the inner life what choice of action is to the outer. In both cases a man is responsible for his choice and must accept the consequences whatever they may be. The primary task of the school teacher is to teach children in a secular context the technique of prayer.
>
> (Auden, 1970, p. 306)

At the heart of this understanding of education is the discipline of attention to *what is* as a means of so placing oneself as to be open to the awareness described above, which is the core of spirituality.

What kind of education can awaken us to these truths, can create in us the ecstasy which takes us out of our taken-for-granted 'knowledge' of things, can put us back in touch with the world by helping us to pay attention to it (beyond all our conceptions of it) and to the awareness of it (which underlies our understanding of it in conventional categories)?

It is to questions such as these that traditional spiritual disciplines have addressed themselves – and they have always done so in *practical ways* which bring the learner up against some antinomy or contradiction of the world of knowledge, or experience, or judgement.

These methods have been deliberate attempts to 'break the spell' of the received frame of reference; to put the person back in touch with what the received knowledge is about in such a way that the 'knowledge' itself is radically called in question; to direct attention to what is present in unprocessed experience; to rehabilitate the experiencing subject who is him- or herself the instrument of perception so that he or she sees things undistorted by the seeing.

If this sets the agenda for education for spiritual development, 'who is sufficient for these things'? The question, itself, is unspiritual in its assumption that this is something we can *do*, can *organize*, for ourselves or others. But it does point us to certain steps we can take to place ourselves in relation to the world of experience so that we may be more open, more disposed to the kind of change that is required. Some pointers to educational contributions to such predisposing conditions are given below.

SO WHAT? WHERE DO WE GO FROM HERE?

Edward Robinson (1977, pp. 76–7) believes, on the basis of conversations with experienced teachers, that a great deal is extinguished in the experience of our children and young people because we, the adults, are spiritually obtuse. We 'see' the world within an interpretative framework and what we 'see' can become impervious to the reality that is around us. The worst thing that can happen is that we lose all awareness of the dislocation between our thinking and our experience and become trapped; we see only what is authorized within this frame of reference. Our need is to learn all over again how 'to see, no longer blinded by our eyes' (Brooke, 1952, p. 131). The very organ by which we see is an organ that distorts what we see. Furthermore, the need to be able to rely on our seeing is so important to us that we will defend its correctness at all costs, even the cost of denying the reality it is supposed to be putting us in touch with.

Now, some such shaping of our perceptions is unavoidable. Without it we could never become human, never be part of any community or able to communicate meaningfully with others. The benefits are immense and varied. My plea is that we resist being so dazzled by its power that we come to be trapped by it in a view of ourselves and of the world which excludes those elements which are most distinctively characteristic of whole human beings.

A good education, together with the influence that shapes us, will also transmit the means by which it can itself come under critical scrutiny and be tested for its adequacy in helping us to relate as whole people to the whole of our experience. An education for life must be one by which we can live.

Where – as in our society – the paradigm of knowing and understanding is one which almost exclusively emphasizes objectivity and rationality of a particular kind, education itself can alienate the learners from awareness of their own experience. It thus is not surprising if there is a conflict between our tuitions and our intuitions; if the things that we are taught have repressed the things that we 'know' at a deeper level. This brings us back once again to the fundamental point that of first importance in spiritual development is *awareness*. And, if the last few paragraphs are even approximately true, that awareness must come about through *ek-stasis* (ecstasy).

This process of being taken outside the 'normal' (pre-structured) way of perceiving is a process of being put in touch with reality – with things as they are in themselves. This is a difficult notion philosophically. It is nonetheless a central facet of spiritual ways that they seek to help those who follow them to disengage from their entrapment in beliefs which are authorized externally rather than on the basis of personal experience in openness to what is there to be encountered directly.

Now, clearly, this kind of radical questioning *could* be subversive of 'normal' educational intentions and unsettling in the extreme. And certainly the advocacy of a particular spiritual way contravenes the intention which governs education (officially, if not always in practice or even consistently in theory) in our open, plural society. (It also, incidentally, would be self-contradictory for the spiritually mature person to advocate, or proselytize in favour of, a particular way – which may be one reason why those most advanced in various spiritual ways seem seldom to do so.)

While these (and other) vexed questions can fairly be raised about the appropriateness of schools taking an interest in the spiritual development of their pupils – and their fitness to do so – neglect of this area of pupil development is undoubtedly damaging. In addition to this, there is much that we can do to provide appropriate conditions and stimuli – *conditions* of spiritual growth – without either claiming advanced status for ourselves, or presuming to 'manage' the direction of our pupils' development. It is in this context that Beck's or Evans's (or some other such) list of spiritual characteristics can be useful. Each invites us to address certain widely accepted aspects of human spiritual development. We can legitimately do so in our schools, I suggest, by concentrating mainly on the development of *spirituality as awareness* and encouraging, but leaving open for personal decision, the matter of *spirituality as response*, both whether it will be made and, if so, in what form. *Spirituality as way of life* is fundamentally the kind of life choice which none of us can presume to make on behalf of others. Yet, again, it is difficult to avoid – or to refrain from advocating – the view that the flourishing, the effectiveness, the integrity (in the sense of integration) of a person's life depends on its cohering around what Erich Fromm has called 'a frame of orientation and an object of devotion' (Fromm, 1980, p. 135). The same, I would hold, is true of the responses which young people make to – or withhold from – their own awareness. As for the awareness itself, it is not in the control of either teacher or pupil. But, certainly, this is the aspect of spirituality with which schools can most appropriately attempt to help their charges.

So what implications can be drawn for our educational contribution to the spiritual development of young people in schools?

First, some telegrammatic recapitulations:

- spirituality involves everyone: being a person means being a spiritual being;
- spirituality has to do with living life to the full and discovering how to become more fully human;
- spirituality is about self-discovery, discovery of others and discovery of the world;
- spirituality is not synonymous with religion; nor is it opposed to it;
- we are feeling our way in attempts to understand spirituality;
- we will need to *learn* what spiritual development is and how we can foster it;
- spirituality covers a wide range of human experience;
- spirituality can be experienced in awareness, in response and in ways of life.

Then, a list of pointers:

1. The school's contribution to spiritual development is *not* a subject on the curriculum; is *not* the preserve of RE; does *not* happen only in assembly. It can/should be happening in every subject/classroom/school activity/relationship. It is not *knowing* something different; it is a different *way of knowing*: it is not *doing* something different; it is a different *way of doing*: it is not *being* something different; it is a different *way of being*.

2. This entails a new quality of *attention* to experience, and the attempt to allow all our concepts and percepts to be brought to the test of genuine correspondence to what is before us – to see things *as they are* by reducing the contribution to our seeing of what *we* have become – an acceptance of and opening up of ourselves to otherness. The same message is conveyed by Auden's words about prayer and attention and the centrality of that attentive attitude to what is 'other' in the process of education.

   In other words the heart of education and the heart of prayer – and, certainly, the heart of spirituality – is the giving of attention to what is not ours to command, to control, to wish other than it is; but ours to submit ourselves to, to learn from, if we wish to be rightly related to reality rather than trying to force reality into some distorted form which will satisfy our ego (and leaving it unimproved). It entails, in turn, the submission of ourselves to what we seek to understand: the silencing and stilling of our clamorous efforts to fit the whole of reality into our existing conceptual framework – making space for what we are studying to 'speak on its own terms' and being ready, if need be, to hear new things that challenge us deeply. How must our educational contributions change if this is to be an important goal?

   This kind of attention is found in a developed and deliberate form in the empathic attention that a counsellor offers a client – letting what is be what it is and delighting in it as it is, without intrusive attempts to alter it or to constrain it into a preconceived expectation.

3. If our culture has systematically extinguished our capacity for spiritual awareness, a large and basic part of our task is to *rehabilitate the instrument of perception* (i.e. ourselves and our pupils) – to bring about a renewal of awareness and recognition and wonder – e.g., the kind of 'So, that's what it means!' experience; 'My God, I knew that all the time. I've only just realized it!'; the 'I know, for I was there', knowledge – direct, first hand and memorable; the recognition of 'I don't know', as an invitation to wonder and to explore; the sense of being *a part* of the world we study and not *apart* from it; learning to know through involvement in; the development and exercise of empathy as a means of 'passing over' to what is other than oneself with a view to understanding it in its otherness; and so on. Many means are available for getting pupils into touch with their own first hand experience. Among them are: awakening the awareness of pupils through challenging 'final' answers; asking for justifications related to experience; reading primary texts for first-hand statements of views; showing different perspectives.

4. Many different methods or techniques can be used in an attempt to assist the ability to see things afresh – to experience 'ecstasy', in the sense of being shaken out of one's normal taken-for-granted view of things – for example, parable; questioning techniques; the creation of situations which create (cognitive or affective) dissonance; the use of Zen Koans or jokes; the presentation of alternative explanations or descriptions or interpretations of the same evidence or situations; perspective taking;

listening in an empathic way; drama, roleplay, miming; silence; meditation; just sitting and looking; and so on and on.

5. Obviously we cannot hope – and should not try – to engage our pupils in learning activities of this sort if we are not prepared ourselves for the discipline of submitting to the reality we claim to be studying:

> *allowing* ourselves to be called in question by it
> *submitting* ourselves to truth which is not yet realized in our awareness
> *committing* ourselves to obligations which are not yet embedded in our practice.

The elaboration of these possibilities in terms of curricular provision awaits another opportunity. I believe, however, that this chapter moves in the direction of providing an educational rationale within which such activities can be seen as contributing to the spiritual (and moral, cultural and social) development of pupils in our schools.

REFERENCES

Auden, W. H. (1970) *A Certain Way*. London: Viking Press.

Beck, C. (1991) *Better Schools*. London: The Falmer Press.

Brooke, R. (1952) 'A Sonnet: Not with Vain Tears'. In *Poems*, ed. G. Keynes (Nelson).

Clark, K. (1986) *The Other Half*. London: Hamish Hamilton.

De Mello, A. (1982) *The Song of the Bird*. New York: Doubleday Image Books.

Eliot, T. S. (1944) 'Little Gidding', from *The Four Quartets*. London: Faber and Faber.

Erikson, E. (1965) *Childhood and Society*. London: Collins.

Evans, D. (1979) *Struggle and Fulfilment*. London: Collins.

Evans, D. (1993) *Spirituality and Human Nature*. New York: SUNY.

Fowler, J. (1981) *Stages of Faith*. San Francisco: Harper & Row.

Fromm, E. (1967) *Psychoanalysis and Religion*. New York: Bantam.

Fromm, E. (1980) *To Have or to Be*. London: Abacus.

Hardy, A. (1978) *The Spiritual Nature of Man*. Oxford: Clarendon Press.

Hertfordshire County Council (1993) *Spiritual and Moral Development Guidance for Schools*. Hertfordshire Education Services.

Kuhn, T. (1979) *The Structure of Scientific Revolutions*. Chicago: University of Chicago Press.

Lamont, G. and Burns, S. (1993) *Initial Guidelines for Values and Visions*. Manchester Development Education Project.

Macquarrie, J. (1972) *Paths in Spirituality*. London: Harper & Row.

Maslow, A. (1976) *Religions, Values and Peak Experiences*. Baltimore: Penguin.

Muir, E. (1983) *Autobiography*. London: Faber and Faber.

National Curriculum Council (1993) *Spiritual and Moral Development: A Discussion Paper*. York: NCC.

OFSTED (1994) *Spiritual, Moral, Social and Cultural Development: A Discussion Paper*. London: HMSO.

Polanyi, M. (1959) *The Study of Man*. Chicago: University of Chicago Press.

Polanyi, M. (1964) *Science, Faith and Society*. Chicago: University of Chicago Press.

Regamey, C. (1959) The meaning and significance of religion. In *Philosophy and Culture East and West*, report of Third East–West Philosophers Conference held at the University of Hawaii, 1959.

Robinson, E. (1977) *The Original Vision*. Oxford: Religious Experience Research Unit.

Scottish Consultative Council on the Curriculum (1981) *Curriculum Guidelines for Religious Education*. Glasgow: SCCC.

Weil, S. (1959) *Waiting on God*. Glasgow: Fontana.

CHAPTER 5

Spiritual development, spiritual experience and spiritual education

David G. Kibble

My young son of eighteen months constantly uses the phrase, 'Wozzat?' 'Wozzat' means many things and is often used as an exclamation on seeing something. One of its meanings is, of course, 'What's that?' Over the last few months teachers have been saying, 'Wozzat?' when confronted with the concepts of spiritual development and spiritual education. Whilst the 1988 Education Reform Act set education within the context of the spiritual development of pupils (alongside their moral, cultural, mental and physical development), it has been the publication of the OFSTED inspection framework and the National Curriculum Council and OFSTED's discussion documents on spiritual development that have made teachers ask themselves what spiritual development and spiritual education might be. In particular, Governing Bodies and members of schools' senior management teams have been scurrying around trying to determine not only what the concepts might mean but also whether their schools' spiritual education, once determined, meets the requirements for the forthcoming inspection.

In the day-to-day operation of a school, spiritual development and spiritual education have not been things which have occupied much of teachers' time or thought. Now they have to and many of us are far from clear in our own minds what the concepts actually involve. It will be the purpose of this chapter to attempt to paint a picture of what spiritual development and spiritual education might be.

RELIGIOUS EDUCATION, MORAL EDUCATION AND PERSONAL AND SOCIAL EDUCATION

Spiritual education might be thought to have close links with RE, ME and PSE. Maybe spiritual education can be 'done' through one or more of these subjects. In order to try to determine the uniqueness of spiritual education, if it has any uniqueness, we need first to determine the aims and objectives of RE, ME and PSE so that spiritual education can be seen to have its own particular aims and objectives, if indeed it has or needs them.

I believe that RE should have three main aims. First, we should encourage pupils to understand a religion 'from the inside', that is to say from the point of view of an adherent of the religion in question. If we are studying Judaism, for instance, then we should aim to educate our pupils so that at the end of the course they understand in some measure what it means to be a Jew. Second, we should encourage our pupils to make some sort of assessment of religion: they must be encouraged to search for truth and falsity. Third, pupils should be able to enter and go along a path that is a search for meaning. Pupils can be helped in their own personal quest for meaning and helped too to recognize their own 'tacit religion', that is, beliefs that they may hold without actually realizing it. (For a more detailed discussion of aims in RE cf. Kibble, 1982, pp. 6–8.)

Moral Education (ME) has its own unique aims. It seeks to have pupils examine and discuss moral issues so that they can be helped to make reasoned moral decisions of their own. Ethical decision-making, however, is not a purely cerebral activity although it has elements of that. For many, ethical decisions are reached as a result of experience of life, as a result of what we might call 'tacit morality', that is, a morality based upon experience, and particularly upon empathy. ME must encourage pupils to act upon such a 'tacit morality'. It should also help pupils to examine the rationale of morality. By this I mean that the pupils should use the tools of reason to examine the basis of morality and to work out for themselves the logic of their own moral presuppositions. (For further details of the concept of 'tacit morality' and of aims in ME cf. Kibble, 1978, pp. 15–17.)

Personal and Social Education has its unique aims too. PSE, aims first to develop in pupils an understanding of themselves. Second, it aims to develop an understanding of society and its institutions. Third, it aims to enable pupils to discuss social issues ranging from topics like abortion and divorce to topics such as crime and healthcare. Fourth, it aims to develop life skills ranging from study skills through presentation skills and assertiveness to debating skills.

RE, ME and PSE have points of contact. All three can rightfully claim to deal with ethical matters and in so doing may examine the concept of an ultimate authority; RE and PSE both ask pupils to consider what it means to be human and what it means to live in communities or in society; RE and ME may rightfully look at codes of conduct; ME and PSE may both look at social problems. Each subject has its own unique and distinct aims, content and rationale but each, too, is closely related to the others: so much so that in many or even most schools the three may be taught through various combinations – Religious Education and Moral Education, RE and PSE, Community Studies or whatever title the school chooses to use.

What needs to be decided at some point is whether spiritual education forms yet another subject to add to the triumvirate or whether it can be encompassed by one or more of the three existing subjects. At first sight it would seem to be at least closely related to RE; in so far as it is something that is intensely personal it would seem to have an affinity with PSE; and the NCC and OFSTED might seem to wish to link it with Moral Education. But maybe spiritual education is something totally cross-curricular which should not be located within any single discipline or group of disciplines.

SPIRITUAL DEVELOPMENT IN RECENT NCC AND OFSTED PUBLICATIONS

The National Curriculum Council's document, *Spiritual and Moral Development: A Discussion Paper* (NCC, 1993, p. 2), makes clear that spiritual development and religious belief, whilst having a connection with one another, are not to be seen as identical. 'The potential for spiritual development is open to everyone and is not confined to the development of religious beliefs or conversion to a particular faith.' It describes spiritual development as having to do with

> relationships with other people, and, for believers, with God. It has to do with the universal search for individual identity – with our responses to challenging experiences, such as death, suffering, beauty, and encounters with good and evil. It has to do with the search for meaning and purpose in life and for values by which to live.

(NCC, 1993, p. 2)

The National Curriculum Council proposes a number of 'aspects' of spiritual development. These are

● beliefs: the development of personal beliefs that may or may not be specifically religious;
● a sense of awe, wonder and mystery;
● experiencing feelings of transcendence;
● a search for meaning and purpose;
● self-knowledge;
● relationships: that is, recognizing the worth of individuals and building relationships with others;
● creativity: expressing one's innermost thoughts through the arts and exercising the imagination; and
● feelings: a sense of being moved.

It is suggested that there are various steps that might be taken in a person's spiritual development. These include recognizing the existence of others; becoming aware of and reflecting on experience; questioning and exploring the meaning of experience; understanding and evaluating a range of possible responses and interpretations; developing personal views and insights; and applying those insights.

The NCC suggests that spiritual development might be effected through the ethos of the school although it fails to spell out how this might be achieved except in terms of moral development. It also suggests that spiritual development will take place through all subjects of the curriculum: questions of meaning will be raised, for example, when looking at questions about the origins of the universe and the uniqueness of humanity. Clearly RE also has an important part to play in this. The report suggests that there will be a number of learning experiences that will contribute to a pupil's spiritual development: discussing matters of personal concern; developing relationships with both adults and peers; exploring the beliefs and values of others; discussing religious and philosophical questions; understanding how decisions are made with regard to spiritual matters;

experiencing what is aesthetically challenging; and experiencing silence and reflection. It is suggested that collective worship will be one of the loci for such learning experiences.

The OFSTED handbook on inspections deals with spiritual development under a composite heading of a pupil's spiritual, moral, social and cultural development. Within this composition, however, we can pick out certain features that relate to spiritual development particularly when read in the light of the NCC document. The handbook amplifies spiritual development in terms of pupils displaying a capacity for reflection and curiosity and a sense of awe and wonder; an ability to discuss beliefs; having relationships that are open; valuing imagination, inspiration and contemplation; and asking questions about meaning and purpose. Again, the handbook, like the NCC discussion paper, highlights the particular place of RE and collective worship (OFSTED, 1993, sect. 5:1).

OFSTED's discussion paper, which includes within it a section on spiritual development, reiterates much of what has already been said but attempts to determine how pupils and students might display evidence of developing spiritually. It suggests that

> pupils may display evidence of having benefited from provision intended to promote spiritual development if, at a level appropriate to their age and ability, they demonstrate such qualities as: knowledge of the central beliefs, ideas and practices of major world religions and philosophies; an understanding of how people have sought to explain the universe through various myths and stories, including religious, historical and scientific intepretations; beliefs which are held personally and the ability to give some account of these and to derive values from them; behaviour and attitudes which derive from such knowledge and understanding and from personal conviction, and which show awareness of the relationship between belief and action; and personal response to questions about the purpose of life, and to the experience of e.g., beauty and love or pain and suffering.
>
> (OFSTED, 1994, pp. 9–10)

Clearly much thought and energy has been put into the above documents. There has been a desire to 'pin down' the nature of spiritual development and to enable school inspectors to determine whether pupils have been given opportunities for such development. There has been a move away from grandiose generalizations towards meaningful and precise statements which teachers, governors and inspectors can work with and which give schools the chance to look clearly and realistically at their own practices. I now intend to examine what spiritual experience might actually mean and then to reflect back on NCC and OFSTED documentation to see whether they have 'got it right'. In so doing I will look at where RE, ME and PSE fit into the picture.

SPIRITUAL EXPERIENCE

Neither the NCC document nor the OFSTED publications succeed in putting much flesh on the concept of spiritual experience. Whilst what the documents say may be good and accurate, teachers need more detail concerning the whole idea of what spiritual experience and therefore spiritual development might mean if they are to develop a policy on spiritual and moral development and education, and even more so if they are to put such a policy into practice in the classroom.

In Britain one of the most well-known studies of people's spiritual experience is that undertaken by Sir Alister Hardy in the 1970s under the auspices of the Religious Experience Research Unit based at Oxford University. His findings and conclusions were published in *The Spiritual Nature of Man* (Hardy, 1979). Simply put, Hardy and his colleagues invited people to respond to the key question as to whether they had ever been 'conscious of, and perhaps influenced by, some power, whether they call it God or not, which may either appear to be beyond their individual selves or partly, or even entirely, within their being' (p. 20).

One woman wrote to the unit explaining how she had had to resign from a job she very much enjoyed. She was very upset about this and was unsure where her future lay. One day she went to Cambridge where she sat under a willow tree in a garden. It was summer and all was very still. As she sat there she felt that time had stopped. She felt able to look at her problems in a new light. New plans began to take shape in her mind. She felt an overwhelming sense of peace. She wrote explaining how 'this peace and strength and support from this encounter has never left me and has slowly grown...' (Hardy, 1979, p. 52). Another woman described a childhood experience: 'At the age of twelve, I was quite ill in bed, I found myself floating up from my body into a ray of sunshine. At the time I thought quite consciously that I was dying, and I remember that the feeling of liberation was joyful beyond anything that I have ever known. I didn't die, of course, but returned quite gently to my body. From that time on I've never been afraid of death' (Hardy, 1979, p. 36).

Hardy found that there were often 'triggers' to spiritual experience; triggers included natural beauty, sacred places, the creative arts, depression and despair (the biggest trigger), illness and death. The experience would often lead to a sense of security and peace, a sense of joy and well being, a sense of certainty, clarity and enlightenment, a sense of a non-human 'presence'. The experience could involve a sudden change to a new sense of awareness, a conversion or a 'moment of truth'.

Other studies have added the triggers of watching young children and childbirth and have identified effects such as a certainty that all would turn out for the good and a sense of wishing to contribute to the needs of others. Other studies suggest that spiritual experience can be an ongoing, developing affair in addition to a 'Damascus road' experience; some people identified no particular trigger for their spiritual experience. (A summary of all the relevant literature may be found in Miles, 1983.)

In order to see how these studies related to day-to-day teaching in the classroom I decided to ask a Year 8 and a Year 10 class Hardy's key question. The Year 8 class was a middle-ability class, the Year 10 class a mixed-ability group. Initially the Year 8 class seemed to have difficulty understanding what such an experience might mean, although once they had given some time to thinking they were as able as the Year 10 group to come up with some experiences of their own. Some of the more interesting and relevant descriptions are given below.

Whilst doing my RE project [on York Minster] in Year 7 I thought that if all of these men had built this magnificent building with only simple tools, and risking their lives every day, that they must have known something that I don't about God and I wanted to know it too and that made me think about whether I believed in God or not and it also made me think a lot about life. (Year 8)

When I got a new telescope I was curiously looking at the stars and I was thinking about how far away they were from earth because most of them were only pin-pricks in the night. Later when I was looking through the book which came with the telescope it said that the nearest stars would be light-years away; this means the distance it takes for light to travel for a year. Also in the book there was a picture of all the galaxies known to man and the Milky Way which we are in which is small when compared to the size of others. I was wondering about how long space did actually go on for. Did it go on for infinity, what happens when it finally runs out? Or is space round, if you travelled forever would you eventually hit earth again? (Year 8)

Sometimes, when I play with my dwarf hamsters I wonder how anything so small and delicate could be made or even live. I have been told about a big bang which created the world but how could that create such a delicate thing so I don't believe that. I often think how things could become from nothing (like in cave man days) into the skills we have today. Also how will it end? And what was here before us? All these unanswerable questions keep me in awe and wonder. (Year 8)

I often think who is controlling me, who makes me think what I think, who makes me do the things that I do. It's as if I'm in someone's chess set and being moved around to suit someone's purpose. (Year 10)

I have had a spiritual experience. I thought if God made us who made God? And I have often wondered if I am really here or not and when I die whether I will just not exist or will I exist spiritual. I have been talking to my grandad and he doesn't lie and he said that he was floating above his body. (Year 10)

My friend and I were walking home and we were talking about summer coming because the sky was really blue. We were looking up at the sky and suddenly realized that it doesn't end and if it did what would come after that. We began to get irritated when we thought about it and so changed the subject, but still in my mind I wonder if it did come to an end or not and if it did what would come after it. Nobody knows. (Year 10)

When I watch hospital programmes and the doctors and nurses are doing everything that they can to save one person's life, e.g. a tramp – who are generally looked at as worthless beings – even though he is close to dying they still try to save his life and make him well again. Even though this is really simple and everyday it still makes me think about how important and how precious life is. (Year 10)

Spiritual experience then has a lot to do with one's feelings or emotions in the face of events and people. It is an affective and reflective response. How do we respond to the question of the validity or truth of such experience? If I undergo an experience that leaves me with a new perspective on the nature of what it means to be a human, how true is that perspective? I believe that a person can, over a period of time, judge whether a particular perspective is 'true' and valid by applying a modified form of the criteria suggested by F. Ferré for the verification of religious and metaphysical systems: internal criteria and external criteria (Ferré, 1972, ch. 2). These may be summarized as follows:

The internal criteria
- *Non-contradiction.* A spiritual belief cannot be said to be true where the belief can be easily contradicted.
- *Inter-relatedness.* A person's spiritual beliefs must exhibit a logical unity: they must fit together in a unified whole.

The external criteria
- *Empirical adequacy.* The spiritual belief in question must 'ring true' with *all* aspects of a person's experience of life.
- *Practical adequacy.* Any spiritual belief must be practicable. A person must be able to live by it in terms of thought and action.

In most cases, of course, such testing will be undertaken quite unconsciously in the face of experience over a period of time. It is experience that will tell whether a spiritual belief is 'true' or not.

Spiritual beliefs have to do with something ultimate, something that is beyond the individual. That something ultimate will be seen at least to be something that is trans-personal, that is, something that is greater than individual persons. For others it will be greater than that: it will be something that is 'religious' in the sense of having an existence or reality that is above and beyond the trans-personal: an existence that is independent of the people who perceive it. This latter will involve something that is believed to be transcendent. For some that will involve God.

SPIRITUAL DEVELOPMENT IN SCHOOL

Michael Beesley described spiritual development in schools, or spiritual education, as 'a life-long process of encountering, responding to, and developing insight from what, through experience, we perceive to be "the beckoning transcendent truth and rightness" and the sacred, mystical or numinous' (Beesley, 1993, p. 27). Bearing in mind my own contention that spiritual belief does not necessarily need to involve transcendence as such – it may involve only something that is what I have termed 'trans-personal' and therefore immanent – I would wish to rephrase the definition of spiritual development as follows: *A lifelong process of encountering, reflecting on, responding to and developing insight from what, through experience, one perceives to be the trans-personal, transcen-*

dent, mystical or numinous. It does not necessarily involve the concept of God.

Beesley suggests that spiritual development in school will involve three things: (1) helping children and young people to *acknowledge* the spiritual experience and learning which they already have; (2) offering them regularly a variety of ways to *explore* and develop this aspect of their being; (3) helping them to find a language, not necessarily in words, to *express* their spiritual experience, learning and insight (Beesley, 1993, p. 23). The first point made by Beesley, having children acknowledge the spiritual experience and learning that they already have, is important. One could argue that *everyone* has spiritual beliefs of one kind or another even though they may not have articulated those beliefs. Indeed, it may be that many are not able to articulate such beliefs: being unable to articulate them does not mean that they do not have them. It may be that they have spiritual beliefs but that they hold them 'tacitly'. To know or believe something tacitly means that a person knows or believes it but is unable to express in words either the belief itself or how or why he or she holds that belief. People know far more than they can tell. (For discussion on the whole idea of tacit knowledge, see Polanyi, 1967.)

Expanding on Beesley, I believe one might contribute to pupils' spiritual development in schools by having pupils sharing, reflecting on and evaluating:

- their own and others' feelings of awe and wonder;
- their own and others' numinous experiences or experiences of the transcendent;
- matters of personal concern;
- their own and others' religious experiences;

and by

- having pupils using and developing their imagination;
- having pupils experiencing what is considered to be aesthetically pleasing and challenging;
- having pupils working to help others, especially the young, the old and the disadvantaged.

CONCLUSIONS

What conclusions can we draw from our look at spiritual education? First, I think we should applaud the NCC and OFSTED's efforts to highlight such a deep and important area of human experience. It is a facet that goes to the very root of our humanity, a facet which can all too easily be overlooked in the hurly-burly of day-to-day living in the fast lane.

Second, we can see how spiritual education has close links with each of the three curriculum subjects whose aims were outlined at the beginning of this study: RE, ME and PSE. It has links with RE in that RE is concerned, among other things, with examining other people's spiritual experience. As well as looking at St Paul's Damascus road experience, Muhammad's experience on Jabal an Noor and the Buddha's enlightenment, it will, as part of its aim to have pupils understand religion from the point of view of a believer, also examine, for example, as my Year 8 pupils did recently, what it means for a Muslim to go on pilgrimage and become a *hajji*. In putting themselves in the position of a Muslim on pilgrimage in Mecca they were asked to describe a Muslim's experience of Allah and the Muslim community by writing home to a friend. Spiritual education also involves RE in so far as RE will be examining matters of personal concern and assisting pupils in their personal search for meaning. RE also examines people's beliefs and philosophies.

In so far as ME is concerned, it will be involved in spiritual education when it examines the basis for morality with pupils. As for PSE, it will be involved in spiritual education when it helps pupils to understand themselves as persons and when it deals with topics centring around human relationships. In this way, however RE, ME and PSE are delivered in the school's curriculum, they will each be involved in a major way in spiritual education.

Third, spiritual education will take place outside these curriculum subjects as well. We have already noted how many pupils point to questions as to the origin and nature of the universe as a trigger for spiritual experiences or thoughts: science may therefore be involved in spiritual education although, unlike RE, ME and PSE, it will not see this as one of its main aims. What science teaches may be a 'trigger' for some. English in particular, but other subjects too in the humanities area, will be involved in having pupils develop their imagination and express thoughts and feelings, thereby giving them tools for spiritual development. Music and the performing arts will enable pupils to experience what is considered to be aesthetically pleasing and challenging and will therefore be involved in the spiritual education process too. A school's community service scheme will enable pupils to work with others. There are, no doubt, other areas in the overt and hidden curriculum where spiritual education takes place. The community of the school itself will certainly be important. We conclude, therefore, that spiritual education in school takes place in many subjects and areas, although RE, ME and PSE will play a particularly important part.

What about collective worship? As one who is philosophically opposed to the whole idea of collective worship I would none the less agree that it could have a part to play in a person's spiritual education. However, collective worship is by no means the sole purpose or even the primary focus of most school assemblies. Assemblies often centre around matters of personal concern, can deal with aesthetics, can be based upon people's experience of awe and wonder or people's religious experience and these, too, can contribute directly to spiritual development.

We need to remember, when we talk of spiritual education in school, that most spiritual education will actually take place outside school. It is experience of life itself which is the great spiritual educator. Yes, we can help pupils to examine, reflect on and evaluate their own and other people's experiences but we cannot give them those experiences, although we can, it must be said, sometimes pave the way. It will be developing pupils' imaginations, giving them access to the arts and having them working with and for people that will pave the way.

Fourth I would have preferred the NCC and OFSTED to have used the term 'spiritual education' rather than 'spiritual development'. The word 'development' suggests that pupils will not be asked to look critically or in an enquiring way at the idea of spiritual experience. Just as when one looks at the literature of the New Testament in RE one might study form criticism and ideas about how the gospels developed, so when one examines spirituality in RE one might examine it from a critical point of view as part of one's study. What was it, for example, that led Muhammad to be so critical of the prevailing polytheism that his experience on Jabal an Noor was so shot through with monotheism? How much do people's spiritual experiences when under pressure or in despair help them to 'accommodate' events that have happened to them? Why is it that studies have shown that more-educated people are more likely to have spiritual experiences than their less-educated counterparts? And is this assertion actually true, or is it just that more-educated people can verbalize their experience better? None of these questions deny the reality of the experience: they help us to set it in its context and to understand something of the nature of such experience. Miles's thesis had as one of its aims to introduce sixth formers to a *critical* study of spiritual experience (Miles, 1983). The inclusion of an element of critical study would lead me to prefer the title spiritual education as opposed to spiritual development alone. The concept of spiritual education adds an extra dimension, and one which is educationally valuable.

I also dislike the link that the NCC and OFSTED have made between spiritual education and moral education. As studies on both sides of the Atlantic have shown, spiritual experiences often have a moral outcome. I remember reading not long ago of a teacher who spent time with one of his own childhood teachers who was dying. The whole experience led him to place less importance on his own career development and more on the value of human relationships. That represented a moral outcome. But a moral outcome is by no means a necessary outcome of spiritual experience. My pupils who talked of wondering at the infinity of the universe did not undergo any significant change in moral outlook. Spiritual education must be seen as valuable in its own right and not merely as a way of improving the morals of the nation's young people.

Finally, schools will need work and time to develop and implement policies on spiritual education. Most schools will already have in place considerable elements of spiritual education: for most a small number of changes or changes in emphasis may be required. Quite possibly the biggest change for some will be in the attitudes of teaching staff who will need to see education as not merely a way of amassing academic certificates or skills to enable pupils to fill their place in society but also as a process to help build pupils and students into more human individuals. There is no doubt that this is part of what education should be about: let us not doubt that it can be achieved.

One trigger of spiritual experience that I have not mentioned is war. I will end with a quotation from an army helicopter pilot who served in the Falklands War and whose words seem to encapsulate much of what spiritual experience is all about:

The Falklands experience has made me review my priorities considerably and things which were important before the Falklands are of total insignificance now. I'm a different person, I think, because my priorities are so different. I'm far more relaxed than I used to be. I used to be terribly ambitious, and now I've found that ambition is totally irrelevant. I look and see that I've got arms and legs, I can see, and I'm very thankful for that, and life is much, much sweeter now.

(Arthur, 1985)

REFERENCES

Arthur, M. (1985) *Above All, Courage.* London: Sidgwick and Jackson.

Beesley, M. (1993) Spiritual education in schools. *Pastoral Care in Education,* **11**(3), 22–28.

Ferré, F. (1972) *Language, Logic and God.* London: Fontana.

Hardy, A. (1979) *The Spiritual Nature of Man.* Oxford: Oxford University Press.

Kibble, D. G. (1978) *Moral Education in a Secular School.* Bramcote: Grove Books.

Kibble, D. G. (1982) *Politics in the Context of Religious Education.* Bramcote: Grove Books.

Miles, G. B. (1983) A critical and experimental study of adolescents' attitudes to and understanding of transcendental experience. Unpublished Ph.D. dissertation, Leeds University.

National Curriculum Council (1993) *Spiritual and Moral Development – A Discussion Paper.* York: NCC.

OFSTED (1993) *Handbook for the Inspection of Schools.* London: HMSO.

OFSTED (1994) *Spiritual, Moral, Social and Cultural Development.* London: HMSO.

Polanyi, M. (1967) *The Tacit Dimension.* London: Routledge and Kegan Paul.

CHAPTER 6

Experience, critical realism and the schooling of spirituality

Kevin Mott-Thornton

INTRODUCTION

I would like to start by attempting to set out what I take to be some of the animating principles behind both the legislative requirement for spiritual development in schools *and* recent official guidance on the matter of implementation.

There have been several attempts by government agencies, of a range of political persuasions, to characterize the area of the spiritual, the most recent being as follows:

> The term needs to be seen as applying to something fundamental in the human condition which is not necessarily experienced through the physical senses and/or expressed through everyday language. It has to do with relationships with other people and, for believers, with God. It has to do with the universal search for individual identity – with our responses to challenging experiences, such as death, suffering, beauty and encounters with good and evil. It is to do with the search for meaning and purpose in life and for values by which to live.
>
> (NCC, 1993, p. 2)

The following aspects of spiritual development are then listed:

- Beliefs
- A sense of awe, wonder and mystery
- Experiencing feelings of transcendence
- Search for meaning and purpose
- Self-knowledge
- Relationships
- Creativity
- Feelings and emotions

> Spiritual development relates to that aspect of inner life through which pupils acquire insights into their personal experience which are of enduring worth. It is characterised by reflection, the attribution of

meaning to experience, valuing a non-material dimension to life and intimations of an enduring reality. 'Spiritual' is not synonymous with
'religious'; all areas of the curriculum may contribute to pupils' spiritual
development.

(OFSTED, 1993)

A number of important conclusions may be reached from a close and
sympathetic reading of these and other government pronouncements and,
having outlined them below, I will regard them as guiding constraints upon
what follows.

1. There is an *explicit* rejection of any attempt to regard spirituality as
the exclusive domain of religion. These characterizations appear to be
attempting to disengage the language of the spiritual from its association
with religion. This enables policy-makers to see the 'spirituality' of the
school as coextensive with its current 'ethos' and opens up the possibility
of secular interpretations.

2. While affirming the connection between spirituality and religion, there
is a thoroughgoing and explicit rejection of any suggestion that the development of spirituality should be aimed at making pupils religious. In
particular, spiritual development is not presented as of necessity involving
the attempt by schools to ensure that all their pupils become adherents of
any particular religious tradition in a closed or illiberal way.

3. As a counterweight to the above considerations, there is a distinct
(but in my view quite anaemic) attempt to ensure that schools do not characterize spiritual development in such a way as to *exclude* any reference to
religious sources of inspiration. It is this emphasis which I suspect makes
the use of the word 'spiritual' by government and its agencies both important and controversial. While the widely touted alternative notion of the
'ethical' is also suitably disengaged from 'religion', it has a much weaker
link with the notion of 'transcendence'.

In a liberal and pluralist society, where opportunity is one of the key
values, one of the many reasons why talk of the spiritual is better than talk
of the ethical is that the former is *necessarily inclusive* of transcendent
sources of lifestyle orientation while the latter *may not* be.

It is worth noting the association made in these characterizations
between spiritual development and an awareness of a hidden or non-mate-
rial/physical/transcendent dimension. This association is both vitally
important and potentially open to misunderstanding.

If it is taken to mean that the visible and material can play *no* role in
supporting spiritual values then there is a danger of building into school
policies a particular and partial view of spirituality and thereby excluding
without criticism or reflection those spiritual traditions which find spiritual
values within the material world. This might lead to a devaluation of the
material and physical side of life. Nor should such remarks be taken to
mean that spiritual development is *necessarily* connected with acquiring
knowledge of some mysterious spiritual substance or establishing a relationship with a transcendent or supreme being, as conceived by various
religious groups. Talk of spirituality as an orientation towards a hidden and
non-material but important dimension, allows us usefully to include *both*

religious and secular ways of thinking and living under the same broad heading.

The emphasis on the hidden and the non-material is necessary as most of the school curriculum is rightly concerned with giving pupils a knowledge and understanding of the material and physical aspects of life. The reality and importance of these aspects of our life are obvious and beyond question. In my view, the hidden and the non-material are not emphasized here in order to suggest that the material and obvious are unimportant. The aim is rather to counter the possibility of an unreflective drift towards the view that material things are the only real and important things, i.e., the *only* possible source of spiritual value, and that immediate personal pleasure is the *only* form of spiritual fulfilment. This is a very real possibility in our society where such a view is promoted actively by powerful agencies.

In view of this the school must acknowledge and take responsibility for its own agency. It has a spiritually formative role to play in ensuring that its pupils both engage in an exploration of their own experience and are enabled to reflect critically on the broad range of traditional spiritual alternatives together with the accumulated human experience that they embody.

These points are extremely important if a consensus is to be established around the notion of spiritual development, since there are those on both sides of the debate with a variety of motives who refuse to accept any notion of transcendence which is not characterized in *purely* religious terms.

4. The use of the term 'spiritual' in recent educational legislation, both in 1944 and 1988, has been motivated by a political desire to unite all those who accept the need for the promotion of civilized values through education in such a way as to include a growing number who would not link those values with adherence to a religious tradition. Following from this is a view that all pupils can benefit from spiritual development, irrespective of their background in any one of a number of religions or in none.

The concept of the 'spiritual' within this legislation is designed to be wholly non-exclusive of any pupil or of any interest group in a way that 'religious' could not be (Priestley, 1985, pp. 112–13).

A WORKING DEFINITION OF 'COMMON SPIRITUALITY'

In this chapter the word 'spiritual' will refer to anything which might be regarded as a source of inspiration to a person's life. It is connected to those things which support and give life to a person's ideals, goals, sense of purpose and identity. The area of life concerned with and influenced by such values could be called spirituality. There is obviously a close connection between spirituality, personality and moral behaviour. Likewise a community might be said to have a spiritual dimension or 'ethos'. Each individual could be said to have a constitutive spiritual aspect (soul) which is nourished by those sources of inspiration, provided by the community, and which, in turn, resources individual aspirations and ideals.

There is a fundamental link between the spiritual and moral dimensions of both personal and social life. The spiritual is connected with that which inspires an individual or group and characterizes and influences their quality of life. These spiritual sources may take the form of beliefs, values, traditions, people or particular experiences and they, in turn, influence the moral and ethical dimensions of our personal lives and the communities of which we are a part.

In some sense the spiritual sources provide the 'food' which gives purpose and meaning to each individual life, influencing the quality of life and moral behaviour.

This spiritual dimension might be regarded as a hidden, non-material source of inspiration. For most religious people the main source of spiritual inspiration will ultimately be God, while for others it might be associated with, for example, a political party, football team, a group of musicians or a piece of art. But in all cases the inspirational quality is probably not reducible to that which could be detected presently by the senses or measured scientifically.

The etymology of the word 'spirit' is suggestive: it is derived from the Greek word for 'breath', i.e., that which gives life to our lives while being constitutive of that life. All this leads to a plausible definition of a common spiritual dimension of human existence which both lines up with our day-to-day use of words rooted in the language of spirituality (e.g., inspiration, aspiration, charismatic, spirited, 'that's the spirit!', etc.) and at one with current educational legislation.

Spirituality is that quality of being, holistically conceived, made up of insight, beliefs, values, attitudes/emotions and behavioural dispositions, which both informs and may be informed by lived experience. The cognitive aspects of our common spirituality can be described, at any particular time, as being a 'framework' of ideals, beliefs and values about oneself, one's relations with others and reality/the 'world'. Logically intrinsic to this framework, and rooted in a notion of what is real and ultimately significant, is some conception of the good life (possibly, but not necessarily, related to a supreme will and agency), which informs (implicitly, via a network of unexamined assumptions/prejudices or explicitly, via rational justification), but may not determine, all action.

This definition has a number of important features:

The definition of the spiritual is non-evaluative. Anyone who has attained a certain minimal level of cognitive development has the kind of spiritual life that is encompassed by the definition. It therefore applies, *at the very least*, to all pupils of ages 7 to 19 in non-special state schools. It will also be noted that the definition leaves open the extent to which any particular or *de facto* framework of belief and value *determines* experience and action.

Being non-evaluative, the definition also accommodates pluralism. It rules out no conception of what might, for any given individual, constitute a good life. It accommodates the secular and even those which are expressed through immoral or amoral lifestyles.

The definition could be applied to any human being. One does not have to be religious in order to have a spiritual aspect.

The definition avoids locating the spiritual exclusively with the mental rather than with the physical, or with the affective rather than the cognitive.

I offer this definition not primarily because it is in line with current or past linguistic usage and certainly not because it breaks through to some pure conception in the realm of ideas. I offer it rather because, in my judgement, it, or something much like it, stands the best chance of establishing the widest possible consensus for the future implementation of policy, without being vacuous. The definition is therefore unashamedly located, consensual and pragmatic. It is one small but important part of the conceptual apparatus required for the construction and implementation of spiritual development policies suitable for state schools in modern Britain.

THE SPIRITUAL DIMENSION, COMMON SPIRITUALITY AND SPIRITUAL DEVELOPMENT

While it is possible to broadly characterize the sources of spiritual inspiration and to give an account of a spiritual mechanism common to all, it is not possible to maintain the same degree of non-exclusivity when the concept of 'development' is introduced. This notion is *intrinsically* evaluative.

This problem is recognized by the recent OFSTED discussion paper (1994), which devotes a whole section to the concept of 'development', with an obvious and natural focus on how school practice in this area might be assessed. On this question three important things are said.

- The school cannot be judged on or expect its policy to result in specific spiritual outcomes, basically because schools are not the only spiritual influence on their pupils.
- There are assessable 'procedural' outcomes of a healthy spiritual policy. Whatever a person's personal values, the ability to express them clearly or reflect on them rationally might be expected to develop and constitute one aspect of school policy open to inspection and assessment.
- The document offers the horticultural notion of 'growth', with its associated ideas of 'nourishment' and 'soil', as a way of thinking of spiritual development that is open-ended, appropriate to the constraints of pluralism.

These comments may be satisfactory as a rationale for the *inspection* of schools, but they may give out an authoritative and misleading signal to the effect that school policies do not require any *substantive* developmental thrust. It might be asked why a school policy should have a substantive developmental thrust. The answer to this becomes clear when it is recognized that certain developmental responsibilities fall upon the school because of the role it has within a liberal and democratic society. It has responsibilities towards society, the democratic process, parents and pupils, all of which have legitimate interests in the values promoted by the school. This is because spiritual and moral values inevitably affect the attitudes, skills, behaviour and well-being of each pupil and are ultimately bound together with the well-being of the community and the wider society. Personal empowerment is a crucial factor in moral and spiritual development but even this is much more than a private matter. An individual can no more flourish in a spiritually dead environment than could a tree in the midst of an ecological disaster.

Liberal educationists will, in my opinion, take a dangerously wrong turn if they cannot see that there is fertile middle ground between two extreme positions on the relationship between the individual and the state. It is perfectly consistent to say that individuals are responsible for bestowing meaning and value on their lives, and to put in place procedures which enable them to do so, while scrupulously giving up any attempt to influence the outcome. Many educationists working with liberal assumptions have a tendency to characterize any such attempt to work this middle ground, especially when initiated by government or its representatives, as authoritarian and an illicit attempt to blame teachers for the ills of society.

From an effective communitarian critique of the extreme individualist liberal position, one might suggest that the state should take steps to ensure that a uniform set of values is promoted in state schools across the country. If promotion of values is inevitable, it might be argued, then someone in Whitehall or Westminster should decide what kind of country Britain should be and take the appropriate steps.

Between these two extremes is a third possibility which recognizes the inevitability of values inculcation and the social character of the individual but rejects the move towards centralized state control which might be thought to follow from the communitarian position. This position might be labelled 'pluralist liberalism' and it is the one most in line with the pronouncements of the current government and its agencies. From this perspective it is the state's responsibility to ensure that pupils are nurtured into a particular and substantive set of values, via a system of legislation, broad guidance and inspection. It is left to others to decide which particular set of values that might be for each individual school. It would, of course, be essential to this position that any 'nurturing' were open and legitimate, the development of appropriate autonomy being one substantive liberal value that would be insisted on centrally.

While there is very little room for disagreement about what constitutes the flourishing of a tree, this is, self-evidently, not the case with a human being; it is this fact which constitutes the challenge of pluralism. Groups and individuals disagree about precisely which values should be promoted in the interests of pupils and the wider society.

The professional response to this must be active rather than passive. The school has a derived responsibility, acting as it self-evidently does both *in loco parentis* and *in loco civitatis*. For better or worse, school policy-makers are inevitably commissioned, in partnership, with the task of setting out and reinforcing, in a legitimate and open way, a *substantive* set of values which will play some part in enabling individuals and the wider community to flourish in their own, perhaps unique, way.

The vast plurality of value systems available in our society presents us with both challenge *and* opportunity. But the challenges will not be met and the opportunities will remain unrealized unless an important distinction is made. While trying to conceive of spirituality in the broadest sense, it is necessary to recognize that some sources of inspiration may indeed be harmful to the individual and/or society. The notion of spiritual and moral *development* requires a school to take up some value-full position about what constitutes the well-being of its pupils.

The definition of the spiritual that I have given above is broadly conceived and could be instanced in an infinite number of ways. Any given instance of such spirituality will be characterized, in part, by a cognitive framework which I shall call a *de facto* spiritual framework. Spirituality, in this sense, is not optional. Each individual has a framework of belief and value which informs, and is informed by, lived experience. For current purposes a *de facto* spirituality is the particular instancing of the mechanism of common spirituality in the life of an individual.

It is essential that we maintain a distinction between the *de facto* manifestations of common spirituality, held consciously or unconsciously by particular individuals, and what might be called *developmental* spiritual frameworks used by those operating within contexts of nurture and education.

The openness which we aimed for in the original definition of the 'spiritual' is not an option when we are operating with a notion of 'development'. Here a non-judgemental openness to an infinite range of possible spiritualities on grounds of pluralism, or a misplaced desire to avoid passing judgement on the spiritual life of pupils, is undesirable since the notion of development *must* incorporate some particular view of human well-being. This is true even if it is characterized negatively in terms of the avoidance of what is harmful.

I am not suggesting that each school should work with a particular complete and positive view of human well-being. At an individual or communal level, we have to recognize that a *de facto* spiritual framework might be secular, materialist or even immoral. But it would be wrong to assume that because we might call this a 'spiritual' framework at some level, we are thereby compelled to accommodate it, *as an ideal*, in the policy for *spiritual development*. Schools should, for reasons set out above, promote a particular set of values. From my perspective it is axiomatic that those values will be grounded necessarily in some ideal view of human well-being and that cannot in turn be dissociated from a concern for the spiritual life of pupils. This concern must, at the very least, regard some forms of common spirituality as harmful.

Developmental frameworks, such as those which might be incorporated within a school's policy on spiritual development, will have to include some *evaluative* element and will have to make implicit judgements regarding the spiritual state of the individuals under its jurisdiction. Even the most pluralist and liberal spiritual development policies will, at the very least, contain certain limits upon the range of allowable ideals of spirituality. Those limits will have built into them certain assumptions about human well-being. Monistic conceptions of spiritual development will embody a particular spiritual ideal, as well as a positive commitment to a range of values and beliefs.

A liberal education policy erected on purely procedural values cannot succeed since it fails at the very least to acknowledge the role which education plays and must play in promoting values and personal characteristics (of, for example, self-determination/autonomy) upon which a liberal society depends for its survival. The values vacuum which might result from such a policy is arguably 'the best yob-creation scheme ever devised'. It is also arguable that just such a view has held sway in Britain for far too long. Liberal education policies will necessarily incorporate *some conception* of the good; the question is exactly how substantive that conception should be.

The judgement as to exactly how pluralist a particular school's policy should be is ultimately, in my view, best left in the hands of policy-makers within each school. Both OFSTED and NCC guidance suggest that the values to be built into a policy will be the responsibility of the school, working in partnership with parents and other interested parties. The danger of the current approach by both the NCC and OFSTED is that, in the name of pluralism, they are keen to emphasize the many and diverse *de facto* manifestations of the common spiritual mechanism, while failing (NCC) or failing properly and clearly (OFSTED) to draw the kind of distinction which I am recommending here. The result of this may be to encourage school policy-makers to adopt a wholly non-judgemental approach to the moral and spiritual development of their pupils, especially when this is combined with the commonly held assumption that the individualist liberalism sketched out above is the only alternative to an unacceptable authoritarianism.

In addition, I suspect that it may be some failure to recognize this distinction which makes several fashionable approaches to spiritual development seem attractive simply because they are apparently more accommodating of the secular world-view so prevalent in the classroom and less judgemental of *de facto* spiritualities (Newby, 1993). I think this is partly true of both the 'experiential' and 'non-realist' approaches which I discuss below.

A MAP OF POSSIBLE POLICY ASSUMPTIONS

There are a range of logical issues which can only be made clear and discussed adequately when a clear distinction is made between 'common spirituality' and spiritual development and when a number of possible developmental policy assumptions are explicitly recognized.

In order both to help school policy-makers get in touch with their assumptions and to place the following discussion in a helpful context, I would like to put forward a theoretical framework for the mapping of any proposed model of spiritual *development*.

Eight dimensions for classifying developmental models of spirituality

1 Source/s   *Tradition — Individual experience*
What are the creative sources of the process of spiritual development? Are traditional beliefs and practices seen as an enabling source or as a

disabling hindrance to spiritual growth? One can imagine answers here ranging from those who say that tradition is the creative source through to those who might claim that 'tradition' is part of the problem, with an 'interactive' mid-position.

2 Location   *Holistic — Dualistic*
Is the spiritual associated with the whole person or with some part/aspect (e.g. 'mind', 'soul', 'inner', 'outer')?

3 Context   *Communal — Individual*
Does the spiritual development necessarily require a communal context?

4 Developmental ideal   *Specific — Non-specific*
Does the policy have specific developmental aims?

5 Conception of human well-being   *Monist — Liberal — Pluralist*
Does the policy incorporate a single set of values, reflecting a single conception of the good life (monism), does it incorporate a single set of values at the procedural level, while enabling individuals to develop one of a range of substantive good life conceptions (liberalism), or does it incorporate a plurality of good life conceptions even at the procedural level (Kekesian pluralism)? (Kekes, 1993)

6 Approach to truth   *Objectivist — Instrumentalist —Subjectivist*
Does the policy aim to facilitate discovery or self-expression? If the notions of 'truth' and 'reality' are used to underpin spiritual development, how are they characterized?

7 Characterization of transcendence   *Realist — Non-realist*
Does the developmental ideal of the policy accommodate or rule out a metaphysically real approach to transcendence? How is the relationship between the immanent and transcendent characterized?

8 Assessment   *Assessable — Non-assessable*
Can the level of spiritual development be assessed? Are the criteria substantive or procedural?

This framework of dimensions should give a useful method of 'placing' any potential model of spiritual development, discussing its educational potential and its philosophical presuppositions. In the rest of this chapter I shall canvass two currently influential models, the 'experiential' and the 'non-realist', which might appeal to liberal policy-makers wishing to avoid the charge of indoctrination and recognizing the plural and secular nature of modern Britain. The discussion of these two models will illustrate in some detail how the framework of dimensions can be used to draw out, set in context and be the basis for discussion of the philosophical assumptions of any particular model.

THE EXPERIENTIAL APPROACH

The so-called experiential approach is already quite influential among a range of Religious Education practitioners as a corrective to the emphasis on the external and public aspects of religion which has prevailed since the early 1970s. According to this corrective analysis, Religious Education, in a bid to gain academic and curricular respectability, has lost sight of its developmental role. In moving from a confessional approach, where nurture of the child into a particular faith was a recognized part of the Religious Education teacher's agenda, to one where religious phenomena are studied in several of their many forms, without preference for any one, something has allegedly been lost. Schools are now recognizing the plural nature of British society and are no longer taking up a position on the truth of the various religions that are studied. However, while this meets some of the educational needs of a liberal and pluralist society, the requirement that schools must play some role in the spiritual development of their pupils has been neglected.

The experiential approach, as presented, for example, by Hammond, Hay et al. (1990), offers a methodology for reintroducing spiritual development into Religious Education and other curriculum areas (see also Marjon, 1990; Mackley, 1993; and Stone, 1992). It consists of organizing activities, like meditation and guided fantasy, which allow pupils to reflect upon their own life experience within the context of what appears to be a purely therapeutic, and apparently cognitively neutral, set of procedural values. The promise of such an approach for those operating with liberal and pluralist values in the state education system is that it offers a way of promoting spiritual development without having to promote any particular set of substantive values.

The experiential approach seems to embody values and assumptions which might be characterized as a neo-romantic attempt to nourish a child's spirituality through a focus on the natural and pure realm of his or her own experience, gathering self-evident values, uncontaminated by the wider society or any 'theological' tradition (i.e. institutions). This suggests an inherent individualism about both the source and context for spiritual development. This is brought out by asking the questions underpinning the first dimension of the framework set out above. The experientialist model, in identifying the *source* of spiritual growth in a reflection on personal experience, is clearly located at the right-hand pole and the individualism which underpins it.

This individualist bias might be thought advantageous when considered in relation to dimensions 4 and 5. One of the apparent disadvantages of the confessional approach to spiritual development is that it presupposes a narrow, particular and traditional conception of human well-being. It is the pluralist context of the common school which rules out the monist approach to spirituality. Controversy and conflict might be avoided by opting for an approach based around personal experience since the truths which might arise from it are connected with what is most immanent and undeniable. In relation to dimension 4, the clear emphasis is towards a developmental ideal that is non-specific, reflecting the fact that the outcomes of the developmental process are not determined in advance.

In a recent discussion of the work of Hammond, Hay et al., Adrian Thatcher (1991) says that the emphasis upon 'inwardness' that characterizes the experiential approach disqualifies it as a suitable candidate for the development of spirituality in schools. Such an approach, he says, is dangerously 'dualistic' and leads to a radical and unacceptable individualism. In terms of the framework of dimensions, the allegation is that the experiential approach *must* be mapped at the right-hand pole of *both* dimensions 1 and 2.

While I accept that this is indeed true of the first dimension, there does not appear to be any *necessary* connection between the experientialist approach and the kind of mind-body dualism that is alleged by Thatcher. His attempt to find evidence for the existence of philosophical dualism in the work of Hammond and Hay *et al.* is, in fact, as I have argued elsewhere (Mott-Thornton, forthcoming), evidence of a failure to appreciate the difference between

- the attempt to locate the spiritual *exclusively* with the private and the inner aspects of human life, and
- the use of the notion of 'inner' experience and looking inwards as an important *aspect* of spiritual development.

The first would seem to associate the experiential approach necessarily with the dualistic pole of dimension 2 and with a wholly individualistic contextualization of spirituality on dimension 3. The second, however, appears to be logically compatible with a more holistic approach to dimension 2 and a communal contextualization of spiritual development on dimension 3.

To support his allegation of dualism. Thatcher cites the writings of Wittgenstein and in particular his so-called 'private language argument' (Wittgenstein, 1953). In fact, Wittgenstein's writings do not show that he disallowed all talk of the inner life as intrinsically dualistic. What they show is that such inner talk only finds its place within language games with essentially public and social criteria. Wittgenstein uses various arguments to show that those philosophers, from Descartes to Russell and the Logical Positivists, who found themselves operating within a dualistic framework were wrong to try to build a foundation for their system of knowledge on the basis of sensation statements. If there is a Wittgensteinian conclusion to be drawn in this area it is not, as Thatcher supposes, that we must stop speaking of inwardness or of inner reflection and concentrate *only* on public behaviour, but rather that we recognize that the notion of 'experience' cannot be *confined* to some ephemeral stuff, somehow distinguishable from, but located within, our bodies.

The location of the experiential approach on the right hand pole of dimension 1, i.e., in individual experience, is attractive to those wishing to operate with a non-monistic conception of human well-being and a non-specific developmental ideal (dimensions 4 and 5). It also lines up nicely with the spiritual writings of many religious mystics who speak in terms of a direct experience of God or ultimate reality. Many have supposed such mystical experiences to be foundational for the spiritual growth of individuals and religious institutions, i.e., they are the experiential and epistemological basis of spirituality and religion. This view of the relationship between experience and religion has been challenged and rejected by a number of writers working in the field of philosophy of religion, most notably Stephen Katz (1978) and John Hick (1967/8).

These writers argue that the framework of values and beliefs which individuals inherit from their religious community will be *reflected in* and may *determine* their experience. This analysis has obvious implications for an experiential view of spiritual development. If correct, it undermines the promising link between individual experience and non-monism, outlined above, since it suggests that individual experience is more a *reflection* of the individual's current values than a critical source through which new and better ones are developed.

This has serious implications for those wishing to use the experiential model for spiritual development in schools. On this view of perception, each person would just have their current views reinforced by reflecting on their own experience. If all experience is tradition-mediated, if not tradition-determined, there is just no logical space, it is alleged, for the foundational purity which is central to the educational promise of the experiential approach. Forces quite distinct from experience, and quite beyond the control of the school, would be the *real* source of any change or development if the experimental approach were to be combined with a disallowal of specific aims.

If this is true, then one can first ask whether this could be truly said to constitute 'development' at all, since the *de facto* spiritual forces which reign in the lives of pupils as they enter the classroom would continue to do so when they leave it. In that case the school would be wasting valuable time and energy on spiritual development in the first place.

It is also necessary for those who wish to adopt the experiential model to recognize and defend the romanticism which underpins their methodology. There is a strong anti-empiricist tradition which would deny that personal experience can provide a pure and sound foundation for any kind of knowledge. While there may still be scope from this perspective for saying that individual experience can provide important material for, and be the context of, spiritual development, it is not possible to assume that the value-laden nature of pupil experience can then be ignored. The burden of proof is now with those who wish to assume that individual experience or the methodologies designed to promote reflection upon it are in some sense 'pure'. There is a prima facie case for assuming otherwise.

THE NON-REALIST APPROACH

In the final section of this chapter I wish to explore another aspect of what I take to be part of the orthodox view among writers on spiritual development. It takes the form of a particular view of the nature of truth and reality, underpinning the process of spiritual growth. It could be described as 'non-realism' and it can take a number of forms. Some of these forms are extremely subtle. I am using the term in its technical sense; it is quite possible for someone to use the words 'truth' and 'reality' and still be non-realist in my sense.

My thesis is consciously limited. I am not concerned here to claim that non-realist spiritualities are wrong. My comments are exploratory and are designed to ensure that certain important philosophical presuppositions, which may animate the thinking of school policy-makers, are brought out into the open and reflected upon in the light of criticism.

At the present time, I believe, an orthodox view has developed which takes it as read that a full-blooded, objectivist sense of truth is inappropriate in respect of human values. This orthodoxy has developed despite several recent decisive refutations of its philosophical underpinnings (Haldane and Carr, 1993).

On dimension 7 the temptation, amongst those wishing to accommodate pluralism on dimension 8, will be to move away from any full-blown notion of the transcendent and to concentrate on that which no one could deny, i.e. a notion of the ultimately real which is based on what is immanent, directly present or undeniable.

On dimension 6, there may be an unreflective tendency to move away from the objectivist pole, with its implications towards the expressive, subjective and non-cognitive, since the notion of objectivity might be thought to imply an agreed notion of the truth which is unlikely to be available to the school community, given its pluralist context.

Liberal policy-makers may feel that there is an inevitable link between a realist position on dimensions 6 and 7 and monism on dimension 5. This impression is compounded by the fact that it is shared by Christian communitarians writing in this area who favour both monism and realism (Hardy, 1981; Haldane, 1986). I want to show that this orthodox view of the relationship between realism and monism is wrong.

In addition, I suggest that, while attractive at one level, the non-realist approach may not be able to do the work which is required of it by liberals. In particular, I would claim that their use of a non-realist approach may in fact contravene the requirements of autonomy and pluralism, which it was intended to fulfil.

Realism in the sense in which I am using it is the view that there is a metaphysical reality which both includes and transcends human language and rationality. It can be characterized in a number of ways and it sets limits on what can be truly said and done. It is not limited to the physical and is interwoven by values which continue to exist irrespective of our acknowledgement of them. At some level, on this view, truth must be defined in terms of a 'fit' (not necessarily isomorphic) between this reality and what is said about it. At the very least, our ability to construct truth, meaning and purpose is limited by a sense of reality which transcends any given individual or community. This approach is represented on dimension 6 as 'objectivist'. In contrast, non-realism is the view that individuals and/or communities are at liberty to construct stories which embody truths, without limit and without any reference to a reality which transcends human rationality. An extreme version of this view is represented on dimension 6 as 'subjectivist'. This is the view that values are ultimately expressions of individual preference.

The most prevalent form of non-realism to be found in the literature on spiritual development is that of instrumentalism or pragmatism. It can be found, for example, built into the analogy of the spiritual journey used by Hammond and Hay (1990) and also in Erricker (1993, pp. 138–9). It is a deceptively subtle form of non-realism because it can utilize the words 'truth' and 'reality', while disavowing any reference to a reality which transcends human rationality or purpose. Basically, instrumentalism says that something is to be regarded as true if it serves the purposes of a human individual or community.

Instrumentalism and spiritual development

The danger with building instrumentalism combined with subjectivism into a school spiritual development policy, as the only definition of truth, is that it is premissed upon presuppositions which undermine the values which liberals working in a pluralist context would wish to uphold. Note that I am not saying that an instrumentalist notion of truth has no place in a spiritual development policy but that there are dangers in using it *exclusively* to define truth within such a policy.

The point I am trying to make here is, I believe, significant but also tantalizingly subtle. I am not suggesting that all school policy-makers should put into place the means for judging negatively any pupil who manifests a *de facto* spirituality which is based upon a non-realist view of values. On the contrary, I think we would have to say that anyone of school age exhibiting such characteristics would have to be judged, in some respects at least, as highly spiritually developed.

The problem, as I see it, is rather with school policy-makers who decide to put into place a developmental ideal which views *de facto* spiritualities based on non-realism as more highly developed than those based on realism.

This may sound odd but it is a very tempting move which might be thought to follow almost automatically from a commitment to pluralism on dimension 5.

Any policy involving the notion of development must take up a position on what constitutes human well-being for all the pupils under its jurisdiction. It must be independent in order to give some characterization of what it might mean to say that something is 'true' because it 'helps'.

In an educational setting it would, I submit, be inappropriate to offer a subjectivist/instrumentalist characterization of this in terms purely of what each individual believes or wills to be in his or her own best interests. One only has to think of some of the more outlandish manifestations of what I have called 'common spirituality' to see that this would be a gross abnegation of professional responsibility. But more importantly, it would itself constitute the promotion of a very particular set of values and a very particular view of what constitutes human well-being, i.e., that it is in children's best interests that they be allowed to decide for themselves what is in their own best interests on the basis of their current beliefs and values.

It is, I think, clear from this that, where it is appropriate, an instrumentalist view of spiritual development must itself rest upon some substantive notion of what constitutes human well-being, which cannot be both instrumentalist by nature, educationally appropriate and able to fulfil the requirements of pluralism and liberalism, since it is by default promoting a single set of values.

At some level, then, it looks as if each and every school policy in the area of spiritual development will have to embody, as critically and explicitly as possible, a consistent and rationally justifiable set of values based around a notion of what constitutes the well-being of *all* the pupils under its jurisdiction. If this set of values is to be open to rational support and criticism, then it must ultimately rest upon a set of truths conceived along realist lines, not merely seen as a set of fairly arbitrary social or individual constructs.

Non-realism and the notion of transcendence

In addition to the problem of the overall rational coherence of the non-realist view highlighted in the last section, I also believe that its exclusive adoption by policy-makers in a particular school might be said to undermine that school's claim to be plural and open. The problem here centres on the non-realist attitude to transcendence.

Non-realism is the view favoured by several moral theorists and radical theologians (Phillips, 1976; Cupitt, 1980) to provide a non-metaphysical basis for moral and religious values. Ideas like 'God', which were traditionally believed to have a metaphysical reference, are reinterpreted to have no metaphysical implications. As the name suggests, such statements as 'God is good' or 'Killing is wrong' can be believed as true but, for such value statements, truth is defined in terms of coherence within a wider socially constructed web of belief, based upon a particular form of life.

It might be tempting, given the pluralist context, to incorporate this view, at some fundamental level, into a school spiritual development policy. Analogous to the 'bracketing' of truths into 'truth claims' in the phenomenological approach to religious studies, it might be thought possible, and altogether more appropriate, to eliminate any metaphysically significant notion of transcendence from a school's policy. If metaphysically realist claims about spirituality are associated with religious fundamentalism and religious conflict, then many will think it highly appropriate, especially in the state school, to abandon full-blooded realism in favour of a privatized view of spiritual truth based upon the notion of what works for any given individual. It might be assumed, in addition, that any alternative realist conception would be necessarily authoritarian and closed.

In response, I would make the following brief points to show why such a move would incorporate a number of significant value assumptions into the policy. These would, ironically, compromise any policy's claim to be pluralist.

- Influential Christian non-realist conceptions of the belief/value dimensions of the spiritual life actually rest on specific, unexamined and highly questionable assumptions about the following:
  - The relationship between the autonomy of the individual, the community and the moral or religious tradition. The view, often implicit in attempts to recommend non-realism in the field of values, is precisely that the only alternative to non-realism is a monist one, allied to the scientific notion of naïve realism which is by its very nature closed. On this view the role of tradition is presented as coercive of the individual. I will return to this in the last section, to suggest a more open and viable alternative picture of what realism might amount to.
  - Science, which is implicitly regarded as having a monopoly on the really 'true' and a veto on any notion of what is really 'real'. Non-realism is therefore usually premissed on a quite specifically realist metaphysic (i.e., that of positivism) which rules out any notion of the supernatural or any cognitively significant notion of transcendence. (Banner, 1990)

- Ironically, while non-realists make much of the notion of personal autonomy, their non-realist model of spiritual development is in danger of violating personal autonomy in the educational field. If it were used as a developmental model of spirituality it would rule out certain *de facto* options by ruling out good-life ideals based upon a realist view of transcendence. (Ward, 1982)
- Although it would be wholly appropriate to give due place to non-realist spirituality as a *de facto* option, it seems very counter-intuitive to suggest, as a non-realist model of *development* logically would, that spiritual development could be truly 'spiritual' while operating in such a way as to *rule out* the notion of divine transcendence as a potential source of spiritual inspiration.
- Pure non-realism, whether in the realm of religion or science, can be shown to be unworkable as well as counter-intuitive. Pure non-realism rests logically on a coherence theory of truth which defines truth as a species of 'belief'. But we can ask, with devastating effect, where that notion of belief is derived from. The only option we appear to have which avoids a reference to correspondence with the 'world' (a metaphysical notion rejected by the pure non-realist) is to say that 'belief' is a 'truth claim', but that leads inevitably and self-evidently into a logical regress without end. The notion of truth, and ultimately of knowledge, might alternatively be mounted on a criterion of 'justified assertability', but would that be sufficient? Did those who once justifiably asserted that the earth was flat, on good coherentist grounds, truly 'know' that the earth was flat? (Cooper, 1993)

Critical realism and pluralism
In order to give the full breadth of pluralist options, our notion of realism has to be a form of metaphysical realism, capable of sustaining the transcendental claims that religious good-life conceptions incorporate.

'Critical realism' is the name of one version of metaphysical realism which claims that true statements do depict reality. It is based upon the view that our web of belief is grounded in communal experience, that our experience has its origins in a metaphysical reality of which we are a part and which remains even when it is unperceived by anyone.

The critical realist position is, however, not tied to a single conception of reality because, in a way that mirrors many mystical religious traditions, it says that our language will never allow us to encapsulate it completely. The charge of authoritarianism cannot be levelled at this view in the way that it could towards a *naïve* realism which claims some uncontestable relationship between our statements about the world and the world itself. As such, critical realism can accommodate a range of views about the world, from the fundamentalist through to the non-realist. It is a better basis for a non-monist policy than any based upon non-realism, since that would self-evidently lack the ability to accommodate any full-bloodedly realist view of the transcendent.

I believe that a commitment to critical realism is an essential prerequisite of any school-based policy which claims to be pluralist and open. This should be clearly and immediately distinguished from the view that all school policies in this area must commit themselves to a notion of human well-being which is rooted in the existence of some metaphysically significant transcendent reality. But it is an essential requirement of pluralism that schools do not operate policies in such a way as to rule out life options based upon a notion of a transcendent reality. In this respect a school policy based *exclusively* upon a non-realist conception of the transcendent will not do, since it would implicitly deny the value or existence of certain sources of spiritual inspiration.

On the other hand, a policy based upon a critical realism which explicitly affirms a notion of truth built upon a metaphysical commitment to a reality which sets limits, but is itself not limited (or exhaustively characterized) by any particular view of it, looks to me like the best basis for encapsulating a broad range of lifestyle options *on their own terms*. Clearly, neither of the versions of non-realism that have been discussed in this chapter, despite their superficial attractions, ultimately seems capable of setting out the necessary limits, making its own presuppositions clear, or giving the broadest range of life-options 'a good run for their money'.

REFERENCES

Banner, M. (1990) *The Justification of Science and the Rationality of Religious Belief.* Oxford: Clarendon Press.

Carr, D. and Haldane, J. (1993) *Values and Values Education.* Fife: Centre for Philosophy and Public Affairs, University of St Andrews.

Cooper, D. E. (1993) Truth and liberal education. In R. Barrow and P. White (eds), *Beyond Liberal Education: Essays in Honour of Paul Hirst.* London: Routledge.

Cupitt, D. (1980) *Taking Leave of God.* London: SCM Press.

Erricker, C. (1993) The iconic quality of the mind. In D. Starkings (ed.), *Religion and the Arts in Education: Dimensions of Spirituality.* Sevenoaks: Hodder & Stoughton.

FARE (Forms of Assessment in RE) Project (1992). Exeter: Exeter University.

Haldane, J. (1986) Religious education in a pluralist society. In A. Thatcher and L. Francis (eds), *Christian Perspectives for Education.* Leominster: Gracewing.

Hammond, J., Hay, D. *et al.* (1990), *New Methods in RE Teaching: An Experiential Approach.* Harlow: Oliver and Boyd.

Hardy, D. (1981) Truth in religious education. In J. Hull (ed.), *New Directions in Religious Education.* London: Falmer Press.

Hick, J. (1967/8) Religious faith as experiencing-as. In Vesey (ed.), *Royal Institute of Philosophy Lectures: Talk of God.* Vol. 2.

Katz, S. (ed.) (1978) *Mysticism and Philosophical Analysis.* London: Routledge.

Kekes, J. (1993) *The Morality of Pluralism.* Princeton: Princeton University Press.

Mackley, J. (1993) *What Is Meant by Spiritual Development and How Can the Secondary School Promote It?* Bristol: Farmington Trust.

Marjon (College of St Mark and St John) (1990) *Educating for Spiritual*

Growth. Video material. Plymouth: College of St Mark and St John.

Mott-Thornton, K. (forthcoming) Language, dualism and experiential RE. *British Journal of Religious Education.*

NCC (1993) *Spiritual and Moral Development: A Discussion Paper.* York: NCC.

OFSTED (1993) *Handbook for the Inspection of Schools.* London: HMSO.

OFSTED (1994) *Spiritual, Moral, Social and Cultural Development. A Discussion Paper.* London: HMSO.

Phillips, D. Z. (1976). *Religion without Explanation.* Oxford: Blackwell.

Priestley, J. (1985) Towards finding the hidden curriculum. *British Journal of Religious Education,* **7** (3), 112–19.

Stone, M. (1992) *Don't Just Do Something, Sit There.* Lancaster: St Martin's College.

Thatcher, A. (1991) A critique of inwardness in religious education. *British Journal of Religious Education,* **14** (1).

Ward, K. (1982) *Holding Fast to God.* London: SPCK.

Wittgenstein, L. (1953) *Philosophical Investigations.* Oxford: Blackwell.

CHAPTER 7

Towards a secular concept of spiritual maturity

Mike Newby

INTRODUCTION

This chapter endeavours to clarify the meaning of spiritual development in the non-religious context of secular life today and attempts to do so by focusing upon the connection between spirituality and the development of self-identity. Since education initiates children into the culture which it reflects, it is most important that attempts are made to clarify what, in the common school, this culture might be. This might then enable schools to express their own commitment to ideals within that culture, and to pursue these more effectively. But, in order that they might engage more perceptively in their work, it is essential that an idea of personal maturity be explicated, even if any explication is bound to fail to give a complete or incontestable account.

The meaning of spirituality is here identified with the development of personal identity, and is distinguished from moral development by its focus upon the psyche as the developing self, which might not always sustain its own integrity by conforming to moral norms. Prerequisite desires for spiritual development will be explained and justified, including the desire for a meaningful life-narrative and engagement with cultural narratives which are authoritative in the spiritual development of others. I shall distinguish these prerequisite desires from the criteria of maturity because, although to some they might seem to amount to one and the same thing, they lack the insights, strength and experiential knowledge that mark out a state of maturity.

I shall distinguish ten features of the spiritually developed person. These are independent of a religious perspective on life, and only militate against certain common, if non-definitive, characteristics of the religious believer. My goal is to assert provisional criteria on the basis of which further debate can proceed. These are not drawn from a hat, but are intended to be authentic reflections of the post-traditional cultural milieu of our time. An essential presupposition is that spiritual growth is meaningful as an idea outside of tightly-defined religious and ideological traditions. If this were not the case, tomorrow's adults would be condemned to a life of inner passivity to the powers which determine their lives, whereas there is, in reality, a hope that they will be able to address, resist and transform such powers for the sake of a greater good.

SPIRITUAL DEVELOPMENT IN A NEW KEY

The debate about spiritual development, now undergoing a hurried revival, requires contributions from secular thought. In the contemporary context, spirituality has become, thanks to the pluralism and post-traditionality of late-modernity, focused upon the preservation of individual, national and international identity rather than religious development, and must become increasingly so if there is ever to be a hope of a united global society. Religious believers now face a challenge to their faith from those philosophical and ethical criteria which are integral to the democratic and humane way of life. Religious educators, for example, are now subscribing to the view that specific religious practices are to be evaluated in terms of a common core of shared values which transcend the boundaries of faiths (e.g. Grimmitt, 1987, 1994).

All spiritual development, which I understand as primarily the development of psychic self-identity, requires the composition of a continuous, coherent and creative life-narrative. In what follows, I will consider those shared elements in the values, beliefs and attitudes of teachers, scholars and citizens in our democratic and humane culture, and show how the embodiment of such in story forms may help children and adults in the composition of their own life-narratives. I shall develop out of this common cultural ethos ten criteria for spiritual maturity. These are not claimed to be anything other than provisional, and they might well be more effectively developed by others. They are important because a concept of maturity is an important prerequisite to any notion of development. Unless they focus upon the end-state they are seeking to develop as educators, teachers and parents will be in no position to progress towards more effective practice.

The secular approach need not, however, imply the demise of the sacred story, but rather its mythic role in the development of selfhood. The major role of religious education lies in the development of the knowledge, understanding and sensitivity by means of which the individual can enhance his or her critical and imaginative powers, thereby informing the composition of a personal life-narrative.

According to the National Curriculum Council (1989), spiritual development is the formation of informed, but personally chosen, answers to questions about the nature and meaning of life. It aims also at self-transcendence, which is reflected in achievements of various kinds, and it relates closely to moral, social and cultural aspects of development. The most recent discussion paper (circulated by OFSTED in February 1994) has suggested the secular possibilities of spiritual development in ways only hinted at by the National Curriculum Council document. Nevertheless, it remains the case that the major emphasis in recent educational legislation has been upon spirituality in a religious, chiefly Christian, sense.

The secular understanding of spirituality requires far greater clarification than it has received to date in the debate about the aims of schooling. Most schools do not have a religious foundation, and they are not initiating pupils into a religious view of life. They see their task as educating pupils rather than initiating them. But, of course, policy-makers have long realized that education cannot be value-free. To write policy documents is not only to commend certain values, it is to explicate that culture into which the school should initiate pupils. The following account attends to values shared by liberal educators committed to an education which seeks to enable the transformation of life-quality through the development of personal autonomy. To acknowledge this need not embroil us in the difficulties arising from attempts to formulate a timeless notion of autonomy (Allen, 1982) for, whilst personal autonomy must be defined from within the cultural milieu of the age, that milieu is no longer traditional. The end-state of maturity we are seeking to define is bound to be thin in content by comparison with traditional conceptions, but it will have to define the ethical limits within which personal identity can become individualized.

This requires, first and foremost, an explication of the value-perspective of our common secular culture as liberal democrats, and to show how these have important implications about the sort of spiritual maturity we seek in ourselves, our pupils and our society. Space prevents detailed engagement in this chapter with problems arising from the tension between these values and those associated with the consumerist lifestyle pervading our society.

SPIRITUAL DEVELOPMENT AND THE OPEN SOCIETY

One central feature of the liberal society is its commitment to openness of enquiry. Integral to this is the valuing of critical and imaginative thought which is not restricted by refusal to question accepted authorities. That this rules out certain religious and ideological attitudes should be clear at the outset. For reasons of tact and discretion, it is unwise to specify offending sub-traditions, as well as politically and socially harmful. It is important, however, if we are to develop an integrative system of values, that we give up pretending to show respect for authorities that inhibit change by repressing unrestrained enquiry. This claim requires no supporting argument unless we remain convinced that the only spiritual hope lies in a revival of tightly-defined tradition, as do some (MacIntyre, 1990; Allen, 1982). Alasdair MacIntyre, the most influential of writers who subscribe to this view, can, as we might expect, give only the vaguest notion of what form the best tradition might take (1988, 1990, ch. 18).

The recent emphasis in government consultation papers upon open and critical enquiry attests to the insufficiency of religious spirituality, at least as it is commonly understood. OFSTED itself comes very close to this perception in its emphasis both upon 'what is supremely personal and unique to each individual' and also upon the importance of 'pressing towards a common currency of shared understandings' (1994, p. 8). Spirituality is, therefore, not simply an individual matter, but one for society to address.

The strength of a nation depends very much upon its sense of identity. A weak, woolly notion of what it means to be British, for example, has led to international anonymity and mediocrity, and suggests an intimate relationship between the idea of citizenship and that of personal identity (McLaughlin, 1991). But what, we must ask, is this identity to be like? What might be the shared features of personal commitment which identify members of a liberal, democratic and humane society and which themselves serve as boundaries to the sort of lifestyle citizens might reasonably adopt? What is to be the personal sense of identity to be fostered in pupils whatever their traditional background? Before developing a response to such questions, it is to be acknowledged that it is not possible to produce any coherent expression of these things in an incontestable form. My conclusions will be challenged, but this chapter serves as a contribution to the debate which forms a vital part of progress towards discovering shared meanings.

Given the need to become open and uninhibited in our critical and imaginative faculties, does this not constitute a secularist, anti-religious ideology? I think not, for two main reasons. First, citizens of a liberal state must, by virtue of the principle of freedom of lifestyle, be entitled to hold, and express, views that constitute a criticism of the *status quo*, provided that such views do not constitute a threat to democratic and humane principles (Lustgarten, 1983). It has to be for the government to decide when this is, in fact, the case. Second, debate about religious meanings will surely be encouraged as part of the quest, not only to adopt shared meanings, but also to adopt those which promise the accommodation of diversity within an overall unity of purpose. To this end, the movement in theology towards expressivism (e.g. Phillips, 1971; Cupitt, 1989; Spong, 1994) as opposed to 'theological realism' has become established. Under such a movement, the various 'Master-stories' (Cupitt, 1991) of traditions can be seen as 'ontologically-shy' (Barbour, 1971) parables of life. This accords with the fact that the post-traditional age is one in which fiction is no longer rated as a poor second to fact as mediator of truths-to-live-by (Cupitt, 1991, p. xi). Under an expressivist umbrella, dialogue can become possible.

SPIRITUAL DEVELOPMENT AS THE DEVELOPMENT OF PERSONAL IDENTITY

If we feel so convinced that our common culture is not religious, and that the development of children into maturity cannot be religious in any realistic sense of the word, why do we continue to speak of spiritual development at all? There are at least five arguments on which my case depends.

First, the spiritual self is the inner person, the self as existing behind its persona as real rather than merely apparent. This is the goal of self-understanding, which seeks to distinguish between the self as a product of the expectations of others and the self as a creative agent, only developing in directions which are chosen and understood.

Second, the spiritual self is unified and coherent. Whilst the apparent self may seem unified, judged in terms of name, dwelling, roles and biography, deeper analysis may reveal a fragmented existence in which the psyche takes on a variety of lifestyles having no coherent theme and, therefore, no unified meaning (MacIntyre, 1990). It is one thing to have a variety of pursuits in life, another to have a variety of conflicting pursuits, entailing inconsistent loyalties, desires and viewpoints.

Third, spiritual development is progress from ill-being to well-being. It is the unfolding of one's most enduring and overriding commitments as a person. Such commitments are undertaken with a view to making one's life have meaning and point, and may in some contexts require resistance to the views of convention for the sake of personal sanity, but will not generally be egocentric. It would not seem to be necessary to waste time arguing against a self-indulgent style of life. I take it that spiritual development can safely be defined as responsible, and with the interests of the community at large in mind (cf. White, 1990, ch. 4).

An instructive complication arises in this connection. Whilst spiritual development has a close relationship with the moral life, it cannot be equated with it. The demands of morality may be either met or usurped without this necessarily indicating the state of a person's psyche. For example, someone may be morally upright according to all conventional criteria, yet dwell in a void in terms of his or her own direction and purpose in life. Conversely, a person may be immoral or unclean when judged according to conventional criteria of respectability, yet, through the owning of such unconventional behaviour, find his or her true being. (This was certainly the experience of Jesus and Gandhi when embracing outcasts. It may also be the experience of homosexually orientated persons.)

Fourth, to conceive of spiritual development as essentially religious is as inaccurate as it is to conceive of it as synonymous with the moral. Indeed, spiritual maturity cannot be religious, if religion is understood in the traditional, realist sense. The religious life, as traditionally conceived, is a life for which the celestial view is pivotal. The believer's life derives its meaning and direction from a theological perspective determining language, thought and values. Once we remove this framework and begin to entertain the notion that God's will is valid only in so far as it can be identified on grounds independent of Scripture and tradition (Hirst, 1974), we sense that the age of religious realism is ending. Agapaistic love either makes sense on secular rational grounds, being worth pursuing for what earthly (however long-term) good it can yield, or makes little sense at all. The appeal to heavenly rewards, as Kierkegaard and his successors have shown, is immature. We would be deeply disappointed to discover that Florence Nightingale worked chiefly for her own eternal security. And today the supernaturalist dogmatic has to be transcended if one is to go on caring in a climate where beliefs evaporate like dew in the critical sunshine.

This position gains further support from the insight, which I believe originates in Freud, especially in his essay 'The Future of an Illusion' (1974), that the preciousness of religious beliefs relates to their nature as comforters and motivators rather than their resistance to critical thought. Freud also subscribed to the view that religious interpretations have a *de facto* indispensability to the well-being of most people. If this is still the case, the process of initiation into the values underlying secular education will threaten the protective cocoon of beliefs into which people tend to retreat at times of crisis. Nevertheless it can also have the effect of enabling self-awareness and self-criticism, through which growth out of this dependency can begin. Furthermore, as one pursues the way of love, so one identifies with suffering and death to the extent that one accepts this for oneself as for all creatures. Life comes to be seen as a gift made more precious and wonderful because of its very brevity and fragility. Once we become freed from our concern that it should go on forever, we can focus all our capacity for wonderment upon the here and now and upon all forms of life, without having to feel sad that they will not go to heaven.

Finally, and in spite of my previous argument, the preservation of the term 'spiritual' serves as an important safeguard against the assumption that religious realism is dead for ever. I am claiming that it is dying as a source of personal meaning, *given the conditions of the present age*. The time could conceivably arise when that is no longer the case, and the investigation of a case for realism must continue. Post-traditional life, given its democratic and liberal requirement, must continue to seek the falsification of its own implications. It remains agnostic about the nature of humankind's eternal good.

PREREQUISITES TO SPIRITUAL MATURITY

If we want to talk about spiritual development as the development of personal identity, what might be the signs of spiritual maturity? Unless we outline a picture of this, we remain unclear in our ideas. First, however, it is necessary to elaborate upon some of the attitudes and abilities we need to develop along the way if we are to aspire to the maturity to which they point.

The desire for knowledge and understanding
I need not, I trust, elaborate greatly upon the importance of a desire to develop depth and breadth of knowledge and understanding. Richard Peters' *Ethics and Education* (1966) remains, nearly thirty years after its publication, the definitive expression of values implicit in this desire. However, the rather negative emphasis upon anti-racism, anti-sexism and so on, which is a part of the current climate, tends to obscure the positive values which we should understand and possess. The search for a better life has degenerated into so much witch-hunting simply because our positive values are under-emphasized.

In short, for Peters the pursuit of knowledge and understanding implies an attitude of openness towards others in order that we may learn. That openness involves freedom of thought and expression, the subjection of any sources of knowledge to critical debate, the valuing of honesty, fairness and equality of opportunity as fundamental to the mutual discovery of the state of knowledge and understanding on any issue. Whilst Peters is not often cited on this matter today, it is Habermas and his 'Ideal Speech Situation' that seem to be a ubiquitous source for academic name-droppers. It seems strange to me that Habermas and the Critical Theorists have dismissed or neglected the liberal position and devalued knowledge as being really a tool for social oppression in the hands of an élite, but have to ascribe to the non-relativity of ethical knowledge in order to condemn oppression and strive for emancipation.

Alasdair MacIntyre's celebrated critique of the liberal tradition, to which Peters's thought belongs, fails simply because he refuses to accept the irreversible globalism of the modern age to which liberalism belongs and to perceive its consequences (MacIntyre, 1988, 1990). The advent of intercultural communications on the everyday and grand scale by means of high technology has changed the face of human culture. By contrast with MacIntyre's cultural conservatism, Richard Peters's emphasis upon rational moral principles can be frustrating in its formality and its subsequent failure to resolve all issues of how we should act. We can therefore agree with MacIntyre that all reason is reason within the horizons of tradition, but the global dimension in human communication has once and for all prevented us from evading the threat of anonymity foisted upon us through our liberal education. Peters's position is that of people who find themselves forced to transcend the confines of philosophical and ethical traditions which are less than global in their appeal. We can now begin to see that the key to personal and national identity lies in shared commitment to those very liberal values which MacIntyre disdains.

I have emphasized 'the desire for' rather than 'the realization of' knowledge and understanding because I would not want to define maturity in terms of formal intellectual competence. Attitudes are more important than achievements here. I would not wish to disqualify intellectual low-achievers from spiritual development, for such people may display high levels of sensibility and self-transcendence. It is not likely, however, that the mentally handicapped person can achieve an all-round spiritual development as envisaged here. His or her excellence may well confine itself to sensibilities and attitudes within a restricted sphere.

The desire for self-understanding

Intimately related to the first prerequisite is the desire for self-understanding. As we are aware, the pursuit of this desire leads to painful self-criticism, yet also to the exposure of bias, unwillingness to imagine things otherwise than we wish them to be, and valuable insights into our capacity for self-deceit. Alertness to the 'reflexivity' of abstract systems of knowledge, as expounded in Anthony Giddens's work (1991), strengthens our own resistance to unreserved acceptance of the deliverances of experts, including ourselves. The doubtfulness of all abstract knowledge extends to the knowledge of ourselves, and we have to strike a balance between deference to all and inflexibility.

The desire for sensibility

Without the desire to develop sensibility to the life of others, our development will remain essentially impoverished. Sensibility towards others must be developed out of our first relationships into a recognition of the autonomy of others and away from a desire to manipulate them for our own ends. Just as Buber presented the 'I-Thou' relationship as extending beyond the human context, so sensibilities will have to extend towards all life if the human species is not to gain notoriety as a pest upon the planet (Buber, 1923).

The desire for continuity, coherence and creativity

We must have a desire for continuity, coherence and creativity in our life-narratives. Discontinuity, taken to extremes, can be illustrated by the view expressed by one of my students. She was opposed to the presupposition that life is a journey, with set goals, threats, struggles, victories and defeats, progress and reversal and a final destiny. Her view was that she wanted to enjoy the moment and avoid introspection and self-appraisal and anything that seemed to tie her down for the future. Her attitude reflects, to some extent at least, the philosophy of Moritz Schlick (1987). The bene-fits of this position are that it delivers one from the accountability that arises from interaction with others, an accountability which grows greater the more intimate the relationship. It ensures that there is little need to identify oneself as the author of certain past events. It also ensures that one's life is not likely to lead to anything of deep value to anyone else. In other words, this nomadic and hedonistic lifestyle lacks that continuity of autobiography which is a necessary prerequisite to our fulfilment as social and cultural beings.

A person's life-narrative tends to be of greater value, both to him- or herself and to others, if it belongs to a longer narrative than the duration of his or her own life. If one leaves something of beauty or special signifi-cance behind for others, then life's meaning will not have died with one's personal decease. A work of art, a deed of heroism, a life of dedication to others, a bequest, having and nurturing children, teaching children, keeping a family history, living a life of single-minded devotion to the solu-tion of a problem: all have significance beyond one's life.

The second major feature of a unified life-narrative is that it must be coherent. MacIntyre shows how actions have their context in practices which endow them with meaning and which allow them to be appraised (MacIntyre, 1990, ch. 12). Engagement in practices can be appraised by reference to standards of excellence. The practices themselves can be appraised only by reference to a wider vision of the good life.

The ongoing narrative of a life signifies its own well-being to another. The occurrence of behaviour which fails to accord with the story others are piecing together confuses them. It will, if unexplained by later events, diminish their faith in the integrity of the author's personality. The story of one's life will also be confusing to oneself and others if it lacks a progressive plot which gives it coherence. This suggests the need for a developing life-ideal, or plan, enabling one to weigh up alternative courses of action, use of one's time and money, particular commitments, etc., in the light of priorities. Such life-planning has much less significance in traditional society since the direction of one's life is largely determined by factors one is quite willing to accept. However, things are quite differ-ent in the modern context, as Jeanette Rainwater shows in her book, *Self-Therapy* (1989), for she builds upon the modern awareness that self-actualization is one's own responsibility, to be systematically managed. In modern life, the absence of a plan is likely to leave the individual entirely in the hands of employers, bureaucrats or fate.

The third aspect of life-narrative is creativity. A person will not simply want to fall in with imposed structures, which are, after all, no more than the mirror of others' expectations. He or she will want to become, at least in part, the author of his or her own narrative. We do not want life simply to consist in things that happen to us. Creativity in life-narrative is synonymous with self-transcendence. It is the struggle towards heights that one worked to achieve more in hope than in expectation of success. Through this struggle, people transcend their own stereotype of themselves, and find themselves worth knowing after all. Teachers spend much of their energy encouraging this self-transcendence in children.

There are some strange paradoxes here which threaten to overthrow conventional assumptions about people's worth and potential. In the context of creative life-narrative many mentally handicapped people go through more pain, exercise more patience and climb higher mountains than the normally endowed. They have the potential to evoke a sense that what makes a life worth living is the same as that which the individual brings to it.

The emphasis on life-narrative, especially on our own composition of it in a continuous, coherent and creative manner, does not pass away with the demise of religion. The ontological insecurity awaiting us at every new crisis, new experience, new social opportunity, is only *allayed* by the protective cocoon of culturally defined routines, doctrines and customs. It is positively *overcome* through the composition of life-narrative leading to the discovery of one's personhood. The developed person is one who has a story to tell of effort, failure, persistence, error, folly, learning, pain and success, and that not just for himself but for others and his country's cause. But this account of the importance of life-narrative is quite incomplete and misleading as it stands. Before anyone can compose a story, he or she must first know stories.

The need for cultural narratives

Closely related to the quest for unity of life-narrative, there is the need for engagement with cultural narratives. Story-forms, whether myth, legend, fairy-story, fable, novel or saga, whether fact or fiction, and however mediated to the hearer, whether through film, book or play, are fundamental to the development of personal identity. They are its food, offering imitative models, challenges to adventure, corrective lessons, desirable goals and philosophies for life. They are not instructional programmes but opportunities for imaginative expeditions, occasioning mental play as the entertainment of possibilities for one's life.

One characteristic of late-modernity is the loss of what Cupitt calls 'Master-stories' (1991). Sacred stories have provided ideals, norms, patterns and destinies endowing individual lives with their meaning. Personal identity was, in the past, clearly defined and spiritual maturity fine-tuned by priest and preacher. If children and adults are to become strong as individuals, they will only find paths to take, qualities to emulate and ideals to fulfil as they engage with story. A culture is identified by its stories.

Late-modernity is blessed with a plethora of stories, emanating from world cultures and made available to all. There is no Master-story, and the Master-stories of the past are perceived for what they are. The issue of their fact or fiction has become peripheral to the issue of their power to inspire the life-trajectory of the hearer by virtue of the lessons, principles and examples they inspire.

MARKS OF THE SPIRITUALLY DEVELOPED PERSON

I suggest that the spiritually-developed person may be identified by the following ten features. These criteria are highly assertive and I acknowledge them to be lacking in extended supporting argument. Nonetheless, they show, I hope, that in the post-traditional context of late-modernity, spiritual development makes sense, that, whilst it has a close relationship with moral development, it is quite distinct, and that there can be such a thing as a life of profound commitment to truth and goodness.

Evaluating stories
The mature identity will have critically responded to a large repertoire of stories from many sources, employing their wealth as influences upon the story of his or her own life. The hearer alone must decide which stories mediate truth. The evaluation of story is not, however, simply a personal matter, for the teacher, at least in the common school, indwells a culture of liberal humanism and chooses each on the basis of a number of criteria, not all of which are literary. Good stories are such as enable the hearer to become enriched and strengthened as a member of global society, and which are true, not only to life as it is, but to its possibilities for us. These:

- furnish insights into human experience and needs, especially of those who may not usually be empathically considered;
- shake partisan and egocentric presuppositions relating to a whole range of issues of personal and social significance;
- inspire paths to self-transcendence as a co-worker with others who seek to enhance the quality of life for all; and
- enable the hearer to distinguish life's facticity (Heidegger, 1962), which must be accepted and conformed to, and life's evils, which must be resisted and overcome.

Listening to wisdom
It follows that another mark of maturity is an ability to listen to the wisdom of many cultures, imaginatively indwelling and critically appraising their truth, 'truth' here being considered as verisimilitude to life's actualities and possibilities. The mature self cannot, in a pluralistic and democratic society, remain loyal to one Master-story or religious tradition alone. He or she is a member, first and foremost, of a humane society transcending the bounds of tightly-defined tradition, yet one who knows that the stories and teachings of world cultures enshrine many principles and insights so easily lost in the preoccupations of the present. It follows from our valuing of openness of enquiry that we will be open to the account of those who

oppose our position and that we will be concerned to preserve their free expression. It is, therefore, important to support the interchange of ideas between people of various persuasions. The problematic of tolerance arises at this point, for openness abhors dogmatism and élitism. Whilst it is important to oppose such things in schoolteachers, the action could not extend to officers of religious institutions without generating social strife.

Appraising effects

The mature person will be able to distinguish between the short- and long-term effects of activities and appraise them as contributing to the well-being of self and others. He or she will recognize those forms of immediate desire-fulfilment which lead to future suffering. His or her self-fulfilment will never be determined solely by considerations of the present and will involve forgoing present satisfactions where these might lead to long-term frustration. Mature people will, for example, be acutely aware of the dangers of the natural appetites whenever these are considered apart from their own and others' long-term interests. I am conscious of serious problems at this point, however. It is quite possible that long-term and community-wide considerations may lead someone to neglect the family. Gauguin and Gandhi are oft-cited examples (Williams, 1981, ch. 1). It appears that there are no safe criteria for judging whether a person's neglect of moral commitments for the sake of a great vision is justifiable apart from its consequences for the well-being of a wider community than would otherwise have been the case.

Reflecting on the future

Reflection upon the future will also encourage a person to live in the knowledge of his or her own ageing and death. Without placing this in the forefront of our knowledge, we will not be able to formulate a balanced perspective on our individual worth in relation to that of the rest of humanity, especially the coming generations. The escape of the mind from the fact of its death is primarily effected in our society by our own abstract systems, which serve to 'sequestrate experience' (Giddens, 1991, ch. 5), so that the ultimate questions about the meaning of our lives are only asked in times of extreme crisis, when it is far too late.

This awareness of the brevity of life must be balanced with the perception that one's contribution to the human colonization of the future can far outweigh the duration of one's own existence, and that this generates a responsibility to the future which will serve as a tool for the appraisal of one's actions in the present.

Finding happiness in that of others

This entails, therefore, living, not for the gratification of one's own immediate or self-seeking desires, but for the gratification of those conducive to the happiness of others. Mindfulness of the constraints of ageing, such as the loss of one's physical and mental agility, need not be disconcerting to the person who finds his or her own happiness in that of others. It is of interest that happiness cannot be understood as pleasurability of feeling, for how can I, as one who rejoices in the happiness of another, simply be glad that he or she is experiencing intense pleasure? The reveller may be engaged in wasteful, harmful or even criminal activities. Happiness is not, essentially, a state of the hypothalamus, but the advance of the psyche into self-transcendence in the context of life's battle with the forces of delusion, distraction and despair. This is not achieved without depth and breadth of knowledge, understanding and sensibility.

Independence of material wealth

Such insights will also enable the mature person to develop forms of self-fulfilment which are not dependent upon the possession of material wealth, which is in both limited and uncertain supply, being one of Aristotle's 'external goods' for which people compete (cf. MacIntyre, 1990, p. 188). One will perceive the superiority of those goods internal to the pursuit of 'practices' which enhance personal and social well-being in so far as they are the source of shared meanings in life. MacIntyre's account of 'practices' (MacIntyre, 1990, p. 187) places emphasis upon the depth of meaning they generate for participants by virtue of the excellences internal to them. (It is a fundamental requirement of a humane society that access to a wide range of cultural practices is not determined by the wealth of participants.)

Wariness of 'external' goods

Spiritual maturity will, it follows, inevitably imply wariness regarding the pursuit of all 'external' goods, such as fame, social standing and wealth. This is perceived to be divisive of society, locally, nationally and internationally. Not only is the pursuit of them likely to lead to frustration and discontent, but it also offers a distraction from the pursuit of goods internal to activities themselves. The will to power, acclaim and possession cannot have pride of place in harmonious society. Therefore these cannot have pride of place in the harmonious psyche, even though the desire to create an influence appears to be a common aspect of human nature. The question to ask is, surely, 'To what end?'

Living with uncertainty

Since the significant ontological certainties relate to the event of death and the mutual interdependence of oneself and others, the mature person will learn to live with uncertainty in a way never expected of religious believers. His or her faith will not be founded upon metaphysical beliefs but upon the ethic of love as the way forward in the task of reducing suffering, enhancing life's quality, and conserving the planet. The enduring problematic is not, however, minor, for the age-old problem of balancing care for self and care for others still remains. There may be times when others must be neglected for the sake of one's own sanity and self-fulfilment but, if this is understood and anticipated, the need to renege on past commitments will be minimized, thus reducing the burden of guilt.

Self-control

Self-control is a quality which must be added to self-understanding if real strength of personality is to be attained. This requires, as the Buddhists teach, a good foundation in the maintenance of an overall perspective on what is important in life and what is not. Hasty actions based upon the passions of the moment cannot characterize the mature personality. Passions may have their place, of course, but, like horses, should only be left to run in a well-fenced field. Self-control cannot be attained without having at the forefront of one's considerations in life a range of elements whch are, to some extent, outside one's ability to determine. The knowledge that much depends on luck, who catches whose eye, and on natural endowments, must have the effect of allaying feelings of bitterness and revenge. Our self-esteem must not depend upon how we are assessed according to conventional criteria. Only those with whom we are most intimate can have any chance of realistically assessing the battles we fight and win in life.

Strength

Strength is clearly going to be a hallmark of the mature self. One attribute central to inner strength is the ability to accept the adverse circumstances in which we find ourselves and exploit them to the furtherance of our own and others' well-being. The truly great are people who have overcome the apparent restrictions of bad fortune, employing it as a foundation upon which to build for the future. I think, for example, of Joey Deacon, the cerebral-palsied victim who succeeded in telling the world his life-story after fifty-five years of inability to communicate, or of the rape victim who has used her experience to enable others to come to terms with their own abuse and to help offenders to realize what they have done.

This last point was made clear to me through my reading of the Parable of the Talents in Matthew's Gospel, chapter 24. For the unfaithful servant, life had ceased to be perceived as an opportunity for self-transcendence. The term 'talent' became, in English after the seventeenth century, the term for a natural gift. Reflection upon the story helped me understand spiritual greatness. Stories conserve cultural values and change people's lives. If we lose the great stories of the past, then we have fewer models which can generate an imaginative view of how the trajectory of our lives might transcend the mundane.

One problem which remains is no small one, to which I referred in connection with Freud's perceptions. God has always been present as author, observer, recorder and motivator to the reader of such stories. On the above account, for the reflective person he has become no more than a powerful fictional device. The stories' demythologized message lives on. But can this be so for the child who is deprived of the opportunity to pass through a theistic stage of development? Even as a temporary structure, to be removed when we 'come of age', God appears to be necessary. But perhaps this problem will dissolve itself in the way that the delusions of childhood always have once initiation into adulthood has been successfully accomplished. As Kieran Egan perceived (1986), the mythic capacity remains with us without dominating us once we have come to perceive it for what it is and we can return to it at will.

CONCLUSION: SPIRITUAL DEVELOPMENT AS THE ULTIMATE AIM OF EDUCATION

If we are to conceive of spiritual development in the essentially secular manner outlined here, relating it to the forming of a personal identity whose first loyalty is to the principles of a humane, democratic and pluralistic society, there might, at first glance, appear to be no need for the term 'spiritual' at all. The focus could, it might appear, be upon the development of healthy and happy selfhood, so that a term like 'personal development' might seem to suffice. There is, however, a pressing reason why we would do well to preserve the term 'spiritual', for this draws attention to the development of an ultimate, overriding perspective on life that influences all one's values and decisions. That is no merely personal matter, for people can only be left alone to make up their own outlooks on life at the cost of the communal, political and moral solidarity on which a democracy depends for its identity. It is only when we seriously attempt to delineate shared elements in the meaning of maturity appropriate to our late-modern circumstances that we become clearer about the ultimate point of education within it. There would be little to be gained from investigating the meaning of component aspects of self-development, such as the moral, political and health aspects, were these themselves given no unitary principles to ensure their mutual coherence.

It is through a clear account of the path that spiritual development is to take that criteria can be furnished for appraising accounts of moral, political and health development. And it is, of course, impossible to proceed along that path without possessing a vision, even an incomplete one, of that maturity which, despite the vast range of our personal differences of choice and capability, we all need to attain.

REFERENCES

Allen, R. T. (1982) Rational autonomy: the destruction of freedom. *Journal of Philosophy of Education*, **16** (2)

Buber, M. (1923, 1958) *I and Thou*. New York: Scribner's.

Cupitt, D. (1980) *Taking Leave of God*. London: SCM Press.

Cupitt, D. (1991) *What Is a Story?* London: SCM Press.

Egan, K. (1986) *Individual Development and the Curriculum*. London: Routledge and Kegan Paul.

Freud, S. (1974) 'The Future of an Illusion.' In *The Collected Works of Sigmund Freud*. London: Hogarth. (first published 1928)

Giddens, A. (1991) *Modernity and Self-Identity*. Cambridge: Polity Press.

Grimmitt, M. (1987) *Religious Education and Human Development*. Great Wakering, Essex: McCrimmon.

Grimmitt, M. (1994) Religious education and the ideology of pluralism. *British Journal of Religious Education*, **16** (3).

Heidegger, M. (1962) *Being and Time*. Trans. J. MacQuarrie and E. Robinson. Oxford: Blackwell.

Hirst, P. H. (1974) *Moral Education in a Secular Society*. London: University of London Press.

Lustgarten, L. S. (1983) Liberty in a culturally plural society. In A. Phillips Griffiths (ed.), *Of Liberty.* Cambridge: Cambridge University Press.

MacIntyre, A. (1988) *Whose Justice? Whose Rationality?* London: Duckworth.

MacIntyre, A. (1990) *After Virtue* (2nd edition). London: Duckworth.

MacLaughlin T. (1991) Citizenship, diversity and education. *Journal of Moral Education,* **21** (3).

National Curriculum Council (1993) *Spiritual and Moral Development: A Discussion Paper.* York: NCC.

OFSTED (1994) *Spiritual, Moral, Social and Cultural Development: A Discussion Paper.* London: HMSO.

Peters, R. S. (1966) *Ethics and Education.* London: Allen & Unwin.

Phillips, D. Z. (1976) *Religion without Explanation.* Oxford: Blackwell.

Rainwater, J. (1989) *Self-Therapy.* London: Crucible Press.

Schlick, M. (1987) On the Meaning of life. Reprinted in O. Hanfling (ed.), *Life and Meaning.* Oxford: Blackwell (first published 1927). Discussed in Hanfling, *The Quest for Meaning* (1987), pp. 35–40.

Spong, J. (1994) *Resurrection: Myth or Reality?* London: Harper Collins.

White, J. (1990) *The Good Life: Beyond the National Curriculum.* London: Kogan Page.

Williams, B. (1981) *Moral Luck and Other Essays.* New York: Cambridge University Press.

CHAPTER 8

Childhood spirituality and contemporary developmental psychology

Rebecca Nye

INTRODUCTION

Contemporary developmental psychology rarely acknowledges the existence of the spiritual domain in childhood, and yet the significance of the spiritual has been increasingly drawn to our attention in recent official education documents. There is considerable confusion concerning the very meaning of 'spirituality' in childhood, and a paucity of guiding principles and relevant evidence to clarify our understanding. In this chapter I draw on current theories and evidence in child psychology. Although not designed to address the question of children's spirituality, these contributions from psychology may serve to inform an emerging understanding of the range and potential of children's experience and expression in the spiritual domain. The three broad areas of psychological research considered are the Vygotskian approach to the relationship between language and thought in developing consciousness, children's theories of mind (i.e. understanding the nature of mental and emotional states in themselves and others), and children's understanding of the fantasy-reality distinction.

CHILDREN'S SPIRITUALITY: A CURIOUS CASE OF NEGLECT

At present the issue of children's spirituality is characterized by questions and uncertainties. There is however one certainty – there is no contemporary general developmental psychology textbook that mentions spirituality in childhood, despite the apparent importance allotted to this dimension of development in British education, where it appears alongside areas that are frequently the focus of psychologists: the intellectual, moral, social and cultural.

Curiously, from the etymology of 'psychology' (the Greek 'psyche' translates as 'soul') one might reasonably conclude that spirituality would be the core study of psychologists. However, its omission is not only true of contemporary developmental psychology, but extends across the whole of academic psychology, at least in Britain. And yet among the most influential founders of psychology as a discipline at the beginning of this century we find William James and G. Stanley Hall, who were both actively involved in the development of a psychology of religion. Having suspected the importance of religious or spiritual awareness and response as a core human psychological phenomenon, they inspired many of their students to treat this area with appropriate attention and give proper place to it in the early parameter-setting of what a psychology of the human mind should study.

Contemporary psychology's avoidance of the spiritual nature of its human subjects is often attributed to the secular taboo concerning religious matters, and the demand that as a science it should avoid controversy at all costs. Religion, like politics, is regarded as a matter of personal predilection, and its metaphysical terms of reference are in any case quite at odds with the logical positivist framework that psychology has tried to adopt. That is, psychology currently assumes a place on the intellectual high ground. However, there were equally fierce intellectual pressures on psychologists such as James and Stanley Hall, since at that point religion held the high ground and was highly suspicious of the interest mere psychologists were showing.

But the facts remain, whatever the intellectual climate. Many human beings throughout history and in all cultures have demonstrated a natural spiritual capacity, and have frequently developed ways and traditions that were intended to nurture this capacity. Even in contemporary Britain, between half and two-thirds of the adult population report having had a particularly memorable spiritual encounter (Hay, 1990), confirming the suspicion of those early psychologists who considered spiritual inclinations a common feature of human beings which therefore ought to be included in a comprehensive account of our psychology. Even the most reductive psychologist who might argue that spiritual inclinations are culturally conditioned delusions that will be replaced by a more scientific way of thinking in the fullness of time, ought to be at least interested to study his dismissive prediction of the imminent extinction of such a long-lasting human characteristic that confers no obvious survival advantage!

I am not that kind of psychologist, and I do not regard spirituality as 'on the way out'. But I am intrigued by all phenomena that contribute something to the apparently unique nature of human psychology, and in particular how such things develop. Spirituality seems such a case. Indeed, in some of the many descriptions of what is meant by 'spirituality', the references to psychological qualities are inescapable. For example, the *Model Syllabuses for RE* (SCAA, 1994) define spirituality as 'the highest expression of the human person', and Guntrip calls it 'the essential personal quality of fully human living' (Guntrip, 1969). This suggests that the study of how this emerges and manifests itself in the early life of a person is a question at the heart of a comprehensive understanding of our developmental psychology.

It seems there are as many attempts to define spirituality as there are articles on the subject. The question of what is meant by spirituality is one to which I cannot claim to have a neat answer. Some clarification of my general conception of spirituality is necessary, however, before I proceed to examine whether developmental psychology has anything to contribute, at least indirectly.

I regard the relationship between the spiritual and the religious as extremely important and developmentally interesting to an understanding of spirituality, but I do not necessarily equate the two. There is of course a problem in what is meant by 'religious' here, for in some loose sense, 'religious' can be an adjective synonymous with spiritual (e.g. as C. G. Jung refers to the psyche's 'religious function'). However, as there seems to be a popular, contemporary tendency to adopt a narrower definition of 'religious' as that pertaining to an established, theistic framework of beliefs, the further linguistic distinction seems necessary (spiritual/religious). Creating such a distinction may prove useful for directing our attention to what is at the psychological core of this area of experience, allowing us to see the foundations of the human religious response on to which religions have been scaffolded. A case for spirituality in its own right is found in the work of Berger (1970), who treats spirituality as experience potentially manifested in a number of ordinary human activities and concerns. These can serve as 'signals of transcendence' and it is likely that this experience constitutes the phenomenology of the spiritual. In turn, this may or may not awaken a religious dimension. Watson (1993) expresses a similar view, although her position includes the belief that the higher ground is found in an acceptance of a religious interpretation: 'People can immerse themselves in the spiritual dimension without being religious at all.'

However, she adds, 'if these signals are really thought about, they can lead people to an awareness of religion', since the signals of transcendence are all normal aspects of life but are 'all at odds with a materialistic understanding of the world, they point to something other – something more ... whether or not such factors develop religious awareness depends on the degree to which people can see a relationship between them and religion and can tease out the implications' (Watson, 1993, p. 71).

Therefore, there seems to be a case for taking 'spirituality' seriously in its own right, and some sense in which this can be understood in a wider perspective than the traditional religious perspective. From a developmental research standpoint, this appears essential. In contemporary society, many children have few opportunities to explore traditional religious perspectives, outside the RE class where so many 'facts' are now covered. Therefore to take children's exclusively religious experiences and expressions as evidence of their spirituality could result in the severe judgement that large numbers of simply inexperienced and non-religious-language-using children possess no spirituality. In the light of the definitions above, which place spirituality at the core of what it means to be human, such a judgement seems inappropriate and drastic. Whilst the traditional religions clearly offer time-honoured languages and symbols to reflect our human spiritual response, these languages and symbols alone do not wholly contain spirituality. As Watson notes elsewhere, just as it is possible to talk about the spiritual without reference to the religious, 'it is possible to talk about God without being spiritual' (1993, p. 56). Children's ignorance of religious language and symbols therefore is not necessarily a bar to their spirituality (though it may become a handicap if the child's own 'language' of spirituality is passed over, and never connected to some kind of shared language allowing validation and exploration of private experience).

It can be argued therefore that the relatively small amount of research that has been done to investigate in this general area has too often focused exclusively on children's 'God-talk' (e.g. Tamminen, 1991, 1992; Coles, 1990; Taylor, 1989). Similarly, what little attention psychologists have given to this area over the years has focused on children's religious thinking and concepts (e.g. Goldman, 1964, 1965; Elkind, 1971; Fowler et al., 1991; Fowler, 1981; Reich, 1992). In taking such an approach, these studies have contributed a disappointingly small amount to our understanding of the emergence or development of spirituality, conceived in the more general, universal sense I have argued for above, at its most basic, that of 'attachment to or regard for things of the spirit as opposed to material or worldly interests. From Latin: *spirare*, to breathe: spirit – the animating or vital principle in man, the breath of life' (*Oxford English Dictionary*).

I wish to argue that this focus on the 'religious' end of spirituality may be developmentally 'off-target', and that evidence for children's early spiritual life needs to be sought amongst their perception, awareness and response to those ordinary activities that can act as signals of transcendence, what Bradford (1994) calls our 'human spirituality'.

There are inevitably problems arising from such an approach; perhaps most seriously, it would seem to deny that some children might naturally experience an explicitly religious awareness from the earliest age. Ideally, psychology will eventually be able to contribute to an understanding of such children, but for the present a search for (what I suspect are) the more common indications of early spirituality seems more pressing, especially as most of the major religious traditions do not seem to report or expect explicitly religious awareness of their youngest members, focusing instead on teaching in preparation, as it were, for the later emergence of religious awareness and encounter. Psychology may already contain useful developmental theories to facilitate the understanding of how some children come to an early realization of their spirituality in a traditionally religious form. In Vygotsky's theory of child development, the expectation of other people and of the culture at large is postulated to be a powerful developmental instrument (Vygotsky, 1978). In his account, learning takes place in the 'zone of proximal development' which is the distance between what the child can do with and without help or encouragement. This emphasizes the importance of the social context of expectation and the provision of sensitively engineered 'help' to reach the expected next level of understanding. This has implications not only for the development of spirituality in a secular culture, in which the provision of 'help' scaffolded on the child's natural spirituality may be overlooked in pursuit of more valued goals, such as those of cognitive and physical development. But the role of social context may also impinge in a restrictive way on the developing spirituality of children within religious cultures, since the powerful model of childhood espoused by that culture may reserve spirituality for adulthood, following a period of pure learning in childhood. For example, the old-fashioned practice of children learning their catechism by heart was once considered a prerequisite of spiritual awakening in Christian culture. Both secular and religious cultures therefore need to address themselves to the discovery of where the child's unaided spirituality can be found, in order to provide the appropriate kind of 'help', with a zone of proximal development, to nurture this according to their particular maturational objectives and language.

Another serious consideration in adopting a general approach for a psychological investigation of children's spirituality, is that expression of the spiritual may be largely dependent on religious language; indeed religion can be defined as metaphors used to verbalize the spiritual (Wulff, 1991). If spiritual consciousness necessarily implicates specialized language, consistent with the view that language is the primary tool of human consciousness, then this would support Watson's suggestion that religious awareness is what arises from conscious reflection on the spiritual experience. However, here developmental psychology can also inform the debate, since there are well-documented complications concerning children's acquisition of word meanings, such that their initial learning of a new word may long precede the development of a stable meaning or internalized understanding of that word (Vygotsky, 1978). The problems that can arise in the use of religious language with children were highlighted in a study by Petrovich (1989), which revealed that when the context did not focus on the religious, what young children meant when they spontaneously used the word 'God' (or similar) was free of anthropomorphic caricature, and therefore relatively mature. However, when the word was introduced by the researcher asking directly, response to what the word 'God' meant was quite different, and invariably along the lines of 'a man in the sky with a white beard'. Petrovich concluded that the anthropomorphic conception was one unintentionally taught to children, and therefore the one they reproduce when adults question them. Thus in structuring an investigation of spirituality around a specialized kind of language, such as the religious, there is a danger that superficially understood, 'taught' responses and associations (perhaps dogmatic or hostile) will be predominant, rather than the intended deeper, personal response to life in spiritual terms.

VYGOTSKY'S CONTRIBUTION: LANGUAGE AND THOUGHT

Whilst such psychological research suggests caution regarding the language used to explore spirituality with children, other psychological approaches to development suggest we cannot simply avoid the issue of language. Vygotsky's contribution to developmental psychology is both profound and intellectually demanding, and contemporary Western psychology acknowledges there is far to go before fully appreciating the implications of his theory (Coles, 1978; Sutton, 1983). However, at a relatively simple level, Vygotsky's convincing research on the role of the *inter*psychological, i.e. context, culture and language, on the child's *intra*psychological architecture and development, offers us a potential model for understanding the interplay of nature and nurture in spiritual development. For example, when a child is exposed to a particular spiritual vocabulary it is likely to have a profound effect on his or her spiritual awareness, according to Vygotsky's analysis in other domains. The different religious traditions obviously provide particular vocabularies to describe the spiritual, and arguably some may be richer or more 'child-accessible' than others. As a clearer picture of the nature of children's spirituality takes form, attention will need to be directed to the problem of agreeing a spiritual vocabulary appropriate to education in a pluralist society, such that all children have an equal opportunity to become aware of a spiritual dimension in themselves and its application to their experience of the world.

At the heart of Vygotsky's scholarship is a serious concern to tackle the highly complex issue of the development of human consciousness in a way that does not immediately reduce it to a series of subsets to be independently investigated, in the hope that an understanding of the independent parts will, in time, reveal the nature of the whole. The endeavour to study our human condition in this holistic way seems pertinent to the subject-matter of spirituality, which as we have seen is often described as a feature permeating the whole person. Vygotsky's theory gave priority to the role of language as the primary instrument in developing the unique form of reflective consciousness that humans possess. He viewed the child's so-called cgocentric speech as critically important in this development, suggesting that eventually this gave way to a fully internalized, new mode of thought which he somewhat misleadingly termed 'inner speech'. This is *not* a silent version of spoken language, rather it is a 'descendant' of language – influenced by the language it emerged from, but quite different in form. Inner speech, he argues, is the mode of thought characteristic of mature human reflective consciousness, to which all the uniquely human psychological accomplishments such as creativity (and one might add spirituality) are indebted. Interestingly, the properties of inner speech identified by Vygotsky seem to bear resemblance to the hypothesized phenomenological properties of the spiritual (e.g. Otto, 1950), in being richly symbolic language consolidated to the point of ineffability and yet highly meaningful.

As direct access to this 'inner speech' is not normally possible, psychological 'tools' must be used in order to elaborate and enunciate the content of inner speech. Tools which were high on Vygotsky's list were those of memory, attention and planning, each of which affords a categorizing of an aspect of time, past, present and future. These are necessary since Vygotsky's investigations of this deep level of human consciousness, the first meeting-place of language and thought, led him to suggest that this consciousness served by inner speech is without a sense of time. Again, unintentionally contained within this psychological model there seem to be echoes of what is understood by the spiritual. Many spiritual technologies, such as meditation, emphasize the aim of reaching a point in which the normal sense of time is transcended in the belief that this creates appropriate conditions for spiritual awareness (Csikszentmihalyi, 1975).

This invites a possible note of caution. These strategies for using the tools of memory, attention and decision-making are still developing in young children, and so these tools are still playing a relatively new role in their everyday consciousness. It may be of dubious expediency and benefit to apply or encourage such developed adult techniques with children. They may need to fully master their organizing effects on consciousness prior to relinquishing them to explore this domain in its strong and pure form.

CHILDREN'S THEORY OF MIND

The most active area of developmental psychology in the last decade is without doubt research concerning the child's theory of mind. In brief, this focuses on when and how children come to have a lay understanding of mental life, in particular the ability to impute mental states (such as beliefs and desires, but also emotional states, see Harris, 1989) to themselves and others. The field concentrates on the cognitive capacities involved in developing psychological understanding (as opposed to social capacities, see Light, 1979, on social sensitivity, or emotional capacities, see Harris, 1989, on empathy). Being such a currently popular field, it is impossible to present it adequately here; however, I shall offer some examples which may indicate why this area could be of use to those interested in the child's spiritual awareness and the psychological foundations on which the spiritual may be built.

Spirituality itself has been sometimes described in terms of applying psychological insight or recognizing one's 'inner life' in relation to physical reality (Mitchell, 1994), or at least relating to a particular aspect of inner life (OFSTED, 1994). Thus, in its investigation of how children come to understand the mechanics of mental life (e.g. how a belief may or may not correspond with reality), theory of mind research may be an important early building block in the construction of an understanding of a relation between material and metaphysical ideas, and how it may be experienced by themselves and others. The essential link, as I see it, between this area of research and children's spirituality is that this area of developmental psychology has concentrated on the problems facing the child coming to understand the invisible reality of mental life, and the driving force this invisible reality has in human behaviour. (In other words, beliefs and desires direct the majority of behaviour, yet another person's belief or desire cannot be 'seen'. This research has found that children appear to take some time to come to a functional appreciation of the existence, role, and characteristics of mental states.) In the same way, educating the spiritual includes coming to an understanding about a kind of reality that is 'invisible'. Even if the child chooses to reject such a notion (that there are aspects of experience which are not fully contained within material reality: a spiritual realm), he or she needs first to be able to appreciate the kind of thing which is being referred to in order to examine this in the light of his or her own experience.

The findings of theory of mind research therefore may suggest ways to build a spiritual understanding on to children's developing understanding of the psychological. In addition, the form of analysis given to these findings – in terms of what underlying processes are necessary for mature understanding of mental life – may inform a much more detailed conception of what kind of spiritual understanding is likely to be within the reach of children at different stages.[1]

A key finding of this research is the inaccuracy of the Cartesian view of the mind as transparent to itself, according to which 'the soul acquires all its information by the reflexion it makes upon itself' (Descartes, 1981), a position that for many years informed the field of social cognition and the development of perspective-taking and empathy (Piaget, 1932). Theory of mind research has shown that the difficulty the child has in perspective-taking is not so much a problem in being able to decentrate sufficiently to 'put yourself in the other's shoes' and then simply introspect to 'read off' the emotion or belief of the other person, but rather an initially profound conceptual difficulty in understanding the very nature of mental states (Astington *et al.*, 1988; Frye and Moore, 1993).

Analysis quickly highlights why this might be tricky. Mental states are essentially non-material, invisible and abstract, yet they contain predictive power if we can learn, despite their intangibility, to treat them as causal 'objects'. This ability allows consideration of the unique properties of the psychological as opposed to the physical world, and the recognition that human action is often based on subjective interpretations of 'objective' reality. An ability to distinguish appearance from reality, seeing from believing and utterance from its interpretation becomes possible if this understanding is organized and applied in a systematic, coherent manner: a theory of mind. In practice, this means that the young child of 3 to 4 years of age fails to understand that beliefs can be different from or misrepresent reality. So when the child is shown that a 'Smarties' tube unexpectedly contains pencils, if we ask 'What will your friend, who hasn't seen inside the tube, *think* is in here?'[2] she incorrectly answers along the lines of reality, i.e. the real but unexpected contents: pencils. But, more than this, the child cannot correctly recall *her own* initial belief about what was in the tube (Smarties) before the tube was opened, as this is now out of line with reality, suggesting her concept of the mental state 'belief' is far from mature.[3] (For a review see Astington *et al.*, 1988 or Frye and Moore, 1993.)

As mentioned above, it has been shown that a variety of mental states present the child with similar difficulties, and this suggests a problem with getting to grips with the role of psychological life in one's own and others' behaviour in general, and the independence and potency of physical and psychological realities in particular. Fortunately for educationists, research shows that this problem normally begins to be overcome just as the child starts school, in his or her fifth year of life. Exactly what developments contribute to this new understanding is still a hotly debated issue, but many agree that underlying the child's emerging abilities in understanding the properties and mechanics of mental life is a significantly more powerful capacity for mental representation (see Perner, 1991). Certainly, the ability to understand that it is possible for the mental or inner life to be disengaged from physical reality, and an emerging ability to represent for oneself aspects of psychological reality (in order to compute increasingly complex mental states, e.g. 'I think, that she thinks, that he's sad') must be assets in developing a spiritual outlook. Not least, such a level of mental representation facilitates reflective awareness, frequently cited as a cornerstone of spirituality (e.g. Watson, 1993) and spiritual capacities (Furlong, 1994).

In summary, this kind of research has made considerable headway in mapping the development of the child's ability to appreciate possibility and relativity, and to conceive of the world in terms of an alternative to a concrete view of reality. Together, these seem to be ingredients of a sense of wonder, another oft-cited defining characteristic of spirituality. The younger child may experience a sense of wonder at some level, but once she is able to represent that experience to herself, to consider the context in which it arose and to bring to mind other material such as memories and ideas (for example, religious concepts), there would seem to be the basis for a radically different spiritual awareness (or to return to Vygotskyian terminology, an aspect of an emerging mature consciousness). And as connections and meanings are created in this process of reflection on the experience, a basis for spiritual growth also takes form.

CHILDREN'S UNDERSTANDING OF FANTASY–REALITY DISTINCTIONS

This is an area of research which is related to that concerning children's theory of mind, since again there is a focus on how the child construes the conventional boundaries of reality (material reality). Examining children's particular understanding of fantasy and reality, however, has revealed a paradox. Contrary to Piaget's traditionally accepted claim of childhood realism, children even as young as 3 and 4 years old can demonstrate an ability to distinguish reliably the properties of real things from those of imagined and supernatural things. That is, when asked questions such as, 'Can you touch a real dog / an imagined dog / a ghost?', children correctly judge that only the real dog can be touched (Estes *et al.*, 1989). They are also able to appreciate some of the properties of imagined entities, such as that they cannot be seen by others, and that they can be non-existent, impossible entities (e.g. that pigs can fly). However, there are other signs which suggest that children's understanding of the relationship between fantasy and reality is far from stable. Jersild (1943) reports that children's fear of imaginary creatures increases between the ages of 2 and 6, and that between the ages of 5 and 12 the child's most common fear is of imaginary or supernatural creatures. A recent study (Harris *et al.*, 1991) found that children as old as 7, whilst able to distinguish the properties of real and imagined items, showed a 'tendency to respond as if an imagined creature could actually exist'. For example, having been shown an empty box and asked to imagine a dog inside, the children then exhibited or verbally expressed curiosity to look inside (or in the case of imagining a ghost inside, they were fearful of the box), suggesting that their understanding of the imaginary and supernatural included the possibility that entities in these domains could become real. The authors conclude 'children system-atically distinguish fantasy from reality, but are tempted to believe in the existence of what they have merely imagined' (Harris *et al.*, 1991, p. 120).

On the one hand, this seems an excellent foundation for spiritual educa-tion since the child of this age will be open to every attempt to foster what is often called a 'powerful' sense of imagination with regard to those areas typically associated with the spiritual (e.g. entertaining ideas about the existence and nature of a transcendent reality, and how one might relate or feel connected to that). On the other hand, this sort of evidence suggests two areas of potential difficulty.

First, a note of caution is suggested by this paradox of understanding and confusion concerning the fantasy-reality distinction. A child may demonstrate certain levels of understanding (e.g. that real and imagined have distinct properties), and possess certain cognitive or other abilities (e.g. reflective thinking), but may lack a sufficiently robust framework or ability for overall control and integration of mental life as it relates to material reality. An exercise designed to foster spirituality, such as guided fantasy, may become a very different experience for the child than that intended by the adult, when the child's apparent understanding of the distinct boundaries of the fantasy and reality is not adequately established.

Second, in Harris's (1991) discussion of how to account for the paradox in understanding the fantasy-reality distinction, he proposes a 'transmigration hypothesis'. This suggests that, for a period, children may be ignorant of the full knowledge of laws governing each domain. Thus they may know something of the properties of each, in the same way as very young children know some of the defining characteristics of boys and girls, yet lack the knowledge that these features are stable, that a boy cannot grow up to become a girl, or in this case that an imagined entity cannot become the real thing. The implication of this is that mature understanding takes the form of 'properly' separating mind and physical reality, accepting the popular, but reductive, message 'it's only in your mind'. Spiritual education, the attempt to nurture a positive and creative regard for the inner life and a sense that it can be valuably applied to outer life, is thus thwarted in the very process of development in this area. The task of spiritual education as this stage is reached may be to challenge the cultural overlay of reductionism ('*only* in your mind'), whilst accepting the child's new level of understanding as progress in its own right.

CONCLUSION

It has been my aim to point to areas of developmental psychology that may be of interest and relevance to our emerging understanding of children's spirituality. A detailed analysis of each potential area is beyond the scope of this chapter, but will be the focus of my future research. Clearly, many of these thumb-nail sketches of potentially relevant psychological research are cognitive in flavour, and as such may seem unusual reference points for exploration of the spiritual. It is certainly not my intention to reduce spirituality to a series of cognitive processes. However, just as it is useful at times to be informed of the cognitive domain in order to understand development in the physical domain (for example, that young children may have difficulty mastering complicated rule-based sports, due not so much to physical limitations as to cognitive limitations), so also the cognitive may impinge on the spiritual domain, *and vice versa*. It has been the error of psychology generally to overlook the spiritual aspect, and its habit to focus exclusively on one domain (the cognitive) at the expense of our understanding of the whole child. It is my hope that the study of spirituality can avoid taking a narrow path, by creatively exploring what scholarship in other areas has to offer.

NOTES

[1] There is, I sense, a tendency to regard the spiritual as outside such developmental strictures that operate on largely logical principles (if ... then ...), whereas the epistemology of the spiritual is usually characterized as antithetical to logic. However, if the child's spirituality is independent of such cognitive developments, the empirical study of children's spiritual responses could afford this position greater credibility, since one might find precocious spiritual responses relative to the child's cognitive abilities.

[2] Countless studies have looked at whether clearer wording can overcome the child's problem with these kinds of task, but the phenomenon seems consistent.

[3] The possibility that difficulty recalling his or her own false belief is simply a memory problem has also been ruled out in a number of parallel studies.

REFERENCES

Astington, J. W., Harris, P. L. and Olson, D. R. (1988) *Developing Theories of Mind.* Cambridge: Cambridge University Press.

Berger, P. L. (1970) *A Rumour of Angels: Modern Society and the Discovery of the Supernatural.* Harmondsworth: Allen Lane/Penguin Books.

Bradford, J. (1994) The spiritual needs and potential of the child and young person: a rationale and discussion. Paper given at International Colloquium on Spiritual and Moral Development: From Theory to Practice. Homerton College, Cambridge, July.

Coles, M. (1978) Preface to L. Vygotsky, *Mind in Society.* Cambridge, MA: Harvard University Press.

Coles, R. (1990) *The Spiritual Life of Children.* London: HarperCollins.

Csikszentmihalyi, M. (1975) *Beyond Boredom and Anxiety: The Experience of Play in Work and Games.* San Francisco: Jossey Bass.

Descartes, R. (1981) *Philosophical Letters.* Trans. and ed. A. Kenny, London: Blackwell. (first published 1639)

Elkind, D. (1971) The development of religious understanding in children and adolescents. In M. P. Stommen, (ed.), *Research on Religious Development.* New York: Hawthorn.

Estes, D., Wellman, H. M., and Woolley, J. D. (1989) Children's understanding of mental phenomenon. In H. W. Reese (ed.), *Advances in Child Development and Behavior.* San Diego, CA: Academic Press.

Fowler, J.W. (1981) *Stages of Faith: The Psychology of Human Development and the Quest for Meaning.* New York: Harper Row.

Fowler, J. W., Nipkow, K. E. and Schweitzer, F. (1991) *Stages of Faith and Religious Development: Implications for Church, Education and Society.* New York: Crossroad.

Frye, D. and Moore, C. (1993) *Children's Theories of Mind: Mental States and Social Understanding.* Hillsdale, NJ: Erlbaum.

Furlong, J. (1994) Spiritual development. Paper given at International Colloquium on Spiritual and Moral Development: From Theory to Practice. Homerton College, Cambridge, July.

Goldman, R. (1964) *Religious Thinking from Childhood to Adolescence.* London: Routledge and Kegan Paul.

Goldman, R. (1965) *Readiness for Religion.* London: Routledge and Kegan Paul.

Guntrip, H. (1969) Religion in relation to personal integration. *British Journal of Medical Psychology,* **42**, 323–33.

Harris, P. (1989) *Children and Emotion.* Oxford: Blackwell.

Harris, P. L., Brown, E., Marriott, C., Whittall, S. and Harmer, S. (1991) Monsters, ghosts and witches: testing the limits of the fantasy-reality distinction in young children. *British Journal of Developmental Psychology,* **9** (2), 105–23.

Hay, D. (1990) *Religious Experience Today: Studying the Facts.* London: Mowbray.

Jersild, A. T. (1943) Studies of children's fears. In R. G. Barker, J. S. Kounin and H. F. Wright (eds), *Child Behavior and Development.* New York: McGraw Hill.

Light, P. (1979) *The Development of Social Sensitivity: A Study of Social Aspects of Role-taking in Young Children.* Cambridge: Cambridge University Press.

Mitchell, P. (1994) Comment as discussant. Given at International Colloquium on Spiritual and Moral Development: From Theory to Practice. Homerton College, Cambridge, July.

OFSTED (1994) *Spiritual, Moral, Social and Cultural Development: A Discussion Paper.* London: HMSO.

Otto, R. (1950) *The Idea of the Holy.* Oxford: Oxford University Press.

Perner, J. (1991) *Understanding the Representational Mind.* London: MIT Press.

Petrovich, O. (1989) An examination of Piaget's theory of childhood artificialism. Unpublished Ph.D. thesis, University of Oxford.

Piaget, J. (1932) *The Moral Judgement of the Child.* London: Kegan Paul.

Reich, K. H. (1992) Religious development across the life-span: conventional and cognitive developmental approaches. In D. L. Featherman, R. M. Lerner and M. Perlmutter (eds), *Life Span Development and Behavior.* Vol. 11. Hillsdale, NJ: Lawrence Erlbaum Associates.

SCAA (1994) *Model Syllabuses for Religious Education, Consultation Document: Glossary of Terms.* London: SCAA.

Sutton, A. (1983) An introduction to Soviet developmental psychology. In S. Meadows (ed.), *Developing Thinking.* London: Methuen.

Tamminen, K. (1991) *Religious Development in Childhood and Youth: An Empirical Study.* Helsinki: Suomalainen Tiedeakatemia.

Tamminen, K. (1992) The multiplexity of religious development of childhood and youth. In *Religious Development:* papers presented on the research of Kalevi Tamminen at symposium on Religious Development. Research Reports on Religious Education, Institute of Practical

Theology, University of Helsinki.

Taylor, J. (1989) *Innocent Wisdom: Children as Spiritual Guides*. New York: The Pilgrim Press.

Vygotsky, L. (1978) *Thought and Language*. London: MIT Press.

Vygotsky, L. (1986) *Mind in Society*. Cambridge, MA: Harvard University Press.

Watson, B. (1993) *The Effective Teaching of RE*. Harlow: Longman.

Wulff, D. M. (1991) *The Psychology of Religion*. New York: John Wiley.

CHAPTER 9

Respect for persons: a curricular crisis of identities

Jasper Ungoed-Thomas

Martin Buber (1961, p. 148), opening a lecture on 'What is Man?', recalled that a certain Rabbi Bunam von Przysucha, one of the last great teachers of Hasidism, once said to his students, 'I wanted to write a book called Adam, which would be about the whole man. But then I decided not to write it.' The rabbi's title, together with his synopsis, suggests questions about gender, spirituality and corruption, just the sort of value-laden, powerful and emotive issues which almost invariably arise sooner or later in any consideration of personhood which is more than superficial. It is perhaps hardly surprising that the good rabbi, who no doubt like many teachers was a cautious individual appreciative of a quiet life, decided that discretion was the better part of valour.

However, if we wish to encourage respect for persons in education, it would be as well not to follow the rabbi's example. Both logically and in practice it is difficult, if not impossible, to teach, learn about or exercise respect for persons in the absence of a secure grasp of what it is one is supposed to be respecting. Accordingly, we have to be clear about what we mean when we talk of persons.

Schools are currently facing a curricular crisis of identities. There is a crisis because too few of those with responsibility for education have much more than an implicit notion of what it is they and others mean when they talk of persons. This situation is contributing substantially to the difficulty many schools are finding in educating students to respect themselves and others.

The crisis arises, not so much on account of flaws intrinsic to education, but because of the difficulty which schools can find in evolving effective responses to powerful external forces. In particular, schools' sense of personal authenticity can be undermined by the historic and continuing attacks on that view of the centrality and moral worth of the individual which has been characteristic of mainstream Western thought.

THE ATTACK ON THE CENTRALITY OF PERSONS

Paradoxically, questioning of the pivotal position of the individual origi-nated in the Renaissance. On the one hand, of course, the period saw the emergence of a confident humanism. The concern of the ancient classical world with the individual was rediscovered.

However, the newly liberated intellect was now at liberty not simply to celebrate, reflect upon and explore its own significance. It was also able to turn its full attention upon questioning its place in whatever scheme of things might be discovered to exist.

There emerged the successive assaults, now deeply familiar but still retaining a capacity to unsettle and provoke, upon many of the major assumptions which enabled persons to be placed centre stage in whatever particular piece of explanatory narrative, theological, philosophical, scien-tific and so on, was being represented. Copernicus, Galileo, Darwin, Marx, Hegel, Freud, all from their differing times and perspectives provided evidence or systems of thought which contributed to undermining belief in the centrality of persons.

Accompanying the dispersion of persons, there developed a sustained and prolonged questioning of their interior coherence and stability. Analysis of what was increasingly seen as a crisis, developed in detailed pessimism to the point where it became difficult to distinguish diagnosis of an identity-threatening condition from forecasts of imminent demise.

Adorno (1973) talked of the 'withering of the subject,' its shrunken consciousness, its loss of awareness, spontaneity and truth. Barthes (1977, p. 143) refers to 'A dispersion of energy in which there remains neither a central core nor a structure of meaning. I am not contradictory. I am dispersed.' For R. D. Laing (1960, p. 47) the predicament of the person lay not so much in diminution or diffusion as in being voided of content. He talked of implosion, of 'The full terror of the experience of the world as liable at any moment to crash in and obliterate all identity, as a gas will rush in and obliterate a vacuum. The individual feels that like the vacuum he is empty. But this emptiness is him.'

The ground was prepared for Lévi-Strauss's (1966, p. 247) rallying cry, 'The ultimate goal of the human sciences . . . [is] . . . not to constitute but to dissolve man.' For Foucault (1970, p. 387), the achievement of that objective was thought to be well within reach: 'Man is an invention of recent date . . . likely soon to be erased, like a face drawn in the sand at the edge of the sea.' While the poet John Ashbery (1992), even more opti-mistic, or pessimistic depending on one's point of view, considered that the foretold demise of the individual had, to all intents and purposes, arrived: 'Just being a person does not work any more.'

THE CENTRALITY OF PERSONS

In contrast to the decentred self stands the centred person. While the latter is certainly no longer the dominant figure it once was, it continues to claim attention.

In particular, in education as more widely, the centred person exerts its influence through the role it plays in our inherited Western culture. Furthermore, despite the attacks, for many it continues to represent an idea of what it means to be human which still both makes sense and commands respect.

Each centred person, in its particularity, is itself the substantiation of a universal, an instance of a given human nature. It is *'l'uomo singulare, l'uomo unico, l'uomo universale'* of the thinkers of the Renaissance.

Centred persons are not essentially dispersed, disjointed, internally disconnected in their constituent parts. While they may under particular stresses lack at certain moments full inner coherence, they always, by virtue of their given nature, have the capacity to achieve wholeness.

The condition of being as an entity is fundamentally moral. A person develops as a whole through a willed, sustained and continuing effort to become at one with a particular founding and guiding principle, identified most usually as the divine, the rational, or the good.

To be moral, persons must be capable of exercising choice. They will be autonomous, or endowed with free will.

THE STRATEGY OF SCHOOLS

Given the inherited value placed on the centrality of persons, and the attack upon it, what should be the strategy of schools?

Education, by virtue of its purposes and its procedures, is inescapably committed to certain general propositions concerning the nature and purpose of being human. Schools really have little choice but to accept, first, that persons are able to improve in ways generally agreed to be worthwhile; second, that different ideals can emerge, and that these have to be treated as potentially worthy of respect; third, that persons have, in however limited a way, some capacity and freedom to choose what sort of person they wish to become; and finally, that the way persons develop is open to influence.

Conversely, schools cannot make any substantial educational use of notions which see persons as having minimal capacity for choice, or as being disintegrated, or as finding themselves existentially overwhelmed by the social or historic circumstances in which they find themselves. The nature of such individuals is manifested not in coherence but in dispersion, not in progress but in dissolution, not in responsibility but in capriciousness. This is not an idea of humanity with which education can readily work, nor one which it can realistically help to develop towards a condition capable of inspiring respect.

What all this means is that schools, whether in theory or in practice, are mainly obliged to rely now, as they have overwhelmingly in the past, on that major Western tradition which sees persons as conscious, inward, private, capable of exercising freedom and responsibility and, if not necessarily situated at the fulcrum of their universes, certainly significantly placed within them.

However, teaching predominantly within and about the main Western notion of what it means to be a person is not an alternative to providing young people with the means to understand the full complexities of modern views of a person, and of how they have reached their present point; it is, rather, a necessary precondition for it. As schools become more secure in reflecting in their activities concepts of a person as centred, so they become better placed to provide pupils with a firmer base from which, as they grow older, they can explore or at least try to come to terms with, notions and feelings of decentredness. Ideas of decomposition cannot properly be grasped in the absence of some prior knowledge of what is composed.

WHAT A PERSON IS

Should one respect all persons? Every one?

A genuine respect for others is only likely to develop where there is a securely grounded belief that such respect is deserved.

There are two aspects of the concept of a person which, like the chains in a double helix, are mutually linked. The first of these is concerned with what all persons, of necessity, are: what has been called a status concept. The second is teleological, and has to do with what persons are capable of becoming, in different ways, for better or worse.

Respect for status, for what all persons intrinsically and inescapably are, should be absolutely unconditional. What, then, can be said to constitute the status of a person?

- For a start, it makes sense to follow the dictionary definition, itself supported by ordinary usage, which understands a person to be an 'individual human being, man, woman or child'.
- The concept of person includes the ideas of 'self' and of 'other'. It is, in normal usage, quite acceptable to refer to oneself and to others as persons. Persons have subjectivity and objectivity.
- Given that persons are by definition human beings, it is evident that creatures other than humans cannot be counted as persons. However, this does not imply lack of respect for other forms of life, or indeed for the physical environment. These, like persons, also deserve consideration. It is just that the rationale for such respect rests on arguments different from, albeit related to, those which justify respect for persons.
- No human can be excluded, on any grounds, from the status of person.
- Personhood cannot, in any sense, be racially exclusive.
- Equally, no one can be declared a non-person on grounds of lack of intelligence.
- All persons have life, and consciousness is an essential attribute of being a person. Such a state may be more or less clear and focused, it may be heightened or dulled, it may be dispersed or intermittent.
- As humans, persons are embodied. However, the influence of our inherited culture has tended to distort, minimize or relegate the significance of the body. This has been perhaps particularly true of the sorts of questions which deal with gender and sexuality. Persons are female or male; they are sexual creatures; they have at one time or another erotic energies and appetites, libidinous impulses and orientations.

Despite the detailed analysis and exploration of such matters in recent years, it can still be true, not least in education, that discussion of personhood is carried out as if all persons were male, or as if sexuality were, at best, a peripheral issue. Any such approaches devalue the status of persons.

- Persons have their being in a social environment.
- Persons are complex and protean. They metamorphose, physically, socially, psychologically. In different times and places they appear in various forms, roles and guises. As the attacks on the centred person have argued, these characteristics may be both cause and effect of confusion and destabilization. On the other hand, the possibility of achieving human authenticity arises from this same capacity to change appearance and identity.

IDEALS

'The education we desire for our children must depend on our ideals of human character, and our hopes as to the part they are to play in the community.' So said Bertrand Russell (1926, p. 10).

The question is, what are, and should be, those ideals? Or, to put it another way, what models or ends of a person do we consider worthy of respect?

There is room for argument over what are the key culturally-inherited ideals of a person which influence schools. I would suggest that they are the Christian, the classical, the rational, and the humanist.

I would further argue that schools also have a working model of what persons ought to be. This draws upon inherited ideals, but is predominantly influenced by contemporary thinking.

Finally, schools are involved in the national debate about what it means to be an *economic* person.

The Christian person

Christianity sees the whole person as an *'anima naturaliter religiosa'*. One feature of this view, given more or less emphasis according to doctrinal position, is of persons as capable of ill-doing; not simply on account of their circumstances, although these may indeed play a part, but on account of the sort of beings persons necessarily are.

Unqualified pessimism about human nature is ultimately nihilistic. For Christians it is, however, counterbalanced, indeed in the last resort outweighed, by what are seen as greater truths. 'We are,' as Cardinal Basil Hume (1991) has expressed it, 'made in the image and likeness of God and are created ultimately so that we might share the life and love of God for eternity. We are a unique whole, a physical reality which is also an immortal spirit.'

In religious terms, what Don Cupitt (1980) has called 'A fully achieved ... spiritual subject' must, ultimately, be a person who has a transcendental purpose and who is so developing that such an aim may be increasingly realized. What then, to a Christian, is the meaning of fulfilment for a person? The first answer which can be offered is that sanctification, a growth in holiness, is what we are about. Such a view can be supported by Bonhoeffer's statement that 'The Christian goal is . . . pure and simple . . . to be as Jesus was.' The second, as St Augustine phrased it, is that 'The contemplation of God is promised us as being the goal of all our actions and the everlasting perfection of all our joys' (*De Trinitate*, Book 1, 17).

It is the nature of Christian personal, spiritual and religious experience which often fascinates. It intrigues, at least in part, because of the paradoxes it seems to suggest. It does not, for instance, appear to be exclusive, but to involve forms of perception and enlightenment reported by followers of other faiths and traditions: there seems to be, in Aldous Huxley's phrase, a 'Perennial Philosophy'. Further, in what could be interpreted almost as a contradiction in terms, it is reported that spiritual fulfilment as a person may be accompanied by an obliviousness of self. For Eckhart there is the 'empty soul', for Simone Weil the 'Decreated Person'.

Spiritual experience may be reflected in a certain personal maturity and integrity. This comes about, according to John Macquarrie (1972, p. 45), because as persons go out from or beyond themselves, the spiritual dimension of their lives is deepened, they become more truly themselves and they grow in likeness to God, who is Spirit. Macquarrie also goes on to suggest that where, on the other hand, a person increasingly 'turns inward and encloses himself in self-interest, the less human does he become. This is the strange paradox of spiritual being – that precisely by going out and spending itself, it realizes itself.'

The classical person

The person was, for the Greeks, an object of the greatest fascination. Greeks portrayed themselves as cunning and self-interested; as courageous, aggressive and ruthless; as highly intelligent and endlessly talkative; as curious and observant; and as proud and dangerously susceptible to over-confidence. The Greek ideal of a person was essentially masculine, and reflected a society in which males dominated.

It was, however, the power, and in particular the destructive power, of the emotions which perhaps most fascinated the Greeks when they observed and tried to make sense of human personality. It was, for the Greeks, a matter of the utmost practical importance to find an ideal of a person which could help in the control or sublimation of the worse passions, while at the same time legitimating and strengthening the virtues.

How, then, was a person to develop in a way which was both morally desirable and socially acceptable? For Plato, all emotions except proper pride were classed as appetites and subjugated to those powers of reason which, if properly used, helped an individual to achieve wisdom through a knowledge of the true and the good. However, for such persons reason became at once dominant and threatening.

At the height of Athenian civilization, before the time of Plato and when it was at its most self-confident, it was generally accepted that the emotions and reason should work together. At best, this would result in a harmonious equilibrium of psychological forces, in a balanced personality. Equally importantly, inner concord would manifest itself in completeness. The Greeks valued the idea of a whole person.

The Greeks had a particularly strong belief in the importance of the person achieving excellence, *arete*. This conviction, although not necessarily incompatible with the ideal of balance and wholeness, was certainly distinct from it. While the ideals of both wholeness and excellence involved the notion of a person as an individual entity and as a social being, achievement of excellence was, in the classical perception, dependent on securing the recognition and approbation of society in a way that becoming a balanced person was not.

The ideal of *arete*, originating in the heroic age of Homer, was almost infinitely adaptable. For the Athenians it was a teleological concept. Persons were born with certain natural capacities. Their ultimate purpose was to develop these as fully as was humanly possible. In particular, abilities should be displayed, tested, refined and strengthened primarily through action.

A Greek came to excel primarily through the exercise of power. This involved the ability to make the most of one's capacities and opportunities; more specifically, it meant employing the skills of political manoeuvre to help one on one's way in whatever fields one desired to succeed.

The greatest prize which society offered for the achievement of excellence was fame. This the Greeks desired with an inordinate passion. Tragically, as the Greeks understood only too well, the longing for fame carried within it the potential to destroy both personal and social balance. Ambition and self-assertion, the usual fuel of any drive for fame, could in principle be guided by reason. In practice, they often proved to be highly volatile elements which might erupt at any time into ruthless behaviour and unjustifiable risk taking. A need to excel could degenerate into an urge to dominate or even humiliate others. And, at worst, it could result in personal destruction, at one's own hand or that of others.

The Greeks had a sense of the wholeness not only of persons but, far more generally, of all those phenomena, whether observed or imagined, which they understood to constitute their universe. They sought not simply underlying realities, but rather one single sustaining essence. The reality which was sought by the Greeks could readily be identified with the Good, and with Truth which it encompassed.

If one was to have any chance of aiming successfully for such a goal, one needed to develop as a person along certain lines. Persons must have the intellectual and spiritual capacity to search for the truth. They must also display the moral qualities of respect for understanding of reality combined with the persistence to acquire the necessary knowledge. 'Unflinching thought,' said Burn (1990, p. 142), in discussing the pre-Socratic thinker Parmenides, 'must lead to truth.'

The rewards for being, or becoming, such a person lay in the journey as well as in the ultimate arrival. For the pursuit of Truth and Goodness itself gave a sense of satisfaction.

In due course, just as Athenian civilization was beginning to decline, this philosophical perspective led to a marked turning inward of attention and to a view of the person which was in contrast to the hitherto dominant ideals. Where they had been both contemplative and activist, and incorporated elements of the heroic and the democratic, this was predominantly concerned with the life of the mind. It offered a mainly intellectual vision of what a person should aspire to be; it was élitist in tendency.

The rational person

During the Enlightenment, or the Age of Reason, persons were, above all else, beings defined by their capacity to *think*. The intellectual foundations on which this image of a person was built was substantially the work of René Descartes.

The Cartesian stance, *Cogito ergo sum*, is individualist and dualist. The process of thinking is carried out unassisted, alone. Identity is established with little or no help from others. Relationships have no significant role to play; meaning comes from an inner world. Because being a person is equated with having the ability to think, any function the body might have is seen as subordinate and not significant. Physical care and exercise are only worthwhile in so far as they ensure that effective functioning of the thinking processes is not impeded. As for feelings and emotions, material and somatic as they substantially are in origin, they need to be kept kennelled. Spiritual, moral and aesthetic awareness arise from the workings of the mind.

Of the various attributes of the rational person, the ability to make choices emerged as the one which perhaps had the most far-reaching practical implications. A person was an individual with the capacity to decide what to think, or even feel, and say on whatever topic engaged his or her interest, be it, in the words of J. S. Mill (1962, p. 137), 'practical or speculative, scientific, moral or theological'.

Such a person was essentially autonomous.

Rational persons had the capacity to take ethical decisions, and to act morally.

The idea of a person as a rational being could command, paradoxically, strong emotional commitment. It was perhaps only to be expected that it would achieve more than a cult – almost a religious – status.

The rational faith attracted followers because of its intrinsic appeal. It also impressed those fearful of the excesses of romanticism, who often saw it as a defence against the turbulence of everyday existence.

The main attacks against the rationalist notion of a person were undoubtedly fanned, but by no means exclusively fuelled, by resentment at the presumption of setting up an ideal which ignored the religious. A major criticism was that the spiritual capacity of the individual to be aware of the numinous, to encounter Other, was effectively denied. The profundities, the wonder, the awe, even the fearfulness of existence were sanitized and tidied away. In their place emerged an ultimately arid preoccupation with the thinking self as the scale by which everything must be weighed and valued.

The humanist person

Humanism is a broad church.

A key axiom of humanism is that persons are essentially incorrupt and free from sin. 'Man's first instincts,' wrote Rousseau (1991), 'are always good.'

Instincts are one thing. Whether one is willing and in a position to follow them can be quite another. While humanists are hopeful about human nature, it does not follow that they are unduly optimistic about the way people are likely to behave.

What then, for humanists, is the ideal of a person? It certainly is distinct from any theological notion since, if humanism has one major defining characteristic, it is that it does not accept belief in a personal God.

The humanist idea of a person is perhaps best exemplified in the work of Carl Rogers. Here we see the characteristic belief in the significance of personal development and its achievement crystallizing into a clear-cut concern with questions of identity and self-fulfilment. 'Each individual,' says Rogers (1967, p. 123), 'appears to be asking himself a double question: "Who am I?" and "How may I become myself?"' Here we also see an approach to an individual's environment which interprets it as potentially a source of both disturbance and support: 'In a favourable psychological climate a process of becoming takes place; the individual drops one after another of the defensive masks with which he has faced life . . . he experiences fully the hidden aspects of himself.'

And here, finally, as the concealed features of the individual human being emerge into the light, we see the characteristics which are most highly valued. The ideal person is one who is 'a sensitive, open, realistic, inner-directed member of the human species'; who is 'creatively realistic, and realistically creative'; who has 'an openness to and acceptance of other individuals'; and who, perhaps above all, is someone who is 'open to all the elements of his organic experience . . . who is developing a trust in his own organism as an instrument of sensitive living' (ibid., pp. 181, 174).

EDUCATION'S WORKING MODEL OF A PERSON

Schools have, as well as inherited ideals, what I refer to as a working model of a person. This does not replace but supplements the inherited ideals. It is 'working' in the sense that it provides an educationally useful notion of what persons are capable of becoming and should become.

The working model incorporates some of the main features of the inherited models. Accordingly, it offers a focus for consensus rather than for conflict.

The working model is dynamic. At its best, it is responsive. However, of its nature it is not a finished product.

The model reflects significant elements of current approaches to interpreting the nature of persons. This helps the educational debate to be conducted, not simply within professional confines, but more generally and in relation to the broader concerns of society at large.

According to the working model, individuals should become whole persons. This means that they have spiritual, moral, social, cultural, mental and physical attributes which should be developed harmoniously and in mutual balance for the benefit of the individual and of society.

The working model sees individual learners as protean, and not readily to be interpreted in reductionist terms. This understanding derives, in part at least, from cognitive social psychology, which portrays humans as infinitely complex learning animals.

The working model tends to perceive persons as beings who gain knowledge and understanding through experimental behaviour. Relatively little emphasis is placed on the role of pure reason and considerably less on revelation. To put it at its simplest, learners are mostly seen as individuals who progress through making guesses which are accepted, modified or rejected in the light of experience. This, in its essentials, is the view argued by Karl Popper.

Individuals who are capable of learning through the intelligent management of trial and error, and through reflection on the results, are bound to have a certain degree of freedom, choice and autonomy. They are accordingly, to some extent, responsible for their own learning.

The working model includes ideas of persons as creative and imaginative beings. In its interpretation of imagination and creativity, it tends to focus on these faculties as enablers of learning and moral sensibility. An ideal emerges which may be represented along the following lines:

- Persons are active participants in the world of the imagination.
- Individuals exercise the imagination, not only to throw light on the nature of that which is, but also to explore and exploit the considerable territory of metaphor for its own sake.
- All living things inherit a created world. Persons are also involved in its creation.
- In this perspective, we originate our personal reality. In so doing, we can come to discover how far that reality is shared with, and how far it is distinct from, that of others. In terms of our own understanding, we can also investigate and evaluate not only the nature of the physical world but also of the social world which has been created in the past, the interpretations of which are carried in and transmitted through the cultures of our society.
- The sort of persistent thought and action which results in creation can, in the final resort, only be sustained by what is perhaps most appropriately described as moral optimism.
- In creating, persons give identity and meaning to themselves, and to their world. Through what they shape and become, they reveal what it is they value. Intrinsic to acts of creation are questions of worth. Through the free play of the imagination and openness to reality, individuals have the opportunity to develop a self and an environment which they believe to be worth working for.

THE ECONOMIC PERSON

The inherited models of a person have tended to disregard economic motivations, aspirations or concerns. Partly in consequence, the idea of humans as economic beings has traditionally been ignored by schools or, where acknowledged, seen as a regrettable reality. There has unquestionably existed throughout education what has been called a 'disdain for *homo oeconomicus*'. Moreover, while such an attitude is less strong than it used to be, it is by no means simply a historical phenomenon. It persists. And, understandably, it has been widely attacked.

The working model is beginning to incorporate ideas of the individual as wealth creator. However, because of both historic and contemporary divergences of view, there is to a large extent no fully-established consensus over what an educationally viable model of an economic person should look like.

What schools require is clear enough. They need a view of a person which, while properly acknowledging attributes and motives appropriate to economic behaviour, is at the same time worthy of respect and generally acceptable.

Schools have been inhibited from developing a positive approach to people as creators of wealth by the existence of strong cultural forces which they have both reflected and helped to sustain. As various authors have pointed out, in particular perhaps Wiener (1981) and Perkin (1989), English society for much of the nineteenth and twentieth centuries has been powerfully influenced by a labour movement, a liberal intelligentsia, a public service, and a professional class whose values and ideologies, however different in detail, have had in common a view of economic activity, especially in the context of free markets, as at best little more than a regrettable necessity.

Today, the influences which questioned the place, purpose and worth of economic effort as a human activity are in decline. In this situation there is a real opportunity for education. The possibility exists of moving away from the dogmatic positions into which numbers of the various protagonists have dug themselves over the years.

Any agreed educational ideal of an economic person cannot be partisan. There exists a wide range of possible forms of economic organization. One can reasonably talk of a social market, a free market, a controlled market, a socialist economy and so on. Each of these is likely to be sustained by rather different notions of what an economic person should be. Clearly, it would be neither right nor acceptable for schools to base their relevant teaching on any one particular economic philosophy and approach. Still less would they be justified in aiming to produce, for example, little capitalists or little socialists.

What then are the main economic ideas of a person?

The free-market person

If one considers first the free-market idea of the economic person, one finds reasonably clear, if rather general, ideas of human nature. To begin with, it is said that persons have a range of interests (not identified or explored by free-market thinkers in much detail), which they pursue more or less regardless of other people's concerns or any wider considerations. More specifically, wants are most likely to be satisfied through the acquisition of financial assets.

The wants of the free-market person are liable, whether taken individually or as a whole, to prove unlimited. There is a restless and insatiable desire for further gratification. A *laissez-faire* capitalist is not likely to have any notion or experience of inner serenity or a balanced lifestyle.

Market capitalism, according, for instance, to Nigel Lawson (1993), is based on freedom and liberty. It follows from this that free-market persons are endowed with the attributes characteristic of free persons. At the least, they have the capacity to make choices.

It is true that the capitalist economy does offer a degree of freedom, albeit greater for the winners than for the losers. However, the ability of the individual, through the enjoyment of freedom, to develop as a person is, in certain respects, limited in a free-market society. People do not have any real opportunity, whether acting on their own or collectively, to attempt to develop according to their aspirations through the creation of forms of social and economic arrangement that differ significantly from market capitalism. The individual who does not wish to be a free-market person is liable to be forced to be free.

Free-market persons are hardly social beings. They have to compete in order to survive, and if possible to prosper. The ability to compete is both their *moyen* and their *raison d'être*. Such individuals have no interest, and hence negligible skills, in co-operative behaviour.

Free-market persons enjoy minimal opportunities to develop any ethical sense. They are likely to see themselves as little more than amoral operators.

Alternatives

Alternatives to the free market rest, as it does, on particular views of *homo œconomicus*. These views are often, explicitly or by implication, critical of the free-market model of the person.

Thus, it is suggested that persons in their economic roles ought to be seen not as isolates but as social animals. Only where this happens, argues J. Gray (1993), can there be a chance of developing that rational approach to planning necessary to create the conditions in which enterprise can flourish and markets operate in an orderly fashion.

Further, some recent research appears to indicate that, if only from a practical point of view, economic persons should be seen as having a sense of and a desire for fairness. As various studies have shown (for example, Blanchflower and Oswold, 1994), a key to making the labour market effective is to respect people's desire for fairness. Where this is ignored, economic inefficiency or disruption may well result.

Economic behaviour is governed, according to Robert H. Frank (1988), as much by the emotions as by rational (but necessarily seldom fully informed) estimates of profit and loss. In particular, humans are capable of altruistic behaviour. This is not simply an optional extra, a sort of fashion accessory for the conspicuous consumer of morality, but a necessary condition of economic success. Frank argues that someone who always pursues self-interest is bound to fail.

There is a well-established view which holds that economic individuals of their nature aspire to find work intrinsically worthwhile, look in fact for 'job satisfaction'. In this tradition, work is seen as an inherent source of human well-being. As Caleb Garth put it, in George Eliot's *Middlemarch* (1994, p. 562), 'You must have a pride in your own work, and in learning to do it well.' And some modern economists are returning to this understanding, developing it and relating it to contemporary circumstances.

As I have argued, no worthwhile educational ideal of an economic person can be partisan. However, it is not easy to achieve a balanced approach. It is this problem, quite as much as cultural antipathy to *homo œconomicus*, which has hindered schools from effectively developing an agreed model of what the economic person might look like.

Nevertheless, it is now arguably just about becoming possible to suggest what the outlines of an acceptable ideal might look like.

The economic ideal

- Persons should expect to work. They have an ability to choose, and this ought to be practised in relation to occupation. Of course, individual circumstances or the way in which the economy is organized and managed may make this difficult or virtually impossible. However, that is a consideration which suggests that society should be run along different lines.
- Persons may have occupations for which, through their own choice or not, they receive little or no financial reward. However, great numbers of those involved in wealth creation wish to receive a reasonable personal dividend for their efforts. Clearly this is absolutely legitimate.
- Persons, cognitively, should have a grasp of key economic concepts such as wealth creation.
- As members of society, all persons should have a worthwhile economic role to play whatever their intelligence, ability, social background, gender or ethnicity.
- Morally, persons should be able to apply relevant knowledge and understanding to economic questions. They should, for example, be aware that a desire to make money is morally neutral, in itself neither good nor bad, right nor wrong. They should know that people ought to make up their own minds about what, in practice, is the golden mean for themselves, as individuals and as members of society, between avarice and the sort of laziness or arid self-denial which erodes the well-being of oneself and others. Above all, they should accept that, as autonomous beings, moral responsibility for personal economic aspirations and behaviour rests with the person and not somehow, somewhere, Beyond, immanent in the mysterious workings of the system.

SCHOOL LEADERSHIP

How then, in practical terms, should schools set about educating students to respect persons?

Schools may be tempted quietly to obscure or ignore any spelling-out of what sort of persons they intend pupils to become. And some at least of their reasons for doing so may appear persuasive.

First, there is the sheer complexity of the situation. It is not as if schools are dealing with one or two straightforward, readily described and communicated models. Second, there is the potential for dissension. People can readily disagree about their ideals of a person, and even more about the implications of trying to educate in the light of such ideals. Schools are naturally wary of becoming arenas of conflict.

However, schools have an obligation to be clear about what sorts of persons they wish students to become, and to communicate that ideal to others. If a school is unsure about its views, or fails to share them with students, parents, staff and so on, then it is hardly in a position to provide education of quality: training, possibly.

So, headteachers and governors need to elucidate their own beliefs about what persons should become. Within the general sense of direction given by a feeling of common purpose, a school should become a forum where contrasting ideals of a person are clarified, common ground discovered and differences respected.

CURRICULUM

Models of a person do not appear in decontextualized isolation, intellectual wares waiting to be chosen according to taste. Personal ideals may, and of course should, be raised up so that they can guide and be emulated. But they are also encountered through the rhythms and accidents of school life. The ideas they represent underpin, sustain and are reflected throughout the fabric of education.

Schools, accordingly, need to be able to identify where the curriculum is promoting particular ideas of a person. Once they have gained an insight into what is occurring, they will be better placed to try to ensure that the whole range of planned educational activities contributes in an openly acknowledged and purposeful way to the development of students as the sorts of persons whom the school community considers to be worthwhile.

There should be little difficulty in discovering where schools have been influenced by the Christian idea of a person. One would look, in particular, to their general aims, to religious education and acts of collective worship, to the study of literature and to their pastoral treatment of pupils.

The study of the classics is disappearing from the curriculum of the vast majority of schools. Nevertheless, in education as elsewhere, one still finds strong traces of the Greek notions of what a person ought to be. To this day, especially perhaps in the aims and objectives of schools, one discovers recurring reference to self-fulfilment, the achievement of excellence, the development of the whole person, the exercise of reason and the particularly Platonic notion that the individual ought to have and develop capacities as moral, truth-respecting individuals motivated above all else by a search for the Good.

On a less exalted note, speech days, silver cups, prizes of all sorts, team photographs, etc., all bear witness to a continuing belief in the importance of encouraging and rewarding a striving for, if not personal fame, at least public recognition. Also still identifiable in some institutions, though more as a covert sub-text of the educational lexicon, are intellectual élitism, the belittling of women and fear of the emotions.

The notion of the rational person has exerted very considerable influence in education. For instance, the encouragement of autonomy remains an important aim for many schools. While it may no longer attract the zealous support it once did, it continues to be widely seen as a worthwhile and valid objective.

The curriculum, particularly but by no means only at secondary level, is as a rule organized so as to promote all-round intellectual development. In this it now receives significant help from the National Curriculum. However, less support is usually offered for spiritual, aesthetic, physical, creative or emotional education. The notion of wholeness, in practice, is visualized mainly in relation to the person as a thinking being. In so far as the focus of concern is on training the intelligence, and this is particularly true of policy at national level, the more substantial rewards and resources are not infrequently allocated to those who show specifically intellectual aptitude.

Choice is frequently seen as a good in itself, as well as a necessary means to the achievement of particular ends. Guidance and advice on the selection of curricular options, exam courses, careers, higher education and post-school activity in general are built into the life of schools. Naturally enough, given the inclination to value those students who are skilled at thinking, the quality of what is available to them is often better than it is for their contemporaries.

Education has traditionally paid little attention to the significance and value of relationships. The needs of individuals arising from their existence as social beings have seldom been thought of as important. Many English schools, at least until recently, have characteristically perceived themselves as places where various separate persons, who ought to be rational even if they are not always apparently so, meet together for the primary purpose of developing their minds.

The influence on schools of humanism, and particularly of humanist psychology, is a relatively recent phenomenon. But it is a considerable one. It has also been accompanied by some controversy.

Humanist-inspired thought and research have played a significant part in moves to child-centred education and the development of pastoral care. Humanists have been particularly active in any consideration of the place of religious education and worship in schools. They have, on occasion, worked together with members of religious faiths in questioning the spiritual validity of the notion of compulsory worship and in seeking to secure that religious education is just that, and not simply initiation into particular dogmas, doctrines and practices.

Humanism brings optimism to education. Believing, as it does, that all individuals are innately good and, moreover, have each their own unique gifts, it proposes that education has both the obligation and the capacity to help pupils develop as fulfilled and moral members of society. Ultimately, humanism holds a democratic rather than an élitist ideal of personhood.

The working model, essentially, contributes to ensuring that what schools are aspiring to help students be as persons has contemporary relevance.

The notion, crucial to the working model, that students should develop as whole persons, spiritually, morally, socially, culturally, mentally and physically, now appears in one form of wording or another in the aims and objectives of the great majority of schools.

Perhaps the most evident influence of the working model is to be seen as a result of the emphasis it places on the person as learner. Both in primary and, increasingly, in secondary schools subject content and method, as well as assessment procedures, take into full account the nature of learning. This has, at times, led to an underestimation of the importance of the logic and disciplines intrinsic to particular subjects. Hence certain of the reservations expressed about child-centred education.

Imagination and creativity, in so far as they are implicitly or explicitly recognized as part of the learning process, nowadays usually, but by no means inevitably, find some place in the curriculum. Nevertheless, ingrained habits die hard. The once overwhelming influence of the rational ideal of a person still inclines many schools to envisage imagination and creativity as not so much fundamental personal attributes as luxury extras, to be acquired from peripheral and often optional timetable activities and indulged once the really serious learning has taken place elsewhere.

Schools do now for the most part accept, despite continuing reservations and controversy, their obligation to the individual and to society to encourage personal economic development. School aims may talk of the economic development of students. In personal and social education, pre-vocational and other courses, in tutorial programmes and through cross-curricular links ways are explored, with admittedly varying success, of promoting economic knowledge and understanding. And work experience, increasingly related to the curriculum, is now usually provided for all students. However, few schools would claim to have evolved all-round successful practice. Good in parts, like the curate's egg, is probably the best that can realistically be claimed.

ACHIEVING RESPECT

The ideals of a person held by a school are significantly influenced by its nature. Thus, schools with religious foundations will intend to educate students as good Christians, or Jews, or Muslims, etc. Public, and some other longer-established schools are likely to nurture both Christian and classical ideals. Schools selecting on the basis of academic ability will be inclined, at least implicitly, to place a fairly high value on the belief that persons should aspire to be rational beings. Comprehensive schools frequently emphasize the importance of educating the whole person.

More generally, any school which is fee-paying, whatever its other ideals, will more probably find itself in tune with economic, and more specifically free-market, notions of a person than one which is not. On the other hand, schools which are not fee-paying will tend rather to see the virtues of humans as social creatures, dependent on and contributing to society.

Schools, as well as making their own stance clear, need to help students to look outwards. Whatever their founding and guiding principles, schools should acknowledge the range of ideals which different people hold regarding the ends of being; and they should offer to students a balanced insight into the ideas of a person valued by those with experiences or perspectives which may be in contrast to their own. Where this is not done, there can be little worthwhile education in respect for persons.

Perhaps the greatest opportunities, and by the same token the greatest dangers, in educating students to respect persons lie not so much with those schools which select their students, on whatever grounds, or with those which in some sense offer a special or distinctive curriculum and ethos, but with those schools which in principle and practice aim to provide for all the children, and the children of all families, in their area.

Now that the direct influence of classical civilization on our culture and education is fading away, it is gradually becoming apparent that it is through comprehensive schools that there flows the main stream of educational traditions and contemporary concerns. It is in these schools that the full range of perceptions of human nature which our civilization has inherited and is exploring can be most fully manifested – what that nature is, what it is capable of becoming, and what it should be.

At best, comprehensive schools provide that richness and variety of understanding of persons which is the foundation upon which any education of quality has to be built. From such schools can come students who are learning a real respect for themselves and for others, arising from informed understanding of how many and valuable are the ways of being to which individuals may aspire.

But where comprehensive schools fail to realize what they can and should achieve, the results are often dismal. Such schools can damagingly lack belief in the importance of what they are doing and in their capacity to succeed. Here, amidst apathy and confusion, students can be counted lucky if they achieve even a blurred vision of what it means to be, and how to become, a worthwhile person.

For all schools, whatever their nature, the challenge is to create communities with the knowledge and confidence to enable students truly to learn to respect persons.

REFERENCES

Adorno, T. (1973) *The Jargon of Authenticity*. London: Routledge.

Ashbery, J. (1992) In I. Murdoch, *Metaphysics as a Guide to Morals*. London: Chatto and Windus.

Barthes, R. (1977) *Roland Barthes*. London: Macmillan.

Blanchflower, D. and Oswold, A. (1994) The wage curve. *Journal of Economic Perspectives*.

Buber, M. (1961) *Between Man and Man*. London and Glasgow: Fontana.

Burn, A. R. (1990) *The Penguin History of Greece*. Harmondsworth: Penguin.

Cupitt, D. (1980) *Taking Leave of God*. London: SCM Press.

Eliot, G. (1994) *Middlemarch*. Harmondsworth: Penguin. (first published 1871–2)

Foucault, M. (1970) *The Order of Things: An Archaeology of the Human Sciences*. London: Tavistock.

Frank, R. H. (1988) *Passions within Reason: The Strategy of the Emotions*. New York: W. W. Norton.

Gray, J. (1993) *Beyond the New Right: Markets, Government, and the Common Environment*. London: Routledge.

Hume, B. (1991) Address to Catholic Secondary Headteachers in the Archdiocese of Westminster, London Colney, 24 September.

Laing, R. D. (1960) *The Divided Self*. London: Tavistock.

Lawson, N. (1993) A paeon of praise to capitalism. *Financial Times*, 4 September.

Lévi-Strauss, C. (1966) *The Savage Mind*. London: Weidenfeld and Nicolson.

Macquarrie, J. (1972) *Paths in Spirituality*. London: SCM Press.

Mill, J. S. (1962) *On Liberty* (first published 1859). In M. Warnock (ed.), *Utilitarianism*. Glasgow: Collins.

Perkin, H. (1989) *The Rise of Professional Society*. London: Routledge.

Rogers, C. (1967) *On Becoming a Person*. London: Constable.

Rousseau, J-J. (1991) *Émile*. Harmondsworth: Penguin Classics. (first published 1762)

Russell, B. (1926) *On Education*. London: Allen and Unwin.

Wiener, M. J. (1985) *English Culture and the Decline of the Industrial Spirit 1850–1980*. Harmondsworth: Penguin.

CHAPTER 10

The child in relationship: towards a communal model of spirituality

Andrew Wright

INTRODUCTION

> Noli foras ire, in teipsum redi; in interiore homine habitat veritas.
> Do not go outward; return within yourself. In the inward man dwells truth.
>
> (St Augustine *De vera Religione*, XXXIX.72)

Despite their origin in late antiquity, these words of St Augustine have a curiously modern ring to them (Taylor, 1992, p. 129). The notion of a spiritual depth within the 'inward man', hovering somewhere below the surface of our normal, everyday consciousness, permeates many of our current post-Freudian perspectives on humanity. We should as a result be alerted to the fact that contemporary debate regarding the 'spirituality' of the 'whole child' does not take place in a vacuum. On the contrary, it is rooted in, and dependent upon, a cultural tradition whose foundations were in part laid by Augustine himself, built upon by Descartes and extended and renovated by those interlinked series of cultural and intellectual movements that are attributed the collective label 'modernism'.

A key feature of this collective tradition is that of the primacy, within philosophical debate, of the individual self as a thinking being: *cogito ergo sum*, and in an ideal state I do so autonomously, self-sufficiently and free from external constraint. Into this notion of personhood is inserted the discourse of spirituality. It is by turning inwards, by exploring the hidden depths of the self, that the individual encounters his or her essential nature, appropriates an understanding of ultimate meaning and truth, and thus confronts the heart of existence as a spiritual being. As a result the spiritual education of the whole child is equated with the expansion of the self-awareness of the individual, the illumination and revelation of an esoteric depth of personal experience that previously lay hidden. Thus we find a recent international educational consultation addressing the thesis that 'education in spiritual growth is that which promotes apprehension of ultimate reality through fostering higher forms of human consciousness' (Lealman, 1986, p. 68).

Cultural traditions are not, of course, static entities, and at our particular point in Western intellectual history the modernist legacy upon which such a notion of spiritual education is grounded is in process of fragmentation as its intellectual and moral shortcomings rise increasingly to the surface. What lies in the future remains in part a matter for speculation, as programmes of post-modernism and critical realism battle for the intellectual high ground. One clear consequence of such fragmentation, however, has been the creation of a critical vantage point from which old-established and previously unquestioned assumptions may be recognized and brought into the open; assumptions that consequently require justification if they are to retain any level of legitimation. Specifically, the fragmentation of modernism means that the twin doctrines of the disengaged autonomous self and the inwardness of a hidden spiritual depth within the whole person can no longer simply be taken for granted.

The present chapter seeks to develop these themes in two directions: (1) by drawing attention, at both fundamental and practical levels, to the limitations of the modernist understanding of the spirituality of the self currently operating within education; (2) by exploring the viability of an alternative understanding that seeks to move beyond the implicit solipsism of modernist spirituality towards a communal spirituality within a framework of critical realism. The latter draws upon the resources of the mainstream of orthodox Christian dogmatic theology in the belief that its insights can supplement and broaden contemporary philosophical developments that attempt to move beyond the limitations of modernism.

THE SPIRITUALITY OF DISLOCATION

A key motivation in the construction of the modern understanding of the self was a desire for enlightenment, a quest for a bedrock of illumination and certainty that could transcend the illusions of superstition and falsehood and provide emancipation from that which Bernstein has termed 'Cartesian Anxiety' (1983, pp. 16ff.). The method was that of a hermeneutic of suspicion, a programme of systematic doubt that sought to question and strip away all that might be false in human consciousness, perception and understanding (Descartes, 1969). Progressively the assumed truth and authority of received tradition, the teachings of church and scripture, perceptions of the external world and relationship with the divine were questioned and placed on one side. The result was a systematic dislocation and isolation of the self from all that surrounds it, a radical disengagement from external reality. The individual stands proud and alone: an autonomous, self-sufficient being, intimately related to his or her thoughts and self-consciousness, yet cut off from communion with other selves, the natural order and the divine. The Enlightenment celebrated this as a genuine achievement, the result of a process of emancipation from misplaced authority. The disengaged self had learnt the courage to trust its own reason. However, from the outset, the emergence of the autonomy of the self functioned in terms of 'freedom from', rather than 'freedom for'.

One of the central results of the creation of the modern self was the acceleration of the conditions necessary for the emergence of modern science (Foster, 1934). No longer in interdependent relationship with the natural order, the self achieved a critical distance from it that made possible a rationalistic investigation that spilled out into technological manipulation (Adorno and Horkheimer, 1979; Gunton, 1985). The dilemma to which such manipulation gave rise, grounded as it was in the divorce between the realms of external scientific objectivity and internal ethical value, was exacerbated as humanity itself became the object of scientific investigation. Where both theologians and philosophers had earlier been united in their acceptance, on either theological or humanistic grounds, of the distinctiveness of humanity over against the natural order of things, the emerging naturalistic investigations of the human species now offered reductionist accounts of humankind as being no more than mere natural animal, a species, furthermore, prey to the whims of instrumental reason.

It is against this background that the modern equation of spirituality with the esoteric depth of human consciousness emerges. Against the background of forms of naturalistic anthropology there developed, via a number of divergent tributaries, a broad stream of thought within modernism that Gadamer characterizes as the 'romantic mirror image of Enlightenment' (Gadamer, 1979). The move involved a turn to what Heidegger described as 'that realm of entities which one distinguishes from Nature by having regard for the way in which man's existence is essentially determined by "spirit" and "culture"' (Heidegger, 1962, p. 431). Retaining the image of the disengaged and autonomous self, its task was to protect the distinctiveness of humanity from the rationalization and reification of science by affirming a spiritual depth within humanity that transcends such reductionist intrusions.

Within this broad romantic movement we encounter a move to rediscover a hidden essence of humanity by returning to a primordial, pre-scientific, perspective in which feeling has priority over reason, and mythology holds sway over the discourses of science. Romanticism revoked the rationalism of the Enlightenment and sought the restoration of a pre-rational mythical antiquity, via 'the conscious return to the unconscious, culminating in the recognition of the superior wisdom of the primaeval age of myth' (Gadamer, 1979, pp. 242–3). Liberal theology, as exemplified by Schleiermacher, made a similar move, attempting to rediscover a religious essence of humanity within that primary religious experience of 'absolute dependence' of which formal religious doctrines are but pale expressions (Schleiermacher, 1958, 1976; contra Lindbeck, 1984). Likewise, phenomenological analysis attempted to transcend the mere external phenomena of human culture and enter into the living noumenal heart and essence of humanity. The same move can be recognized in existential distinctions between authentic and inauthentic existence, and in post-modern rejections of any closure of human potential and freedom in the form of a metaphysic of presence.

It is in this dual movement, of the affirmation of the isolated self and the protection of its essential distinctiveness in the face of reductive rationalism, that the contemporary debate regarding spirituality functions. Over against a rationalistic hermeneutic of suspicion, humanity, it is argued, must rediscover a hermeneutic of faith: faith, that is, in the transcendental spiritual depth of the individual self. This is achieved by the supplementation of the rational, scientific and objective with the creative, aesthetic and subjective. 'Truth within spirituality will then be detected less by argument and proof and more by symbol, story, parable, poem, "allegory" sound, gesture, movement or form' (Webster, 1990, p. 357; cf. Starkings, 1993; Harris, 1988). Inherent within this framework is a distinction between the public, objective truths of science and the private, subjective truths of the aesthetic and spiritual realms. This 'had the effect of giving rise to a romantic idealism where the human spirit could range at will, uncontrolled by scientific evidence or knowledge' (Torrance, 1980, p. 27).

In this context post-modernism, rather than being a decisive break from modernism, may best be understood as the perpetuation and culmination of the romantic mirror-image of Enlightenment rationalism. Thus when Foucault seeks to free humanity from the logo-centric metaphysic of presence rooted in the image of the dislocated self, expressing the hope 'that man would be erased, like a face drawn in sand at the edge of the sea' (1989, p. 387), the irony is that the free play of unconstrained language that emerges merely serves to reinforce the isolation of self-reflection from external reality. As Taylor points out, post-modernism 'reflects that the underlying ideal is some variant of that most invisible, because it is the most pervasive, of all modern goods, unconstrained freedom' (1992, p. 489). Rather than achieving freedom from the constraints of the modernist construction of the self, what the post-modernists 'end up celebrating instead, not entirely by design, is the potential freedom and power of the self' (ibid., p. 488). Thus the process of disengagement is taken a stage further: the self is freed from any limiting construction of its essence, whilst the language it uses stands under constant erasure, emancipated from the constraints of any logo-centric reference or meaning. Hence we arrive at a post-modern spirituality that may be equated with an unconstrained play of private experience and language, divorced from any demand that such spirituality relate appropriately to anything beyond the inner depths of the spiritual pilgrim: 'in the inward man dwells truth'.

FREEDOM AND CONSTRAINT IN SPIRITUAL EDUCATION

If the basic framework of this account is correct, and if the romantic move towards an acceptance of the value of an esoteric spiritual depth within the individual is accepted as a legitimate one, then the role of education may be seen as being pre-determined by the framework itself. The process of an education in spirituality is thus understood as both supplementary and remedial. It seeks to deepen the spiritual experience of pupils in the face of the dry bones of a spiritually decadent, materialistic and instrumental culture, operating as 'an antidote to the slow seeping poison of the unvivid spiritual life, [and] its tendency to slide into the banal clichés of an unexamined religiosity' (Jenkins, 1993, p. 27). The child, it is assumed, is immersed in, and suffers from, the constraints of a rationalistic, reductionist, bureaucratic and spiritually sterile culture. Indeed, the major function of the curriculum is, from such a perspective, precisely to inform and legitimize such an immersion. Induction into such a limited culture alone inevitably fails to address the needs of the whole child, and thus must be supplemented by a spiritual education that offers a counterbalance to such constraints. Spiritual education will then make the attempt to enable the child to transcend such limitations by stimulating an awareness of his or her own spiritual nature, of his or her own inward encounter with truth. 'The teacher's task is to open the pupil's mind and experience to hidden possibilities' (Hay, 1985, p. 147; cf. also Hay, 1982; Hammond, Hay et al., 1990; Thatcher, 1991).

In adopting such a programme, education perpetuates, by default, the dualisms inherent within modern culture and extended by post-modernism: the dualism of self and external reality, and of external fact and internal value. The result is that the spiritual realm of value floats free of any relationship with the facts of external reality. To discover one's own hidden depths is in essence an isolated, subjective and autonomous process. There is here no criterion for truth beyond that which the individual chooses to adopt as an act of pure preference, no moral constraint beyond that of the uncritical and uninformed conscience. The key problem is the failure to accept that 'such recognition of the spiritual in life necessarily involves assessment of what is spiritually significant and pertinent and what is spiritually debasing' (Holley, 1978, p. 144). Such education may indeed emancipate the whole child from the constraints of modern society, but freedom that exists purely for its own sake, without reference to external reality, quickly becomes cancerous. There is a danger, if such programmes do indeed enable pupils to encounter a hidden depth to their existence, that the child is left with no viable framework for interpreting, evaluating and understanding such depth. There is an esoteric, gnostic, anti-realistic thrust to much contemporary education practice that borders on the nihilistic and anarchic.

A single example of the problems created by such a dualism must suffice here. Teachers, it can be argued, find themselves in constant danger of sending out contradictory signals to pupils in the field of moral education. On the one hand schools are clearly committed to the advocacy of a public morality. In terms of the effective management of everyday social relationships within the school community, the schools' responsibility for the moral progress of society at large, and explicit programmes of moral education, the teacher's role must be to induct pupils into a set of public codes of ethical behaviour. Such a fundamental duty applies regardless of the extent to which programmes of moral education expect pupils to achieve a critical appropriation of such social norms and expectations.

Yet on the other hand, the moral dimension of spiritual education requires the child to turn away from the public realm and focus in upon the depth of his or her own private moral insights. There is, of course, the possibility that what the child discovers there may conflict with the schools' public social norms. Such a process may indeed be positive, raising, to give but one (though common) example, issues of sexuality that the public face of the school – despite the achievement of 'political correctness' in other areas of its life – has consistently failed to address. It must, however, also be accepted that the process may be a negative one, revealing ingrained depths to the child's being that are simply unacceptable and require challenging. The rhetoric of esoteric spirituality consistently fails to recognize the actuality of the 'dark side' of human nature, despite its self-evident reality within a society living in the shadow of the Holocaust. The roots of this omission are to be found in Rousseau's romantic assertion of the natural goodness of humanity, and his rejection of the Christian doctrine of original sin. The act of relegating spirituality to the private sphere thus fails to offer criteria and interpretative frameworks through which such spirituality can be evaluated, assessed and developed positively. The dualism between public knowledge and private consciousness represents a problem that modernism itself has been unable to find solutions to, far less the hard-pressed classroom teacher.

If the advocates of the approach to spiritual education described above are to avoid such dangers, then they must be able to give an account of the relationship between mainstream education as induction into public culture and knowledge and supplementary education as the stimulation of private spiritual potential. It is by no means clear that they are in a position to do so. Indeed, there is little evidence that contemporary programmes of spiritual education have been able to develop a philosophical justification that transcends the old conflicts between traditionalist, subject-based theories of education as induction into culture, and progressive, child-centred theories of education as the process of fulfilling the potential of the whole child. In a political environment in which legislation has imposed the former and eclipsed the latter, it is possible to read programmes of spiritual education as existing in, and representative of, the twilight of educational progressivism.

TOWARDS A SPIRITUALITY OF COMMUNION

That Augustine fundamentally shaped the theological and secular perspectives of the Latin West is beyond doubt (Taylor, 1992, pp. 127–42), as is the fact that his legacy is currently the subject of profound debate not only by philosophers within the emergent tradition of critical realism, but also by Christian theologians (Gunton, 1993; Jungel, 1983). Within this debate, it is suggested here, lies the possibility of discovering resources that may aid the transformation of the current structures of spiritual education. There is space here only to focus on theological questions, in particular those of Augustine's relationship with his received theological tradition (Gunton, 1991).

If the notion of spirituality as an esoteric inner depth within the self has its roots in the thought of Augustine, then the divergence between Augustine and his received Patristic Christian heritage, especially that of the Cappadocian Fathers, takes on a special significance. In this earlier tradition we encounter an understanding of the self and of the spiritual that, without any requirement to adopt a specifically Christian perspective, suggests ways in which the spiritual educator might move beyond the flaws in the modernist framework.

Augustine's anthropology was clearly dualistic, setting the material, physical body over against the immaterial, spiritual soul. As Taylor points out, Augustine 'sees the soul as potentially facing two ways, towards the higher and immaterial, or towards the lower and sensible' (1992, p. 137). Given this distinction, the path of spiritual development was always going to be inwards, entering into the depth of the soul, rather than outwards towards external reality. The body is contingent and expendable, the soul immortal and eternal.

This perspective stands in marked contrast to the holistic anthropology of Christian antiquity that can be traced back beyond St Paul to the earliest Hebraic traditions. We find here no distinction between body and soul, since the self is understood as an undivided unity. When Paul distinguishes between flesh and spirit his concern is not to contrast the material and immaterial, but rather two distinct ethical/religious orientations of the whole person: a life of sin under the older order of Adam and a life under the new order inaugurated by Christ and distinguished by a renewed relationship with God. 'To set the mind on the flesh is death, but to set the mind on the Spirit is life and peace' (Romans 8:6). The spiritual life of humanity is thus concerned not with the internal contemplation of the soul in an attempt to avoid the corruptions of the physical body, but with the nature of the relationship of the whole person to the divine. To achieve this it is necessary to look not inwards but outwards, to orientate the whole self to the reality that lies beyond it. If it is true that 'the whole person, body, mind and spirit, and not merely a part, is definitive of human being' (Gunton, 1993, p. 48), then it follows that we must reject the belief 'that we know ourselves not by observing our relatedness with the other but by some kind of introspection' (p. 202; cf. also Yu, 1987).

This understanding of the orientation of the whole self to that which is external to it may be taken a stage further. Christian theology operates with the fundamental belief that humanity is created in the image of God, and thus it follows that the understanding of the nature of God as Trinity will inform any perspective on the nature of humankind. Augustine's approach to the Trinity involved primarily psychological categories: relationships within the divine being were seen as analogous to those within a self-reflective mind. Just as the trinitarian mind of God was sufficient to establish the divine identity, so, it followed, the inner psychological processes of the individual enabled the establishment of human self-identity. Augustine here was setting himself over against the social analogies developed by the Cappadocian Fathers: 'the three persons of the Trinity exist only in reciprocal eternal relatedness. God is not God apart from the way in which Father, Son and Spirit in eternity give to and receive from each other what they essentially are' (Gunton, 1993, p. 164). If, then, the identity of the divine is dependent not upon self-reflection but on communal relationship, it follows that human identity is grounded not upon displacement from the world but on the nature and quality of the relationship of the self with that which is external to it. We are who we are as human beings in terms of the formative processes of our developing relationships not just with ourselves, but with other selves, with the natural world, and with God. It is, then, not merely that the whole person needs to look outward to obtain any depth of understanding, but that the self is actually constituted and formed by the developing nature of its communal relationships.

Since the Enlightenment the language of spirituality has shifted its point of reference from the divine to the human: anthropology came to replace theology as the fundamental locus of spirit (Feuerbach, 1957). So long as the anthropological perspective focuses upon the image of the dislocated self, then the spiritual realm is located within the depths of the individual. Once the self is understood as existing essentially as a being in communion, then the question of the location of the spiritual becomes an issue. If the Christian tradition equated the spiritual realm with the place of divinity, and modernism grounded spirituality within the disengaged self, what are we to say of the location of spirituality in a context in which both options are under threat, one because the Christian tradition is no longer a fact of public consensus, the other because the limitations of the self constructed by modernism are clearly recognizable? Again, Christian doctrine suggests a possible solution to this issue.

The primary reference to spirit in Christianity has always been to the third person of the Trinity. The Spirit is both agent of the creation and sustainer of the universe; the vehicle of divine providence who reveals the nature and ways of divinity to the prophets and seers; the one who holds humanity in relationship with God. 'The Spirit's distinctive work in the world is, by relating the creation of God through Christ, to give direction to its being and beings' (Gunton, 1993, p. 205). This clearly presents a major problem for education since the existence of the trinitarian God of Christian belief is a disputed issue, and certainly not one upon which public education might currently be grounded. However, if the truth of Christian belief cannot be guaranteed, then the placing of such belief under suspicion does raise a fundamental and very public question, that of the ultimate purpose, meaning and end of reality.

Paul Tillich's redefinition of divinity as 'that which is of ultimate concern' is of value at this point (1978, pp. 211–17). It is important though to understand it in a strongly realistic sense: not as 'what is of ultimate importance to me in terms of my subjective perception of the depth of my being', but rather 'what is ultimately true about the nature of the reality I indwell'. The former reading is in danger of slipping into misplaced, blinkered illusion, the latter demands a spiritual striving towards a true relationship and communion of the self with the world. 'Thus ultimate concern needs to be linked with the question of ultimate truth: are the things that I am ultimately concerned about in harmony with the way ultimate reality actually is?' (Wright, 1993, pp. 44f.). The spirituality grounded in a realistic understanding of the communal nature of the self thus addresses the spiritual question of the true nature of reality and the individual's proper relationship with the actual order of things (Thompson, 1990). Spirituality thus may be understood as transcending the limitations imposed by an unconstrained internal quest and the imposition of any form of religious imperialism.

The insights of Christian theology may be summarized thus:

● the whole person is not to be understood as a dualistic combination of body and soul, and hence the direction of our spiritual endeavours needs to focus outwards towards external reality, not merely inwards towards a solipsism of self-contemplation;

- we are the persons we are in terms of the nature, appropriate or inappropriate, of our relationships with other selves, the natural order, and the existence – or non-existence – of a transcendent divine realm;
- the spiritual quest of humankind is concerned with the attempt to look outwards and, in communion with external reality, strive to relate appropriately with the open question of the ultimate and true nature of reality.

RELATIONSHIP AND ULTIMACY IN SPIRITUAL EDUCATION

Such an understanding of spirituality suggests a very different programme of 'spiritual' education from that developed within the framework of the attempt to reveal a hidden gnostic depth within the individual consciousness.

- Such a notion of spirituality demands a programme of spiritual education that is not merely remedial, seeking to supplement the limitations of a dry, arid, soul-destroying curriculum. Rather, the central spiritual issues are precisely those raised by the mundane subject-studies the pupil encounters day in and day out. In so far as all learning, whether implicitly or explicitly, inevitably asks the questions of ultimate truth and meaning, and of our stance towards them, so it follows that all education is spiritual in nature. Spirituality is embodied in the whole of the curriculum. The mystery of the world cannot be reduced to the level of an esoteric gnosticism. Both the Judaeo-Christian-Islamic tradition(s), and the secular Enlightenment that sprang from it, understood reality to be by its very nature public and available for investigation, even if human knowledge may be at best contingent. Thus Webster is absolutely correct when he points out that 'this mystery is there for all to wonder at, and it is within the everyday knowledge of the ordinary school curriculum' (1990, p. 358).
- Just as individual subject areas work with public criteria of truth and tackle realistic questions that transcend individual whim and preference, it follows that spiritual education must also be concerned with the understanding of the way things actually are in the world and the appropriateness of our relationships to such truth. That in a modern pluralistic society such truth is a matter of dispute does not deny the public nature of the various discourses through which truth is articulated and discovered. Rationality will always be provisional and contingent, whether within the discourses of science, theology or any other realm of human intellectual endeavour. The striving for meaning cannot be short-circuited by a descent either into a premature idealism or an arbitrary, anti-realistic plurality of truths.
- The process of spiritual education may then enable the school as a learning community to transcend the limited aims inherent in contemporary education, whether this be in either its 'traditionalist' forms as mere vocational training, social development, cultural induction and academic achievement, or its 'progressive' concern for bringing to fruition the potential of the individual. Education for spiritual develop-

ment need not reject any of these concerns, but rather may take them up beyond any narrow parochial concern and relate them to questions of ultimate truth.

CONCLUSION

This chapter has been able to do no more than draw attention to flaws in the current fabric of spiritual education and suggest the possibility of weaving a new tapestry. In so doing it offers a tentative suggestion of what it might mean to spiritually educate the whole child. A spiritually educated child must be more than one with a highly developed sensitivity towards his or her inner experiential depth. Rather, the whole child will be able to utilize the learning that is central to education in a way that allows him or her to develop communal relationships with themselves, with society, with nature, and with the presence or absence of divinity in a manner that takes seriously the ultimate issues of the truth and meaning of the world we have been thrown into, and that is informed, articulate, literate and above all realistic.

REFERENCES

Adorno, T. W. and Horkheimer, M. (1979) *Dialectic of Enlightenment.* London: Verso.

Bernstein, R. J. (1983) *Beyond Objectivism and Relativism: Science, Hermeneutics and Praxis.* Oxford: Blackwell.

Descartes, R. (1969) *Discourse on Method and the Meditations.* Harmondsworth: Penguin. (first published 1637)

Feuerbach, L. (1957) *The Essence of Christianity.* New York: Harper and Row. (first published 1841)

Foster, M. (1934) The Christian doctrine of Creation and the rise of modern natural science. *Mind*, **43**, 446–68.

Foucault, M. (1989) *The Order of Things: An Archaeology of the Human Sciences.* London: Tavistock/Routledge.

Gadamer, H.-G. (1979) *Truth and Method.* London: Sheed and Ward.

Gunton, C. E. (1985) *Enlightenment and Alienation: An Essay Towards a Trinitarian Theology.* London: Marshall, Morgan and Scott.

Gunton, C. E. (1991) *The Promise of Trinitarian Theology.* Edinburgh: T. & T. Clark.

Gunton, C. E. (1993) *The One, the Three and the Many: God, Creation and the Culture of Modernity.* Cambridge University Press.

Hammond, J., Hay, D. *et al.* (1990) *New Methods in RE Teaching: An Experiential Approach.* Harlow: Oliver and Boyd.

Harris, M. (1988) *Teaching and the Religious Imagination.* New York: Harper and Row.

Hay, D. (1982) *Exploring Inner Space. Is God Still Possible in the Twentieth Century?* Harmondsworth: Penguin.

Hay, D. (1985) Suspicion of the spiritual: teaching religion in a world of secular experience. *British Journal of Religious Education*, **7** (3), 140–7.

Heidegger, M. (1962) *Being and Time*. Oxford: Blackwell. (first published 1927)

Holley, R. (1978) *Religious Education and Religious Understanding. An Introduction to the Philosophy of Religious Education*. London: Routledge and Kegan Paul.

Jenkins, D. (1993) 'And she supposing him to be the gardener . . .': spirituality, the arts and the open secret. In D. Starkins (ed.), *Religion and the Arts in Education: Dimensions of Spirituality*. London: Hodder & Stoughton.

Jungel, E. (1983) *God as the Mystery of the World: On the Foundation of the Theology of the Crucified One in the Dispute between Theism and Atheism*. Edinburgh: T. & T. Clark.

Lealman, B. (1986) Grottos, ghettos and city of glass: conversations about spirituality. *British Journal of Religious Education*, **8** (2), 65–71.

Lindbeck, G. A. (1984) *The Nature of Doctrine: Religion and Theology in a Postliberal Age*. London: SPCK.

Schleiermacher, F. D. E. (1958) *On Religion: Speeches to Its Cultured Despisers*. New York: Harper and Row. (first published 1799)

Schleiermacher, F. D. E. (1976) *The Christian Faith*. Edinburgh: T. & T. Clark. (first published 1830)

Starkings, D. (ed.) (1993) *Religion and the Arts in Education: Dimensions of Spirituality*. London: Hodder & Stoughton.

Taylor, C. (1992) *Sources of the Self: The Making of the Modern Identity*. Cambridge University Press.

Thatcher, A. (1991) A critique of inwardness in religious education. *British Journal of Religious Education*, **14** (1), 22–7.

Thompson, R. (1990) *Holy Ground: The Spirituality of Matter*. London: SPCK.

Tillich, P. (1978) *Systematic Theology*. Vol. 1. London: SCM.

Torrance, T. F. (1980) *The Ground and Grammar of Theology*. Belfast: Christian Journals.

Webster, D. (1990) A spiritual dimension for education? In L. Francis and A. Thatcher (eds), *Christian Perspectives for Education: A Reader in the Theology of Education*. Leominster: Gracewing.

Wright, A. (1993) *Religious Education in the Secondary School: Prospects for Religious Literacy*. London: David Fulton.

Yu, C. T. (1987) *Being and Relation: A Theological Critique of Western Dualism and Individualism*. Edinburgh: Scottish Academic Press.

CHAPTER 11

'Spiritual' minus 'personal-social' = ?: a critical note on an 'empty' category

David Lambourn

INTRODUCTION

I wish to sketch some argument and offer illustrations which might support the proposition that, for most educational purposes, the term 'spiritual' has no useful remainder when distinguished from 'personal-social'. I intend by this to imply that the recent introduction of the term 'spiritual' into official educational discourse, to say nothing of school inspections, by the former Secretary of State, John Patten, is unnecessary, rests on a category mistake and is therefore confusing and likely to be counter-productive in an educational setting.

THE 'SPIRITUAL' AND THE 'PERSONAL'

The term 'spiritual' has a history which may be traced to its New Testament use, and therefore some comments on that use might be in order here. I know of no New Testament use of 'spiritual' (*pneumatikos*) in antithesis to 'bodily' (*somatikos*), nor in antithesis to 'natural' (*physikos*). However, there are occasions when 'spiritual' (*pneumatikos*) is set in antithesis to 'carnal' or 'fleshly' (*sarkikos*), and in New Testament usage *sarkikos* denotes what we would probably refer to as 'only human nature'. In this antithesis, *pneumatikos* denotes those aspects of human being which are not limited to the merely biological and, in this respect, we should perhaps best understand *pneumatikos* as denoting what we have come to mean by 'the personal'. A further related term, *psychikos*, denotes the life of a body. *Psychikos* and *sarkikos* may be said to describe both what is common to human beings and that by which individuals may be distinguished, but not to describe that knowledge of others which arises from interaction between persons. By contrast, *pneumatikos* ('spiritual') implies interaction at a fully personal level. (It might be illuminating to approach this issue through Leonard Hodgson's (1956) question: 'What must the truth be, and have been, if people like that thought about it as they did?')

What do I mean by 'persons' and 'the personal' here? In the social sciences a number of perspectives have been elaborated: a person becomes that at which they play, becomes that as which they are addressed; a person is perceived as a repertory of roles, each one properly equipped with a certain identity; identity is socially bestowed, socially sustained and socially transformed. The person is a social construct, the product of socialization, etc. Social anthropology has described persons as the product of culture and as actors within culture. In another sociological perspective, 'the self is rather a process, continuously created and recreated in each social situation that one enters, held together by the slender thread of memory' (Berger, 1966, p. 124). We may take different parts of the work of Erving Goffman (1969) to illustrate some sociological views of the person. The title, *The Presentation of Self in Everyday Life*, itself contains notions of the person as actor, as also writing the script and being the director. Drama teachers are familiar with this perception, transformed into personal-social education (PSE), and are aware of its power. Elsewhere, discussing the effects of socio-economic structures and the use made by sociologists of role analysis, Goffman writes:

> It is a basic assumption of role analysis that each individual will be involved in more than one system or pattern and, therefore, perform more than one role. Each individual will, therefore, have several selves, providing us with the interesting problem of how these selves are related. The model of man according to the initial role perspective is that of a kind of holding company for a set of not relevantly connected roles; it is the concern of the second perspective to find out how the individual runs this holding company.
>
> (1961, p. 90)

Perhaps it would be possible to offer this perception to pupils in our secondary schools to help them choose appropriate strategies for managing their identity in their many different, and often otherwise unrelated, roles. (See also Watkins, 1993, for a useful elaboration of many 'selves' in an educational context.) For our purposes there are limitations in role theory, for if we attempt to subsume all personal behaviour through the concept of role, and if the education of the young is seen as a form of conditioning for the performance of adult roles (as the NCC seems to suggest) then the concept of a person might simply be degraded to that of a dependent variable, an outcome which I feel would be intolerable.

It is not necessary here to elaborate any special view as to what constitutes a person. I am content to accept many descriptions which are already widely known. For various purposes I prefer to understand 'person' to refer to human beings who are agents acting in the world (as opposed, that is, to Cartesian thinkers), for whom no adequate description may be made without consideration of the relation to other persons, as evidenced by the 'I and Thou' of Martin Buber (1937), or the view elaborated by John Macmurray. (As teacher in a personal relationship with a student I meet the student both as support and as resistance to my action; in this meeting I exist as person. I am both dependent upon and limited by the other – a description which fits my experience of the classroom well.)

Harré and Secord (1972) use models from Strawson and Hampshire in developing their view that humans, like other animals, are able to monitor their own actions, but unlike other animals, are also able to monitor their own monitorings and, further, are able to give accounts of these. This seems to be a very powerful description and may be seen in much that we experience in education. The interplay of action and reflection has long been a principle of effective learning. The introduction of Records of Achievement, particularly when the learner has the primary responsibility for their completion in preparation for subsequent negotiation with the teacher, has offered a formal situation in which one's monitoring may be monitored by oneself. Many find this activity a more effective tool in aid of learning than the completion of records of attainment. Eric Berne's (1966) *Games People Play*, possibly the most helpful exploration of a relational form of psychoanalysis, uses the device of a multi-self model of the person, and that of a game, in such a way as to set up the possibility that we may monitor our own self-monitorings.

A TYPOLOGY OF PERSONAL-SOCIAL EDUCATION

Conscious that we are developing a demanding picture of the 'personal-social', we will need some terms to describe it. As an example, we might usefully borrow and adapt a proposal put forward by Charles Elliott (1989) that we could categorize forms of the Christian tradition into three types – a structure which might have some validity in other areas of human endeavour. He proposed that we consider Religions of Reaction, Accommodation and Resistance. By analogy, we might adapt Elliott (pp. 231ff.) in order to characterize personal-social education (PSE) somewhat as follows:

A PSE of Reaction would be one supporting individual personal development through a strict code of life, prohibition of alcohol and drugs, modesty of dress and language and other forms of self-presentation, strict sexual ethics, hard work, a view of male headship of family and a close knowledge of inerrant authorities which/who could be relied upon to guide the industrious through all life's critical choices of action and behaviour. Practitioners, typically, would fear that political and moral power are probably on the wane and shun the questioning of authority, an authority which is properly hierarchical. Wealth and attainment are seen as the touchstones of success. The world is seen as one offering significant opportunity, within which lack of success is evidence only of a moral inadequacy.

A PSE of Accommodation would be one which adapts itself to the prevailing ethos, often seeking to Christianize, to a more or less radical degree, those secular fashions it incorporates . . . is tolerant of much that upsets the PSE of Reaction such as sexual permissiveness, abortion, feminism. Liberal in mind, tolerant and inclusive in temperament, it would wish to affirm the world in which it finds itself as something essentially good. It is therefore at ease with the powers that be, for it would be constitutionally incapable of challenging them at a level deep enough to discomfort them. It will tut over their peccadilloes rather than rage against their injustices.

A PSE of Resistance would be concerned with an analysis of power and authority. It would be concerned that students should have self-respect. While one student is oppressed, we all are. Justice would be the driving force behind the experience: justice for the poor and the marginalized and, closely allied, the issue of the role of women. It would be concerned to see a critical view of language as important: the linguistic undertaking of the PSE of Resistance is more fundamental, more self-conscious and a great deal harder than that of the PSE of Accommodation. What is at stake is the uncovering of the role of everyday language in affecting the way power is distributed and used. Associated with that goes an attempt to change the level of consciousness of the whole school culture. One part of the agenda, then, of the PSE of Resistance is exactly to resist the way in which language is used to legitimate abuses of power by those who oppress others. Personal-social consciousness comes alive when it responds to the realities of the students, when it seeks to meet the needs that no other institution or system is meeting – or is capable of meeting. The form tutor might say that his or her task was so to work with the students that they acquire sufficient self-respect to start to question the structures that oppress them. A PSE of Resistance would be concerned with a flourishing art criticism, literary criticism, drama criticism, with philosophies of art and science, all of these being institutional examples of monitoring one's own monitorings. The best examples known to me of work in education which incorporate such values are those developed by Paulo Freire (1972a, 1972b, 1976).

A FULLY PERSONAL PSE

An underlying theme of this chapter has been to allow for the possibility that a fully personal conception of the student would involve the recognition of the students' own projects within their own social and economic world. The notion of project here is an important one deriving from such writers as Jung, Cooper and Sartre, that a person's action is viewed as a product of intentionality: I do not so much discover who I am, but rather choose who I am to be. The trick is to know how to fashion, in the present, a future from the past. A corollary of such a view would seem to be that the focus of personal-social education would rather turn away from the question of the teacher's care of, or control over, the students, and towards the students' own developing grasp of their lives, their skills and their abilities to influence them, for themselves. An example may be seen in the World Studies Project's (1976) definition of social education as 'a way of working with young people such that they come to acquire the skills and concepts they will need in order to become active agents of change in their own lives' (p. 5). For such a development to be successful it would require other changes: that students have the opportunity to practise skills of assertiveness and that instances of Williamson's notion of pastoralization, where 'the tutor frequently uses the relationship of mutual trust . . . to deflect legitimate grievance away from the inadequate types of learning experience offered within the school' (Williamson, 1980, pp. 172–3), should be ended, for it is a euphemism for oppression. Spotting such instances would be the kind of activity espoused by Postman and Weingartner (1969), in which they elaborated Hemingway's notion of 'a built-in, shockproof, crap-detector'.

Within a fully personal perception of the students, the teacher would feel obliged to try to see their situation as comprehensively as she could. She would wish the functions, intended or otherwise, of the institutions by which they are surrounded – and this includes the language we endeavour to teach them – to be seen clearly. Carl Rogers's notion of unconditional positive regard seems to me to be very relevant, but short of a solution, to David Hargreaves's trenchant opinion that: 'Our present secondary system, largely through the hidden curriculum, exerts on many pupils, particularly but by no means exclusively from the working class, a destruction of their dignity which is so massive and pervasive that few subsequently recover from it' (Hargreaves, 1982). I am aware of many teachers in all phases of education who are explicitly attempting to develop their classroom practice through the concept of unconditional positive regard, with much success. My thesis here is that a fully personal perception of the students will require that we acknowledge and recognize each of them, for to have one's existence ignored amounts to having it denied, and we may hope that a healthy child will continue to provoke a teacher or parent to an act of discipline rather than be ignored – but with assertiveness skills the ignored students would have additional, and less disruptive, routes available to secure their needs. A deviant identity is often preferred to being treated as less than a person. Expressed within the terms of transactional analysis, negative strokes are preferred to no strokes.

A CATEGORY MISTAKE?

Since the (then) Secretary of State for Education encouraged the publication, by the National Curriculum Council, of *Spiritual and Moral Development: A Discussion Paper* in April 1993, many colleagues have begun the difficult task of trying to bring some kind of conceptual order to the 'vital underpinnings of all aspects of school life (which) should provide a foundation for adulthood and our society in the future'. It is difficult to imagine, in an educational context in the UK, a use of the term 'spiritual' which does not widely connote the idea of God. The term might therefore be subject to some of the same cautions as are held to apply to that connotation.

I wish here simply to draw attention to a phrase, owed to Coulson (1954), which might usefully be redeployed in relation to the discussion document. Coulson wrote of the 'God of the gaps':

> There is no 'God of the gaps' to take over at those strategic places where science fails; and the reason is that gaps of this sort have the unpreventable habit of shrinking. When Descartes located the soul in the pineal gland, all was well until the real purpose of this particular gland was discovered. Then there was no room for the soul, and people began

to doubt whether there really was such a thing. What is more, even when it was there, it was hard to see why it was not subject to familiar physico-chemical laws.

(p. 20)

By analogy, I want to insist that there is no 'spirituality of the gaps' either. This applies as well to our knowledge of people as to the natural sciences. Consider some statements from the discussion paper:

The term (spiritual development) needs to be seen as applying to something fundamental in the human condition which is not necessarily experienced through the physical senses and/or expressed through everyday language.

(NCC, 1993, p. 2)

As a teacher, am I to concern myself, and the students, with something we cannot detect, nor speak about, and presumably not whistle either? Whatever these things are, will they cease to be 'spiritual' when they do come to be described in everyday language?

Among the many aspects of spiritual development suggested by the discussion paper is:

A sense of awe, wonder and mystery – Being inspired by the natural world, mystery, or human achievement.

(ibid., p. 2)

This is one of a number of items listed which, if taken together, might be said to have the force of a programmatic definition (Scheffler, 1960), and, as with any programmatic definition, should be closely examined. A programmatic definition, unlike a stipulative definition, is not concerned with facilitating communication, with economy of utterance, nor with providing explanatory accounts of meaning, as are descriptive definitions which may be judged by reference to pre-definitional usage. Programmatic definitions, according to Scheffler, should be inspected not for their effects in enabling economy of utterance, nor for their relevance to prior usage, but rather for the moral and practical questions raised by the programme of action which they imply. The NCC discussion paper deserves to be treated as one offering a programmatic definition and should be so treated.

This definition identifies spiritual development with 'being inspired'. 'Inspiration', in its etymology at least, is closely related to 'spiritual' so, as definition, this particular aspect of spiritual development might be said to be bordering on the tautological. If tautological, then one term or the other is redundant; which shall we choose? Whatever other comment we might wish to enter here, we may take it that this is a further example of invoking a 'god (spirituality) of the gaps'. Were we to arrive at descriptions of a sense of awe, wonder and mystery as valuable commonplace experiences within the terms of other disciplines, would they cease to be aspects of spiritual development? As an antidote to this suggestion from the discussion paper, an alternative perspective may be found, *passim*, in *Born Curious* (Hodgkin, 1974).

Again, from the NCC discussion paper:

Experiencing feelings of transcendence – feelings which may give rise to belief in the existence of a divine being, or the belief that one's inner resources provide the ability to rise above everyday experiences.

(ibid., p. 2)

If a persuasive account may be given of such feelings, in terms of cognition or social or developmental psychology, will these feelings be removed from the area of spiritual development? Will the Chief Inspector no longer have to report to the Secretary of State? Will the inspection companies no longer be required to comment?

If fresh description, or further explanation, may remove features of 'spiritual development', then the 'vital underpinnings' and 'foundation' begin to feel very much like shifting sands – not the material on which I would care to try to build a curriculum, but possibly the perspective offered here provides an alternative.

I hope it will be accepted that resisting a 'spirituality of the gaps' is both theologically appropriate, and of pragmatic and tactical value.

Perhaps one of the most helpful, and politically sensitive, pieces of writing following John Patten's use of Section 1 of the 1988 Act has been the introduction by HM Chief Inspector of Schools (HMCI) Stewart Sutherland, to the OFSTED discussion paper (1994):

[This publication] reflects the fact that successive pieces of educational legislation have at their centre the belief that education in this country is not only about the gaining of knowledge and the acquiring of essential skills (though of course it is about those things), but also about *personal development in its fullest sense*.

(p. 1; emphasis added)

Professor Sutherland continues:

That fullest sense is, in the wording of the 1992 Schools Act, one which encompasses the 'spiritual, moral, social and cultural' development of all pupils.

The copulative structure here has the effect of saying 'the spiritual, moral, social and cultural development of pupils *is* personal development in its fullest sense' – giving a more flexible and practical interpretation Section 1 of the Act. Using the metaphor of an 'Ariadne's thread' to guide pupils through the 'moral maze', Sutherland suggests that this thread consists of two closely interwoven strands of which the first is personal relationships and the second is the school curriculum, and suggests that:

there is a responsibility incumbent on all those concerned with designing or implementing the curriculum – that of *ensuring that what is taught and how it is taught are contributing as fully as possible and in a positive way to all aspects of pupils' personal development*.

(p. 2; emphasis added)

Within the conventions appropriate to documents of this kind, HMCI could hardly have described the role of 'the personal' in education more strongly. Education is about personal relationships plus whatever else is chosen that will, in method and content, support personal development. I find this description of education and the role of 'personal development in all its fullness', more satisfying, more enabling, more liberating and more demanding than the categories 'spiritual, moral, social, cultural' which seem to me, somewhat ironically, to be more constraining and obfuscatory.

Jack Priestley, Principal of Westhill Colleges, Birmingham, concluded an address to a recent conference of inspectors and advisers of social education with the comment 'What I think I am saying is that if PSE needs RE then the opposite is equally true.' This conclusion seems to come very close to matching my opening proposition that, for most educational purposes, the term 'spiritual' has no useful remainder when distinguished from 'personal-social'.

CONCLUSION

I can conceive of nothing which remains in the category 'spiritual' after the 'personal-social' has been distinguished. However, that is not to say the term might not still have use. I can imagine that it might serve, like any metaphor, to 'focus' attention on an area, and it could serve as an organizing device in certain circumstances. But even in these cases, I would be suspicious that it was being used to smuggle something in which perhaps should be examined more explicitly.

REFERENCES

Berger, P. (1966) *Invitation to Sociology*. Harmondsworth: Penguin.

Berne, E. (1966) *Games People Play*. London: André Deutsch.

Brandes, D. and Ginnis, P. (1986) *A Guide to Student-Centred Learning*. Oxford: Blackwell.

Brandes, D. and Ginnis, P. (1990) *The Student-Centred School*. Oxford: Blackwell.

Buber, M. (1937) *I and Thou*. London: T. & T. Clark.

Coulson, C. A. (1955) *Science and Christian Belief*. Oxford: Oxford University Press.

Elliott, C. (1989) *Sword and Spirit: Christianity in a Divided World*. London: BBC Books.

Freire, P. (1972a) *Cultural Action for Freedom*. Harmondsworth: Penguin.

Freire, P. (1972b) *Pedagogy of the Oppressed*. Harmondsworth: Penguin.

Freire, P. (1976) *Education: The Practice of Freedom*. Harmondsworth: Penguin.

Goffman, E. (1961) *Encounters*. Indianapolis: Bobbs-Merrill.

Goffman, E. (1969) *The Presentation of Self in Everyday Life*. Harmondsworth: Penguin.

Hargreaves, D. H. (1982) *The Challenge for the Comprehensive School*. London: Routledge and Kegan Paul.

Harré, R. and Secord, P. F. (1972) *The Explanation of Social Behaviour*. Oxford: Blackwell.

Hodgkin, R. A. (1976) *Born Curious*. New York: John Wiley.

Hodgson, L. (1956) *For Faith and Freedom*. Oxford: Blackwell.

National Curriculum Council (1993) *Spiritual and Moral Development: A Discussion Paper*. York, NCC.

OFSTED (1994) *Spiritual, Moral, Social and Cultural Development: A Discussion Paper*. London: HMSO.

Postman, N. and Weingartner, C. (1969) *Teaching as a Subversive Activity*. Harmondsworth: Penguin.

Rogers, C. (1969) *Freedom to Learn*, 2nd edn., Ohio: Merrill.

Scheffler, I. (1960) *The Language of Education*. Springfield, IL: Charles C. Thomas.

Watkins, C. (1993) *Whole-school Policy and Practice*. Coventry: NAPCE.

Williamson, D. (1980) Pastoral care or pastoralization? In R. Best, C. Jarvis and P. Ribbins (eds), *Perspectives on Pastoral Care*, pp. 171–81. London: Heinemann Educational.

World Studies Project (1976) *Learning for Change in World Society*. London: One World Trust.

Part 3
Cases and Contexts

CHAPTER 12

Spiritual education and public policy 1944–1994

Peter Gilliat

STATEMENTS OF SPIRITUAL POLICY

The 1944 and 1988 Education Acts provide important statements of policy in placing on the national education system general responsibilities for spiritual development. The preamble to the 1944 Education Act required that:

The statutory system of public education shall be organised in three progressive stages to be known as primary education, secondary education, and further education; and it shall be the duty of the local education authority for every area, as far as their powers extend, to contribute towards the spiritual, moral, mental, and physical development of the community by securing that efficient education throughout those stages shall be available to meet the needs of the population of their area.

In the 1988 Education Reform Act the preliminary section on the curriculum stated that schools must provide

a balanced and broadly based curriculum which
(a) promotes the spiritual, moral, cultural, mental and physical development of pupils at the school and of society; and
(b) prepares such pupils for the opportunities, responsibilities and experiences of adult life.

There is visible continuity here as the 1988 statement echoes the 1944 list of dimensions for development with the significant addition of 'cultural'. However, it is the differences that illustrate the changes which have occurred over the 44-year period. In the 1944 Act the responsibility for spiritual development was placed firmly in the context of the reorganization of the education service into primary, secondary and further. The duty of local education authorities (LEAs) 'to contribute towards the spiritual . . . development of the community' was to be achieved through the provision of efficient education to meet the needs of the local population. In other words, one of the purposes of the national education service as provided by LEAs was the general spiritual development of society. In contrast, the

1988 Education Reform Act placed the responsibility for spiritual education within the context of the school curriculum; although the words 'and of society' appear, the emphasis is clearly on the development of individual pupils. So the idea of spiritual development as one of the underlying values of the national education service had become by 1988 the more focused notion of individual development as one of the requirements of the school curriculum.

One further contrast illustrates a change in what governments think they can achieve through legislation. Whilst the intention of the 1944 Act was far-reaching, the language was modest. The section referred to LEAs contributing 'so far as their powers extend' and by implication recognized the role of other institutions such as the Churches and the family. The language of 1988 was more ambitious and here the curriculum of individual schools was required to 'promote' spiritual development.

THE FORMATION OF POLICY

The policy background to the two Acts was very different. The first was passed in wartime by a coalition government. There was broad agreement on the need of a new legal framework for a better education service which enhanced provision and expanded opportunities. Careful planning and extensive consultations with the LEAs and the Churches beforehand meant that there was near-unanimous support in Parliament. In contrast, the 1988 Act was passed by a 'reforming' Conservative government, which had just won its third general election the year before. The main thrust of the legislation was the establishment of a free-standing, independently managed and publicly funded system of schools and colleges. The LEAs and the Churches had severe misgivings about many aspects of this programme of devolution and deregulation. In some ways the National Curriculum, also part of the 1988 Act, ran counter to the government's market philosophy, but was introduced with the declared intention of guaranteeing and raising standards.

References to spiritual development in both Acts were something of an afterthought (Souper and Kay, 1982; Alves, 1991), and were only included during discussions on overall educational purposes. In 1944 they were introduced at the committee stage in the House of Lords as a result of an amendment introduced by Viscount Bledisloe. He said that when for the first time religious education and an act of worship were to become obligatory, this could not be done 'without it being intended to develop the things of the spirit'. He went on to say:

> Surely we ought to incorporate in the Bill words which indicate our conviction that it is the Christian ethic and that it is spirituality which we want to advance in every stage of our national education if we want to promote the morality as well as the other virtues of our race.

The inclusion of spiritual education in 1988 was not a matter of debate in Parliament, unlike religious education and the act of worship. The preliminary section on the requirement to provide 'a balanced and broadly based curriculum' did not form part of the government's original draft of the Bill;

it was only included at a later stage when formally introduced to the Commons.

It is perhaps understandable that spiritual education was not part of the policy-makers' immediate priorities in framing legislation, because on both occasions they were concerned with far-reaching structural changes to the national education service. However, in 1944 there was evidence that the wartime government did want to acknowledge the spiritual dimension, in that the white paper *Educational Reconstruction* (Board of Education, 1943, p. 36) commented:

> There has been a general wish not confined to representatives of the Churches, that religious education should be given a more defined place in the life and work of the schools, springing from the desire to revive the spiritual and personal values in our society and in our national tradition.

The paper did not define 'the spiritual values . . . in our national tradition' but probably referred to that essentially Protestant tradition with its sense of moral duty and its respect for religious freedom guaranteed by legislation stretching back to the 1689 Toleration Act. Wartime brought to the surface of people's thinking an awareness of the importance of that tradition and the use of the word 'spiritual' acknowledged this.

In 1988 a similar process was at work within the narrower context of the curriculum. Whilst the consultation document *The National Curriculum* (DES, 1987) made no reference to spiritual education, its eventual inclusion was consistent with a national curriculum which reasserted a subject-based approach with origins stretching back at least to the nineteenth century (Moon, 1994). This reassertion of the national tradition can perhaps be best understood in the context of a government anxious about its performance in raising educational standards in relation to those of other countries, and in articulating an adequate national identity as part of the long-running debate about relations with Europe.

SPIRITUAL POLICY AND RELIGION IN SCHOOLS

The link between spirituality and religion is clearly a close one, and for much of the period 1944–1994 there has been the underlying public assumption that by teaching religion in schools provision was being made for spiritual education. As is well known, religious education (RE) occupies a unique statutory position. In the first place it was the only subject which was addressed in the 1944 Act, whereas in 1988 it was the only statutory subject to be left outside the National Curriculum. Secondly, together with collective worship it was the only subject from which parents could withdraw their children, that is until the 1993 Education Act gave parents similar rights in respect of sex education. This implicit acknowledgement that religion involved matters of conscience and commitment was underlined by the link in the 1944 Act between what was termed religious instruction and collective worship under the overall title of religious education. 'Instruction' was dropped in the 1988 Act, although provision for the subject and for worship was still dealt with together under the title of religious education. Thirdly, it was the only subject with its own local curriculum arrangements which developed in the 1920s and 1930s and were laid down in the 1944 Act through LEA-convened Agreed Syllabus Conferences and Standing Advisory Councils on Religious Education (SACRE). These arrangements were further developed and strengthened in the 1988 Act.

This is not the place to explore either the background or the detail of the religious clauses in the two Acts. Suffice to say that the 1944 clauses were seen as part of the carefully negotiated religious settlement which included the new system of voluntary aided and voluntary controlled church schools. The 1988 clauses arose in rather different circumstances (Alves, 1991). The original bill made few direct references to religion in schools and it was not until it came to the House of Lords that important additions and changes were introduced. The first set of amendments safeguarded the position of RE in relation to the National Curriculum by introducing the notion of the basic curriculum, but the real argument came over the desire by some members to describe the subject and worship more precisely. This resulted in the Act's requirement that any new agreed syllabus must 'reflect the fact that the religious traditions in Great Britain are in the main Christian whilst taking account of the teaching and practices of the other principal religions represented in Great Britain'; the Act also required that collective worship 'be wholly or mainly of a broadly Christian character'.

The dangers of trying to give this kind of precision to the statutory requirements for RE and collective worship were foreseen in the 1944 debate, and again it was in the House of Lords that the issues were high-lighted (Souper and Kay, 1982). It was Bishop Bell of Chichester who observed that 'there is nothing to require that religious instruction according to an agreed syllabus should be in any particular faith'. Lord Selborne, who was in charge of the bill in the Lords, replied that it was the government's intention that it should be Christian instruction and worship but that to include the word 'Christian' in the Act itself could create difficulties; for instance, in the event of a dispute the courts might have to decide on what was Christian. He used the same argument in favour of 'spiritual' in the preamble to the bill when some peers urged the insertion of 'religious' instead.

Jack Priestley, in his 1985 paper 'The Spiritual in the Curriculum', provided interesting evidence about the use of the word 'spiritual' in the 1944 Act. On the intentions of the legislators he quoted Canon Hall, Chief Officer of the National Society, who worked very closely with Archbishop Temple on the legislation, as saying:

> The Churches were in such a state at the time we thought if we used the word 'spiritual' they might agree to that because they didn't know what it was. They all had very clear ideas about what religion was and they all knew they didn't agree with anyone else's definition of it.
>
> (Priestley, 1985, p. 28)

So the use of the word 'religious' was recognized as divisive whilst 'spiritual', although difficult to define, was regarded as more likely to unite people.

SPIRITUAL POLICY AT NATIONAL LEVEL 1944-1988

The major concern of central government during the first 30 years of the period 1944-1988 was the expansion and growth of the education service. It had to meet the needs of the post-war generation and then of a growing population, through building and reorganization programmes and eventually through raising the school leaving age to 16 in 1972. This 'securing of efficient education', with its encouragement of greater opportunities, could be seen as contributing to the 'spiritual development of the community' as envisaged by the 1944 Act. In 1971 R. A. Butler, when writing about the 1944 Act, observed that 'succeeding decades had brought great quantitative growth and much qualitative improvement to education' (Butler, 1971). However, he also listed what he regarded as five unfulfilled promises of which the most important was 'the perfunctory and uninspired nature of religious instruction' which had begun 'to imperil the Christian basis of our society'.

Expansion and growth continued to be the major concern of central government until the mid-1970s but before then ministers of the Crown had begun to show a greater interest in what was actually going on in schools and classrooms. In 1963 Edward Boyle asked the Central Advisory Council to inform him on developments in primary schools, and the subsequent Plowden Report, published in 1967, exercised considerable influence. The establishment of the Schools' Council in 1964 began to make some impact on the level of educational debate at the Department of Education and Science (DES), as well as promoting important national curriculum development projects including ones on religious and moral education. The national inspectorate (HMI) also started to exercise greater influence through its publications which increased dramatically whilst Sheila Browne was Chief Inspector from 1974 until 1983 (Lawrence, 1992).

It was in one of these HMI publications that spirituality reappeared in the 1970s as part of the educational debate about the design of the curriculum. Initially discussion centred on secondary education, with HMI arguing the case for a common curriculum up to the age of 16 in what became known as the first of the red books, *Curriculum 11–16* (DES, 1977b). HMI developed a matrix view of the curriculum whereby areas of experience (content) were set against elements of learning (knowledge, concepts, skills and attitudes) which were fully set out in *The Curriculum 5 to 16* (DES, 1985a) as part of the *Curriculum Matters* series of booklets. In 1977 eight areas were listed in alphabetical order 'so that no other order of importance may be inferred'; this contrasted with the lists in the statements of policy in the 1944 and 1988 Acts where spiritual was placed first on the implicit assumption that it might pervade the others. The 1977 list included aesthetic and creative, ethical, linguistic, mathematical, physical, scientific, social and political, and, finally, spiritual. In 1985 technological was added, ethical became moral; literacy had been added to linguistic, and social and political had become human and social.

In the *Supplement to Curriculum 11–16* (DES, 1977c) an attempt was made to define these areas of experience. For seven of the eight areas a single description was provided but for spiritual two contrasting accounts were offered. The first suggested that spiritual should be 'defined in terms of inner feelings and beliefs' and always 'be concerned with matters at the heart and root of existence'. The second described the spiritual area of experience as 'derived from a sense of God or of Gods' and claimed that it was 'a meaningless adjective for the atheist and of dubious use to the agnostic'. The definitions for all the areas were developed and included in the 1985 HMI booklet (DES, 1985a), although in all instances they were clearly linked to individual subjects so that the spiritual section contained substantial references to RE. The first definition of spiritual from 1977 was the one taken forward in 1985 with references to 'feelings and convictions about the significance of human life'. The description also recognized 'that there is a side of human nature and experience which can be only partially explained in rational or intellectual terms' and that 'dance, drama, music, art and literature witness to the element of mystery in human experience'.

The development of government policy on the curriculum from Prime Minister James Callaghan's speech at Ruskin College in 1976 to the Education Reform Act in 1988 can be traced through documents such as Shirley Williams's Green Paper *Education in Schools* (DES, 1977a), Mark Carlisle's paper *The School Curriculum* (DES, 1981) and Keith Joseph's policy statement *Better Schools* (DES, 1985b). The first two referred to the idea of a core curriculum of English, mathematics, science, modern foreign language and RE, and all three developed lists of appropriate aims for schools which found their way into LEA and individual school curriculum statements up and down the country. The 1977 Green Paper suggested eight aims including instilling 'respect for moral values, for other people and for oneself, and tolerance of other races, religions and ways of life'. The 1981 list was reduced to six but still retained the 'respect and tolerance' aim with the inclusion of religious as well as moral values. It was the only aim which suggested that schools might 'instil' these values but in the 1985 list it changed to 'helping' pupils 'develop personal moral values, respect for religious values, and tolerance of other races, religions, and ways of life'. Spiritual education did not appear in these DES documents except for a reference in *The School Curriculum* (DES, 1981) to the place of RE which 'provides an introduction to the religious and spiritual areas of experience'. When it came to the 1987 consultation paper on the National Curriculum (DES, 1987) 'areas of experience', including the spiritual, were ignored in favour of a subject-based curriculum.

SPIRITUAL POLICY AT LOCAL LEVEL 1944–1988

Like central government, LEAs saw their major task during the period 1944–1988 as carrying out their statutory duty to make adequate provision for education, which would then 'contribute to the spiritual development of the community'. Until the mid-1970s LEAs were largely preoccupied with providing sufficient school places, and for developing and reorganizing secondary education along comprehensive lines. Their level of concern for the content and quality of the curriculum varied, depending on the tradition and size of the LEA. Likewise the level of resources was uneven across the country, as was the provision of inspection and advisory services, curriculum policies and guidelines, and in-service training.

This unevenness extended to LEAs' specific responsibilities for agreed syllabuses and their general support for RE. After 1944 many LEAs did prepare new syllabuses but others continued their pre-war arrangements (Hull, 1975). The content of the new syllabuses continued the nurturing tradition of teaching the Christian faith through a study of the Bible and the history of the Church. As the Hampshire *Syllabus of Religious Education* (Hampshire Education Committee, 1954) said in its introduction, RE was not a subject like others but aimed to make children practising Christians. Hampshire did not offer advice on collective worship in its agreed syllabus, but many LEAs did. Bristol, for instance, proclaimed, 'let the assembly be direct, fresh, warm, poetic – a religious experience in which all staff and children may feel themselves at the footstool of the Lord' (Bristol Education Committee, 1960).

In the 1960s and 1970s, in common with some other subjects, RE began to take closer account of what was known about the ways in which children's thinking developed, as well as the context of pupils' own lives and experiences. There was also a widening of the RE curriculum to include some of the other major religions of the world, although Christianity continued to be the main area of study. It was Birmingham's 1975 syllabus which broke new ground with its approach to the study of world religions and its references to non-religious 'stances for living' (Birmingham Education Committee, 1975). Hampshire's new agreed syllabus, *Religious Education in Hampshire Schools* (Hampshire Education Authority, 1978), also demonstrated some of the changes when it stated: 'the principal aim of religious education . . . is to enable pupils to understand the nature of religious beliefs and practices, and the importance and influence of these in the lives of believers'. It went on to make the point that 'it is no part of the responsibility of a county school to promote any particular stand-point, neither could an exclusively Christian content do justice to the nature of the subject'. Hampshire's syllabus was adopted by over 20 other LEAs prior to 1988. It and many other syllabuses represented considerable curriculum development in the subject, which could now point to its educational rationale rather than its statutory protection for its place on the timetable. LEA guidance on collective worship from the same period also emphasized the educational nature of the activity and drew the distinction between a school assembly and an act of worship as conducted within a religious community (Avon County Council, 1978).

In a closely related area of the curriculum, some LEAs supported initiatives which helped to develop what was increasingly called personal and social education (PSE). The government's review of *Local Authority Arrangements for the School Curriculum* (DES, 1979) indicated that LEAs gave very varied support to developments in moral, health, careers and social education. On a wider issue the review reported that there was general acknowledgement of the importance of promoting racial understanding, a topic which raised difficult questions of attitudes and values in some LEAs. In the mid-1980s the government accepted the Swann Committee's report on the education of children from ethnic minority groups, *Education for All* (Swann Report, 1985), which presented an inclusive view of education and the curriculum and insisted that multicultural understanding should permeate all aspects of a school's work. In one or two areas during the 1980s LEAs promoted peace-education policies, which included amongst their aims encouraging 'attitudes that lead to a preference for constructive and non-violent resolution of conflict' (Avon County Council, 1983). Central government distrusted this kind of local initiative (DES, 1985b) and the provisions of the 1986 Education (No. 2) Act included a statutory constraint on the teaching of political issues. This Act also intervened in the increasingly controversial area of sex education by stipulating that it should have regard for moral considerations and family values. The government was gradually being drawn into legislation on the curriculum which culminated in the 1988 Education Act.

PROMOTING SPIRITUAL EDUCATION 1988–1994

Implementing the requirement to promote spiritual development was not a major priority for schools immediately following the 1988 Education Reform Act. They were more concerned with subject demands as dictated by the timetable for the introduction of the National Curriculum. However, some LEAs produced new agreed syllabuses and most of these adopted the National Curriculum pattern of key stages, attainment targets and programmes of study (National Curriculum Council, 1993). Many of them referred to spiritual development in their attainment targets. Hampshire's new syllabus aimed to develop 'an awareness of the spiritual dimension of life' (Hampshire County Council, 1992) and Avon called for 'reflection on and response to the spiritual dimension of life' (Avon County Council, 1993). In some ways this represented a continuing element within RE from the 1960s but it also drew on development work during the 1980s, much of it derived from the University of Nottingham Religious Experience Research Project (Hay *et al.*, 1990).

At national level the new Department for Education (DFE), with John Patten as the Secretary of State from April 1992 to July 1994, attempted to promote spiritual education in two ways. In the first place the 1993 Education Act extended the 1988 structural changes to the national education service with measures to encourage the growth of grant-maintained schools. The White Paper *Choice and Diversity* (DFE, 1992) that preceded the Act set out the government's views on the need for an education service that provided greater diversity of schools and more choice for parents. Within this context strong support was expressed for voluntary schools 'which provide powerful reinforcement of the spiritual and moral dimension of education'. The paper also placed emphasis on a school's 'set of shared values', with the implication that parental choice would ensure the promotion of acceptable values by individual schools. More generally, others have argued that support for the common school is in decline and that a more differentiated education system may be more appropriate to the needs of a pluralist society, where a core civic education programme could replace current arrangements for religious education and collective worship (Hargreaves, 1994).

In contrast, a second strand in John Patten's promotion of spiritual education was to pursue the centralizing tendency of the 1988 Act, which was characterized by the introduction of the National Curriculum. This was the attempt to 'give a further impetus to the development of RE in schools' (DFE, 1992). The 1993 Act tightened up the requirements for LEAs to convene Agreed Syllabus Conferences and SACREs, and in January 1994 a DFE circular *Religious Education and Collective Worship* was issued (DFE, 1994). This provided detailed and complex interpretations of the sections in the 1988 Education Reform Act which had tried to define the place of Christianity in agreed syllabuses and collective worship. The circular emphasized that RE should reflect 'the Christian heritage of this country' and that 'the relative content devoted to Christianity should predominate', a view which aroused considerable anxieties within religious communities and beyond. On collective worship the circular overruled the more general approach promoted in earlier LEA documents in favour of a narrower definition which emphasized the Christian tradition, again a view which provoked widespread concern. Overall, the circular, whilst wishing to strengthen spiritual values in schools, reopened old controversies by trying to insist on particular definitions which did not command general support.

INSPECTING SPIRITUAL EDUCATION 1992-1994

Meanwhile the Office for Standards in Education (OFSTED), set up in 1992 with Stewart Sutherland as Chief Inspector during its first two years, began to report on aspects of spiritual education. Its first report on RE and collective worship for the year 1992-93 (OFSTED, 1994a) concluded that 'the major issue is the widespread non-compliance with the Education Reform Act and the low status accorded to RE in school plans'. In only half the primary schools was RE overall satisfactory or better, and whilst RE was offered to all pupils at Key Stage 3 it was only provided for all pupils in about a quarter of the schools at Key Stage 4. On collective worship, 'although provision was made conscientiously, few schools provided a sufficiently strong spiritual focus' in the primary sector, whilst in the secondary sector 'few schools met the requirement to provide a daily act of collective worship'.

Under the provisions of the 1992 Education (Schools) Act there was a specific requirement for OFSTED to report on pupils' spiritual, moral, social and cultural development. This has proved a difficult area to inspect and the different versions of OFSTED's Framework in the *Handbook for the Inspection of Schools* illustrate some of the problems. The original 1992 version linked spiritual and moral development, and used the same evaluation criteria as if there were no distinction between the two. The 1993 version brought the four aspects of pupils' development together into one section, underlining their interconnection, but offered separate evaluation criteria for each, so recognizing the distinctions. The 1994 version introduced further changes following consultation on an OFSTED discussion paper, *Spiritual, Moral, Social and Cultural Development* (OFSTED, 1994b). This version now requires spiritual development 'to be judged by how well the school promotes opportunities for pupils to reflect on aspects of their lives and the human condition through, for example, literature, music, art, science, religious education and collective worship, and how well the pupils respond' (OFSTED, 1994c, p. 21). Current guidance on the inspection schedule describes spiritual development as relating 'to that aspect of inner life through which pupils acquire insights into their personal existence which are of enduring worth', and states that 'spiritual is not synonymous with religious'.

ISSUES FOR THE FUTURE

The DFE under John Patten and OFSTED under Stewart Sutherland gave spiritual education an enhanced profile which highlighted two major issues which have surfaced from time to time over the last 50 years. The first concerns the relationship between 'spiritual' and 'religious', and the need to clarify the contribution of RE, alongside other subjects, to pupils' personal development. Following the Education Reform Act in 1988 the position of RE in schools has remained vulnerable and weak (OFSTED, 1994a). The status of being part of the basic curriculum has proved to be a token gesture to its importance, and the absence of any national framework, apart from the current legislation, has continued to lead to competing expectations about the aims and purposes of RE. In this situation it has been very difficult to clarify the particular contribution that the subject might make to pupils' spiritual development. The *Model Syllabuses for Religious Education* (SCAA, 1994), endorsed by the leaders of the six major religious communities, may provide some national guidance. However, they are only advisory documents for the use of LEAs and of themselves do not give RE the priority and resources necessary to develop the subject effectively.

The contribution of other subjects to pupils' spiritual development was scarcely recognized in the original National Curriculum documents on the core and foundation subjects, and the new slimmed-down versions show little evidence of any greater attention to it. The new curriculum arrangements for Key Stage 4 limit the statutory requirements to the three core subjects, physical education and short courses in technology and a modern foreign language, and by implication devalue the remaining National Curriculum subjects of history, geography, art and music, four subjects that can make very important contributions to pupils' spiritual development. This priority given to particular subjects at Key Stage 4 puts in jeopardy the 1988 declared concern for 'a balanced and broadly based curriculum' and compromises the commitment to promote pupils' spiritual development.

The second major issue highlighted by the enhanced profile given to spiritual education by the DFE under John Patten and OFSTED under Stewart Sutherland concerns the place of spirituality within national overall purposes for education. The growing fragmentation of the education service, encouraged by government reforms, has tended to reduce the importance of policies on overall purposes, save that of 'choice and diversity'. Furthermore, the drift within the National Curriculum arrangements to emphasize utilitarian and scientific/technological values has done little to support spiritual education. The attempt by the DFE under John Patten to promote spiritual values by emphasizing the place of RE and collective worship within the context of the country's Christian heritage has sharpened controversy. In particular, the Secretary of State's reminder to headteachers that 'the law on collective worship is not my law, not Patten's law, it is Parliament's and it goes back 50 years' was not well received (*The Times*, 3 June 1994). It failed to take account of earlier implicit interpretations of the law which favoured wider definitions and reflected the growing plurality of beliefs and values. This issue promises to become a long-running tussle with growing demands for changes in the law, with similarities to the debate that took place over Sunday trading.

OFSTED under Stewart Sutherland provided a different perspective and began a process of promoting a consensus on the meaning and importance of spiritual education. OFSTED's different versions of its Framework in the *Handbook for the Inspection of Schools* make it clear that spiritual development is a whole-school and whole-curriculum issue, and not just the concern of RE and collective worship. In its discussion paper OFSTED acknowledged the need for public discussion and debate about the overall purposes of education; it recognized that 'successive pieces of legislation have had at their centre the belief that education is not only about the gaining of knowledge and the acquiring of essential skills, but also about personal development in its fullest sense' (OFSTED, 1994b). As part of this debate OFSTED emphasized the need 'to press towards a common currency of shared understandings' on spiritual development. This debate, drawing on the language of spirituality, deserves to continue so that a new consensus can be established which reflects educational aspirations once associated with religion and which unites people from different traditions and with different values.

REFERENCES

Alves, C. (1991) Just a matter of words? The religious education debate in the House of Lords. *British Journal of Religious Education*, **13** (3).
Avon County Council (1978) Assemblies. *Agreed Syllabus File*. Bristol: Avon CC.
Avon County Council (1983) *Peace Education: Guidelines for Schools*. Bristol: Avon CC.
Avon County Council (1993) *Mystery and Meaning*. Bristol: Avon CC.
Birmingham Education Committee (1975) *Agreed Syllabus of Religious Instruction*. Birmingham: City of Birmingham.
Board of Education (1943) *Educational Reconstruction*. London: HMSO.
Butler, R. A. (1971) *The Art of the Possible*. Harmondsworth: Penguin.
Bristol Education Committee (1960) *Syllabus of Religious Education*. Bristol: City and County of Bristol.
DES (1977a) *Education in Schools*. London: HMSO.
DES (1977b) *The Curriculum 11–16*. London: HMSO.
DES (1977c) *Supplement to Curriculum 11–16*. London: HMSO.
DES (1979) *Local Authority Arrangements for the School Curriculum*. London: HMSO.

DES (1981) *The School Curriculum*. London: HMSO.

DES (1985a) *The Curriculum 5 to 16*. London: HMSO.

DES (1985b) *Better Schools*. London: HMSO.

DES (1987) *The National Curriculum*. London: HMSO.

DFE (1992) *Choice and Diversity*. London: HMSO.

DFE (1994) *Religious Education and Collective Worship*. Circular 1/94, London: Department for Education.

Hampshire Education Committee (1954) *Syllabus of Religious Education*. Winchester: Hampshire CC.

Hampshire Education Authority (1978) *Religious Education in Hampshire Schools*. Winchester: Hampshire CC.

Hampshire County Council (1992) *Visions of Life*. Winchester: Hampshire CC.

Hargreaves, D. (1994) *The Mosaic of Learning: Schools and Teachers for the Next Century*. London: Demos.

Hay, D. *et al.* (1990) *New Methods in Religious Education: An Experiential Approach*. London: Oliver and Boyd.

Hull, J. (1975) Agreed syllabuses, past, present and future. In N. Smart and D. Horder, *New Movements in Religious Education*. London: Temple Smith.

Lawrence, I. (1992) *Power and Politics at the Department of Education and Science*. London: Cassell.

Moon, B. (1994) The National Curriculum: origins, context and implementation. In B. Moon and A. Shelton Mayes (eds), *Teaching and Learning in the Secondary School*. London: Routledge and Open University.

National Curriculum Council (1993) *Analysis of Agreed Syllabuses for Religious Education*. York: NCC.

OFSTED (1994a) *Religious Education and Collective Worship 1992–1993*. London: HMSO.

OFSTED (1994b) *Spiritual, Moral, Social and Cultural Development: A Discussion Paper*. London: HMSO.

OFSTED (1994c) *Handbook for the Inspection of Schools*. Revised May 1994. London: HMSO.

Priestley, J. (1985) The spiritual in the curriculum. In P. Souper (ed.), *The Spiritual Dimension in Education*. Southampton: University of Southampton Department of Education.

SCAA (1994) *Model Syllabuses for Religious Education*. London: SCAA.

Souper, P. and Kay, W. (1982) *The School Assembly Debate: 1942–1982*. Southampton: University of Southampton Department of Education.

Swann Report (1985) *Education for All*. London: HMSO.

CHAPTER 13

Religious Education, spirituality and the acceptable face of indoctrination

David W. Rose

INTRODUCTION

Whilst it is possible since the 1944 Education Act to discern periods where the emphasis in discussion and practice lay on the term 'religious' and then on the term 'education', the debate latterly has revolved around the term 'spirituality'. This chapter is concerned to discuss the emerging use of the term spirituality in religious education.

The increased emphasis on the term 'spirituality' has arisen within religious education especially within the last decade, in the context of 'what it means to be religious'. This appears to be the position arrived at historically by many LEAs and their Agreed Syllabuses of religious education, though the issue of assessment in RE has raised fairly fundamental questions as to its feasibility and, in the minds of some, its desirability.

In the period since the 1988 Education Reform Act there has been a tendency within the media and the political arena for the term to be equated with Christianity. This shift, which cannot be educationally justified, is having a profound effect in educational circles.

In what follows I shall argue that the spiritual rights of children deserve a broader educational context for debate. Recent government initiatives and the SCAA documentation (1994) may make a contribution, but a concerted effort is needed by those involved in RE in its broadest sense to ensure that the term is not hijacked from its rightful place within broadly based RE. Failure to achieve this will render religious education vulnerable to the accusation that it is adopting an indoctrinaire approach to our children.

THE CONTEXT

The 1988 Education Reform Act requires that the curriculum for a maintained school be a balanced and broadly based curriculum which

(a) promotes the spiritual, moral, cultural, mental and physical development of pupils at the school and of society; and

(b) prepares such pupils for the opportunities, responsibilities and experiences of adult life.

(1988, Section 1 (2))

The procedures for promoting such curricular development are contained
within the requirements laid out in subsequent sections of the Act, and
these reinforce earlier legislation. At the time of the 1988 Act, the
Secretary of State for Education, Kenneth Baker, had not intended to
repeal the requirements of the 1944 Education Act in relation to religious
education and therefore had not intended initially to include any reference
to religious education. Under intense political pressure from the House of
Lords, he relented and amendments were made to the bill; hence the resulting legislation, with its ambiguities in relation to acts of worship and lack
of clear definition of terminology. Research I undertook in 1992 on the
constitution of SACREs and how a faith stance comes to be deemed acceptable for inclusion within a LEA reveals the inadequacies and confusions
surrounding the precise mechanisms and requirements for religious education in the curriculum (Rose, 1993).

The promotion of the spiritual development of pupils, via the curriculum,
is not defined and this absence of a precise interpretation of the legislation
has given rise to a general 'free-for-all' with those apparently possessing
power seeking to retain it, and those without it striving to obtain it. The
first half of 1994 has seen the rationale and *raison d'être* for religious
education being seriously damaged by subjective, quasi-educational
opinion being put forward by those with self-interest and vested interests
at heart. It is my contention that we shall be witnessing a new form of religious indoctrination unless religious education remains firmly rooted
within an educational framework. For more than a century, religious education has had to guard itself against the accusation of indoctrination and
being indoctrinaire in approach. Recent events appear to suggest that pressures external to the subject are being brought to bear to influence its
content. These influences do not show a clear educational rationale and
various factors have given rise to this uncertainty.

The steady encroachment into religious education is not a mere reflection of the Tory government's 'back to basics' campaign, nor is it simply a
reflection of the upsurge in fundamentalism across the world. Contributing
factors may include the imprecise wording of the 1988 legislation; its
subsequent interpretation by the DFE (formerly DES); a desire to organize
religious education as a means of improving society (this was part of the
immediate post-war rationale for the inclusion of RE in the curriculum,
reiterated by Margaret Thatcher in the late 1970s); or a hankering after the
'good old days' (which probably never existed) by a society which has
forgotten the maxim that today's 'bad old days' are the 'good old days' of
tomorrow! Consensus of opinion within a pluralistic society, as recognized
by the 1988 legislation, must be arrived at by agreement based on educational considerations, not on *force majeure*. It may be argued that the
emphasis needs to return to the spiritual rights of the child, and of children
growing up within Britain today. An educational rationale needs to direct
the debate.

RELIGIOUS EDUCATION AND INDOCTRINATION

In educational circles the term indoctrination has tended to be used narrowly, in a negative and pejorative sense, and the idea that indoctrination is incompatible with education is well-established. Teachers are instructed by legislation to refrain from indoctrination. The requirement in section 26 of the 1944 Education Act that the religious instruction to be given in county schools must not include any distinctive catechism or religious formulary is a re-enactment of the 1921 Education Act which itself was included in section 14 of the Elementary Education Act of 1870 (the so-called 'Cowper Temple' clause) (Taylor and Saunders, 1976, p. 118).

On the issue of indoctrination J. P. White (quoted in Cox, 1983, p. 102), places greater emphasis on the intention and method rather than on the content of that which is taught. He states,

it is teaching with the intention that the pupil will believe what is taught in such a way that nothing will subsequently shake his belief.

In considering the issue of indoctrination, Hull (1984) writes

considerations of content and social context enable us to distinguish indoctrination from socialization, the latter seeking to create conformity with accepted social mores and attitudes, whereas indoctrination is concerned with cognitive conformity . . . indoctrination attempts to bypass the reason.

(p. 167)

Hull argues that

the public dissemination of political and religious views by advocates of those views (evangelists or party political broadcasters) is not an educational activity, but it need not be an attempt at indoctrination either.

(p. 167)

He discerns an intermediate process, that of nurture. The dangers of indoctrination within nurture are apparent, especially within a society whose legislation recognizes the plurality in its representatives and expressions of faith. I suggest that current pressures and influences should be of concern to those involved in religious education. This situation is potentially one of a new style of indoctrination in which politics and religion are brought together in the realm of religious education, tending to blur the philosophical/linguistic distinctions which could be identified a decade ago.

The previously narrow interpretation of terminology has meant that when teachers positively use indoctrinaire approaches it is not referred to as indoctrination. Cox (1983, p. 102):

To be an indoctrinator the person trying to impart the doctrines must be in a position which influences the learner.

B. G. Mitchell (1967) argues that there have been attempts in the literature to root indoctrination in:

(1) a certain method of teaching,

(2) a certain content of teaching, and
(3) a certain aim of teaching.

In relation to (1) the positive dimension of indoctrination should not be overlooked. For example, no questions are raised about the indoctrinatory role of the teacher with regard to health and safety issues, or equal opportunities, yet such a role is disallowed in relation to religious education.

Within the current RE debate it is (2) and (3) that are being disputed. Should Christianity dominate religious education? The cultural heritage argument for Christianity was recognized by many LEA syllabuses long before it was required by legislation. My research (Rose, 1993) has shown the lack of clarity in understanding and practice by LEAs in the way they allow faiths to be represented on SACREs, as well as in the way content is selected for teaching in schools.

The 1988 Education Reform Act recognizes, requires and legitimates a pluralist approach to RE. In bringing together the RE curriculum and the collective act of worship, where the latter is seen as an extension of the former, the ERA challenges the *status quo*. Historically, Christianity has underpinned society in the UK. The 1944 Education Act recognized this. By contrast the current legislation recognizes that whilst Christianity permeates the history of the UK there are other principal world faiths which also need recognition. The DFE, in attempting to clarify the vagueness of the 1988 legislation, for example with its statements relating to worship (Circular 1/94), has suggested practices that may be unworkable and ultimately challenged in law.

The DFE (Circular 1/94) states on its cover that

> this guidance does not constitute an authoritative legal interpretation of the provisions of the Education Acts or other enactments; that is a matter for the courts.

One can understand its inclusion, yet when this document is used to enforce 'political' views it does a disservice to education generally and religious education in particular. Recent comments indicate that a narrow entrenched approach to RE may well be unenforceable in law, and should it come to litigation the effect on curriculum RE will be to erode further the gains for its status, hard fought over the past few decades.

Bibby (1994) argues that the only grounds for intervention following an inspection of the act of worship would be on the basis of underachievement. Responsibility for the act of worship rests with the headteacher and governors, not the Secretary of State. As the law stands, active participation in the acts of worship cannot be a requirement of a teacher in a school. Great uncertainty about the nature of the duty of governors means that any court order would need to define the duty, so that what must be done can be clearly identified. Culpability in law rests on failure to carry out an order. Bibby (1994) writes,

> further legislation would be required to enable a Secretary of State to compel schools to undertake daily worship.

Publication of the SCAA *Model Syllabuses for Religious Education* in early 1994 (SCAA, 1994) promoted and provoked widespread debate about the proportion of time to be spent on Christianity, and the nature of the daily act of worship which should be held in schools. At the SCAA launch of the draft syllabuses on 25 January 1994, Baroness Blatch, for the government, urged that religious education in the classroom be an extension of the role of the family. She used the term 'nurture' in her argument, especially for the promotion of Christianity. Rev. Dr Stephen Orchard, a United Reformed minister and a member of the SCAA Monitoring Group, argued publicly that he did not want teachers of religious education doing his job, which by its very nature clearly involves a legitimately biased indoctrinaire approach. He recognized the inappropriateness (and illegality) of this approach for the county-school classroom, a fact seemingly overlooked by the government speaker.

Political pressure towards one faith against others should be checked and tempered by educational principles and justification. The exertion of pressure in favour of one faith in the context of the legal recognition of a plurality of faiths within society may be divisive. Indoctrination is illegal yet the pressures put on religious education, by politicians and factions within faith communities in the last few years, seem to herald a new form of 'social indoctrination' by groups within a pluralist society.

It would appear that attitudes towards the place and nature of religious education are becoming more critical and more entrenched, and it is difficult to see how this is to be avoided under present legislation. As Harries argues,

> religion is a matter of faith and conscience . . . for any law to be effective, its terms must be defined or the law lacks meaning and is therefore unenforceable . . . it seems to me that there is simply not enough common ground in the Britain of the 1990s for there to be any realistic expectation that this law, as presently interpreted, will be obeyed.
>
> (Harries, 1994)

As Dye (1980, p. 19) puts it:

> the most important thing to remember is that the personal integrity of the pupils must be respected, and that it is their right to be responsible for their own spiritual futures.

THE CHANGING UNDERSTANDING OF SPIRITUALITY

The passage of time from the 1944 Education Act to date has seen various changes in emphasis for religious education. In the period up to the 1960s the emphasis was on the content of the religious education and this dominated the legal processes and requirements made for it. In the late 1960s and 1970s the emphasis shifted more to the educational framework of religious education – an era of change when the concepts of religious education and religious studies replaced religious instruction. At this time the phenomena of religion were explored, especially at secondary level. The early 1980s witnessed a religious education which focused on what it meant to be a practising member of a faith (or a non-theistic stance for living). During this decade the dynamics of 'living' a faith entered the classroom in a significant way.

Throughout this period, though receiving limited attention, the term 'spirituality' co-existed. Whilst the spiritual is a recognized dimension of knowledge, legally recognized and required, there is no consensus as to its accepted meaning. The Croydon Agreed Syllabus (1992, p. 3) states,

> the concept of spiritual . . . is at the heart of religious education's contribution to the whole curriculum. Spirituality is not the sole domain of RE; it is encountered and expressed in English Literature, Art, Music, Drama . . . but RE constantly returns to this important area of human experience.

It goes on to define the constituent elements of spirituality as including values, beliefs, authority, lifestyle, symbol and ultimate questions, within a context of plurality as required by the ERA.

According to the Ealing Agreed Syllabus (1989, p. 6),

> 'spiritual' refers to the inner motivations, feelings and beliefs that can raise questions about the mystery of life and evoke a sense of awe and wonder. An appreciation of the spiritual is integral to human life.

The NCC paper (NCC, 1993, p. 3) considers that

> The term needs to be seen as applying to something fundamental in the human condition which is not necessarily experienced through the physical senses and/or expressed through everyday language. It has to do with relationships with other people, and for believers, with God. It has to do with the universal search for individual identity – with our responses to challenging experiences, such as death, suffering, beauty, and encounters with good and evil. It is to do with the search for meaning and purpose in life and for values by which we live.

Some of the constituent elements of spirituality identified by NCC are: beliefs, sense of awe, wonder and mystery, experiencing feelings of transcendence, search for meaning and purpose, self-knowledge, relationships, creativity, feelings and emotions.

The SCAA draft *Model Syllabuses for Religious Education, Consultation Document – Glossary of Terms* (1994) has in its published glossary of terms two definitions of the spiritual (p. 44):

(1) The highest expression and activity of the human person deriving from whatever source.
(2) Sometimes used more selectively to refer only to what relates explicitly to God.

(Interestingly, the glossary does not explain who makes this selection, and the final published glossary (July 1994) omits this section on general terminology completely.)

In discussing the link between the ERA and spirituality the editor of *British Journal of Religious Education*, John Hull, writes that the emphasis on the spiritual could be helpful, but it all depends upon the interpretation of the term.

The emphasis on the spiritual could mean little more than a further intrusion into education of the Government's concerns for the creation of a cult appropriate to the needs of late industrial society. In that case, spirituality will simply mean pupils will be encouraged to become more competitive, self-assured and independent in outlook . . .'

(Hull, 1988, p. 121)

The intensely personal dimension of spirituality is highlighted by Richardson (1988, p. 132) when he writes,

spirituality involves not only self-knowledge but also seeing the world as it objectively is, unaffected and uncoloured by one's own projections, hopes, resentments, desires, self-pity, one's own buffeting and wounds from involvement in politics.

Over the past few years various writers have expressed concerns over (apparent) political interference in religious education. The issue of spirituality, instead of being a basis for ongoing dialogue and debate, has become a source highlighting inner fears and doubts in relation to political pressures.

The International Year of the Child was 1979, for which John Bradford of the Church of England Children's Society produced a discussion paper on the spiritual rights of the child (Bradford, 1979). In this, and a subsequent paper (Bradford, 1984), he notes how the 1948 Universal Declaration of Human Rights used the term 'religious' but by 1959 the Declaration of the Rights of the Child adopted the term 'spiritual', well before its more common usage in RE today. Bradford suggests that in the context of children and young people the term spiritual means 'a growing attunement to and rapport with the transcendent values and ultimate realities of life' (Bradford, 1978, p. 4). He postulates five spiritual rights for children, whilst recognizing that they are moral not legal rights:

- the right to the best of the spiritual heritage of the culture into which he or she is born;
- the right to express his or her spiritual belief in private and/or public without discrimination;
- the right to deepen, doubt or alter the spiritual commitment into which he or she is being nurtured or educated;
- the right to schooling, family life and other institutional support complementary to his or her spiritual development;
- the right, especially in early life, to such protection from spiritual damage and handicap as is reasonable and appropriate.

These rights are summarized as those of initiation, expression, choice, support and protection. As they are rooted in the faith traditions from which they derive, it is far too easy to lose sight of the intended participant – the child. Bradford distinguishes between the 'rights of action' and 'the rights of recipience'. With the former he cites the right to worship as one pleases and for the latter he cites religious education. It may be suggested that current legislation confuses these rights with requirements.

CURRENT DEVELOPMENTS

A return to healthy debate dealing with the key issues in relation to spirituality and spiritual development is necessary. These issues include the nature and definition of the very language we use: the extent to which the concepts of spirituality in the various Faiths are represented, and the basis on which their arguments are founded. Is the system of education itself founded on constant values such as fairness, justice and recognized educational principles?

In 1992 I conducted a survey of SACREs nationally (Rose, 1993). It is apparent that faith communities gain representation on SACREs through a variety of disparate practices by LEAs with no central cohesion or policy being required other than those required by statute. The nature of the religious education content selected for the classroom and the percentages of time spent on each faith shows no logical coherence. Local discretion, being permitted, has resulted in diverse practices which do not help the longer-term development of religious education. Questions now need to be asked as to how representative the faiths are themselves and on what basis their arguments for representation are founded. It appears that it is necessary to reinforce our educational system with constant values such as fairness and justice allied to recognized educational principles.

Alongside these local differences in policy and practice, the academic debate as to the nature of spirituality is well under way. The key issue revolves around the nature and definition of the language used.

R. Richardson (1988, p. 132) asks the question:

> What is spirituality and spiritual tradition within the different Faiths? What is the interconnectedness of spirituality and everyday community life?

Starkings (1993) questions,

> What are we to say about personal and corporate spiritualities now, in an age when faiths and cultures are thrown into ever-increasing contact, mutual influence and contradiction, and when (for much of the western world, at least) formal religious adherence seems less prevalent than it was?

When the NCC (1993) considered the 27 new agreed syllabuses produced since the ERA, it concluded:

> In NCC's view, no single syllabus matched all the legal requirements, although it must be emphasized that, if syllabuses are to meet this requirement in the future, DfE must issue further guidelines as to the interpretation of the law.

How ironic that the NCC has not provided a clear interpretation of the meaning of statute and yet was quite prepared to be critical of LEAs for their failure to comply fully with the legal requirements! (Incidentally, in my research there was not one LEA which felt it did *not* comply with the legislation contained in the ERA.)

The 'draft' SCAA model syllabuses (January 1994) made several significant contributions to the debate. SCAA at least attempts to suggest an overall pattern of content for RE across the key stages, with a time allocation for each. Of major significance has been the inter-faith dialogue and contribution to the chosen RE content. The positive effect of the various faiths being consulted and included in the decision-making process has, however, been lessened by a high level of public comment which has not been based on accepted educational grounds. Various influences, including the media and a number of prominent politicians, standing outside religious education directly, are being marshalled to affect the nature and practice of RE in the state sector. This new style of 'indoctrinaire' and biased manipulation has heightened fears and doubts for RE on a broad scale. Rather than the plurality of faiths, recognized in legislation, being unified in a common educational purpose, questions about fairness, equitability, mutual understanding, the act of worship and the very nature of religious education are being debated in a hostile, entrenched manner which will not serve the longer-term status and development of the subject.

The statutory structures for religious education lack real coherence. Local discretion in selecting content for religious education has its value but not at the expense of a national coherence which would aid stability. National and local structures allow for too much manipulation of a neo-indoctrinaire type by the media, local politicians, fringe religious groups and government pressure.

At the launch of the SCAA *Model Syllabuses for Religious Education* on 5 July 1994, Archbishop Carey stated,

> the aim of religious education is not indoctrination and winning of converts; it is about education.

Bishop Konstant, on the same occasion, argued that

> as religious education is part of the basic curriculum, it must be educationally sound.

The SCAA launch was accompanied by a range of media 'hype', most of it unhelpful to RE. The following are typical of the newspaper headlines at the time:

> Evangelicals to oppose the Teaching of Other Faiths (*Daily Telegraph*, 6 July 1994)

> Kids of 5 get Islam lessons in new RE course (*Sun*, 6 July 1994)

> Tories Fear Teaching 6 Religions (ibid.)

> I Believe in the Father, Son, Mohammed, Moses, Buddha, Vishnu . . . (*Today*, 6 July 1994)

> How Minority Power Now Rules Our Lives (*Daily Mail*, 6 July 1994)

> Religious Leaders agree on RE syllabus (*Independent*, 6 July 1994)

RE Guidelines put Christianity First (*The Times*, 6 July 1994)

RE Syllabuses Broadly Welcomed (*Times Educational Supplement*, 8 July 1994)

The new syllabuses, as portrayed by large tracts of the media, are viewed as fairly extreme, left-wing, opposed to Christianity and socially divisive. The media generally appear to have missed the whole *raison d'être* for religious education and its place within the curriculum.

CONCLUSION

Religious education is at a crossroads. RE should be enabling children to develop the spiritual dimension of their education and equip them for life in a plural society. The voice of the religious educationist, whether academic or classroom practitioner, must be heard at this crucial moment in time. The debate may move away from the percentage of time each faith should have within the school curriculum, into how best religious education can achieve even 5 per cent of curriculum time. This is the presumption behind the model syllabuses and may be a starting point for LEAs when revising their Agreed Syllabuses.

It is also necessary to achieve adequate resourcing and an increasing number of qualified teachers for the subject of religious education. Above all, we must arrive at a consensus definition of the nature and meaning of spirituality so that the vacuum that currently exists cannot be filled and exploited by those with a political or dogmatic axe to grind, for whom RE itself is of secondary interest.

REFERENCES

Bibby, P. (1994) Powerless to act. *Times Educational Supplement*, 29 April.

Bradford, J. (1978) *The Spiritual Rights of the Child*. Church of England Children's Society.

Bradford, J. (1979) Spiritual rights. In J. M. Sutcliffe (ed.), *A Dictionary of Religious Education*, London: SCM Press, 1984.

Cox, E. (1983) *Problems and Possibilities in Religious Education*. London: Hulton.

Croydon (1992) *A New Agreed Syllabus for Religious Education in Croydon Schools*. London: Borough of Croydon.

DFE (1994) *Religious Education and Collective Worship*, DFE Circular 1/94. London: DFE.

Dye, T. (1980) Indoctrination. *Association for Religious Education Bulletin*, **33**.

Ealing (1992) *The Ealing Agreed Syllabus of Religious Education*. London: Borough of Ealing.

Harries, J. P. (1994) A matter of conscience not law. *Times Educational Supplement*, 1 July.

HMSO (1988) *The Education Reform Act*. London: HMSO.

Hull, J. (1988) Editorial. *British Journal of Religious Education*, **10** (3).

Hull, J. (1984) Indoctrination. In J. M. Sutcliffe (ed.), *A Dictionary of Religious Education*. London: SCM Press.

Mitchell, B. G. (1970) Appendix B, Indoctrination. In *The Fourth R: The Durham Report on Religious Education*. London: National Society and SPCK.

National Curriculum Council (1993) *Analysis of Agreed Syllabuses for Religious Education*. York: NCC.

Richardson, R. (1988) Spiritual direction and political endeavour, *British Journal of Religious Education*, **10** (3).

Rose, D. W. (1993) Sacre blur. *Times Educational Supplement*, 16 December.

SCAA (1994) *Model Syllabuses for RE, Consultation Document: Glossary of Terms*. London: SCAA.

Starkings, D. (1993) *Religion and the Arts*. London: Hodder & Stoughton.

Sutcliffe, J. M. (ed.) (1984) *A Dictionary of Religious Education*. London: SCM Press.

Taylor, G. and Saunders, J. B. (1976) *The Law of Education*. London: Butterworth.

CHAPTER 14

Where angels fear to tread: discovering children's spirituality

Clive and Jane Erricker

INTRODUCTION

The research in this chapter is a small part of the *Children and Worldviews Project* which is investigating the way in which children learn.

This research stems from a belief that the way in which children learn cannot be separated from who they are and the experiences that have shaped that identity. The experiences, and their interpretation by the child form the machinery by which all subsequent experiences (including formal learning experiences) are moulded and readjusted in order that the child can make sense of them. This machinery, made up of all previous experiences, forms the child's world-view – the window through which he or she looks out on the world and that protects his or her being. This belief owes something to the Piagetian concepts of assimilation and accommodation:

> Through assimilation the child takes in information about the outside world and modifies it to fit in with his own understanding and experience, whereas by accommodation he changes and develops his own understanding thus fitting in with objects and events in the external world.
>
> (Sylva and Lunt, 1982, p. 164)

However, it is now widely acknowledged that Piaget's theory does not take sufficient account of the complexity of the processes at work.

The process approach to education (Blenkin and Kelly, 1987) advocates a view of knowledge that is essentially tentative and suggests that the essence of education is the facilitation of the development of skills and not the transfer of a traditionally agreed body of knowledge which may not endure. The transfer theory of knowledge makes exactly that assumption: that knowledge is something unchangeable and unchanging and that the job of the teacher is to transfer this knowledge from his or her mind to that of the learner. The assumption is also made that the knowledge is transferred in its pure form, untainted by its passage through the teacher's mind and its reception in the learner's.

This obviously cannot be the case. Each person must re-interpret and adjust the knowledge as it passes into his or her sphere of perception. If we ignore this then we make dangerous assumptions about the nature of what is taught and what is learned.

The personal construct theory of learning suggested by Kelly (1986) takes this into consideration.

It holds that an individual invariably approaches any situation in life with a personal theory of explanation.

(Brown *et al.*, 1986)

Thus the acquisition of a new concept by a learner involves the interpretation of that new concept within the existing framework. The framework is altered by the acceptance of the new idea and the whole process is repeated until the learner is comfortable with his or her understanding. Knowledge is therefore context-dependent.

The personal construct theory and the related process approach to education both see learning as beginning with existing knowledge, and therefore the interpretative framework, of the learner. If a teacher wishes to start where the learner is, then some idea of the learner's existing knowledge is required. In a classroom situation this is taken to mean that which has been previously taught. But as we have seen, this does not take into consideration the adjustment of those taught ideas by the frameworks of the learners. If these ideas, either taught or caught, are ones which deal with existential issues, then we may be said to be considering children's spirituality.

We wish to access these frameworks: to gain some understanding of the way in which children attempt to understand and come to terms with these important existential issues. After looking at the information provided by conversations with children we developed the idea that the way to access children's understanding is to look at the metaphors that they use when talking about these important issues.

Metaphor's essential role is a cognitive one, sustained by our need to explain and understand through comparison.

(Cooper, 1986, p. 144)

We thought that they would use metaphors from their existing experiences and understanding and that this would help us to access their frame of reference. We do not expect their frames of reference always to appear the same. The child in the classroom being 'good' may see himself very differently as that same child in the playpark being a 'hero' to his gang. He is operating in a different situation and occupying a different role and we would expect him to use different metaphors.

METHODOLOGY

Quantitative research tends to rely heavily on a hypothetico-deductive, scientific paradigm with an emphasis on the verification of an already established theory. Such research requires a hypothesis that can be tested and data that can be quantified and possibly subjected to statistical analysis. Variables need to be manipulated and controlled. There is a need to have controls for the sake of comparison and to feel that the sample is chosen to cover as much of the range as possible. The method must be seen as rigorous, heading towards a definite 'proof' that can then be applied generally.

We were concerned that this methodology was not appropriate for our research and we adopted a qualitative approach.

> Qualitative research (is) . . . an umbrella term to refer to several research strategies that share certain characteristics. The data collected has been termed 'soft', that is, rich in description of people, places and conversations, and not easily handled by statistical procedures. Research questions are not framed by operationalizing variables; rather they are formulated to be investigated in all their complexity, in context. While people conducting qualitative research may develop a focus as they collect data, they do not approach the research with specific questions to answer or hypotheses to test. They are concerned as well with understanding behaviour from the subject's own frame of reference. External causes are of secondary importance. They tend to collect their data through sustained contact with people in settings where subjects normally spend their time.
>
> (Bogdan and Biklen, 1982, p. 2)

The lack of a tight idea of a testable hypothesis or question to answer means that the theory is 'grounded' in the data collected. The notion of grounded theory was put forward by Glaser and Strauss in 1967.

Thus we went into this research with the idea that we should allow the children to speak to us in as natural and unstructured a way as possible and that these data should allow us to construct theory.

Data were collected by unstructured interviews using Key Stage 2 children in four schools: two multi-ethnic schools in Southampton, a Catholic school in Southampton and a multi-ethnic school in Hounslow. Children were interviewed in small groups, usually of four or five children, or in pairs, and the conversations were tape-recorded.

EXPLORING CONCEPTUAL FRAMEWORKS

As an example of the potential of this kind of study, one interview with Kelvin and Damien will be described and analysed.

Damien and Kelvin are pupils at an inner-city primary school in Southampton. The school is situated in the centre of a development mostly of high-rise flats. The population is ethnically mixed, containing Indian, West Indian, Chinese and Caucasian people. Many of the pupils at the school come from socially-deprived backgrounds and their families have an understandably ambiguous attitude towards authority. Many of the children are also emotionally deprived and make demands on the staff of the school to compensate for this.

There is a comparatively high number of statemented children at the school and the staff/pupil ratio allows for the individual attention that such children require. The dedicated and committed teachers produce an atmosphere that is caring, supportive and non-judgemental and that attempts to prevent the parents' feeling marginalized.

Teachers, governors and parents were informed of the research, permission was sought and we were available for further discussion if anyone required it. The headteacher and class teachers were very interested and supportive and the research has been discussed with them regularly. Their perception and insight into their children's thinking has been a constant inspiration.

As an initial stimulus the two children were asked to draw a circle on a sheet of paper and, within the circle, to draw someone who matters to them. Damien did this task, Kelvin said he couldn't draw well and just wanted to talk.

Kelvin's response

K. I like having a gang. People get scared of me. They try to take us on but . . . there's more of us and there are big boys. Lee can't take us on [*Lee's a big boy*].
Q. Where do you go with your gang?
K. Walk about the estate. David's a trouble-maker on the estate. His Dad's name's Sid. His Dad's been in prison. When he's in prison we'll beat him [*David*] up. He tries to get us to do shoplifting. He's big. I beat him up at the disco. He was bleeding. He felt gutted.
Q. Who's in your gang?
K. I don't want to tell you . . . it's a secret.

Later Kelvin explains how he likes violence. He is sitting playing with a pair of scissors as though they are a weapon.

Q. Do you like violence, Kelvin?
K. Yes, I like kung fu films. [*He also watches violent adult videos and had mentioned earlier that he has a book with stories about God.*]
Q. Kelvin, tell us about the book you mentioned earlier.
K. A kiddies' Bible.

He talks about how his parents used to go to church.

Q. Do you both believe in God?
Kelvin and Damien. Yep.
Q. Can you tell me why?
K. 'Cos you should and it's a good reason to do it. He gives you food and all that. If you believe in God, God the father as well. He's the one who made us.
Q. Does believing in God mean being good?
Kelvin and Damien. Yeah.
Q. Okay, give me an example of being good.
K. You see David H, he's on the devil's side, right. And he pushed Jonathan Y into the river. Me, Paul, Desmond and Jason, we jumped into the river and saved him.

Q. What makes you think David's on the devil's side?

K. Because he nicks motorbikes and all that . . . if you talk about a devil, right . . . the devil swoops down somewhere in your room and tries to get you to do things. He tries to get you to hurt the angel in the other ear, right.

Kelvin demonstrates having a devil and an angel on each shoulder.

K. He sits on my shoulder and he says things and he flies away and I've killed the devil I have.

Q. So, are you telling me the devil sometimes whispers in your ear?

K. Yeah, to tell me naughty things.

Discussion

Here we can try to see how Kelvin is interpreting his social reality through a framework that he has constructed. His framework seems to be constructed from three sources:

- the 'kiddies' Bible'
- the violent videos
- his experience of life on the estate

Within this framework Kelvin has given himself a heroic role – he's put himself on the side of the 'good guys' – which allows him to fit together his belief in God and the violent videos. He has been told that God wants him to be good.

In the context of his school life, this story does not help him. Kelvin is continually in trouble for aggressive activity which ensures his survival on the streets, and his scenario of the battle between God and the devil played out in his own mind does not fit with the behaviour required in school. Whose side are the teachers on? Whilst appearing to be enabling in one context, Kelvin's metaphors do not allow him to operate effectively in another.

There is a temptation to regard Kelvin's ideas as an unnecessary projection, merely a self-justification of his behaviour and attitudes, but they also have a purchase when he is concerned about significant events in other's lives.

Damien's response

Damien's circle shows two figures with a bag between them.

D. I like helping old people, carrying their food and help them get up the stairs.

Q. Why?

D. Because they're old and they can't live very long, old people.

Q. Is that a problem?

D. (*nods*) Because they die and people feel sad. My grandad died the other day. I think he had a heart attack in the hospital. I think he had cancer in his lungs and he had bad ribs.

Q. Did you help him?

D. Yes, I was bringing him letters saying get well soon.

Q. But he didn't get well.

D. No, he died. He went in a deep sleep and he died.

Q. Where do you think your grandad is now?

D. He's in the grave.

Q. So he's just dead?

D. (*nods*) We often go up to the grave to see him.

Q. How long ago did he die?

D. About six months ago. I don't remember all of it.

Q. When people die does life just stop for them or do they go somewhere else?

D. Life just stops for them.

K. I think they go back to God. Become an angel. It is true.

Q. How do you know that, Kelvin?

K. I've got a big Bible.

Q. Damien, you're not sure about your grandad. Is it possible to be in touch with your grandad now?

D. I'll always be in touch with him.

Q. How will you stay in touch with him?

D. By prayer, I pray for him every night before I go to bed. I say, please God could you make my grandad be alive soon. I want to see him.

Q. Do you think it's possible for him to be alive again?

K. He's still alive, Damien. He's an angel.

D. I know he's flying around now probably.

Q. Where are the angels, Kelvin, are they with us or somewhere else?

K. At night they come. They're in the air. They never come in your house.

D. They look in through the window.

K. When my mum dies I'll put some blood in [the grave] and then she'll stay alive a bit longer. 'Cos I don't want her to die. When my mum dies I might want to go with her.

D. Yeah, stab yourself.

K. I'm not too scared to do it, you know. I'll do it right now . . . . Yeah, I'm not allowed to, am I?

Q. Is that because you love your mum?

K. (*nods*)

Q. And what do you think will happen to your mum when she dies?

K. She'll become an angel, I'll want to come and see what her'll be like. I'll wait for her. I'll wait for a long time till I dies and then I'll be the same.

Discussion

Here Kelvin brings his framework to bear on Damien's problem. Despite the differences between them there is a close friendship. Damien acknowledges this by playing with Kelvin's idea of angels but it is not convincing for him.

Despite his belief in God and the hope he invests in his prayers, Damien has no concept of heaven that he can employ in the context of his loss. At the same time he can still speak of being in touch with his grandad though his grandad is not alive.

In this interview we see children struggling to make sense of very large existential issues – the relationship between good and evil, and the loss of a loved one. We suggest that the metaphors they use give us some clues as to their existential framework, Kelvin's angels helping him with loss and his devils helping him with the existence of violence and hate. We can also get a sense of Damien's refusal to accept Kelvin's explanation as an interpretation of his own experience. However, we have not had time to explore Damien's framework further. It may be that Kelvin can express his ideas, using language we can understand, while Damien has metaphors of his own that we haven't yet accessed.

THE SUGGESTION OF GENRE

From this and other data we are developing a concept of *genre*. This idea is borrowed from the world of literature and cinema, in which it describes the style of the book or film. The genre determines, to an extent, the characters found in the work, the setting and what is allowed to happen. Examples of genre are the western, the detective story and the romance.

We would like to suggest that children operate within genres – that they approach life with a set of attitudes and ideas which constitute an identifiable package. We can tentatively assign children that we have interviewed to a list of various genres that we have identified. They include:

● The 'my little pony' genre – typified by a Disneyesque approach and a deep interest in the welfare of animals.
● The all-American kid whose life revolves around theme parks, Macdonalds and consumerism.
● The family-centred genre where relationships within the family are all-important.
● The hard man (like Kelvin above) whose life includes a lot of violence and conflict.

We are not suggesting that children always operate in one particular genre. I am sure that we can all switch our genre at different times and in different places. However, we feel that identification of the relevant genre must help to understand a child's approach to his life. One thing we have not yet found is a genre based purely on religious tradition. But perhaps we have been talking to children in the wrong places to uncover that.

Kelvin's genre is one of conflict. It is what he sees in his reading of different 'texts', from whatever source, and it identifies the way in which he sees his role in his social life. He also chooses 'texts' which support this role in terms of the genre they project, such as the videos he watches, the kung fu films. Whatever he is presented with at school in terms of social situation or that which he is required to learn, he will attempt to interpret within this framework.

Equally, Damien is not open to explanations of future reconciliation with his grandfather because his storying of events does not include the expectation of an afterlife. We can see this at a later stage in the conversation:

D. We're getting older, Kelvin, every year we're growing dead. Grown-ups get older and we get older.

Q. Does getting older make you feel good or not?

D. Sad, I wish I was a baby and then I would live a bit longer.

K. I don't want to grow up.

D. I want to stay eight.

Q. What's good about being eight?

D. You've got more toys. When I grow I want to stay eight.

Q. What about old people? Why is it not so good for old people?

D. Because they die soon and it's not so good for the other people. We're lucky but we might die or something.

Therefore he will not existentially engage with any attempt to introduce such a possibility. The genre of his narrative is one in which ageing implies decrepitude and extinction. Being young offers hope and a possibility that age denies.

NARRATIVE, METAPHOR AND GENRE

The understanding of the term metaphor is highly varied and needs to be explained so that its function is clear. If it is understood as having a purely decorative value it cannot be said to be a means by which we come to know things, but only as a way of expressing, more poetically, what we already know. A further understanding of metaphor relies on a distinction between empirical enquiry (commonly understood to be the basis of scientific investigation) which gains us knowledge of an 'objective' world, and poetic language which is a matter of 'subjective' apprehension. If we hold to this distinction metaphor falls into the latter category and therefore can be dismissed as having no purchase on 'knowledge', i.e., no epistemological function at all. Neither of these notions of metaphor serves us well. When involved with ontological concerns and, in this case, children's ontology, metaphor becomes highly significant because it acts as a way of making meaning, of constructing sense and pattern out of experience.

Samuel Levin, in discussing the nature of conceptions, suggests they can operate as functions of phenomenological behaviour. He states:

> In its epistemological sense a conception is a rationalization of how the world is organized; in this sense the notion has an objective cast. The phenomenological sense, on the other hand, has a subjective tone: in this sense the notion represents how we as individuals relate to – how we play our roles in – the organization that we make of the world.
>
> (Levin, 1988, p. x).

He goes on to explain the role of metaphor in this respect, relating his study to Wordsworth in particular.

> It is by extracting from the particular and characteristic conceptions that Wordsworth expresses in his metaphors that we arrive at his general conception of how the world is ordered.
>
> (Levin, 1988, p. x)

We are concerned with a similar venture to Levin's in asking how we can enquire into the conceptual constructs of children without imposing upon them criteria belonging to a particular body of knowledge which already operates within a specific epistemological paradigm. Following Levin, metaphor becomes the means of access to children's world-views by virtue of being the vehicle by which they construct and express their conceptions derived from their experiences.

Here we are working with the hypothesis of 'bricolage', to use Foucault's term, in which, by analogy, we may understand the child to be selecting from his or her experiences as a builder determines what raw materials are useful for a particular construction and then how they can be used in conjunction: Do they fit together and what shape and structure do they result in? Identified in this process are the relationships and influences that children draw upon to make explanations of events, circumscribed by their enculturation. It is at this point that genre becomes a useful theoretical term.

We have referred to 'frames of reference' varying according to the particular circumstance in which the child finds him or herself and the different roles played in those circumstances. Genre is concerned with different types of narrative. It determines what characters, roles, plots and outcomes are possible according to the way in which we story events. There is a narrative already in place: at home, in school, with friends. Effectively this narrative belongs to a genre: a type of story, which operates according to certain possibilities.

Narrative itself, therefore, employs different metaphors according to the genre. The three terms together, narrative, metaphor and genre, provide us with a structure by virtue of which we can analyse children's conversation about their world.

PROBLEMS AND POSSIBILITIES OF THIS KIND OF RESEARCH

Trying to do this kind of research presents a variety of problems. The difficulties of working with people, with all their inconsistencies, are magnified when those people are only seven years old. You cannot depend on their co-operation or their concentration during the interview and they can easily be distracted or bored. Alternatively their desire to co-operate is so great that the purpose of the interview is completely thwarted. In one interview not quoted here and conducted in a school library, the children found books to show the meanings of words like space and world rather than relating their own ideas. This also indicated the possible lack of confidence that these children had in their own ideas, bowing to the authority of the 'book'.

Accessing children's thinking as we have been trying to do is a time-consuming process. You have to establish a relationship with the child before there is enough trust for the child to speak freely. This involves visiting a school fairly frequently and becoming familiar to the children before even trying to interview them. A facilitating environment is necessary and a child may be more comfortable at home or may be able to express his or her ideas more easily in church or temple. Robert Coles found that children felt certain topics appropriate to certain environments, as we suggested above.

In order to avoid putting ideas into the children's heads or giving the impression that there is a right answer to a question, the style of questioning has to be very open-ended and the interview child-led. Again this makes the process very time-consuming and often frustrating when the interview takes a direction all its own. The important point to note is that if you are trying to find theory that is grounded in data, there should be no intention in terms of outcome. The interview goes where it goes and the theory comes from that. The interviewing process, indeed the whole research, involves an element of risk because it is not entirely in the researcher's control. This has parallels with the whole concept of process education, which is essentially child-led.

The question of the nature of truth becomes an issue. When children talk about their understanding of a concept like heaven, are they telling me the 'truth'? Are they talking about their real understanding, their understanding today (which will be different tomorrow), what they think I want to hear, what someone else has told them and which must therefore be correct (especially if the someone else is an adult), or some imagined fantasy? It is necessary to view this research in such a way that the concept of truth, in the accepted sense, becomes irrelevant. It doesn't matter into which of the above categories the children's offered information falls: what matters is what lies behind that information and how they are attempting to communicate it.

We could ask a child for the same information by different methods and strive for reliability in that way, but we suspect that the information would be different each time. A different truth would be appropriate in each situation as the variables of mood, feelings and perceptions all change.

We suggest that each of us tells different stories each time we talk about issues and concepts that are important to our being, to our sense of identity. Our stories are tailored to fit the situation, even if that situation is simply internal and our audience only ourselves. Children are no different. Today I feel like Superman and my story stresses the heroic; tomorrow I may be in church and feel like a saint. Thus we must look instead for a process held in common, not a consistency of information. How are these children trying to express their identities and their spirituality? What metaphors are they using and where have they found them? How does this affect their understanding of new concepts that teachers try to teach them? How can teachers allow and help children to express themselves and how can they use that information to help children deal with existential issues?

CONCLUSION

This chapter has presented an analysis of how children work with their own ontological paradigms, with metaphors drawn from their enculturation and the authority figures in their lives. It focuses on themes of loss and conflict and how children attempt to resolve these in the construction of their personal narrative. The conclusions drawn can only be tentative but suggest that teachers must take account of the need to deconstruct children's storying in any attempt to educate them, especially in the domains of values education and spirituality.

This is not seen as a matter of defining particular curriculum areas but of underpinning an approach to education as a whole curriculum enterprise.

We feel that by listening to the children speaking and trying to find structures and systems in the way in which they construct their metaphorical frameworks, we may come to a better understanding not only of their understanding of religious and spiritual matters but of learning in general.

NOTE

The Children and Worldviews Project is a collaborative venture involving Clive Erricker from Chichester Institute of Higher Education, Danny Sullivan and John Logan from LSU College Southampton and Jane Erricker from King Alfred's College Winchester. A research assistant, Cathy Ota, works with the team.

REFERENCES

Blenkin, G. and Kelly, A. V. (1987) *The Primary Curriculum*. London: Paul Chapman.

Bogdan, R. and Biklen, S. (1982) *Qualitative Research for Education*. Boston: Allyn and Bacon.

Brown *et al.* (eds) (1986) *Science in Schools*. Open University Press.

Cooper, D. (1986) *Metaphor*. Oxford: Blackwell.

Glaser, B. and Strauss, A. (1967) *The Discovery of Grounded Theory*. London: Weidenfeld and Nicolson.

Kelly, A. V. (1986) *Knowledge and Curriculum Planning*. London: Harper.

Levin, S. (1988) *Metaphoric Worlds*. London: Yale University Press.

Sylva, K. and Lunt, I. (1982) *Child Development*. Oxford: Blackwell.

BIBLIOGRAPHY

Coles, R. (1990) *The Spiritual Life of Children*. London: Harper-Collins.

Donaldson, M. (1963) *A Study of Children's Thinking*. London: Tavistock Publications.

Erricker, C. and Erricker, J. (1994) Metaphorical awareness and the methodology of religious education. *British Journal of Religious Education*, **16** (3), 174–84.

McFague, S. (1987) *Models of God*. London: SCM Press.

Madge, V. (1965) *Children in Search of Meaning*. London: SCM Press.

Rorty, R. (1982) *The Consequences of Pragmatism*. Hemel Hempstead: The Harvester Press.

Sacks, O. (1982) *Awakenings*. London: Picador.
Sontag, S. (1989) *Illness as Metaphor and Aids and Its Metaphors*.
  Harmondsworth: Penguin Books.
Wood, D. (1988) *How Children Think and Learn*. Oxford: Blackwell.

CHAPTER 15

Talking to young children about things spiritual

Elaine McCreery

INTRODUCTION

This chapter is a summary of work from January to June of 1994. It represents part of a study being undertaken towards a research degree. The study focuses on the notion of spiritual development in young children.

The beginning of my interest in this area is probably related to three events.

- Some time ago I undertook a study to examine the response of primary schools to the 1988 Education Reform Act regarding collective worship (McCreery, 1991). Among other things, I found that schools often saw part of the value of worship as being able to contribute to the spiritual lives of children. What was also clear was that this sense of 'developing the spiritual' was not clearly articulated; more, it was some kind of feeling of something that was of value. Schools had not explored the concept in any great detail, but there was still a sense that the spiritual needed addressing and worship was part of this.
- Some time after this I was talking to a colleague who is experienced in early years education. I asked her if there was any sense in which teachers of young children believed they helped to develop the spiritual. She felt that although it was never made explicit, many teachers would say that within the work they do with young children, a lot of the activities might be contributing to spiritual development. For example, many early years classrooms do work with nature, studying animals, growing plants, etc. Yet when I turned to books on early years education, there appeared to be little reference to notions of the spiritual.
- A further source of interest to me was the growing number of books and articles, possibly in response to the 1988 Education Reform Act, which aim to promote spiritual development. These offer activities which teachers can do with children in the classroom and which are supposed to develop the spiritual. The activities are very similar in all

these publications and tend to focus on the idea of personal reflection on events and situations. Some appear to be similar to activities used in psychotherapy. I was interested to know how such activities had been identified as good for developing young children spiritually.

Other recent material offers an insight into the spiritual lives of children. For example, work by Robert Coles, recently published in *The Spiritual Life of Children* (Coles, 1992), gave a good picture of children's thoughts from the age of about seven upwards. I was interested in the picture of children younger than this. Can we find out what notions of the spiritual children have at the age of four or five?

Work described by Edward Robinson in *The Original Vision* (Robinson, 1977) suggests that people who remember spiritual awareness from their childhood were often unable to talk about it. Furthermore, many of these people also say that it was only as they became adults that they recognized the significance of such events. This might suggest, therefore, that any attempt to discuss 'spiritual' matters with very young children is fruitless.

At the same time, many people who have worked with young children, and of course many parents, can recount stories where very young children have raised questions of a 'spiritual' nature. Such questions often arise out of a particular situation or event which leads the child to question what it already knows in an attempt to understand that which seems to conflict with previous experience.

The issue which most interests me is this. Teachers are charged with promoting the spiritual development of children, and now we see materials being developed with this aim in mind. However, not only is the notion of 'spiritual' itself a complex and much-debated term, but as yet there is no evidence to show the relationship between designed activities and spiritual development. How do we *know* that we are developing the spiritual?

Consideration of these events has led me to reading around the whole area of the spiritual within an educational context. There are obviously many questions to be explored, and one of the key ones for me was, what do we know about the spiritual development of young children?

I decided that one way forward was to enter into conversations with 4- and 5-year-olds to see if they could tell me in their own words what they believed about the world as they know it.

AIMS AND METHODS

The purpose of the investigation was to identify methods for entering into young children's conception of the spiritual. In this context the term spiritual is taken to mean, *An awareness that there is something other, something greater than the course of everyday events.*

In planning the investigation I set out:

- to use situations which the children may have experience of, whether directly or second-hand;
- to use a range of activities and materials which the children would be familiar with through school; and
- where possible to allow children to use their own words, avoiding

words which might influence their answers, particularly religious language.

Experiences

In choosing experiences which I hoped would be familiar to children, I wanted to locate conceptions of the spiritual within regular childhood experience. A great deal of work can be found which relates to adult spirituality and much appears to be related to adults questioning the world in which they live and, in particular, asking questions relating to the 'ultimate'. I wanted to discern what represents the 'ultimate' in children's lives. What questions do they ask about the world, what meaning do they find in life, how do they explain the unexplainable? In order to do this, I could not *give* them questions, I needed to discover *theirs*. The task, therefore, was to present the children with situations arising from events with which they might be familiar, and encourage them to identify the questions.

I needed to consider what events or situations in a child's life are likely to raise questions about the spiritual in a child's mind. It seems to me that a child of between three and five is beginning to explore his or her world in several places at one time. The most influential places are likely to be: home, school and television.

Taking each one separately, what 'spiritual' aspects might arise in each?

Home is the place where children first learn about their own identity and role in life. They start to learn about relationships and others' roles and they begin to find answers about the world in which they live. Events or situations they may have encountered might include birth and death, love, trust, joy, sadness, special occasions, religion, etc.

In *school* the child first begins the relationship with the unknown world of strangers, who may have different ways and meanings to those at home. The child must learn to co-operate and communicate with a variety of people and may need to learn to take his or her turn in getting attention. Events which might lead to reflection of the spiritual may include classroom activities, e.g. nature study and stories, and situations in which the child may encounter danger, failure, reward, companionship and success, as well as many of the things first encountered at home.

No study of children's lives today can be complete without consideration of the impact of *television and video*. Even those children whose TV watching is closely vetted by parents will still be aware of popular culture through other children. Today's children have access to worlds far-removed from their own in distance and in time. They also have access to fantasy worlds which go far beyond the fantasies of their story books. Through TV children will have encountered difference, especially of cultures, values and beliefs. They will have some knowledge about violence and death, social taboos, very noble behaviour and despicable behaviour, tremendous suffering and uplifting charity.

Activities

In choosing to use activities that the children were familiar with through schooling, I wanted to make sure I was not introducing them to strange situations or activities. I wanted to find out if, in their usual activities in school, they had some notion of the spiritual. At this stage I did not want to attempt to develop the children 'spiritually', only to trace the development of their conceptions thus far. Using familiar activities would, I hoped, make them comfortable in a situation which was not usual. I was a relative stranger who would be taking them out of their classroom to tape their conversations.

The young child's school activities are rich in potential for exploration of the spiritual – perhaps more than any other age group's. In contrast to older children, their timetable is more flexible, the teaching methods more open and the content more exploratory and creative, and many classroom activities are likely to give rise to exploration of the spiritual. In painting, drawing, sorting, matching, play, story, singing and so on, the children are beginning their encounters and responses with themselves, other people, and the world around them. There is no need to introduce artificially constructed activities to address the spiritual; in children's minds the barriers which define subject areas are not yet drawn, everything is 'life'.

Language

An important factor in children's learning is the acquisition and development of language. The issue of language in connection with the spiritual is a complex one. In the past, researchers have concentrated on talk with young children in order to evaluate their spiritual awareness. There are difficulties with this. Adults struggle to explain the spiritual in verbal terms and throughout history have built up many ways of communicating spiritual insight, of which language is only one. At the same time, part of the reason why the spiritual has suffered neglect is that adults cannot find words to describe it which can be universally understood or accepted. A further complication is the fact that until recently most discussion of the spiritual has concentrated on religious traditions, using religious language and imagery to convey meaning. This would require children to have a working knowledge of such language before they are deemed to be spiritually aware. There is great danger here that children may be able to repeat such language without understanding it, or at least not building the same meaning into it as adults do. Does this also mean that children outside religious traditions are less likely to develop spiritually because they may not be initiated into the language?

While language must be a feature of the study, I resolved that it should not be the only means of communication. I wanted to explore other ways in which children might demonstrate an awareness of the spiritual. This is potentially much more demanding, for it is far easier to interpret children's conversation than, say, their drawings or movement.

One last point about language. I was determined that as the researcher, I would not give children the language to express themselves or to respond to my questions. I wanted to learn what terms the children use to express their spiritual knowing. I wanted to avoid offering them terms which were meaningless to them, distorted their expressions or led them to the conclusion that all I was after was 'God stories'. Children are quick to give us what they think we want and become skilled at this at an early age. If they used a religious language themselves, then I would explore it with them, but I would not furnish them with it. This made the research task even more difficult, not because the children might not be able to say something, but because I had to restrain myself from making religious (in my case, Christian) links. So, for example, in talking about death I had to find some way of finding out children's thoughts about life after death without introducing the concept itself. If I asked, 'What do you think happens when we die', the notion is introduced to the children that something indeed *does* happen.

THE STUDY

The world of the spiritual is often related to encounter and response. It is related to human beings trying to find meaning in the world as it appears to them. Three main encounters seem to provoke spiritual reflection:

- encounter with self
- encounter with others
- encounter with nature

Activities were chosen which would help the children relate to these three types of encounter in contexts which they were likely to recognize.

Activity 1: Pictures

This session took place in the school hall, sitting on benches and with people passing through. The atmosphere was not conducive to talk and the children moved around a great deal, unable to keep attention on the task. I showed the children posters of the natural world including landscapes, insects, animals and plants. I asked them questions about what the pictures showed, if they had seen such things and where. Then I asked about how these things had got here and how they had come to be. Their answers were very vague and they kept moving away from the questions to tell me all sorts of details about events in their own lives. I learned about what they had done at the weekend and how they came to have cuts on their knees, but very little else.

I concluded that the task was too abstract for them, and did not relate to concerns immediate to their own experiences. So after several pleasant but unrewarding chats (as far as my study was concerned), I abandoned the task. However, I did learn from it. First, an appropriate atmosphere needed to be established which included seating the children at tables to prevent them wandering about. Second, I needed to tape conversations so that I was not constantly trying to jot down what was said in unreadable shorthand. Third, I had to use content which the children could quickly relate to and which held their attention for a length of time.

Activity 2: Story

This activity proved to be far more successful. It initially involved me telling an invented story, discussing it and then asking the children to draw pictures from it. I invented a story about a little girl and her cat. I described how the girl loved the cat and cared for it and how eventually it was killed. I had a much clearer notion of what I wanted from the children.

I wanted to gain some insight into their notions of life and death, but I wanted to avoid determining their answers by giving them my understanding of the concepts. The question I asked the children after the story was, 'Julie was very sad after her cat was killed, what could we say to her to make her feel better?'

Here is an extract of a conversation with Kerry, Stephanie, Chantal and Darren which followed my story:

Me What could we say to Julie to make her feel better?
K. To get another kitten.
S. Or get a puppy.
D. Tell her it's gone up in the sky.
S. My gran had a dog and it's gone in the sky.
D. My nana Pam is up in the sky. She stays there every day.
K. She's with Jesus.
C. And God.
K. My little sister died when she was a baby.
Me Did she? That must have been very sad. What's it like in the sky?
S. There's puppies and kittens.
Me What happens to the kitten when it's in the sky?
K. You can't come back.
C. They put you in a hole and you get flowers.
D. Then they take you to hospital.
C. No, you have to stay in the hole.

From this brief conversation it is possible to identify certain aspects of the children's understanding of life and death. We see that they quickly relate the story to events in their own lives, the death of pets, grandparents and even a baby sister. They understand that once you are dead you cannot 'come back'.

They have some knowledge about burial procedures and some notion of the dead going into the sky, which they relate to what they know about Jesus and God. One notion that appears here and appeared frequently in other discussion about death is the connection of death with hospital.

On another occasion I used the children's story, *Badger's Parting Gifts* (Varley, 1992), to explore the notion of life and death. Here is an extract from a conversation with Stacey and Jeffrey, aged 4 and 5.

Me Stacey, you've just said that God's going to make him alive again. How does he do that?
S. He's got magic power.
Me So what do you think happened to Badger?
S. He's going to be alive.
Me And would his friends see him again?
S. and J. Yes.
Me Is that what happens when people die, do they come alive again?
S. and J. Yes.
(Discussion about colour of pens)
Me So do you know people who've died and come alive again?
S. Yes, my mum told me.

Me What did she tell you?

S. She told me God makes people alive. My grandad and my nana died.

J. My grandfather died. He was at Ghana. He can't be alive anymore.

Me They don't come back to life? You don't see them again?

S. I don't know where they are, but my daddy and my mummy, and Kelly and Steven know where their hospital is. But we haven't seen them for a long time. (*At this point Stacey seems to be getting upset*)

J. And do you know what? My grandfather is alive now.

Me Is he? Is that a different grandfather?

J. Yes.

Me Badger's friends were sad when he died. How did they make themselves feel better?

J. Because they had a dream about Badger and they said thank-you and they feel happy.

S. The mummy badger should have a baby badger.

J. There's a badger and there's one. (*Pointing to the book, the two find other badgers*)

S. They should pray for Badger.

Me What should they say?

S. They should say 'I miss you Badger'. That's what I would say.

J. Can we do some drawing now?

Here, Stacey has some notion that her grandparents are in a hospital which she cannot go to. Do young children associate hospitals with dying? We also see once again concepts of God, and the notion that God makes people alive again.

Activity 3: Difficult questions

The last activity I tried was to ask the children about difficult questions. Here I was aiming to find out if children of 4 and 5 have started to ask the so-called 'ultimate questions' that we see identified in Agreed Syllabuses for RE. I introduced the children (Lauren and Kim) to my nephew, whose picture I had brought along. I told them a little about him and then said that he often asked me some difficult questions. I began by asking them to guess what questions he asked. This proved to be very difficult for all the children, but when they did answer, their questions were very practical.

Me What kinds of questions do you think Adam might ask me?

L. How old is your mum?

Me That's a good question. Could I find out the answer to that question?

K. Yes, easily. You could just go to your mum and just say the age.

Me What other difficult questions might Adam ask me?

K. How do you make paper?

Me Yes, that is a tricky question. Do you know how to make paper?

L. I know how to make fire.

Me Do you? Let's think about the paper first, then the fire. How do you make paper?

K. You get a square and you put the paper in the square and when you've done that you put it in some water, and you leave it to dry.

L. Well how do you make cardboard paper?

Me Perhaps you need to put more paper in?
L. and K. Yes . . . .
Me Now you said you know how to make fire.
L. Right, well you get a piece of metal, and you get a piece of wood. Then you scrape it with the metal and fires comes out.
Me OK. Are there any other ways of making fire?
K. Yes, by stones. Of if you have a lighter you can get a fire easily.
L. And buy matches.

In order to move on I told the children some of the questions that my nephew asks me. The first was, 'How did all the world get here?' Most of the children attributed this to the world of God and his power to create things. Some responses demonstrated a questioning of this assumption, as can be seen from this later conversation with Kim and Lauren.

Me Kim, what do you think?
K. God made the people.
Me Who is this God?
L. He's in the sky. And Jesus made them.
Me What do you think?
K. He made things. Some people think he made apple trees. And worms can get in the apple tree.
Me Who made the worms?
L. I don't know. How do you think God made us?
Me What do you think?
L. I don't know. By cotton wool?
K. No.
Me How do you find out about God?
K. You can't find out.
Me So how do you know about him? How did you find out about him?
K. I didn't. My dad told me.
Me What else did your dad tell you about God?
K. Nothing else.
Me He just told you that he's there?
K. Yes. How did God make himself?
Me That's an even harder question, isn't it?
L. God made himself first and then he made Jesus.
Me What do you think of that, Kim?
(*Kim nods but he doesn't look convinced by Lauren's suggestion.*)

Other children had obviously been told something quite different, but it still left them with unanswered questions. See this thought from David:

Me What questions do you think Adam asks me?
(*No response*)
Me Let me tell you one that he asked. Where did all the world come from?
D. I know, because my mum told me. It came from a big bang.
Me What do you think, Ibrahim?
(*No response*)
Me So, David, there was a big bang and all the world got started –

> **D.** How come there was no people alive and then suddenly they got . . .
> alive? That's what I don't understand.

Later in this conversation I asked the children another of my nephew's
questions, 'What's at the end of the sky?' Some of the children talked of
heaven and space, and went on to tell me about ET and spaceships. David
and Ibrahim had other ideas:

> **Me** Let me look at another question Adam asked me. I know, what's at
> the end of the sky?
> **D.** There isn't an end of the sky.
> **Me** There isn't an end? It just goes on? How far does it go on?
> **I.** Ten hours.
> **D.** It goes on for the whole world.
> **I.** Maybe a year – infinity.
> **Me** Infinity – what's that?
> **I.** That means you've finished all your numbers.

These young children demonstrate an understanding of the notion of infinity and appear to be quite at ease with the concept. They challenge my
question, refusing to give me a tangible answer, and instead offer me a
much more abstract concept.

SOME ISSUES

The aim of the work I have done so far has been to start to identify possible methods for exploring children's notions of the spiritual. Thus far, it
appears that the use of stories which relate to their own lives is very
rewarding. I have still to try other methods, such as using the natural world
by taking the children outside or bringing natural objects in. I also intend
to get them drawing and painting, but again, the difficulty will be to focus
their drawing without determining the results by putting ideas into their
heads.

I have also begun to refine the techniques of gathering the data. I have
found that talking to just two children at one time is easier when it comes
to transcribing – children's voices sound remarkably alike on tape! But
equally it is better to have two children so that they respond to each
other's statements and feel more confident.

Collecting this data is very enjoyable, especially when you are taken into
the home corner and made tea during the conversation. The challenge
arises when you begin to analyse what the children have given you. How
great is the danger of putting one's own interpretation on their answers? Is
their understanding of terms the same as mine? And given their more
limited vocabulary, how far can I get into their understanding of concepts?
Do they think and conceive of ideas far more than their language allows
them to express?

In the past it has been suggested that work with young children on spirituality is difficult because they were not considered to be spiritually aware.
What empirical work there is tends to focus on children much older than
those I worked with (e.g. Coles, 1992). What I have learned so far is that

these 4- and 5-year-olds have started to sort out their experiences of the world, and have begun to ask questions about the bits they don't understand. Further work like this is needed to explore children's spiritual understandings so that eventually teachers will have some indication of what it is they are trying to do. From this work so far, it would seem that development of the spiritual needs to start with the questions children ask as they begin their encounter with the world. Teachers need to find ways of encouraging such questioning and then exploring issues as and when they arise. It is in this way that teachers can feel sure that they are addressing the spiritual in a way which has meaning to young children.

My future plans are to extend the work I have done so far to a larger number of children, in different settings such as church schools, state schools, urban and village, to see if there are common features in the understandings of children who are receiving different experiences. I will be using the story-telling methods and trying out others. My ultimate goal is to see if there is a way to devise appropriate activities in school which may serve to promote the spiritual development of children at key stage 1.

REFERENCES

Coles, R. (1992) *The Spiritual Life of Children*. London: HarperCollins.
McCreery, E. (1991) 'An investigation into the effects of the 1988 Education Reform Act on collective worship in primary schools.' Unpublished MA dissertation, Roehampton Institute, University of Surrey.
Robinson, E. (1977) *The Original Vision*. Oxford: Religious Experience Research Unit.
Varley, S. (1992) *Badger's Parting Gifts*. London: Picture Lions.

CHAPTER 16

Modern spirituality, moral education and the history curriculum

Gavin Baldwin

Since the advent of the National Curriculum there has been a tendency to view education and, in turn, the learning of children in terms of discrete subject areas. In spite of cross-curricular themes this has led to a fragmentation of the image of the child as a holistic learner. In this chapter I accept the notion that learning of subjects must be linked and set within an understanding of the child's overall well-being and development. I therefore intend to explore the links between the study of history and the education of those facets of personality which might be called 'spiritual' and 'moral'.

INTRODUCTION: FINDING AN IMAGE

Coming to the areas of spiritual and moral education from history teaching I feel in need of an image around which to organize my thoughts. If education is to have any lasting impact it must effect changes in children's learning which are relevant to their future lives as adults. In the fields of ethics and spirituality the implication is that these adults must be able to operate with autonomous dispositions to the spiritual and moral needs of themselves and their community. To a certain extent, then, the image that emerges is one of a soothsayer attempting to divine the future from the gizzards of the present.

Such an image, however, lacks the systematic and logical ethos which I want my thoughts to possess. I turn instead to the archaeologist who methodically uncovers and pieces together with imagination (makes sense of) ways of life and patterns of being. For this is what I want to attempt. What ways of life will children face as adults in the twenty-first century and what patterns of spirituality and morality will be appropriate to them? How can we as teachers help children to gain a spiritual and ethical perspective, illuminating their daily lives, and is there a special role for the study of history to play in this enterprise?

I must emphasize, however, that this is an image of an archaeology of the future, an attempt to pre-construct the society to come from the fragments of the present. It is a method turned on its head, as it were, with a whiff of danger, for lying within my image is the lure of a past Golden Age of great spiritual insight and moral certainty.

My image needs focusing. I want, tentatively, to offer four layers of meaning in answer to these questions:

Layer 1: The foundations
What do I mean by spiritual and moral?

Layer 2: The fragments of structure
By examining the present can definitions of spiritual and moral education be developed which might have relevance in the future?

Layer 3: The culture
How can moral education in particular be developed?

Layer 4: The purveyors of culture
Is this potential for moral education acknowledged by teachers?

LAYER 1: THE FOUNDATIONS

What do I mean by spiritual and moral?

'Spiritual' I take to be the realm of meaning and experience arising from the abstract, non-corporeal, immaterial identity of people. This may be manifest in the soul, the muse, God or intuition; the nature of its reality may come from chemical reactions in the brain or belief in and a certain conceptualization of experience. In essence it may be that which sets us apart from plants and minerals.

'Moral' I take to be people's responses to such questions as: How ought I to live? What ought I to do? It is concerned with the notions of 'Good' and 'Right' which seem indefinable as discrete concepts. In practical terms morality is concerned with contracts and agreements of human intercourse which may or may not be said to be, or agreed to be, 'good'. Associated concepts might include justice, truth, and respect for others.

The concept of 'spiritual' can be said to be prior to 'moral' in that moral considerations only come about between creatures with a spiritual identity. Natural disasters are not generally held to involve moral considerations whereas any contact between spiritual entities will.

The connections between 'spiritual' and 'moral' may manifest themselves, therefore, at a number of levels. If the spiritual is personified in a Godhead who dictates a certain moral code, as in the Ten Commandments, then to the fundamentalist the union of these concepts is absolute. For individuals who are concerned with developing and negotiating their own 'good life' or moral code, the abstract nature of themselves and others will form an element in such development.

Such definitions are personal: an excavation, perhaps, into my own understanding and an attempt to mark out common ground, to map the foundations.

LAYER 2: THE FRAGMENTS OF STRUCTURE

By examining the present, can definitions of spiritual and moral education be developed which might have relevance in the future?

The abstract definitions excavated in the previous section need to be contextualized if they are to be helpful in developing structures or approaches to spiritual, and in particular moral, education which might be relevant to children in the future.

I will, first of all, offer a rapid analysis of trends in modern society which might be called postmodern. Here I am indebted to David Harvey's *The Condition of Postmodernity* (1989).

Modern capitalist society, dominated by rapid capital accumulation, can be seen as disjointed, dislocated and fragmented. Economic and technological developments have meant that the process of production can take place simultaneously in many parts of a shrunken world. There is a compression of our notions of time and space. It is rare, for example, for workers to see the completed objects to which their labour contributes. This, and the rapidly changing needs of a workforce in terms of numbers and skills, leads to uncertainty and insecurity and a confusion of identity.

Additionally the old certainties of class and religion, for example, which helped to confirm a secure vision of self and others, have collapsed or are undergoing radical reformulation. The boldness of modernism with its 'new' developments in architecture, painting, sculpture, music and literature, etc. has given way to a pastiche of styles drawn at will from a mental *'musée imaginaire'* (Jencks, 1984). These images are collected from all ages and all parts of the world as one might select tins of soup in the supermarket. The identity which we might once have felt in our own narrowly-defined culture has given way to an almost overwhelming richness.

The same process of free selection to suit the consumer might also be seen in the choices people make from various religious traditions to enable their own spiritual quest.

The development of such an atomized and dislocated society can be mirrored by popular dance forms. The inter-relationships of folk and courtly dance mirror a stable and mutually dependent society. As coupledom became more dominant so the waltz, foxtrot and jive took their place. Now discothèques are peopled by individuals dancing in narcissistic abandon or at best in physically non-connected groups where individual display is the norm.

If such separateness is a trend in modern society this has repercussions for our concepts of spirituality and morality. Can we unearth fragments of thought which might help us to analyse this? I will follow Ernest Gellner (1992) in supposing three possible responses: religious fundamentalism, relativism and Enlightenment rationalism. Each is problematic in its application to moral education.

Religious fundamentalism is typified by a belief in the absolute truth of divine revelation in an unadulterated form. Spiritual and moral responses are absolute and not open for negotiation. Moral education would be to follow the teachings of the faith as they are indisputably true. This leads to an unfragmented society bound securely by one spiritual ethic. It does not need to be an underdeveloped society, since the experience of fundamentalist Islam

> demonstrates that it is possible to run a modern or at any rate modernising, economy, reasonably permeated by the appropriate technological, educational, organisation principles, *and* combine it with a strong, pervasive, powerfully internalised Muslim conviction and identification. A puritan and scripturalist world religion does not seem necessarily doomed to erosion by modern conditions. It may on the contrary be favoured by them.
>
> (Gellner, 1992, p. 22)

How could such a response be relevant or operable in a pluralist society which shows every possibility of becoming more so? The very intolerance of such a view makes it unsuitable as a foundation for general moral education in 'common' schools in a society with many competing ethical formulations.

Relativism. Gellner sees this represented in its current form in postmodernism, which he dismisses as an intellectual fad. Of concern to me is its relative notion of Truth. Gellner describes postmodernism as being 'hostile to the idea of unique, exclusive, objective, external or transcendent truth. Truth is elusive, polymorphous, inward [and] subjective' (1992, p. 24). It leads, in Gellner's argument, to a moral nihilism which might be unavoidable. In terms of moral education this is extremely problematic, but an approach whereby individual spiritual and moral responses are accountable to no more than the ideology of the individual, and should all be held of equal worth, has a certain attraction in a pluralist society. Moral education founded on such a premise might answer the concerns of those who worry about moral liberty in the schooling of the young.

The attraction of *Enlightenment rationalism* is that it acknowledges an approach to the world in the form of scientific rationalism which transcends cultures and acknowledges an objective truth. Unlike fundamentalism, however, there are no revelations and no privileged absolute knowledge. All evidence must be treated impartially (Gellner, 1992, p. 84). Ethically the obligation is to be rational and to treat all like cases alike. Thus there is system of appeal, an understanding of rational thought that can be used to defend or attack a moral argument against a system of concepts/values which are held to be universalizable. The challenge of rational defence of an ethical argument may be a worthy principle for moral education, but for the development of a moral code or position which might seek its foundation in a concept of 'good', Enlightenment rationalism is problematic.

This approach has given rise to Liberal notions of values which, Ross Poole argues in *Morality and Modernity* (1991, ch. 4), are not part of the objective world but a matter of individual choice. The more choices of what constitutes the good life, the more potential conflict between persons which must be moderated by notions of 'right' and 'justice'. These concepts become more urgent than that of 'goodness' *per se*.

The project of Liberalism is to construct an account of justice which resists the subjectivity which it allows to the good. . . . The principle of justice is sought not in the fabric of the external world, nor in the content of individual desire or choice, but in a structure of human thought and action.

(Poole, p. 71)

We subject ourselves to justice because we are rational beings.

The principles of right are in this sense self imposed and their restrictions, self-restrictions; they are therefore the products of freedom.

(ibid.)

Poole argues that the concentration of Liberal thought on justice rather than the good life, which it leaves to the 'domain of individual choice' (p. 85), has meant that it has little of worth to say on the 'vast range of moral issues which concern not restriction and obligation, but guidance and advice' (p. 85). We need to provide reasons why people ought to be just (p. 86) and must locate the concept of justice within an account of 'good'. 'Justice must be conceived not as a constraint upon individuals pursuing their good, but a component of it' (p. 86). This requires a theory of inter-subjectivity as a foundation for a theory of justice as a good. The identity of self needs to be seen as part of a network of relations with others (p. 87). The prevalent condition of individuality which I have outlined above needs to develop into a certain concept of community as yet unclear. This could well become the project of the education of the whole child.

This is particularly interesting given the argument above that 'spiritual' is prior to 'moral'. The idea could now be modified to argue that in order for a spiritual identity to develop, an appreciation of the spiritual nature of others is essential, and this may give rise to a theory of intersubjectivity as a foundation for a theory of justice as a good.

The three responses outlined above all offer certain contexts for the concepts of 'spiritual' and 'moral' and give rise to their own forms of related education. There is not space here to pursue the implications of each of our archaeological artefacts, interesting as this might be and necessary for a full picture. Instead I will construct notions of 'spiritual' and 'moral' which have echoes in the three alternatives and move impatiently on to uncover the next layer.

The concept of spirituality which I favour is that arising from the individual, working through a religious manifestation if they should so desire. The present interest in New Age religion may be evidence of people looking for a collective spiritual experience which traditional responses may fail to fulfil. The key point is that the expression of spirituality grows from the individual and is not modelled/trained/conformed from without. In that sense it may be both relative and rational. It cannot, however, be truly fundamentalist because here spirituality is subjugated to belief and is therefore not independent or questioning of that belief.

What of modern morality? I follow Ross Poole (1991, pp. 51, 52) in identifying a split ethic in modern society. Accumulative capitalism makes a virtue of acquisition at all costs and rapid consumption. This suits the fragmented nature of modernity suggested above. In contrast to this is the virtue of caring for family and friends in the small community with which we still identify, the home. Here we may develop the intersubjective notion of good justice as a solution to the Liberal failure. When linked to individualized spirituality this discovers the individual, as the source of spiritual and ethical concern, faced with greed as a virtue on the one hand and love on the other. Where does this leave moral education?

I would argue that moral education must nurture the individual's ability to understand his or her own moral position and that of others and to become critically aware of the assumptions which underlie such principles (Vokey, 1990) and which might help to make sense of seemingly incompatible moral positions in a rapidly changing society. There may be a set of underlying philosophical principles, left over from the Enlightenment, which might help as considerations in making moral decisions in situations which are rapidly changing and which call for renegotiated contracts between individuals and societies.

Before I proceed with my dig, I want to wrap up one consideration and rename another. I hope to have uncovered a contemporary and problematic context/definition for 'spiritual' and have indicated its application to a modern crisis of 'moral'. I wish to subsume spiritual concerns within the moral and shift from talking of moral education, which carries overtones of moral teaching and implies an imposed moral code, to the notion of ethical inquiry. This is a more open-ended process of continuous questioning and justification which enables the independent spiritual and moral growth of the child.

LAYER 3: THE CULTURE

How can moral education in particular be developed?

Arising, as it must, from the structure of the present, how can this form of reflective ethical enquiry be realized? I choose the study of history as my example, as I feel that it has a particularly interesting role to play in the ethical development of children, offering as it does the opportunity to examine real ethical issues 'at one remove'. What follows is a reconsideration/summary of arguments already put forward by me in 'A Dearing Opportunity: History Teaching and Moral Education' (Baldwin, 1994).

The role of history in ethical enquiry can be analysed by considering

- the *process* of historical investigation
- the *content* of the history curriculum
- the *role* of the history teacher as moral agent

I will attend to each in turn, highlighting possibilities and problems.

The process of historical investigation

There is a potential conflict here between the notion of historical objectivity and ethical enquiry. It rests on the assumption that history is an objective discipline and therefore should not concern itself with the moral considerations of past events. This notion is only tenable if history is seen as a selection of inert facts leading to an absolute truth. If a more relativist view of history is taken which sees the historian as a constructor of narratives about the past, with greater or lesser objectivity, then the moral narrative becomes another in a set of illuminating possibilities.

The role of the history teacher may also be seen as problematic. How can he or she maintain the objectivity of the historian, resting, however precariously, on an acknowledgement of ideological interest, and involve the children in investigating the moral implications of past events? There may be a conflict here between the role of the teacher as historian and as a teacher of the whole child, responsible not just for the development of the child's historical understanding but also for his or her moral and spiritual education. It may well be that in practice such distinctions are mere niceties. How do you teach about the Holocaust and refrain from moral judgement? Will the facts speak for themselves in an age when the extermination camps and the 'final solution' are denied by neo-fascists? How do you avoid, however, using your power position as a role model to influence unduly the ethical considerations of children?

The solution to this problem might well come from a methodology where procedures are clear and all points of view are explored with equal seriousness through group discussion. The Community of Enquiry developed by the Philosophy for Children work of Matthew Lipman provides such a model for this form of ethical enquiry through the study of history. (Models for discussion are considered by Robert Fisher in *Teaching Children to Think*, 1990, ch. 6.) I will return to this issue later.

Having acknowledged these potential dilemmas, let us now consider the process of historical investigation and its potential for ethical enquiry.

In order to investigate the past, children need to draw conclusions from historical sources and understand the relative nature of secondary accounts. To do this successfully they need to develop historical imagination or empathy. Hilary Cooper defines historical empathy as 'the achievement of understanding the ways in which people in the past have thought, felt, and behaved differently from us because of their different knowledge bases and because of the different social, political and economic constraints of the society in which they lived' (Cooper, 1992a, p. 12).

Cooper identifies three areas of psychological research which illuminate children's development of historical imagination and an understanding of people in the past (Cooper, 1992b, ch. 2). It is interesting that these areas of creative thinking, changing perspectives and psycho-dynamics are equally essential to their development of moral and spiritual understanding. By making sense of the actions of others, children will be able to develop their own moral values. Through the development of historical imagination children may come to understand that belief systems other than their own have existed and do exist, and through the analysis of decisions taken according to such systems and the resulting outcomes, we enable children to reflect upon their own implicit belief systems and the likely consequences of their moral actions.

There is a potential problem here. What happens if, through empathetical exercises, children exhibit behaviours which are contrary to basic moral principles of justice, for instance by beating beggars or promoting slavery? As long as these behaviours are acknowledged as springing from a past belief system and discussed in a community of ethical enquiry, children are able to develop their own moral perspectives in 'real' situations. The crucial lesson is that what might have been acceptable within one moral code at a given time, may not be acceptable at another time. When did the keeping of slaves become a widely-acknowledged moral concern? There were always critics of the practice but it was only when definitions of humanity and theories of supremacy of one race over another changed that the abolition of slavery achieved popular assent. It is not a question of 'better' values in absolute terms but of different values in different societies.

In terms of interpreting historical sources, children need to understand the belief systems which gave rise to them. Sources which make explicit the moral code of the time, Mayhew's *London Labour and London Poor* (1851) and Pepys' *Diaries*, for example, indicate changing attitudes to basic philosophical issues and different social contracts, and raise children's awareness of consistent moral behaviour different to their own.

History is also concerned with alternative secondary accounts of the past, which inevitably include implicit or explicit values dependent on the prevailing moral code at the time of interpretation. As such, history can be read as a moral discourse ensuring an awareness of moral undercurrents in our response to the past. It may be necessary to make these explicit to help children understand their own moral positions.

The content of the history curriculum and ethical enquiry

Given that any curriculum is a selection from culture, then that selection may reveal ethical concerns current in the culture at the time of selection, particularly those concerns of the selectors themselves. The curriculum, then, is partial and may be interrogated to uncover its own moral stance. In general terms we may ask if the curriculum is broad enough to allow for the impartial examination of events, by offering as many perspectives and interests as possible, thereby attempting some objectivity and consideration of historical 'truth'. Does it offer interpretations of liberty and consequent ideas of justice, as well as examples of struggles for liberty and consideration of those groups who are still oppressed? Is it in fact free enough to allow pupils to make their own selections and thereby express their own moral principles? Is this selection representative of, and influenced by the communities of the school?

Our present National Curriculum for History has recently undergone yet another transformation which might indicate something of the ideological position of this particular group of selectors from culture. It is interesting to note the removal of 'Exploration and Encounters' from Key Stage 2 (DFE, 1995). This provided children with the opportunity to examine what happens when two contrasting systems of belief clash. Its potential for ethical enquiry and political education were enormous.

Opportunities remain, however, for considering ethical issues within the processes of history outlined above. At Key Stage 1 children may be given the opportunity to practise their own developing ideas of moral judgement.

The necessity to distinguish between fact and fiction allows children to consider the consequences of real and fictional moral action. What are their own moral motives and in turn those of the wolf in the story of the three pigs?

Key Stage 2, for all its anglo-centrism (an area for ethical enquiry in itself), allows for the consideration of slavery in Ancient Greece, the implications of colonialism in the Victorian study unit (not actually prescribed but possible if teachers so wish) and changing attitudes and permissiveness in the 1960s.

Key Stages 3 and 4 specifically encouraged children to 'study the ideas, beliefs and attitudes of people in different societies, relating them to their circumstances' (DES, 1991, p. 34). In the latest revision the final phrase has been dropped (DFE, 1995, p. 11).

The beliefs and influences of the medieval Church are to be considered at Key Stage 3, alongside those of the twentieth-century world, which allows for the study of the Holocaust and the plight of refugees. This offers many opportunities for children to reflect on the moral perspectives of others and themselves. Clearly at this level there is opportunity for developing ethical enquiry through the study of history.

One final caveat. There is a danger that historical appreciation of a different belief system will be marred by its comparison with contemporary mores. It is essential to guard against judging the past either as a Golden Age of decency or as having less progressive social contracts than our own. It is essential for children to distinguish between historical moral analysis and judgement of the past. In the first case a belief system may be explained, understood and its suitability to its own era recognized. Judgement, however, can only be justified in terms of chronologically accurate expectations.

By exploring the operation of different moral codes it is hoped that children's own moral choices will be given greater substance, and by carefully teasing out the difference between moral analysis and judgement they may be better equipped to understand the moral positions of others in conflict with their own.

In terms of my archaeological excavation I hope that I have shown how the fragments of individualized spirituality and morality might give rise to a culture of reflective ethical enquiry through the discipline of historical investigation in both its process and its content. I would argue that the study of the past inevitably confronts children with moral concerns; these may be left unacknowledged or explored in all their richness in order to understand historical enquiry better and develop the spiritual and moral autonomy of children. Such opportunities enable a deeper development of the whole child in that they lead to greater self-knowledge and therefore greater self-identity.

The role of the history teacher as moral agent

The role of the teacher as a moral agent is essential in this. I have already considered a methodology of community of enquiry which sees teachers as facilitators and enablers of considered philosophical discussion. As such they are the arbitrators of a set of values which include patience and a respect for the opinions of all contributors. They also teach a disposition to philosophical process which demands careful definition and clarification of terms. Given this, there is, however, an expectation of equality and an objective that eventually the teacher will be no more or less than any other member of the group whose opinions will carry no more or less weight than anyone else's. This may be an uncomfortable position but it is one where teachers can still justify their own perspective and allow the children to develop their own.

Much more could be said about the desirability of such an approach. Some would argue that until children reach a certain level of maturity and experience they are not in a position to develop their own ethical positions independently, regardless of the rigour with which their peers and teachers demand justification. There is a possibility here for relativism to get out of hand. On the other hand the opportunity to practise such argument in a community can only lead to more ethically articulate adults. I am prepared to take the risk.

Such is a description of the culture arising from the fragments of structure we uncovered at layer 2. We have already detected traces which indicate the importance of the purveyors of this culture. The next level of our excavation will reveal what they, the teachers, think about the relationship between the study of history and ethical enquiry. As such it will indicate further work to be done and make possible a tentative assessment of teachers' preparedness for their moral agency in educating the whole child.

LAYER 4: THE PURVEYORS OF CULTURE

Is this potential for moral education acknowledged by teachers?
In order to gain some insight into teachers' awareness of, and attitudes to, history teaching as a potential area for ethical enquiry, I carried out a small-scale survey of teacher trainees. It would be interesting to discover if experienced teachers viewed the matter differently. What follows is a discussion of this survey.

One hundred and twenty-seven students were surveyed: 90 in their third year, from across subject areas, including 30 studying history, and 37 in their second year, including 34 historians. Previous experience of the course does not seem to have affected the responses, although further analysis is necessary to verify this.

The survey was carried out in seminar groups, thus providing a 100 per cent response. It was divided into three parts, students remaining ignorant of each stage until it was introduced. I wanted to discover whether they were conscious of the possible connection between history teaching and moral education without prompting. I therefore introduced the work as preparation for discussion on reasons for studying the past, and students were asked to draw up their own personal lists without conferring. This was stage one.

Stage two was introduced by distributing a list of 31 reasons for studying the past. These were to be marked according to whether the student felt them to be important and essential, quite important but not essential, and not essential at all. Within this list were reasons relating to skills, knowledge and understanding of the past as well as those relating to moral education, i.e.:

- to understand people who have backgrounds different from your own;
- to be a good citizen;
- to be more tolerant of other people;
- one can learn moral lessons from the past;
- it reinforces concepts of liberty and justice;
- by examining belief systems in the past we can come to understand beliefs and values different from our own and can therefore cope with moral conflict.

It is immediately obvious that these terms are so open to interpretation that the subject matter is not really suited to such a crude research tool, but I hope that the findings will indicate problems and trends which can be pursued later through interviews.

In the third stage students were asked to indicate their attitudes (strong agreement, agreement, indifference, disagreement or strong disagreement) towards a list of 17 statements about the connection between the study of history and moral education.

Bearing in mind the problematic relationship between the interpretation by respondents of such abstract concepts and the crudeness of the questionnaire as a research tool, the results are as follows. Without prompting, 517 reasons for studying the past were recorded; only 2 mentioned the word 'moral' but 25 could be said to deal with ethical issues such as the understanding of different beliefs, attitudes, and values of people in the past and their development. Other responses referred to rule-making, tolerance, citizenship, human rights, the reintroduction of attitudes and opinions from the past and the development of reasoning. These issues are only loosely linked and make up only approximately 5 per cent of the total response.

At a second level a number of responses talked of identity; either understanding how one's own culture had developed or that of another. There may be moral implications here in the light of what I said earlier about spirituality and identity and the formation of an ethical relationship or contract with another. There were 107 such responses, accounting for approximately 20 per cent of the responses. It would appear from this level of the enquiry that students do not clearly identify wider implications and potential for ethical enquiry within history teaching.

Stage Two
At the second stage of the survey the results are, perhaps not surprisingly, confusing (see Tables 16.1 and 16.2). In response to 'Can learn moral lessons from the past', 35 per cent thought it important, 44 per cent quite important and 20 per cent not important at all. This shows that when presented with the possibility students are willing to accord it some importance. In response to 'It reinforces concepts of liberty and justice', which one might suppose to be ethical concepts, only 21 per cent held it to be important; of these 70 per cent had supposed *moral lessons* to be important but surprisingly 24 per cent of those who thought *moral lessons* important thought *liberty* and *justice* not to be important at all. Clearly a confusion. Is it that history shows so many examples of injustice and lack

Table 16.1 Responses expressed as raw scores

Statement	Important	Quite important	Not important
Can learn moral lessons from past	45	56	25
It reinforces concepts of liberty and justice	27	51	47
Cope with moral conflict	64	41	21
Understand people of different backgrounds	93	31	3
To be more tolerant of others	48	54	25
To be a good citizen	7	25	94

of liberty that students do not see the positive side of the concept?

More encouragingly, however, in response to 'By examining belief systems in the past we can come to understand beliefs and values different from our own and can therefore cope with moral conflict', 50 per cent thought this important, 32 per cent quite important and 17 per cent not important. Disappointingly, 13 per cent who thought *moral lessons* important thought *moral conflict* not to be important at all.

The opportunity to 'Understand people who have backgrounds different from your own', was recognized as important by 73 per cent of respondents and learning *tolerance* as important or quite important by 80 per cent. 'Good citizenship' was not, however, a popular concept in relation to studying the past as 74 per cent held it to be not important at all. Clearly the relationship between historical study, ethics and citizenship needs exploration.

Despite the obvious confusions and methodological problems, I do feel that there is enough evidence here to suggest that when students are confronted with notions of the opportunities for ethical enquiry within history teaching there is a level of acknowledgement which may indicate a burgeoning awareness of moral agency in this area.

The third stage of the survey gives some insight into the students' perceptions of moral education (see Tables 16.3 and 16.4). Sixty-seven per cent of respondents registered agreement (28 per cent of these strongly) that 'Moral education is about learning right from wrong', 89 per cent agreed (37 per cent of these strongly) that it was about 'understanding a variety of moral positions and then choosing one's own', and 91 per cent

Table 16.2 Responses expressed as percentages

Statement	Important	Quite Important	Not Important
Can learn moral lessons from past	35	44	20
It reinforces concepts of liberty and justice	21	40	38
Cope with moral conflict	50	32	17
Understand people of different backgrounds	73	24	2
To be more tolerant of others	38	42	20
To be a good citizen	6	20	74

N.B. Percentages are expressed to the nearest whole number; some non-responses.

Table 16.3 Responses expressed as raw scores

Statement	Strongly Agree	Agree	Indifferent	Disagree	Strongly Disagree
Moral education is about learning right from wrong	19	48	11	17	5
Moral education is about understanding a variety of moral positions and then choosing your own	33	56	6	3	1
Moral education prepares children to cope with moral conflict	36	55	7	2	0
History shows a variety of moral positions in operation and enables us to compare them to our own beliefs and experiences	16	65	10	7	0
By understanding differing belief systems in the past children can understand differing belief systems now	13	65	13	7	1
Children can practise moral judgement by judging the action of people in the past by present-day standards	4	35	17	27	17
Children can practise moral judgement by judging the action of people in the past by standards of that time	10	57	20	9	2
By considering moral dilemmas in a historical situation children can develop their moral perspectives in real situations	15	61	14	6	2

Table 16.4 Responses expressed as percentages

Statement	Strongly Agree	Agree	Indifferent	Disagree	Strongly Disagree
Moral education is about learning right from wrong	24	61	14	22	6
Moral education is about understanding a variety of moral positions and then choosing your own	42	71	8	4	1
Moral education prepares children to cope with moral conflict	46	70	9	2	0
History shows a variety of moral positions in operation and enables us to compare them to our own beliefs and experiences	20	83	13	9	0
By understanding differing belief systems in the past children can understand differing belief systems now	17	82	17	9	1
Children can practise moral judgement by judging the action of people in the past by present-day standards	5	45	21	34	22
Children can practise moral judgement by judging the action of people in the past by standards of that time	13	73	26	12	2
By considering moral dilemmas in a historical situation children can develop their moral perspectives in real situations	19	77	18	8	2

N.B. Percentages are calculated to the nearest whole number. Some non-responses.

agreed (40 per cent of these strongly) that it should 'prepare children for coping with moral conflict'. There was only a polarization of opinions on the nature of moral education from 3 per cent of respondents and only 1.5 per cent disagreed that it 'prepares children for coping with moral conflict'.

Again, there was largely agreement that 'History shows a variety of moral positions in operation and enables us to compare them to our own beliefs and experiences' (81 per cent agreed, 19 per cent of these strongly) and that 'By understanding differing belief systems in the past children can understand differing belief systems now' (78 per cent agreed, 17 per cent of these strongly).

When asked to respond to statements about moral judgement there was an almost equal positive and negative split over 'Children can practise moral judgement by judging the action of people in the past by present day standards' (39 per cent agreed, 10 per cent of these strongly; 44 per cent disagreed, 40 per cent of these strongly); the strength of disagreement acknowledges an awareness of anachronism but maybe ignores the likelihood of moral judgement being made implicitly. There is much stronger support for the notion that 'Children can practise moral judgement by judging the action of people in the past by the standards of that time' (67 per cent agreed, 15 per cent of these strongly).

Finally, 76 per cent of students agreed (20 per cent of these strongly) that 'By considering moral dilemmas in a historical situation children can develop their own moral perspectives in real situations'.

CONCLUSION

I am not claiming much for this survey because there are clearly conceptual and interpretative problems which are particularly obvious at stage two. There does, however, seem to be an indication that whilst students do not see the possibilities for ethical enquiry when first asked to list reasons for studying the past, once they become conscious of these issues and organize them in some way there is a fair amount of acknowledgement, even acceptance. There is clearly much work to be done in developing an awareness in teachers of the rich potential for educating the whole child. The discipline of history is set against an ethical background and implicit moral issues arise. There is an enormous opportunity here for developing children's moral and spiritual autonomy at the same time as acknowledging history as an ethical discourse.

What should I do with my excavation into the future? Do I cover it over and sell it off to property speculators or open it to the public? I hope that I have made clear my operating concepts of 'spiritual' and 'moral' and set them in a contemporary context which acknowledges the atomization of individual experience. I hope that I have at least acknowledged the problems that lie here for ethical enquiry as part of the education of the whole child. From these structural fragments I have attempted to examine a culture of education which can bring together the mutually beneficial areas of historical, ethical and spiritual enquiry without losing integrity. It may be that the purveyors of this culture can be brought to a more conscious awareness of the work in hand. A teacher's moral agency is no light burden but, to return to the split ethic of modern society, it is caring and not grasping and it operates best within a community where children can come to identify 'justice' and 'right' as good and see the good of others as essential to their own good.

The study of history in the way I have advocated should allow children to develop ethical ideas by reflecting on real moral concerns. By founding this ethical enquiry on concepts of 'spiritual' and 'moral' in relation to the individual, and advocating autonomy in the field of spiritual and moral concern, I hope that we may equip children for the ethical renegotiations necessary for the rapidly changing world in which they will live.

REFERENCES

Baldwin, G. (1984) A Dearing opportunity: moral education and the teaching of history. *Teaching History,* **76** (June), 29–32.

Cooper, H. (1992a) Young children's thinking in history. *Teaching History,* (October), 8–13.

Cooper, H. (1992b) *The Teaching of History.* London: David Fulton.

DES (1991) *History in the National Curriculum.* London: HMSO.

DFE (1995) *History in the National Curriculum.* London: HMSO.

Fisher, R. (1990) *Teaching Children to Think.* London: Simon and Schuster.

Gellner, E. (1992) *Postmodernism, Reason and Religion.* London: Routledge.

Harvey, D. (1989) *The Condition of Postmodernity.* Oxford: Blackwell.

Jencks, C. (1984) *The Language of Postmodern Architecture.* London.

Poole, R. (1991) *Morality and Modernity.* London: Routledge.

Vokey, D. (1990) Objectivity and moral judgement: towards agreement on a moral education theory. *Journal of Moral Education,* **19** (1), 1–21.

CHAPTER 17

Headteachers' perceptions of their role in spiritual education: some empirical data and a discussion

M. A. Warner

INTRODUCTION

Much is said and written about what schools should do about spiritual education, as though schools (and not those teaching in them) devised policies and implemented them. In particular, I suggest that the role of the headteacher is much underestimated by those who speak and write in this way. The head of a school has an enormous responsibility for creating an environment which enables children and young people to understand the spiritual side of their nature. Education can damage or awaken children's natural awareness of the spiritual within themselves. Some children come out of the school experience so damaged by it that they have lost all faith in themselves, others and ultimately in God.

As head of a church school in an inner-city environment, I found that staff interpreted the word 'spiritual' in both religious and secular ways, depending on their own experience. As the spiritual development of children is one of the requirements of the 1988 Education Act I decided to research into the understanding headteachers had of this requirement, taking the three meanings of the word I had found to be most frequently used:

- the religious sense of an 'other' dimension to life and our understanding of and relationship with God;
- the concern of teachers who are unfamiliar with the 'high spirits' of many inner-city children, and the ways in which these can be developed positively;
- helping people to be 'in good spirits' through appropriate provision.

My aims were to address three sets of questions:

- How do heads understand their role in providing equal opportunities for all pupils to experience a religious perspective to life?

- How does the head maintain children's natural sense of fun whilst guiding them away from actions which hurt themselves and others? What is the head's role in ensuring that teachers can make the necessary discriminations?
- What are the factors which at present prevent children's well-being in school and how are they being addressed? What factors are most successful in ensuring an environment which promotes well-being in pupils?

Although each of these could have been researched separately I decided to take the underlying beliefs and experiences that had influenced me as a head and see how far other headteachers found that these influenced them.

I began my research by writing to headteachers who were fellow-students and to others whom I knew to have a particular interest in the subject I had chosen. Seventeen letters were sent out and nine returned. These were followed by interviews lasting forty minutes each, based on their own written responses. The heads were from C of E, RC and state schools.

Using my own experience as a head and the information I had now collected, I compiled a questionnaire and sent it to 275 heads of Church of England schools in the Dioceses of London and Southwark. (The results of the questionnaire survey are summarized in the Appendix. See pages 239–41 below.)

The writing up of the research reflects the original three interpretations of the word:

- Spirituality:
  Worship and religious education
  - Assemblies
  - Religious education
  - Church and school
- 'High spirits':
  Social development and pastoral care:
  - Opportunities for leadership
  - Pastoral care
- 'In good spirits':
  - Curriculum provision and environment
  - Curriculum
  - Building and site

As the section on Church and school refers specifically to church schools and the churchmanship of the local church, i.e. traditional/liberal/evangelical, discussions on this aspect of the research are not included in this chapter, which has a wider brief.

CONCEPTS OF SPIRITUAL EDUCATION

In seeking to define the spiritual I have found Dudley Plunkett's work helpful. He says:

If we take the spiritual to imply the divine [this raises the question] what do we mean by the divine? We may think of a universal force, a power independent of humanity, a creator whose creatures we are, a source of existence outside space and time, a non-personal entity, or a personal God who knows us individually and has claims on us. The minimum accommodation to the spiritual would be to grant that we are not totally conditioned or determined by our physical experience and senses. If we go beyond this, it is to acknowledge that we know the spiritual as a greater force, that is we can only know it by acknowledging our human limits. In fact if we do not see that we are ultimately dependent on a greater power, we cannot recognise divine existence. If on the other hand we subordinate human reason to the divine, then it follows that our individual and collective wills, purposes and destinies are not the most important elements of reality. We will be looking for intimations of a greater value and purpose than we could ourselves conceive. Ultimate reality and truth may not be ours to know, but what if they are known by an infinite, all-knowing God?

Such a value synthesis . . . has profound implications for education. If for example there was a widely and sincerely held belief that human beings were creatures of a loving God, destined to a spiritual existence beyond material existence, then the knowledge and service of that God would necessarily be included in any educational programme. The rational element of education would simply have to make space for a larger purpose.

(Plunkett, 1990, p. 23)

To many, God is the known guiding force of their lives, and for them the spiritual dimension of human experience has not disappeared. Like Plunkett, we may wonder why it was that it 'virtually disappeared from the repertoire of contemporary writers about education' (*ibid.*, p. 3). It could be that the development of 'psychology and the psychic by-ways' was one of the reasons for this reluctance to write, as Plunkett suggests (*ibid.*). Feeling that we need to explain everything, we are no longer prepared to wait on the will of God and recognize his hand in our everyday lives. In a world of experts we have lost the wonder of a child so necessary if the spiritual is to be realized.

We in education need not only to teach but also to learn from children. They have much to teach us. 'Thinking along with the thinker is, if undertaken seriously, a painful (as well as a thrilling) wrestling' (Webster, 1982, p. 70). We need to question to find the truth, but in questioning we have no need to dismiss the unexplainable. As Plunkett says, 'What is being discussed is strictly speaking ineffable: it cannot be confined by logical, rational discourse because it is concerned with a different dimension of reality' (Plunkett, 1990, p. 3).

I would agree with Plunkett (1990, p. 5) that the word 'secular' to describe the school curriculum jars, but would not agree with his presumption that the word 'spiritual' in relation to the curriculum refers to its non-secular dimension. If God is Creator and interested in the whole of his creation, this 'secular' must merely mean the areas of life where his presence is not recognized. To those with a religious faith no part of the curriculum or life is secular. The spiritual development required by the Education Act is an opening of minds to this fact, it is not something apart from it. As one headteacher put it 'it is an "awakening"'. We are secular until we recognize God in the world. He is there whether we choose to recognize him or not and that is why so much is good in what some would not claim to be religious.

Once we begin to see beyond the rational we also further our understanding of the difference between right and wrong, good and evil. If we believe in God the Creator who cares about what he has made and has a purpose for it, guiding it by the example of prophets and his son Jesus and the invisible force of his spirit, we cannot but care that each child we teach has the opportunity to become the person God intended him or her to be. We need to give each child the life skills needed for the environment in which he or she will live and encourage children to develop the particular talents they have been given. In helping each child to understand the purpose of his or her own experience, and by ensuring that provision is made which will provide adequately for it, the so-called spiritual and secular dimensions of the curriculum are both addressed: the former giving meaning to the latter.

If medieval Europe believed in a unifying purpose to life (Jaki and Capra, cited in Plunkett, 1990, p. 7) how much more should we believe in such a unifying purpose in the world now? Today we think in global terms and neighbourhoods reflect the rich variety of peoples previously found in separate countries. In learning how to live together we learn God's purpose for the world. It is the job of the educator to make sure that what is learned is good. This we can only do by communicating with each other through reason and experience. Prince Charles's much-publicized wish to be 'Defender of the Divine', expressed in an ITV interview (Dimbleby, 1994), must surely make sense in the light of the above analysis. Here an openness to the possibility of different routes to a common understanding of spirituality needs to be protected, but so also does the child, who can be drawn away from good by those whose so-called spirituality harms rather than heals.

> Some argue that truth emerges from conflict but I think this is only true for a very limited kind of truth. Truth for living comes from openness to others, experience of sharing and loving, and an acceptance of what we are.

> (Plunkett, 1990, p. 15)

In my experience this thirst for conflict which seems so prevalent in our present society, sometimes even veiled under the cloak of justice, does less than loving, listening and acting positively.

HEADTEACHERS' PERCEPTIONS

It would appear that much is being done by heads to help support the 'spiritual life of young people' in our schools. Many different approaches are being taken, related to the understanding of these needs by headteachers and the communities in which they find themselves. Although headteachers

are seldom explicit about their understanding of the spiritual area of
school life, each has an implicit understanding. This is exemplified in the
views of nine heads representing humanist and Christian beliefs in state,
Roman Catholic and Church of England primary and secondary schools
(Warner, 1990, ch. 2).

One head wrote:

> The spiritual awakening and development of pupils is central to the total
> life of the school. I think it is important to state that this should not be
> confused with social and moral training, though in a Christian environ-
> ment this is going to be coloured by religious belief. As Head I would
> ensure that all pupils were taught to pray and were helped to appreciate
> prayer as a means of communicating with God and establishing a real
> relationship with Him.

She spoke of the sense of awe and wonder in the created world and in relationships which lead to an awakening to the presence of God in his world.

Comment. In the inner-city environment it is sometimes difficult to
develop this sense of awe and wonder in the natural world; however, the
care and concern for one another of people who have lived in such areas
for any length of time are certainly reflections of the love of God. Those
such as heads, responsible for the spiritual development of their charges in
such areas, need to foster the development of caring relationships; but
they may also have a duty to act together with other local community
leaders, helping to improve the quality of the environment and represent
their communities to those with the power to put things right.

Another head observed, 'When we produced our guidelines, people
wondered why we called it spiritual and moral and chose to separate the
two and yet at the same time keep them together.' In this Church of
England school the two were seen to be 'part and parcel of the same thing'.

Comment. This contrasts with the view of the first head who, it would
appear, understands the spiritual as being a relationship with God and
moral as being a relationship with human beings. The spiritual will influence the moral but it does not follow that they are 'just . . . part and parcel
of the same thing'. By providing for moral development in schools we are
not necessarily providing for the spiritual dimension of life.

Another head stated that: 'Children of other faiths and religions come
here to a religious school rather than the secular school.' This head was
not specific as to the reasons for this, other than that the school was selec-
tive.

Comment. In my own experience as a head asking Moslem parents why
they had chosen a church school rather than a state school nearer their
own home, I was told, 'We want a school where God is mentioned.' With
the new Religious Education syllabus can this now not happen in all
schools? If it does not, may we not be depriving a further generation of a
reality still unknown to many? If it does, will it be from the viewpoint of
one RE teacher who saw the study of religion as being the study of strange
people doing strange things, or from a wish to live in harmony with our
neighbours and learn from them, possibly coming to know God better in
the process?

One school had, in the interviewer's mind, great potential for inter-faith dialogue but it seemed that the teachers' lack of knowledge was holding development back. The head said:

When it was originally said that everyone would have to do RE in the classroom lots of people said, 'No, we're not going to.' However, whether they were going to teach RE or not, all went away to look for suitable material and for a while provision was made for those who felt uncomfortable about teaching it, with the result that there is [now] only one person who will not teach RE.

Comment. Here again I would suggest that the children may well be in advance of the teachers in knowledge and experience. A willingness to learn from others was already present in the school and will have developed over time. Without teachers who have a wider knowledge than most, it is difficult to speed up the process. A willingness to learn from the pupils and encourage them to learn from each other will develop understanding if approached in an open and accepting way. In this same school much was also being done to encourage parents of different faiths to attend school assemblies.

R. Cant's question was echoed here, 'Would it not be better – more realistic and more effective – to cut out the obligatory periods of worship, and leave the children free to go to church and learn to worship there?' (Cant, 1965, p. 10). I believe that it is in allowing schools to find their own way that progress will be made, not by putting up barriers by legislating against them, but by legislating *for* them and providing such support as SACRE in difficult situations. We are surely helping towards a better understanding of our fellow human beings if we try to understand them rather than if we refuse to do so, living in suspicion of our next door neighbour who worships in some 'strange' way about which we know nothing.

Another interview showed a different way forward. Both the chairman of governors, who was also the rector, and the head agreed that religion is caught, not taught, and the basic source of spiritual input is through assemblies. The head enlarged on these thoughts by saying, 'Children learn because they have religious experiences or they see others experiencing religious experiences. They experience what it means to worship in a meaningful way.' He explained that parents of children who come to his school say, 'Faith is an integral part of human experience; the way people behave and think. It is something you "catch" in the same way as you "catch" a way of speaking or dialect simply by being in a community which has a faith as a basis of existence.'

Comment. Where teachers do not join in the hymns or mark books before assembly begins, or where they look out of the window when hymns or prayers are being sung or said, it is unlikely children will learn to pray or learn what prayer is all about. To the secular, worship may become worship of the child. There is that danger in the 'show and tell' assemblies that parents are invited to. To those of faith, worship is praise of God for what he has done for us and 'show and tell' assemblies can be combined with thanks to God for the different gifts he has given us. They are very different concepts and lead to very different attitudes in life. As the head of the above school said, 'We should remember what is required of people who subscribe to any religious faith: that they love God, they love their neighbour and they do good works and all those sort of things, and so find the opportunity of praising God.' This is a dimension of life missing in much of our present society which has humankind at the centre.

Another head describes the 'spiritual side of the way we're trying to work', and goes on to say that 'it is deeply spiritual what happens there because of the emotions . . . it's that deep feeling'.

Comment. The religious experience can indeed be an intense experience but one also needs to ask whether what is being described is therapy rather than spirituality. God's healing power may work in this way but as Dobson wrote: 'Emotions – can you trust them?' (Dobson, 1982). To those who see spirituality as being concerned with a more reflective form of worship as described by Main or Cornwall, such emphasis on emotions could be unnerving and unhelpful. However, there is an important place for jubilation in praising God and this particular Evangelical approach is a way forward for those of a more extrovert nature. A way which seems able to combine successfully both the reflective and the jubilant is found by many at Taizé. In the words of Brother Roger:

> With time, contemplation begets a happiness. And that happiness, proper to free men, is the drive behind our struggle for and with all people. It is courage, energy to take risks. It is overflowing gladness.
>
> (Roger, 1974, p. 104)

Another interview gives a practical religion point of view, where one's own philosophy influences what one does. The head explained:

> The view you have of what is spiritual development relates to your own philosophy of life. It does in my case anyway, [and influences me] as a teacher. It's linked with what I think education is. I don't think spiritual development is a narrow churchy thing where you are just talking about God. I think it encompasses broader things. I think it is an appreciation of higher things such as tolerance, compassion, understanding, beauty in literature, music and anything which draws the child out of him or herself and lifts him or her above the mundane, which ordinary life can be. It is also the appreciation of other views and opinions.

The head later acknowledges that she is a Quaker, saying, 'I think it influences [me] in terms of the philosophy of the school, as it's based on my beliefs.' She comments, 'A lot of teachers are Quakers and I think it is because the philosophies of education are very similar to the philosophies of Quakerism.'

Comment. Whether it is fair to others not to share the origins of that philosophy, so that others too may share it if they wish, would be my question here. I wonder whether the philosophy has become so practical that although God is the source of it he is not acknowledged as such. We may ask not only is this being fair, but is it being *true*? Quakerism does, after all, have its roots in Christianity and has developed from those original roots.

The understanding of God's love of oneself as shown in a further interview is an important factor in a society which pulls the individual in many directions. 'God's love for you should make you independent of other people's opinion of you and therefore allow you to deal with their distress and anger in a way which isn't just responding to it as a result of your own distress and anger,' commented one head. That sureness and security which is also open to 'answering that of God in everyone' is an understanding which again will influence the running of a school and the education of the children in it.

Comment. The head's emphasis on *damaging* or *nurturing* children's spirituality as opposed to *developing* children's spirituality represents, to my mind, a much more realistic way of educating the spiritual potential in a pupil. We shall all in some way damage each other, as none of us is perfect, but if we remember that the spiritual life, i.e. God's relationship with the individual, began long before the child came to school and that our job is to ensure to the best of our ability that it is not damaged but nurtured, we shall provide, as requested by the Education Act 1988, Section 6 (1), for the child's spiritual development. This development is, after all, between the child and God, but is also something which we can encourage or discourage, 'damage' or 'awaken'. In the words of the last headteacher quoted, it is in 'developing a child's thinking and behaviour that the child will come closer to or further from the love of God'.

DELIVERING THE SPIRITUAL CURRICULUM

Worship and Religious Education

The first implication for education if we take process theology seriously is that worship stands at the centre of the response to the religious vision. Whitehead has said that 'the power of God is the worship he inspires'. If we are to become sensitized to the aims of God, to the 'commanding vision', we must start with worship. Here is where we find the ground for hope, even in the midst of so much that seems to deny such optimism . . . Children belong in worship when they feel themselves as persons who share in the community.

(Miller, 1990, p. 256)

Question 1a of the questionnaire (see p. 239) sought to find out where headteachers' priorities lay with regard to choosing themes for assemblies. In most schools this time is probably still known as 'assembly' and not 'worship'. It was disappointing to discover that even in church schools there was little overall planning for this important time of the day. In all other areas of the curriculum forward planning is now accepted practice but it appears that this time, which should be influential to the life of schools, is planned only a week in advance in most cases. It is good to see that the new Framework in the *Handbook for the Inspection of Schools* makes clear that:

The school should have a record of the themes and content of its acts of worship.

(OFSTED, 1994, 5.1)

However, I should like to see OFSTED go further and require evidence of long- and short-term forward planning which allowed space for the unexpected.

In some schools four out of five of the assemblies are used as teaching times rather than worship. It would appear from such practice that daily worship as such is not the order of the day even in church schools. However, worship in church is an important part of a church school's role:

> Tradition is one thing. Living it is quite another. The best way to learn about Orthodoxy is to put this book aside and visit an Orthodox Church.
> (Hackel, 1971, p. 29)

But children should also learn that they can worship wherever they happen to be.

There seems to be some confusion as to whether assembly is for the most part an RE lesson. If this is so, the experience of worship may be missed. If, however, children are not shown from whence the values of the school come, they can hardly be expected to hold on to these values in later life.

> Religious education must perform two tasks. First, it must honestly present religion for what it claims to be – the response of human beings to what they experience as the sacred. When religion ceases to be that, it is in its own terms corrupt. Secondly, religious educators must help pupils to open their personal awareness to those aspects of their experience which are recognized by religious people as the root of religion.
> (Hay, 1985, p. 142)

From the results of the questionnaires it would appear that more time could be spent in creating an atmosphere in which guided reflective prayer might become more central to the life of the school. Many inner-city children live in very noisy and crowded conditions and this time of quiet might do much to help them develop an inner silence. Children can be encouraged to take the habits of prayer into their homes if encouraged to pray regularly at school. If a head feels unable to lead the school in prayer, then a time of reflection on one's actions and concerns under the following headings might be a step forward:

● Thinking of something wonderful
● Thinking of something you are sorry for doing
● Thinking of something you are thankful for
● Thinking how you can help another person
● Thinking how you can help yourself

It would certainly 'promote opportunities for pupils to reflect on aspects of their lives and the human condition', as expected by the Framework in the *Handbook for the Inspection of Schools* (OFSTED, 1994, 5.1).

However, the thoughts of a secondary school head about praying in smaller groups are of interest in this respect:

> The very teaching which teachers and learners engage in is just as mysterious as knowledge itself. It is much more dependent on the imagi-

nation, insight, feeling, intuition and vision than is usually admitted or realized. For instance, there is a well known psychological sequence of stages or moments which occurs when a person is presented with a problem about which he is deeply concerned, or when he is called to think creatively . . . The decisive point in this psychological sequence is the pause. What happens? Where a new configuration of ideas occurs it seems to be quite serendipitous; it is 'given' . . . the religiously simple might view it as an area for the activity of the Holy Spirit. The scholars who approach this all need to find the need to use their most abstract concepts.

(Loder, 1966, quoted in Webster, 1985, p. 15)

With regard to religious education lessons, J. M. Hull writes:

The fact that religious education is the only voluntary subject indicates its centrality in family life and in the individual conscience; the fact that it is the only compulsory subject indicates its centrality in community relations and the life of society at large.

(Hull, 1985, p. 102)

In the light of the headteacher interviews and their answers to the questionnaire, I offer the following recommendations:

- Religious education schemes need to be updated so that they are more relevant to pupils in inner-city areas.
- Secondary school successes in the teaching of religious education should be shared.
- The experiences of schools 'starting from scratch' should be shared
- It would appear that giving an incentive allowance to teachers of religious education has a positive effect on the work of the school. This could be noted by schools which do not consider religious education a priority.
- Teachers of religious education should be encouraged to teach a second subject or aspect of the curriculum which is of particular interest to them, thereby emphasizing the fact that RE is both a curriculum area to be studied in its own right and that it is within all curriculum areas.

Social development

The questionnaire asked about three areas of social development (see Appendix, p. 240):

- leisure activities
- leadership opportunities
- responsibilities

Schools can foster links with other organizations to develop leisure activities as well as promoting them themselves. The fact that 52 headteachers considered the encouragement and promotion of leisure activities to be a low priority in London, and eight considered that the school gave it no support at all, gives cause for concern. A school should be able to offer:

- a personal knowledge of a child's particular strengths which could be developed in a setting outside the classroom;
- expertise in a variety of fields;
- professional knowledge which should assist the development of links between school and local clubs and Adult Education Institutes so that school relates to the world outside.

Two questions (7b and 7c) were concerned with the ability to be part of any group. Leaders will emerge whatever the group. We need to give opportunities for leadership and we need to nurture a sense of responsibility in specific ways. This ought not to be just left to chance. Although heads appear to provide for the former, the latter seems to be somewhat overlooked.

Pastoral care

Many professionals are involved in the pastoral care of children. Not only are the head, teaching and non-teaching staff responsible, but where necessary the Education Welfare Officer, Social Services and other 'outside' agencies may be involved.

Watkins and Wagner state that 'the most effective pastoral care is clearly related to the major goals of the school – the intellectual and social development of all young people' (Watkins and Wagner, 1988, p. 158). They take the major goals of a school's pastoral system to be:

a providing a personal point of contact for every pupil and his/her parents;
b offering support and guidance for pupil achievement and development (including personal-social development);
c monitoring pupil progress and performance across the whole school;
d providing colleagues with information to adapt teaching, and promoting a responsive school system.

(Watkins and Wagner, 1988, p. 159)

My research reflects in part the last goal: gaining information about the use of two 'outside agencies' involved in some schools and enquiring about the head's perceptions of teacher/pupil relationships and his or her own role. In special schools, and to a lesser extent in mainstream schools, the expertise of medical and speech specialists will also play an important part in informing pastoral care. The contribution these professionals make to the pastoral system of a school invites further research, as I have found that they do not always relay decisions made about a pupil as much as one might wish.

Pastoral care may well address all the four goals noted above but the balance will vary from pupil to pupil and from time to time according to his or her most immediate needs. Although pastoral care must be at all times for all pupils, it is of particular importance at times of crisis. Those working for 'outside agencies', having legal powers, are not always the people to whom a family in difficulties will turn, and the role of the local clergy, who often know the family through community events, can be of assistance in church schools. They are also valued by local state schools when good relationships are fostered.

One head commented that where a chaplain had been appointed specifically to their large split-site secondary school, important developments were taking place, as he was available to counsel both staff and students when needed. In the same way a deaconess appointed to liaise with a primary school brought additional expertise and knowledge. A secondary school, on the other hand, changed from being known as a 'difficult' school from which parents shied away to one which was sought after by many, when a full-time EWO was appointed. This visible sign of caring could be a necessary factor in changing the ethos of a school. I suggest that these specific relationships should be encouraged in more schools for the benefit of all. With schools now responsible for their own budgets, such appointments could well be considered.

From the results of the questionnaires it appears that the tendency is for all staff in a school to be held to be responsible for pastoral care. Job descriptions reflect this fact. In some schools the SEN Co-ordinator takes some responsibility, but in larger schools the deputy head or one of the senior management team has ultimate responsibility. In secondary schools the heads of year often play a particularly important role, but form tutors oversee the day-to-day pastoral care of the pupils. Those close to working-class pastoral situations know that the damage *caused* by the education system is something from which many find it impossible to recover. Lomas writes of the boy of fourteen who, before he committed suicide, wrote a moving poem about his experience of being forced into conformity which crushed his own creativity (cited in Webster, 1985, p. 19). The natural spontaneity and unashamed vitality for life of the inner-city child are a positive force which, if care is not taken, can often be ill-directed.

The attitudes of teachers are paramount in developing good relationships. As one head commented,

> The quality of relationship between teacher and pupil will rub off on the pupil-to-pupil relationships. That is not to say that if teachers treat children well, all the children will necessarily treat each other well, but if they do, I think there is a much better chance of that actually happening. Whereas if teachers are seen to manhandle pupils or shout at them, the pupils will react in a similar way.

> What the teacher is, is as important as what the teacher knows, a fact widely acknowledged in 1944 but equally widely ignored today.
>
> (Priestley, 1985, p. 115)

Not all headteachers share the same attitude towards their own role in pastoral care. One primary head explained that she knew the job was going to be tough as the previous head had been 'very much a counsellor rather than an educationalist'. She explained to the staff that her own attitude was

> that a lot of the children had tremendous problems, appalling backgrounds and not very good living conditions, and however sympathetic the staff might be, and sympathetic they must be, they could not solve their problems. We have to educate them. It's the only thing we can do. The only fair thing we can do is to give them an opportunity to move out

of this. That is the balance we have to have. We can't go on the counselling side too much.

While this futuristic view may have something to commend it, the child has
to come to terms with the here and now as well as the future. Without
counselling he or she may never reach the future.

In contrast, another head described how she would 'talk to the children
if somebody has been in a bit of trouble. Obviously it's my job to make
them see the point, but I'll sit and talk to children about it. I'll probably
bring in my faith and how that helps me.' I asked her, 'Do you see the counselling side as important?' She replied, 'It works together. There is no
divide between counselling and making them see the point, as far as I'm
concerned.'

It could be argued that the head who wished to 'give them the opportunity to move out of this' was being rather short-sighted. Should not heads
be concerned for the improvement of the locality rather than creating root-
less people?

> Human beings need territory to make a life for themselves. Therefore,
> they must have the right to live somewhere. And where better, normally,
> than the place where they were born and have grown into adult members
> of the community. Usually they will feel that they belong there.
>
> (Beran, 1990, p. 157)

It is by seeing the child in the context of his wider environment that we can
best provide the pastoral care needed to assist in his full development. The
child's neighbourhood is not only her physical, cultural and social 'home'
but also provides for her spiritual needs. When setting up pastoral care
systems we need to have this overview in mind.

Curriculum

The National Curriculum has focused our minds on what is to be taught,
ensuring that a child's education is not dependent on the possibly limited
knowledge and interests of the class teacher. The following quotations,
which refer to a number of areas of the curriculum, serve to remind us that
there is something much richer and more profound about the curriculum
than a contents list or the ticking off of attainment targets:

> The tendency to use 'curriculum' as if it were a synonym for 'education'
> has crept up on us so slowly that we have hardly noticed it. It is one of
> those small bewitchments of the language which may appear trivial but
> can have wide-ranging consequences. Curriculum is one half of the educa-
> tional process: the other half is the people concerned in that process.
>
> (Priestley, 1985, p. 117)

> The perception that knowledge is embedded in mystery is not the posses-
> sion of a gifted view, attained at the conclusion of a lengthy academic
> process. The mystery is there for all to wonder at, and it is within the
> everyday knowledge of the ordinary school curriculum . . . Some teachers
> are likely to approach the mystery through their own subject areas.
>
> (Webster, 1985, p. 14)

> Humanist and Existential outlooks imply that artistic activity is conducive to spirituality . . . A curriculum which stresses spirituality would therefore give pride of place to art and drama.
>
> (Kay, 1985, p. 133)

> Truth within spirituality will then be detected less by argument and proof and more by symbol, story, parable, poem, allegory, sound, gesture, movement or form.
>
> (Webster, 1985, p. 13)

The results of the questionnaire survey suggest that headteachers share something of these wider views. (See Question 9 in the Appendix, pp. 240–1.) Although thirty-nine headteachers replied that they considered the school provided fully for the specific talents of all pupils, over twice that number were not satisfied. It may well be that it is 'a laudable but unattainable target', as one head wrote, but as such it is still something for which we should be striving.

The difficulty of motivating some children is a real one for many teachers, particularly those not used to inner-city children's often pent-up energy. As the *Faith in the City* report records:

> Teachers do not understand black children and their backgrounds. They do not recognise horse play as horse play.
>
> (General Synod, 1989, p. 303)

This could equally apply to many white children, but the question must then be asked, 'When does fun become foolishness?' Teachers who are part of the same culture are very much needed in inner cities, but to leave education to that one culture may also restrict the children, who also belong to a wider world. Schools need to recruit a variety of teachers, but each will need to be willing to learn from others. Yet a meeting of cultures even in a staffroom is not always without its problems.

The relationship of the curriculum to the world of work is high on the agenda now. Amongst other developments the 'work experience' weeks in a secondary school can be beneficial to students and staff in opening their eyes to a part of the world they may know little about.

The dictionary defines talent as 'power or ability of mind or body viewed as something divinely entrusted to a person for use and improvement'. As I have argued before:

> In providing for the development of talent in a school we must think of all aspects; the development of academic and physical skills and the development of the creative nature. Only when all are provided for will the child be able to express himself fully, grow in self knowledge and become the complete person he was created to be.
>
> (Warner, 1979, p. 4ff.)

Building and site
Seventy-six headteachers reported that their buildings and site are a contributing factor in the spiritual life of the pupils. (See Question 10 in the Appendix, p. 241.) They also appear to affect the spiritual life of the

cleaners. In one school at 7.30 a.m. a cleaner working on his own could be heard singing his heart out with Alleluias to God's glory along a spotless corridor!

The age of the building is of little importance, many of the older ones being described in such ways as 'an old building which we love' or '1847 building with tremendous atmosphere'. On the other hand, a modern building may provide better for those with physical special needs, thus providing for their spiritual needs at the same time (see DES, 1980, 1984).

Some of the main findings regarding heads' perceptions of the school building or site damaging the spiritual life of pupils are as follows:

- a large site with two buildings requiring excessive movement of pupils;
- limited size of teaching areas and therefore not enough space for small group work;
- crowded playground;
- grey inner-city wall, ugly site, poor physical environment;
- deprived area in run-down estate with a small amount of play space;
- spiritual darkness of the area;
- claustrophobic, overlooked by next-door sex shop;
- a busy snooker hall and a main road nearby.

Positive responses show that heads are very appreciative of the natural surroundings of many schools. The number that have gardens or 'green' areas is most encouraging when one considers that these are all city schools. Two heads stress the importance of staff creating 'a happy spiritual atmosphere' and one notes that 'our Christian attitudes pervade school life'. In such circumstances even the darkest places can be changed.

Factors which also contribute to the spiritual life of the pupils are, we are told, the proximity of the school to the church. For one the nearby Hindu temple added another dimension. When the school site is used by other groups in the community this is also thought to be beneficial to the spiritual life of all.

It would appear from this part of the research that cramped conditions of either building or site are the most damaging factor in the spiritual life of young people, along with the absence of a place of quiet and noisy or obscene surroundings. Old buildings may have a negative effect if not well-kept, but most headteachers cherish ones that have been well cared for.

In the light of this information I recommend:

- that any new church school built should be near to the local church;
- that more is done to regulate acoustics in some buildings;
- that where conditions are 'cramped', more should be done to remedy this, either by extending the site or reducing the school roll;
- that those concerned with the school in any way should be vigilant about the outlook, seeking to change anything which could harm the spiritual life of the children;
- for schools without 'natural surroundings' an adjoining site should be purchased where possible, and designed for school and community use.

CONCLUSION

Recent concern that the spiritual development of pupils needs to have a higher profile in schools is to be welcomed. Heads are aware of the variety of influences which affect the development of the whole child and are attempting to address many of them. It is therefore important that the voices of individual heads, who know the communities in which they work, are heard. The headteacher's role is fundamental in providing for the spiritual life of young people in school.

If we accept that the spiritual life of a pupil relates to the whole child, then each head should ensure that a knowledgeable and well-trained teacher of religious education is appointed whose expertise should include the ability to lead or advise on collective worship when such skills do not already exist in the school. Collective worship and religious education are the rock on which spirituality is nurtured. If schools are to provide a firm foundation for both present living and life's journey then the broad and balanced curriculum, the social and pastoral development of the child and the environment of the school all need to be addressed. The life which is promised through spirituality has a deeper source than any one aspect of education, and the experiences pupils have, both in school and outside it will either help to nurture or to damage that understanding.

REFERENCES

Beran, H. (1990) Who should be entitled to vote in self-determination referenda? In Warner, M. and Crisp, R. (eds), *Terrorism, Protest and Power*. Aldershot: Edward Elgar.

Cant, R. (1965) The nature of worship. In Jones, C. M. (ed.), *School Worship*. University of Leeds Institute of Education Paper No. 3.

DES (1980) The renewal of primary schools. *Building Bulletin* 57. London: HMSO.

DES (1984) Designing for children with special educational needs: ordinary schools. *Building Bulletin* 61. London: HMSO.

Dimbleby, J. (1994) *Charles: The Private Man, the Public Role*. ITV interview.

Dobson, J. (1982) *Emotions: Can You Trust Them?* London: Hodder & Stoughton.

General Synod (1989) *Faith in the City*. London: General Synod of the Church of England.

Hackel, S. (1971) *The Orthodox Church*. London: Ward Lock Educational.

Hay, D. (1985) Suspicion of the spiritual: teaching religion in a world of secular experience. *British Journal of Religious Education*, **8** (1).

Hull, J. M. (1985) Editorial. *British Journal of Religious Education*, **7** (3).

Kay, W. K. (1985) Variations on a spiritual theme: man in a multi-faith world. *British Journal of Religious Education*, **7** (3).

Loder, J. E. (1966) *Religious Pathology and Christian Faith*. Philadelphia: Westminster Press. Parts 3 and 4. Quoted in Webster 1985).

Miller, R. C. (1990) Theology and the future of religious education. In Francis, L. J. and Thatcher, A. (eds), *Christian Perspectives for Education*. Leominster: Fowler Wright.

OFSTED (1994) *Handbook for the Inspections of Schools*. London: HMSO.

Plunkett, D. (1990) *Secular and Spiritual Values: Grounds for Hope in Education*. London: Routledge.

Priestley, J. G. (1985) Towards finding the hidden curriculum: a consideration of the spiritual dimension of experience in curriculum planning. *British Journal of Religious Education*, **8** (1).

Roger, Brother (1974) *Struggle and Contemplation*. London: Mowbray.

Warner, M. A. (1979) 'The organisation of a school to provide for the development of talent, appreciation of limitations and a growth towards sociable independence.' Unpublished work for Diploma in School Management Studies, College of Preceptors.

Warner, M. A. (1990) 'The head's role in providing for the spiritual life of young people.' Unpublished Master's dissertation, Roehampton Institute, Surrey University.

Watkins, C. and Wagner, P. (1988) *School Discipline: A Whole-school Approach*. Oxford: Blackwell.

Webster, D. H. (1982) Awe in the curriculum. *Perspectives* 9. School of Education, University of Exeter.

Webster, D. H. (1985) A spiritual dimension for education? *Theology*, **88**, 721.

APPENDIX

Information collated from the questionnaires sent to headteachers of Church of England schools in the Dioceses of London and Southwark (Warner, 1990).

Assemblies (see p. 229)

1. a. Are assembly topics usually chosen:

	Always	Most usually	Sometimes	Seldom	Never
i. because of the religious teaching they provide?	23	72	37	0	1
ii. because of the Biblical teaching they provide?	10	38	77	5	0
iii. because of the 'incidents' in the life of the school?	2	6	100	18	1
iv. because they relate to general class teaching?	7	14	62	32	7
v. because they are part of an overall assembly plan?	long-term 10; annual 8; termly 68; weekly 16; none 16; NA 2				

b. Do you ever have end-of-the-day assemblies with evening prayers and/or hymns?

at the end of term 33; monthly 1; weekly 16; never 51

2. Are hymns or religious songs mainly chosen:

	Always	Most usually	Sometimes	Seldom	Never
a. for the tune?	1	16	54	37	11
b. because the theme goes with the assembly topic?	18	88	27	2	0
c. for the teaching that the words of the hymn provide?	7	35	65	3	0
or d. we seldom or never use hymns or religious songs.	5	1	1	3	2

3. Would you consider prayer to be an important part of your school's worship?

Yes 82; not particularly 3; no 1

	Always	Usually	Sometimes	Not usually	Never
a. Do you teach children to pray?	50	34	29	12	3
b. Do you pray with the children?	85	42	6	2	0
c. Do you give the children time to reflect before prayer?	8	32	67	24	2
d. Do you have i. silent prayer	9	10	78	26	5
ii. extemporary prayer	7	31	65	17	10
iii. children's prayers	4	22	90	12	2
iv. set prayers	13	21	91	19	9
v. grace with meals	58	15	6	13	41
vi. 'end-of-day' prayer in class?	school policy 32; individual class policy 72; no 34				

Religious Education (see p. 229)

4.   a.   Is there a member of your staff specifically responsible for religious education?   Yes 114;   no 24

      b.   Does it carry an incentive allowance?   NA 17; No 72; A 19; B 18; C 7; D 4; HT 2; DH 2
         (HT Headteacher, DH Deputy Head, Incentive allowances A – most responsibility, then B, C, D.)

Questions 5 and 6 not included here.

Social development (see p.231–2)

	High priority	Low priority	Not at all
7. a. i. How far do you consider the school encourages and promotes positive leisure activities?	65	52	8
ii. How is this done?	Examples given: 83		
b. i. All children are given opportunities to develop leadership skills.	99	13	2
iii. Some children are given opportunities to develop leadership skills.	34	23	10

	School policy	Class policy	No policy
c. i. All children are given responsibility for a particular job in the classroom.	41	64	26
iii. The oldest children are all given responsibility for a job around the school.	54	14	41

Pastoral care (see p. 232)

	Yes	No	Shared
8. Has your school an appointed:			
a. chaplain whose sole responsibility is your school?	21	102	14
b. education welfare officer whose sole responsibility is your school?	24	102	30
c. member of the teaching staff (other than the head) specifically for pastoral care?	37	96	1

Curriculum (see p. 234)

9. a. Is there any area of the curriculum you believe would
        contribute to the spiritual life of pupils which at the
        present you are unable to provide?   Yes 40   No 84

        If Yes:
            i.   What is it?   NA 9; example given: 35
            ii. What would you need in order to provide it?   NA 9; example given: 23

    b. Do you consider the school provides fully for the
        specific talents of all pupils?   Yes 39   No 80

        If no:
            i.   What would ensure this happened?   NA 6; example given: 93

Building and site (see p. 235)

10. Do you consider your school building:
    a. i.   contributes to the spiritual life of the pupils?   Yes 77   No 37
        ii. why?   Example given: 91

    b. i.   damages the spiritual life of the pupils?   Yes 16   No 75
        ii. why?   Example given: 34

    Do you consider your school site:
    c. i.   contributes to the spiritual life of the pupils?   Yes 79   No 29
        ii. why?   Example given: 82
    d. i.   damages the spiritual life of the pupils?   Yes 10   No 65
        ii. why?   Example given: 27

Part 4
Developments and Applications

CHAPTER 18

Spiders and eternity: spirituality and the curriculum

Derek H. Webster

INTRODUCTION: EXPERIENCE

When I was thirteen and had erupted in acne, there was an experience in school which memory has never rinsed out. The physics laboratory was always gloomy, always cramped and its overseer, Mr Tyson, impenetrable. One autumn morning, attempting to unriddle the coefficient of expansion of a metal rod, I found things especially depressing. Trapped between tedium and fear, I glanced outside. Clouds hurried endlessly across a cold sun.

Then it happened. Unshuttered, sunlight flared across the school field. Damp earth and grass were lit as a thousand spiders' webs rippled for the wind. Each, hanging with dew, reflected a rainbow light. The angle was crucial. Sitting awkwardly but still, I managed to hold it and watched the miracle disappear and return – again and again.

Mr Tyson's finger accused the emptiness of my notebook. After school that afternoon, detained to complete the experiment, I tried haltingly to share my vision. Unresponding, Mr Tyson's blank stare taught me that education was not about those things which brought joy and were ineffable, but about things that were public and measurable. From that time I began to understand that education had to do with the objective and the general and not with the subjective, the sensuous or the imaginative. With bitterness I realized that education was abstract, not personal, that it held no place for poetry. Cycling home alone in dark, beating rain, I wept that the spiritual had fled from schooling. It was, I was told, an emotional fantasy which would disappear with the acne.

Of course Mr Tyson was wrong – though I did not understand why until I had finished school years. He had fallen into that trap of which Wittgenstein warned in *Philosophical Investigations* (1958, p. 48). A picture held him captive and he could not move outside it. What he believed education to be was simply a particular metaphor expressed in authoritative language – not its reality. Yet it was a powerful metaphor and it condemned me at the time to what Paulo Freire called a 'mystification' (1985, p. 116). This 'consists in making the world appear different from what it is and, in the process and by necessity, of imparting an artificial consciousness'. Obviously this is something that has happened to others during many centuries and in many places as political theory, economic necessity and class division have shaped youngsters to be unknowing advocates of particular collective aspirations (Giroux, 1983, part 2). Too often they have become tenants in the ideological edifices raised by others rather than architects shaping their own lives.

When I became a teacher, the legacy of this experience was a deep mystery which can be expressed in the question:

> *What is the curricular response to the reality*
> *of the spiritual dimension of education?*

There would be wide agreement that the spiritual dimension of education may be conceived of as:

- that context which reminds us of what we most deeply are as human beings;
- that context which brings us to the outer edge of our understanding and leaves us with questions;
- that context which suggests our ultimate values.

(Starkings, 1993)

Yet how is a curricular response to be spun from this? A way forward appears when it is seen that central to these contexts are three matters. They concern:

- the value set upon people
- the Beyond and the approach to it
- the value of dialogue

Having first established the significance of these foundations, the curricular implications which arise from them can then be considered.

FOUNDATIONS

People

A primary focus for the spiritual dimension is the significance of people. It shows that there can be no final reduction of any youngster to the descriptive analyses offered by the human sciences. For, as Nicholas Berdyaev (1954, p. 45) puts it, a person

> is quite a special kind of being, not on a par with other realities.

People are open and creative in different ways. Their stories are distinctive and will not easily fit the structuralist assumptions which underlie pre-defined 'stages' or deterministic theories of development. As Paul Tillich (1953, p. 109) says:

> Man resists objectification, and if his resistance to it is broken, man himself is broken.

If child psychology is understood as a study of the events and experiences in youngsters' lives, in other words if it is contextual, teachers are allowed to value the wide variations, the astonishing inconsistencies and the provocative contradictions in youngsters' life stories, which they see day by day in their schools and colleges. Barrow (1986, p. 77) is too sharp when he asserts that,

> though we have some plausible generalisations about education, we do not have anything worthy of the name of a body of general laws about child psychology . . . that are also of practical value.

Yet he signals an important problem. A helpful response to it from parents and teachers is to ask continuously: 'How do we learn from children?' It would be sad if a Byzantine obsession with the statistical minutiae of stage theory obscured the 'becoming' of young people, for then Eliot's words (1963, p. 222) would be true:

> And the children in the apple tree
> Not known, because not looked for.

Yet the hard currency of the view that man is the unanswerable question is that it so values the human person that it commits itself very deeply to political and social change. It takes seriously the fact that one in ten babies in the world dies before its first birthday; that of those children who survive, another 4 per cent die before their fifth birthday; that 10 per cent of all children reach school age with a serious physical or mental handicap whose cause is usually malnutrition; that there are more than 800 million illiterates on the planet.

Despite the fact that it is always difficult to feel the force of statistics at the personal level, Alphonso Lingis's words (1994, p. 157) remain unbearably true. A person

> becomes the brother of the other when he puts himself wholly in the place of the death that gapes open for the other.

The mortality of others concerns us all. This is particularly so when death is both senseless and needless, as is so often the case with the poorest people in developing nations. The links which bind us together are clear. We are given to the world in places vacated by others; we walk the paths trodden by others; our enterprises in life are traced out by those who did not have the opportunity to realize them themselves. Our possibilities are always given to us by others. We can see in the arrangement of things diagrams of the skills of others which we can choose to reinscribe within our own lives. And one day when our own end comes, we too will leave others to sing our songs.

All of this forces into unwilling minds the fact that humanity is a single entity and of such intrinsic value that global responsibility and co-opera- tion has to be taken seriously. As the third millennium approaches it is becoming increasingly obvious that the only future humankind has is as a united humanity on a sustainable planet. So it is that some educationists, who cannot be accused of being bizarre futurologists, already see the importance of internationalism, while others (Muller, 1991, and Andrews, 1994) plan for a global education. However at the heart of all of this lies the view that:

> This Jack, joke, poor potsherd, patch, matchwood, immortal diamond,
> Is immortal diamond.
>
> (Hopkins, 1970, p. 106)

In his own simple and profound way Pablo Casals expresses the same dazzling truth:

> The child must know that he is a miracle, that since the beginning of the world there has never been a child like him and in all the future there will not be another child like him. He is a unique thing . . .
>
> (Quoted Muller, 1991, p. 57)

The Beyond

The spiritual dimension takes seriously the notion of the Beyond and sees that 'infinities meet in the finite' (O'Donoghue, 1979, p. 177). It allows for the undiscovered in human potential, acknowledging what is unknown and can only be disclosed in a free future. Teilhard de Chardin, commenting on the task of psychology in human living, suggests:

> Now the time has come . . . for exploring and tapping the mysterious cores where still lie untouched the most powerful energies of human beings.
>
> (1970, p. 111)

Stanislav Grof's exciting work is a sophisticated attempt to do just this (1975 and 1985).

But there is a curious methodological problem in attempting to speak about what is unknown and about what some would argue is ultimately unknowable. Standing behind the bars of the senses, how can a person 'say' what lies outside all perception and understanding? The words of the Mystic Doctor continue to ring true (Peers, 1964, p. 22f.):

> Who can write down that which He reveals? Of a surety, none . . . It is for this reason that, by means of figures, comparisons and similitudes they . . . utter secret mysteries. No words of holy doctors . . . can ever expound these things fully.

Inevitably speech will need to become symbolic and analogical, often poetry will enter.

Each realm of knowledge deals with this, with what lies outside its legitimate frontiers but which is its mysterious grounding, in its own way. (Theology, for instance, speaks of God as that unconditioned *a priori* behind all knowledge, One whose sheer incomprehensibility is more clearly seen by believers when they behold face to face (Rahner, 1975).) What this does – for the spiritual dimension has a strange dynamism – is to drive people from the brightness of what they know into that mystery where they seem not to grasp but to be grasped, where they reach the limit of rationality and seem pressed to adoration. Though not necessarily before a God or gods, for there is a flourishing and securely-grounded secular spirituality in contemporary culture found in literature and art, poetry and mathematics, the sciences and architecture (e.g. Capra, 1975; Ozment,

1969; Pibram, 1971; Valle and von Ekartsberg, 1981).

Educationists will want to know how the movements towards deeper mystery are made. Experience suggests two approaches. The first is a freshness of perception and the second a humility of method.

Freshness of perception. It is clearly right that learning and performance should be judged and measured in schools. But it is perhaps more important to try to discover *what* inspires learning and performance. In 1943 Thomas Mann was in Switzerland preparing to write *Dr Faustus.* He contacted the distinguished theologian Paul Tillich and asked about education. Tillich's reply emphasized its daemonic character (Wyatt, 1988). Life was paradoxical and ambiguous, it was exciting and joyful as well as tragic and passionate. The job of education was not to smooth out its mysteries, but to open eyes. Education was always provisional, constantly travelling, always on the way facing hope and contradiction. It was an example of John Henry Newman's view that to be perfect is to change continually.

Those who can approach the strangeness of life whilst retaining a freshness of perception about experience, may well be enabled to encourage youngsters to peer with excitement at the challenge of the Beyond – though this is something which is suggested rather than clearly delineated, evoked rather than analysed. The experience is common enough. Take as an example musicians playing Beethoven's late string quartets at a concert. Experts from a dozen fields could give an analysis of the whole performance down to the last measurable item. But all of the physiologists and physicists, electricians and acousticians, musicologists and instrument-makers could not capture and reduce the one central, only worthwhile and all-important element in the performance – the individual's experience of listening to (or playing) Beethoven's music. Description and analysis do not convey what takes place in any meaningful way at such a level. Though perhaps the poets put it best (Reid, 1978):

> The point is the seeing – the grace
> beyond recognition . . . Manifold, the world
> dawns on unrecognising eyes.
> Amazement is the thing
> Not love, but the astonishment of loving.

Humility. Educationists need a humility which can grant that, in working with children, their first axioms and most cherished theories may only capture half truths and may even turn out to be wrong. It could be helpful for them to reflect on the experience of Robert Coles (1992, pp. 24–5). His research was concerned to understand the children of the Hopi Indians in the USA. After six months of unsuccessful work with them in school, he was about to give up. The youngsters seemed unco-operative, taciturn and impassive. Because he continued to find them distrustful and shy, he concluded that they were uneducated, socially isolated and culturally deprived.

His own understanding finally started when a Hopi mother, who worked as a volunteer in the school, said to him: 'The longer you stay here the worse it will get.' Then she explained to him that he was asking the children about thoughts which they put aside when they entered school, for to them this was the building where they learned to read and write. They would never talk about the private events of their lives or their feelings in a school. It was only when Coles moved beyond the school, went into their homes and made personal friends with them and their families, that he was able to begin to understand these youngsters and start his research. He had to put aside the assumptions of a first-class Western scientific and psychiatric training and, quite literally, sit at the feet of the Hopi children in order to learn from them.

Dialogue

At the very heart of the spiritual dimension lies testing dialogue. It drives those who try to respond to what lies in this extraordinary dimension, to a pondering of those great questions that are rooted in human existence. The styles of the answers may vary, the symbols change, the theories move from the magical to the scientific, and the philosophical ideas wear new clothes, yet always the questions are the same. Can evil be accounted for? Why does my friend suffer? What is my duty? Will my neighbour receive justice? Who is my neighbour? How can I live with impulses within myself which seem to be so contrary? How may the State be best governed? Do the gods exist? How shall I face death? What is beauty? What is truth? As R. S. Thomas puts it (1992, p. 19):

> What
> does the traveller to your door
> ask, but that you sit down
> and share with him that
> for which there are no words?

These are the questions whose answers give us our humanity. Teachers have then to assist their youngsters to discern who they are, by setting them on a search and walking with them for part of the journey. But it is the youngsters' own search and it is their answers which they must find – not their teachers'. It is in this faith, in this great assumption – that there are answers and that life is not finally absurd – that values blossom. If the search is seen to be unimportant then the end is a moral failure. It is put succinctly by the Czech intellectual Vaclav Havel (quoted Bullock, 1990, p. 672) to his wife Olga in one of his letters from prison:

> The tragedy of modern man is not that he knows less and less about the meaning of his own life, but that it bothers him less and less.

CURRICULUM

When all of the myths are shredded and all of the slogans trumpeted, the only role the curriculum has is to enable youngsters to become human beings. Of course, in the sense that they belong to the species *homo sapiens* they are already human. But in another sense they must be enabled to become truly human – for they can very easily become less. The only purpose the curriculum has is to help youngsters make sense of themselves and the worlds in which they live. It shows them who they are. It achieves this by doing four things.

A knowledge of spiders

The curriculum which is sensitive to the spiritual dimension of education imparts a knowledge which sets a context for pupils' lives in time and space. Local history and geography, the sciences and mathematics, as well as their own and others' languages, give to youngsters the contours within which their existence can be understood. The sensitivity is shown as there is a recognition that in the content of the curriculum much key knowledge is seen to be open and tentative. (There is not so much *the* scientific viewpoint as the viewpoints of several scientists.) Knowledge must move easily beyond national boundaries, and educationalists must be permitted to raise the idea of a global core curriculum (Muller, 1993). But knowledge alone carries an ambiguity. How is it to be regarded and used? Immediately there is a step into the world of values. These cannot be ignored, particularly in science. In the requirement that the National Curriculum Science Programme should give attention at key stage 2 to 'the welfare and protection of living material' something remarkable has happened. Here is 'a Schweitzerian plea for reverence for life . . . a Gandhian message of respect for all living things' (Andrews, 1994, p. 59).

It is curious that knowledge raises questions whose answers seem to lie outside any knowing. This is a point which is well expressed in Anthony de Mello's story of the philosopher and his disciples (1982, p. 4, adapted).

> Sitting talking with their Master one day, his disciples were full of questions about the Absolute.
> Said the Master: To us it is both unknown and unknowable.
> All that is said about it, each answer to your questions, is a distortion of its truth.
> They were bewildered and said: Then why do we speak about it?
> The Master asked: Why do birds sing?
> Then he waited a long time in silence.
> Slowly some of his disciples realized that birds sing, not because they have a conceptual statement to impart, but because they have a song to sing.
> A few others were even aware that the Absolute was not to be understood, but was to be listened to – as one listens to the wind in the trees.
> However, the most humble and quiet disciple was the wisest.
> In solitude he found that the Absolute awakened in his heart what was beyond all knowledge.

Of course both theology and philosophy know of that *a priori* which is a non-conceptual, non-explicit, non-systematic and non-reflective awareness (Rahner, 1969). As the story suggests, this is not something which can be caught in the intellectual net and subsequently inspected – for it is itself that which gives rise to the net and the means of inspection. So it is never properly grasped or made an object of human knowing. It is given. Bernard Lonergan puts a complex point in a friendly way when he says:

'Explanation does not give man a home' (Lonergan, 1958, p. 547). So each field of knowledge rests on canons that are not finally derivable from within itself, but transcend its subject matter, criteria and methodology.

This transcending foundation, however, is not something only intellectuals can locate. Youngsters in the classroom both find and feel it as, for instance, their work with microscopes and telescopes raises for them the question of what lies beyond the boundaries of sight and the limitations of human intelligence. They find it as they study their own maturation processes and – perhaps looking at a series of photographs of themselves taken at different ages – ponder the mystery of who they *really* are and so raise the great question of human identity. Although younger pupils do not always have the language to articulate the problems raised by the idea of a transcending foundation, it is clear that they feel the force of the questions it poses (Robinson, 1976).

Anthropods of the order Araneida

The curriculum which is sensitive to the spiritual dimension of education offers opportunities for youngsters to develop those skills which enlarge their thinking. So they learn to read and have opened to them endless horizons. They learn how to reason logically and conquer problems of both a practical and a theoretical nature. They are encouraged to think imaginatively and find that they inhabit new worlds. They become creators themselves. And Silas the Maze-Maker reminds his hearers (Webster, 1993, p. 105) that:

> Creators . . . rub sleep from their eyes and gaze at the shining . . . [they] begin a pilgrimage on earth which is only fulfilled in heaven . . . [they] remove old gates, walk in fresh meadows . . . inhabit paradoxes and create love.

As opportunities are seized and skills develop in (say) literature, music or art, youngsters locate that transcendent dimension – George Steiner calls it a 'real presence' – which underwrites so much which is of compelling stature. It is evident in literature from the *Oresteia* and *The Brothers Karamazov* to David Jones's *Anathemata* and the poetry of Seamus Heaney; and in art from the caves at Altamira to Rembrandt, Kandinsky and Marc Rothko. But for some it is in music

> that we are most immediately in the presence of the logically, of the verbally inexpressible but wholly palpable energy in being that communicates to our senses and to our reflection what little we can grasp of the naked wonder of life. I take music to be the naming of the naming of life. This is beyond any liturgical specificity, a sacramental motion.
>
> (Steiner, 1987, p. 217)

There is a happy democracy in the spiritual dimension, for it is sensed not only by those intellectuals with refined tastes but also by those who are simple enough to have developed the skill to sit still and let be.

> Late one winter afternoon I was walking to a class . . . I noticed the beginnings of what promised to be one of the great local sunsets . . . the

sky was starting to burn and the bare trees were black as soot against it. When I got to the classroom the lights were all on and the students were chattering . . . when . . . on impulse . . . I snapped off the classroom lights. I am not sure that I have ever had a happier impulse . . . and as soon as it went dark everything disappeared except what we could see through the windows, and there it was – *the entire sky on fire* . . . You might have thought that somebody would have said something, you might have expected a wisecrack or two, or at least the creaking of chairs as someone turned round to see if the old bird had finally lost his mind. But the astonishing thing was that the silence was as complete as you can get in a room full of people, and we all sat unmoving for as long as it took the extraordinary spectacle to fade slowly away. For over twenty minutes nobody spoke a word. Nobody *did* anything. We just sat there in the near dark and watched one day of our lives come to an end . . . And I am not being sentimental when I say that it was a great class because in one way the sunset was the least part of it. What was great was the unbusyness of it . . . we were not just ourselves . . . but we were in some way also each other looking out at it. We were bound together by the fact of our being human, by our splendid insignificance in the face of what was going on out there . . . If we can bear to let it be, silence can be communion at a very deep level indeed, and that half hour of silence was precisely that, and perhaps that was the greatest part of it all.

(Buechner, 1975, p. 613)

The cognitive developmentalists are probably right in what they say about the maturation of children and their growing grasp of complex skills. But perhaps more important than their results is a question about *what* they select for observation and measurement. Their work often demonstrates that they have what has been called an Acquired Immunity to Mystery Syndrome (Robinson, 1987, p. 81). If they were to listen to children as they are – and to their own silences perhaps . . .

Spider's web: beauty or death?

The curriculum which is sensitive to the spiritual dimension of education is one which helps youngsters to recognize the dynamism of meanings which are important in their lives. It analyses competing value systems; it considers the varied interpretations of social experience; and it examines variations in cultural understanding. It is often in situations where the foil of life is tautly stretched that youngsters consider the significance of questions which are given by such contexts.

The advent of a new baby into a family, the overwhelming strangeness of fresh places and people, the pain that mental or physical suffering deals, grief at the death of a pet, a friend or a close family member, the pressures which duty brings, the obligations which conscience imposes, can all draw pupils towards that dimension which lies at the heart of things. They can also feel that void which is in the deepest part of themselves. There they may fashion answers which help them to live with integrity. There they may create an approach which helps them to deal with conflicting truth claims.

The most popular resolution to so many of the problems encountered is a form of relativism. Yet the hard currency of the view that there are many meanings, each one with its own dynamism, is this: powerful institutions establish truth for others. Always this matters – for personal integrity matters. However, where this is denied, as it can be by very powerful political institutions, the spiritual dimension is threatened. Its most extreme case is that of the torture of its citizens by a state, an occurrence which is currently frighteningly widespread. Within a lifetime many can chant a sad litany of the names of the 'client states of the advanced powers' – El Salvador, Peru, Angola, South Africa . . . – who have mutilated their 'subversives, fanatics, maniacs, and terrorists' (Lingis, 1994, p. 145).

Those who affirm the relevance of the spiritual dimension of education to living in today's world have to be prepared to argue for necessary and universal values and combat moral relativism. It is an argument which is seldom put in staffrooms by teachers because relativists seem to hold all the aces. Yet it is an argument which is stronger than often supposed.

The argument in a simple form begins by defining a value as a state which could be rationally chosen by a free person. Now value is tightly stitched to both *freedom* and *knowledge*. People cannot choose something unless they are free to do so and know what it is. If then people accept anything as a value at all, they must grant that the *freedom* which enables them to choose any values, and the *knowledge* which shows them what their possible choices are, are themselves values. In order to use their *freedom* properly and make sensible choices, people must reason, therefore *rationality* is a value too. So then those who understand what value means must accept that *freedom*, *knowledge* and *rationality* are quite basic values. (For example, a woman who wants to be a really good mother can only do this, if she is a woman, if she understands what this choice means and if she knows how to handle expertly the situations this choice involves.)

But why should people make choices? The only answer is because they want to – and behind this lies the wish for *happiness*. *Happiness* is always an excellent reason for people to choose something, provided it doesn't bring unhappiness to others or spoil their own future happiness. And because unfailingly it makes sense to aim for *happiness*, so it too becomes a further basic value. Yet if people are to get what they want, they will always need other people. None of these four values is possible without the *co-operation* of others. (A person cannot play in a brass band alone; there can be no happiness which either directly or indirectly does not involve others; if a person is to gain knowledge he or she must be taught; if a person is to develop rational abilities he or she must be shown how to do this.) *Co-operation* then becomes a fifth value.

Although *knowledge*, *freedom*, *rationality*, *happiness* and *co-operation* are not all the values that there are, these are the universal and necessary ones. This means that those who value anything at all *must* value these five, for they emerge from the very idea of what a value is. Of course at one level such a conclusion is quite trivial. But that is just what would be expected if the argument is correct – for everyone will consent to these values. Yet at another level such a conclusion is a fundamental step, for it means that values are not just personal preferences or reflections of subjective states. So if teachers in their schools prosecute, in a co-operative way, rational purposes which are freely chosen, they pursue what is good. It is objectively right for them to engage with these purposes. It further follows that it is objectively wrong for them to work in their schools in ways which deny these basic values. They may not, then, engage in activities which foster ignorance, enslave others, encourage foolishness, advance pain and promote enmity – nor may states (Ward, 1985 and 1989).

Getting along with spiders

The curriculum which is sensitive to the spiritual dimension of education encourages in youngsters social competence and sensitivity to others. It helps them develop moral insight, understand the commitments of others and become confident in social situations. This curriculum presents activities over a wide continuum, moving from the importance of narrowly dyadic relationships to the broadest of societal ones. But once again the ethical context is paramount, for values are powerfully inlaid in education, especially when people work together to achieve what is good, argue for change, express judgements and make choices.

The curriculum, as it seeks to be true to its spiritual foundations, tries to reflect those values which are cherished in democratic societies. Preeminent among them are cognitive, communal, aesthetic, moral and personal values. The first is present because knowledge is a large part of education and involves a search for truth which has regard to evidence, honest practice and critical thinking. Communal values have a place, because all life is shaped and given its richness by society and to receive its gifts pupils need to see what the duties and responsibilities of citizenship are. Moral values are included because there are ways of behaving which, if learned, can be life enhancing. Personal values are emphasized because in compassion and respect, in freedom and fortitude, are elements which give meaning to life. The aesthetic values, in lifting eyes to what has beauty, can involve people in truth, turn their faces towards larger visions and show them the poetry set within their own living.

Important though it is to set out the value markers in this way, the pupils and teachers who distil the curriculum through their living and thinking will find no fulfilment without beginning to understand that it is through self-giving that self-realization comes (Niebuhr, 1965, p. 107). Where there is no self-giving in human life, effects can be tragic. For instance Matthew Mendel's account of the impact of sexual abuse on boys in *The Male Survivor* (1995) is terrifying – despite its impeccably objective argument presented through tables, statistics, percentages and numerous academic references – but it does at least allow people to be personally detached. But the distinguished Quaker John Lampen will not allow this. In his Swarthmore Lecture he reminds his readers of the young girl of four who 'lives but a few streets away'. She is 'listening to the movements of a man in the room; in a moment he will be pulling her out of bed, and she will know from the taste of his penis whether it is her father, her brother or her uncle' (1987, pp. 11–13). Small wonder that the protest of Job – 'Why hast Thou done this?' – echoes from innumerable tongues through the centuries. And it is a question which still awaits an answer.

Where there is self-giving the results enable a picture of humanity to emerge which carries hope and which schools will foster in the work they do. Much that goes on in the life of the school and the local community will fuel this. Yet very occasionally an experience is so quintessentially set within the spiritual dimension that it demands to be pondered and remembered in a special way – particularly when it comes from an unexpected source. A professor of philosophy at Pennsylvania State University writes:

> One night, sick for weeks in a hut in Mahabalipuram in the south of India, I woke out of the fevered stupor of days to find that the paralysis that had incapacitated my arms was working its way into my chest. I stumbled out into the starless darkness of the heavy monsoon night. On the shore gasping for air, I felt someone grasp my arm. He was naked save for a threadbare loincloth . . . He seemed to have nothing, sleeping on the sands, alone. He engaged in a long conversation with a fisherman awakened from a hut at the edge of the jungle and finally loaded me in an outrigger canoe to take me, I knew without understanding any of his words, through the monsoon seas to the hospital in Madras sixty-five miles away. My fevered eyes contemplated his silent expressionless face as he laboured in the canoe, and it was completely clear to me that should the storm become violent, he would not hesitate to save me, at the risk of his own life. We disembarked at a fishing port, where he put me first on a rickshaw and then on a bus to Madras, and then he disappeared without a word or a glance at me. He surely had no address but the sands; I would never see him again. I shall not cease seeing what it means to come to be bound with a bond that can never be broken or forgotten, what it means to become a brother. How indecent to speak of such things in the anonymous irresponsibility of a writing he cannot read and a tongue he cannot understand.

> (Lingis, 1994, pp. 158–9)

CONCLUSION

In one way the argument underlying this chapter is no more than a commentary on the question which many centuries ago, Socrates asked of Athenians in the *Apologia*. He was critical of them and asked why they spent so much time acquiring money, reputation and honour and gave so little thought to truth, understanding and the perfection of their souls (Tredennick, 1954, p. 61). That this is a perennial wisdom is evident from R. S. Thomas's poem 'The Casualty' (1984, p. 60).

> I had forgotten
> the old quest for truth
> I was here for. Other cares
> held me.

In the current emphasis on means in education in Great Britain, ends have been set to one side. Instrumentalists and pragmatists have rewritten its agenda. In veering more and more towards a machinery for social control, education is losing its transcendent ends. All of this results in what Peter Abbs calls 'a massive denial of spiritual energy, of intellectual enquiry, of aesthetic beauty and public virtue' (1994, p. 1). The curricular response to the spiritual dimension is to fashion in the classrooms interactions between teachers and pupils which emphasize the value of being and encourage what speaks of wisdom, truth and life in its widest sense. It is a response which takes seriously the words of Moses in Christopher Fry's play *The Firstborn* (1970, p. 100):

> Shall we live in mystery and yet
> Conduct ourselves as though everything were known?

The ghost of Mr Tyson must not be allowed to put poetry to flight again. For it is only poetry and imagination, intuition and prophecy which have the audacity to excavate buried questions about the meaning of life, destiny, the gods, immortality, justice and responsibility to our neighbours. Without poetry education has no vision, is deprived of the only means of setting proper ends and inhabits the dark room of positivism. The spiritual dimension of education which poetry serves is not then a colourful fantasy, it is the true sunrise of wonder in human living. It enshrines a reality whose mysticism is beautifully captured by Wendy Cope (1992, p. 83):

> And suddenly this paving stone
> midway between my front door and the
> bus stop
> is a starting point.

Note

This chapter is a revision and further working of some material which originally appeared in *Curriculum*.

REFERENCES

Abbs, P. (1994) *The Educational Imperative*. London: The Falmer Press.

Andrews, R. (1994) *International Dimensions of the National Curriculum*. Stoke-on-Trent: Trentham Books.

Barrow, R. (1986) The concept of curriculum design. *Journal of Philosophy of Education*, **20** (1).

Berdyaev, N. (1954) *The Destiny of Man*. London: Bles.

Buechner, F. (1969) *The Hungering Dark*. Quoted in J. Westerhoff, Learning and prayer. *Religious Education* (1975), **70** (6).

Bullock, A. (1990) The Edward Boyle Memorial Lecture. Proceedings of the Royal Society of Arts, *RSA Journal*, **138** (5410).

Capra, F. (1975) *The Tao of Physics*. London: Collins.

Coles, R. (1992) *The Spiritual Life of Children*. London: Harper Collins.

Cope, W. (1992) 'New Season'. In *Serious Concerns*. London: Faber and Faber.

Eliot, T. S. (1963) 'Four Quartets'. In *Collected Poems 1909–1962*. London: Faber and Faber.

Freire, P. (1985) *The Politics of Education*. London: Macmillan.

Fry, C. (1970) *The Firstborn*. Oxford: Oxford University Press.

Giroux, H. A. (1983) *Theory and Resistance in Education*. London: Heinemann.

Grof, S. (1976) *Realms of Human Unconscious*. New York: Dutton.

Grof, S. (1985) *Beyond the Brain*. Albany: State University of New York Press.

Hopkins, G. M. (1970) *The Poems of Gerard Manley Hopkins*. W. N. Gardner and N. H. MacKenzie (eds). Oxford: Oxford University Press.

Lampen, J. (1987) *Mending Hurts*. London: Quaker Home Service.

Lingis, A. (1994) *The Community of Those Who Have Nothing in Common*. Bloomington and Indianapolis: Indiana University Press.

Lonergan, B. J. F. (1958) *Insight*. London: Longmans.

Mello, de A. (1982) *The Song of the Bird*. Anand, India: Gujarat Sahitya Prakash.

Mendel, M. P. (1995) *The Male Survivor*. London: Sage.

Muller, R. (1991) *The Birth of a Global Civilization*. Washington, DC: World Happiness and Co-operation.

Muller, R. (1993) *New Genesis*. Washington, DC: World Happiness and Co-operation.

Niebuhr, R. (1965) *Man's Nature and His Communities*. New York: Scribners.

O'Donoghue, N. D. (1979) *Heaven in Ordinare*. Edinburgh: T & T Clark.

Ozment, S. (1969) *Homo Spiritualis*. Leiden: E. J. Brill.

Peers, E. Allison (trans.) (1964) Prologue to *The Spiritual Canticle*. In *The Complete Works of St John of the Cross*. London: Burns & Oates.

Pibram, K. H. (1971) *Languages of the Brain*. Englewood Cliffs, NJ: Prentice Hall.

Rahner, K. (1975) *Theological Investigations*. London: Darton, Longman and Todd.

Rahner, K. (1969) *Hearers of the Word*. London: Sheed & Ward.

Reid, A. (1978) Growing, flying, happening. In *Weathering*. New York; Dutton.

Robinson, E. (1976) *The Original Vision*. Oxford: Religious Experience Research Unit.

Robinson, E. (1987) *The Language of Mystery*. London: SCM Press.

Starkings, D. (1993) *Religion and the Arts in Education: Dimensions of Spirituality*. Sevenoaks: Hodder & Stoughton.

Steiner, G. (1989) *Real Presences*. London: Faber and Faber.

Teilhard de Chardin, P. (1970) *Building the Earth*. London: Avon.

Thomas, R. S. (1984) *Later Poems 1972–1982*. London: Papermac.

Thomas, R. S. (1992) *Mass for Hard Times*. Newcastle upon Tyne: Bloodaxe Books.

Tillich, P. (1953) *Systematic Theology*, vol 1. London: Nisbet.

Tredennick, H. (trans.) (1954) *The Last Days of Socrates*. Harmondsworth: Penguin.

Valle, R. S. and von Ekartsberg, R. (1981) *The Metaphors of Consciousness*. New York: Plenum Press.

Ward, K (1985) *Battle for the Soul*. London: Hodder & Stoughton.

Ward, K. (1989) *The Rule of Love*. London: Darton, Longman and Todd.

Webster, D. H. (1993) *Sands of Silence*. Slough: St Pauls.

Wittgenstein, L. (1958) *Philosophical Investigations*. Oxford: Blackwell.

Wyatt, J. (1988) Academic formation: Paul Tillich's own account. *Journal of Higher Education*, **1** (1).

CHAPTER 19

Helping to restore spiritual values in abused children: a role for pastoral carers in education

Jean-Pierre Kirkland

Childhood, as in Happy, Safe, Protected, Innocent Childhood, does not exist for many children.

(Holt, 1975)

THE CONTEXT

Since the publication by the DES of Circular 4/88 in 1988, the abuse of children has become an important issue for teachers and other carers in the educational field. Of course, concern regarding this issue had been growing for many years, but it took a major incident such as the child abuse cases in Cleveland to cause that concern to be translated into action planning. Local education authorities responded, in most cases almost immediately, by appointing a senior official to take overall responsibility and charge, plus oversight for action, training and liaison with the newly-forming Area Child Protection Committees. Teachers were then trained with varying degrees of intensity; some authorities trained school co-ordinators or liaison teachers; others embarked on headteacher training; others attempted to reach whole school staffs. This training was then extended in some areas to ancillary staff, to governing bodies, to youth workers and to parents. The result overall, no matter how patchy or widespread the training may have been, is that child abuse has become as familiar a phrase to carers in education as appraisal, National Curriculum and records of achievement.

Child abuse falls into four main categories: child sexual abuse (CSA), physical abuse, emotional abuse and neglect (also called failure to thrive). In the case of the last three, physical abuse, emotional abuse and neglect, the signs can often be detected through careful monitoring and watchfulness, with some thoughtful questioning. Although it is often very difficult to determine and assess emotional abuse, and often highly complicated to ascertain what actually forms evidence for neglect, the physical abuse cases are much more definable. They are also the much more dangerous ones, as they may be, and indeed often are, life threatening and therefore action has to be taken quickly. Sexual abuse, on the other hand, is almost impossible to detect other than through changes in behaviour (unless the child is subjected to a medical examination). Changes in behaviour are, of course, often the result of problems other than abuse, such as drug use, parental/relationship difficulties and a large range of changes associated with puberty and adolescence. The job accepted by teachers and other carers and the resultant responsibility is an enormous burden, and one which needs careful attention. Whatever the form of abuse, however, one clear outcome is apparent: abused children, amongst many other things, suffer an undermining, and in the more prolonged or severe cases, an almost total destruction of a pattern of spiritual values.

There are probably as many different definitions of spirituality as there are days in the year and because of this it is very difficult to be objective in defining this area. Many of the more humanistic psychologists added their definitions to the already unclear and imprecise ideas which were floating about. For instance Bucke (1923) refers to spirituality as 'cosmic consciousness'; Maslow (1970) called it 'being-cognition'; Ouspensky (1934) called it 'the perception of the miraculous'; Fromm (1986) refers to spirituality as 'to be' rather than 'to have'. Assagioli (1975) claims that all activity which drives the human being forward towards some form of development – physical, emotional, mental, intuitional, social – if it is in advance of his or her present state, is essentially spiritual in nature.

It is not my intention to enter the debate about the nature of spirituality. The way in which it is being used here is not necessarily in any purely religious sense, rather in that wider concept which incorporates virtues and personal values. I would like to examine spirituality from a child's-eye point of view, and leave the more philosophical, sophisticated debate to others.

Children do experience things which give them deep feelings of well-being, feelings of 'magic' (Kirkland, 1988a), things which give them a glimmer of hope for the future; they develop value systems of their own which incorporate emotions and feelings such as love, honesty, loyalty, devotion, trust, integrity, joy, tenderness, kindness, tolerance, empathy, and warmth; they experience moments of intensity where beauty and under-standing are prominent; and many experience religion with all its powerful and mystic messages. As the child matures, these experiences and value systems change: some aspects are neglected, others grow and blossom. But for the constantly-abused child hiding in a world of threats and false promises, unaware or aware yet afraid, those very values and positive experiences are replaced by a distinctively darker and more evil system of 'values', with any notion of virtue discarded during the process of the abuse.

Abused children often become detached and present themselves as loners or isolates with resultant selfish characteristics. Many become emotionally disturbed and are prone to quite extreme manifestations of feelings – from very high to very low. Some become aggressive and vicious. Love can often be replaced by coldness, honesty by cheating, loyalty by unreliability, devotion by indifference, trust by suspicion, integrity by lying, joy by depression, tenderness by violence, kindness by aggression, tolerance by selfishness, empathy by uncaring and warmth by frostiness. Such children can become extremely difficult both to understand and to control in a teaching sense. They 'turn off' their studies and work, lose concentration and motivation and then fail to achieve. They become disruptive or unreachable in extreme cases. In other cases, they silently survive. What also tends to happen to these children is that, because of their behaviour changes, other children begin not to want to play or mix with them; 'normal' children start to isolate them, taking on many of the behaviours associated with the abused themselves: lack of warmth, little empathy, no trust and open hostility. This inevitably tends to alienate the abused child further. In cases of neglect, the children are isolated from peers on the grounds that they smell or steal or are always 'on the cadge'; in other cases, where the abused children fail to conform to a peer norm of dress, e.g. wearing trendy trainers or tee shirts, etc., they are ridiculed and rejected. My own observations whilst working with adolescents in a large inner-city comprehensive school in the 1980s showed that even one or two abused or suspected abused children in a group of thirty could lead to quite dramatic changes in group dynamics, and if the numbers of abused/suspected abused grew beyond two, the effect was quite unpredictable.

All of this can lead to long-term complications within groups or whole classes, and places heavy burdens upon teachers and other carers themselves. How many teachers can afford to spend hours following up petty bullying or ragging incidents, or spend days counselling children about behaviour or socialization issues? What effects does the abused child have on group unity in the classroom, or on co-operative group work of a curricular or developmental nature? The answers are fairly predictable: groups which once functioned well in play or at work cease to be effective; attempts to reconcile differences eat into curriculum time and detract from overall performance and achievement. Teachers and carers themselves are put under greater emotional strain as they try to find a solution whilst dealing with the other thirty children's needs within the classroom, and the other 101 jobs needing to be done. Stress levels rise amongst teachers, carers and pupils.

SPIRITUAL NEEDS

What is very apparent to me, and was certainly so when I was a practising teacher working with adolescents in an academic and pastoral capacity, was that groups containing numbers of abused or suspected abused children developed *special spiritual needs*. The abused child has had her or his life dramatically altered; the child's serenity, peace of mind, contentedness, personal growth and development have been fundamentally affected. Abused children have been subjected to an intense trauma in their lives and many then experience Post-Traumatic Stress Disorder (PTSD). It is estimated that overall perhaps 21 per cent of children who are abused may suffer PTSD, and where there has been any sexual maltreatment, the incidence rises to over 31 per cent compared to 13 per cent for children suffering physical abuse alone (Famularo *et al.*, 1989). There are no estimates available for neglect or emotional abuse, but it is very clear that such young people suffer huge reductions in their self-esteem, and often in their self-confidence. PTSD was first defined in 1980 by the American Psychiatric Association, who in a third revised edition of their *Diagnostic and Statistical Manual* (DSM-III-R) (APA, 1987) set out five criteria for diagnosing PTSD. These are:

- the 'client' must have witnessed or experienced a serious threat to his or her life or physical well-being;
- the 'client' must re-experience the event in some way;
- the 'client' must persistently avoid stimuli associated with the trauma or experience a numbing of general responsiveness;
- the 'client' must experience persistent symptoms of increased arousal;
- symptoms must have lasted at least a month.

The resultant disorders which present themselves to educators cause either a painful symptom (distress) or impairment in one or more important areas of functioning (Duckworth, 1987). These disorders include clinical psychiatric syndromes such as anxiety, depression and PTSD, personality disorders such as paranoia, antisocial or obsessive compulsive disorders, physical disorders, and severe psychosocial stressors such as in the first criterion above. Scott and Stradling (1992) argue that prolonged persistent maltreatment which is not necessarily dramatic (i.e. neglect and emotional abuse) may also cause PTSD symptoms to arise. The important and essential message here to teachers and carers is that this is a very complex area and a highly-specialized field under the general umbrella of counselling itself, and it would be extremely dangerous, not to say foolhardy, for staff to undertake counselling of children with PTSD without a great deal of specialized training, experience, support and supervision. Few school counsellors are likely to have had the relevant degree of training and experience for this work, and should think very seriously about getting involved in a one-to-one situation with these young people. There are specialists about, particularly within Social Service Departments, the Health Service or private counselling practitioners, who have the relevant experience, training qualifications and supervision/support facilities available. What teachers and carers need to do is practise their skills in those areas where they excel: in the classroom and related areas of the school where they are in an ideal position to address the spiritual needs of the whole class, incorporating the special spiritual needs of the abused children.

The special spiritual needs in abused children arise out of the nature of the harm and hurt that they have suffered or still are suffering. The general behaviour manifestations alluded to earlier will serve to illustrate the deep-seated damage which has been done, and which could go on being done. The signs or symptoms of abuse across the four categories may be summarized as follows:

- aggressive behaviour and temper tantrums;
- emotional detachment and isolationist type behaviour;

- either over-compliance or a state of frozen watchfulness;
- disturbed sleep and/or night terrors;
- depression;
- eating disorders verging on the anorexic, or obesity;
- regression;
- self-harm and attempted suicide;
- running away, physically and emotionally;
- poor concentration and under-achievement;
- lateness coupled with persistent absences;
- medically unexplained illnesses such as bed-wetting, soiling, migraines, abdominal pains, etc.;
- avoidance of school activities;
- reluctance to leave school at the end of the day;
- attention-seeking behaviours and gaze aversion.

In the case of neglect, children may be 'smelly', poorly dressed, have dirty hair, little bodily sustenance, no pocket money, etc. Emotionally abused children may become very selfish and 'clingy' and jealous of others' friendships. Sexually abused children often use sexualized language at an age which is not commensurate with proper understanding, coupled with sexualized behaviours. Physically abused children may be reluctant to change for games or PE because of bruising or scars, and are often absent on days when those activities take place. The picture is a fairly awful one not only for the child, but for other children who come into contact with these strange and often anti-social behaviours, as well as for teachers, carers, youth workers and other adults.

As adults we often get in the way of appropriate action, simply by allowing our own prejudices and educational background to influence our thinking: 'It couldn't happen in that nice family', or 'They've supported the school open days and parents' evenings for five years and always show concern, so it's never happening there'. Abuse does happen irrespective of class, income, culture, education or intelligence, and we therefore need to be alert, open-minded and vigilant in order to recognize it, monitor it and take action. But we also need to be aware that a lot of abuse may well never surface even in terms of generalized concern. The idea of meeting special spiritual needs is not therefore a one-off venture, but rather part of a more structured curriculum approach which will benefit everyone.

A CURRICULAR RESPONSE

The concept of special spiritual needs began to take shape and was emphasized and clarified in my work with young people in residential settings (Kirkland, 1988b). My research showed that it was possible to create atmospheres promoting the spiritual without drawing attention to specifics. This was then translated into classroom practices whereby it became possible to address the special spiritual needs of abused children whilst creating a positive and healthy learning and teaching environment for the whole class. A package of stress management techniques for young people was introduced into the scheme of the personal and social education programme as part of this initiative. This was not originally designed deliberately to help the abused child; rather it became apparent that such an approach did in fact begin to meet the needs of the abused young people as well as help cater for the needs of the rest of the class. The importance of this is that no attention is drawn to the abused child, nor is there any real detraction from pupil-centred approaches to teaching.

In order to approach this subject area, careful thought and planning are essential. I recommend that the stages outlined below are followed in part or in whole.

- It will be necessary for someone to take charge of the development of a scheme of developmental work in this field. The designated person responsible for RE, or PSE, or health education might be appropriate.
- The school's child protection liaison teacher or co-ordinator needs to be closely involved, along with other interested people such as the school or area nurse, someone from the governors, the head, pastoral staff, a youth worker, a consultant or adviser, etc.
- The group will need to define 'spiritual' carefully in the light of the school's mission statement, reflecting the school's aims and objectives.
- A series of group work based strategies for curriculum delivery need formulating, with links into existing classroom practice and Acts of Collective Worship.
- Some time for staff meetings or training days needs earmarking in order to familiarize colleagues with the purpose and philosophy of the scheme, and to consult over matters of suitability and appropriateness for delivery.
- Guidelines or a policy document will need ratifying by the governors and publishing for all the staff.
- The scheme needs implementing with very careful monitoring built in; decisions about monitoring the effect on all the class versus the effect on the abused/suspected abused child need to be clarified and appropriate decisions and strategies adopted.
- The overall scheme needs evaluating periodically.

It should be remembered that this is not an attempt to introduce materials about protection issues. Those are quite separate and require thinking through in a different way (Elliott, 1984).

The gathering together of appropriate stimulus and development material to cater for special spiritual needs is a fascinating area of research. There is much excellent PSE material in print, and by using selections of these the scheme can be greatly enhanced. Since this is a sensitive and quite difficult area within which to work, it is important to examine the dimensions of the exercise. I suggest that the important principles are as follows:

- the scheme is aimed at all the children in the school/year/class etc.;
- the impact will be greatest upon those with special spiritual needs;
- the scheme is not designed to encourage either prevention or disclosure, although both could conceivably occur;
- the scheme is unique to your school and its perceived needs;

- all children have an entitlement via the 1986 Education Reform Act to 'spiritual development';
- abused and thus spiritually deprived children deserve better from life and therefore have a special entitlement to access this area of their lives;
- it is *our* society, for which we are all equally responsible, which has caused the abuse and spiritual deprivation to occur, and it is therefore our corporate responsibility as carers or teachers to help restore this vital area to the children concerned.

The importance of acknowledging these principles is that they will help to clarify thinking and to formulate both planning and action when special spiritual needs issues are being addressed.

The emphasis is on technique and methodology rather than content. This is quite deliberate as I believe teachers to be the best judges of the content matter appropriate for their class and school. Thus the following model, when used with appropriate stimulus material, will go a great way in developing an appreciation and understanding of aspects of spirituality in young people of all ages:

- First, an atmosphere needs creating which will promote the aims of the session or lesson. It may be necessary to calm children down, make them mentally more relaxed, or liven them up if the class or group are flagging. Warm-up exercises are very useful and can be good fun, too, as well as a learning experience, provided that the purpose of the preliminary exercise is properly explained (Brandes and Philips, 1977; Brandes, 1982).
- Second, some form of stimulus can be introduced, such as a video, poem, reading from a book, the Bible or newspaper, a song or other music, or some combination of these. This raises awareness and highlights issues for what follows.
- Third, structured discussion or debate, which can be whole group/class or smaller, carefully chosen sub-groups. Scribes, chairpersons, etc. can be appointed, with the aim of some outcomes being reported back.
- Fourth, structured discussion leads to the whole group sharing and discussing, with opportunities for the young people to express their feelings if circumstances permit.
- A further possibility is a creative task based upon the outcomes of the discussion: designing posters, writing and acting a small play, composing and singing a song, followed by another opportunity to share, but this time with more emphasis on feelings.
- After learning points have been emphasized and possibly recorded, the process may culminate in a period of calm, meditation, relaxation and fantasy, with a final sharing of outcomes and feelings.

It is when the young people have freedom of expression and opportunities to share their feelings and emotions, and through the development of mind in meditation and fantasy, that the spiritual qualities, virtues and values begin to emerge. I would like to expand upon some of these briefly, but before doing so, it should be emphasized that this is not an attempt at enabling abused children to disclose the nature of the abuse; should this occur, then teachers and others need to follow the guidelines laid down by the school, LEA and Area Child Protection Committee. This is purely and simply an attempt to provide the conditions necessary for the growth of spiritual feelings.

SOME STRATEGIES

Music

The first method I would like to expand upon is the use of music both as stimulus material and in the form of creative songwriting/performing which has much potential for helping to restore damaged or missing spiritual qualities. The words of folk-songs and certain 'political' songs contain powerful messages about the society in which we live, and give classes and groups many opportunities to explore sets of values and ideas which contain both overt and covert references to spiritual qualities. Examples are anti-war songs, cruelty to animals, songs about relationships, drugs and alcohol, as well as songs which highlight more major world problems such as starvation, imprisonment, torture, repression and discrimination. Provided that the teacher extracts the information appropriately and then relates it to the everyday life of the class, the opportunity for debating rights and wrongs, sharing ideas, listening to others, tolerating the opinions and values of others and empathizing with particular groups or individuals, will emerge in a way which is healthy and affirmative. The effects on the 'normal' children are noticeable; on the abused, marked. Often, the opportunity to listen to carefully-chosen pieces of music, coupled with creative writing or art, can produce feelings of great spiritual intensity which often have a cathartic or healing effect (Watson and Drury, 1987). Rogers (1967) claims that persons given the opportunity to search for 'the good life' (as opposed to the 'bad life' of current or past abuse) would be those from whom creative products and creative living emerge.

Relaxation

Second, using relaxation in the classroom can be a very revealing and new experience for many children (Leech and Wooster, 1986). The lives of so many children are hectic and busy, and stresses do result. Amerikaner and Summerlin (1982) found that learning-disabled children (I suggest that abused children fall into that category) who were taught to relax were better able to cope with stresses. Relaxation techniques such as muscle detoxification and regulation of breathing are easy to learn for the teacher and quite straightforward to practise. These forms of relaxation and others have led to the reduction of hyperactivity (McBrien, 1978) and to the reduction of anxiety and increase in the levels of thinking (Morris, 1977). Such effects pave the way for the promotion of the spiritual and often lead naturally to the next method.

Meditation

The third approach is via the use of meditative techniques. Many children get stressed quite easily and the use of meditation to relieve stress is both justifiable and very popular, once it is established and culturally accept-able. The abused child is likely to be far more stressed (distressed) than the rest of the class. Providing children with the space and calm to focus the mind, reflect upon experiences and share the feelings engendered by the session with others, is again moving towards promoting the growth of many of the spiritual qualities which may be lacking. Conditions have to be quiet and relatively peaceful for effective meditation to take place, and with careful forward planning this can be achieved for the short periods required. One very effective technique is in the use of the Mettabhavana practice of meditation (Kennedy, 1985) or the development of loving-kind-ness. This is a five-stage meditation which focuses on self, then a friend, then on to an acquaintance, moving next to someone who is difficult in our lives, and finally on to the whole of creation, emphasizing positive and loving messages at each stage.

Fantasy

One final approach I will recommend is the use of guided or scripted fantasy. Oaklander (1978) is a real source of inspiration for those who wish to explore this method in more detail. Taking children 'out of themselves' for short periods of time on a mind trip or fantasy journey is a pleasurable and exciting experience for young people (and adults, too!). The tech-niques are not difficult to learn; the scripts can be prepared by teachers to suit the purposes they desire, and I have found that every age of pupil from 6 up to 18 has benefited from this technique. After relaxing the group, with their eyes closed, the teacher reads or talks them through an experience or journey. Children can be taken to 'a safe place', to the seaside, into the country, on a ship, to a desert island and many other places. Psychosynthesis employs similar techniques in order to achieve a 'spiritual awakening' (Assagioli, 1975, p. 40) and this is reinforced as 'the ways and means for evoking and cultivating a spiritual awareness and vision of life' (Whitmore, 1986, p. 13). Provided the classes and groups are given the appropriate structures for debate, free expression and plenary sharing, whether this latter be of ideas or of creative outcomes, guided fantasy can provide an excellent means of promoting spiritual growth.

The methods outlined in brief above can and do work for a majority of the children in any class and there are probably many others which are equally valuable. But the fact that groups and classes are embarking upon development work together is in itself a great vehicle for the promotion of spiritual qualities. Group work means listening and sharing and participat-ing; the child who has suffered the abuse is made to feel welcome again; her or his ideas and suggestions can be listened to; their contributions are valued; they have opportunities for expressing their creativity; they will begin to feel part of a group and develop a sense of belonging just by being there; they will hear debate about honesty, love and understanding; they will observe tolerance and warmth amongst their peers; in all likelihood they will be invited to offer their contributions; they will begin to feel good about themselves; they may even begin to feel safe again and respond by calming down, respecting others in authority more and eventually begin-ning to trust their own once-damaged feelings. Going this far may be as much as we can do as teachers and carers. We are not, by and large, specialized counsellors; we may have an excellent range of counselling skills to offer and by employing these in ordinary situations may well be able to restore some degree of sanity to the damaged lives of those we care about, and for whom we have great concern.

CARING FOR THE CARERS

Taking care of teachers and carers is also of fundamental importance. The education system has been notoriously bad at providing counselling for staff, even though the degree of responsibility for sensitive issues has grown enormously for many professionals and the nature of dealing with these areas frequently changes. Stress levels amongst teachers are very high and breakdowns are very much on the increase. Add to this the very sensitive nature of having to deal with abused children and their families, perhaps having to attend case conferences and liaise with multidisciplinary agencies, and there is a clear danger of adding to existing stress and break-down levels.

Using some of the above techniques can actually help some individual adults cope better themselves with the issues confronting them. Even so, teachers and carers who must work through abuse issues as professionals also need professional support. I would like to see established in cluster groups of schools, within LEAs or across phases, a support mechanism with a qualified and experienced backup service. Where schools have opted for Continuing Professional Development Schemes, there is often the backup of a Staff Assistance Programme (Kirkland, 1994) similar to the Employee Assistance Programmes (EAPs) which are becoming more and more in evidence in industry. A Staff Assistance Programme would include the provision of a counsellor who would be able to take on board the personal issues raised for teachers by cases such as abused children. It seems strange to me that many Social Services Departments, the police, probation and health services have such a provision, yet education does not. If our aim is to become effective teachers and carers trying to restore the damaged spiritual qualities in abused children, then surely we need our own support systems so that we feel comfortable, capable and competent in helping to complete that most complicated of all jigsaws, the whole child.

REFERENCES

American Psychiatric Association (1987) *Diagnostic and Statistical Manual of Mental Disorders*, 3rd revised edition. Washington, DC: APA.

Amerikaner, M. and Summerlin, M. (1982) Group counselling, learning and disabled children: effects of social skills and relaxation training on self-concept and classroom behaviours. *Journal of Learning Disabilities*, **15** (6).

Assagioli, R. (1975) *Psychosynthesis*. Wellingborough: Turnstone Press.

Brandes, D. (1982) *The Gamester's Handbook II*. London: Hutchinson.

Brandes, D. and Philips, H. (1977) *The Gamester's Handbook*. London: Hutchinson.

Bucke, R. (1923) *Cosmic Consciousness: A Study in the Evolution of the Human Mind*. New York: Dutton.

DES (1988) *Working Together for the Protection of Children from Abuse: Procedures within the Education Service*, DES Circular 4/88. London: DFE.

Duckworth, D. (1987) Post-traumatic stress disorder. *Stress Medicine*, **3**.

Elliott, M. (1985) *Preventing Child Sexual Assault*. London: Bedford Square Press for NCVO.

Famularo, R., Kinscher, F. and Fenton, T. (1989) Post-traumatic stress disorder among maltreated children presenting to a juvenile court. *American Journal of Forensic Psychiatry*, **10**.

Fromme, E. (1986) *Psychoanalysis and Zen Buddhism*. London: Unwin.

Holt, J. (1975) *Escape from Childhood: The Needs and Rights of Children*. New York: Ballantine.

Kennedy, A. (1985) *The Buddhist Vision*. London: Rider.

Kirkland, J.-P. (1988a) Developing adolescent friendships in residential settings. *Values*, **3** (2).

Kirkland, J.-P. (1988b) 'Residential experience.' Unpublished M.Ed. thesis, Nottingham University.

Kirkland, J.-P. (1994) *Continuing Professional Development: A Scheme for Schools*. Altrincham: Positive Attitudes.

Leech, N. and Wooster, A. (1986) *Personal and Social Skills*. Exeter: Pergamon Press.

Maslow, A. (1970) *Motivation and Personality*, 2nd edn. New York: Harper and Row.

McBrien, R. (1978) *Using Relaxation Methods with First Grade Boys*. Washington, DC: American Personal Guidance Association.

Morris, J. (1977) Meditation in the classroom. *Learning* (December).

Oaklander, V. (1978) *Windows to Our Children*. Real People Press.

Ouspensky, P. (1934) *Tertium Organum*. New York: Knopf.

Rogers, C. (1967) *On Becoming a Person*. Boston: Houghton-Mifflin.

Scott, M., and Stradling, S. (1992) *Counselling for Post-Traumatic Stress Disorder*. London: Sage.

Watson, A. and Drury, N. (1987) *Healing Music*. Dorset: Prism Press.

Whitmore, D. (1986) *Psychosynthesis in Education*. Wellingborough: Turnstone Press.

CHAPTER 20

Learning about life: teaching about loss

Louise Rowling

INTRODUCTION

In recent years there has been pressure on the school curriculum to accommodate social and health issues that traditionally would not have been seen as appropriate for schools but as the concern solely of families. Loss and grief is one of these issues. This chapter will describe some findings that have emerged from research into teaching and learning about loss and grief in a secular context in secondary schools. The findings for teachers and students indicated a 'spiritual' dimension to the learning environment in that, for both groups, it provided the opportunity to consider their views about life as they discussed loss.

When it comes to talking about death with young people in the family or in schools, there is still a great deal of hesitancy (Dyregrov, 1991; Raphael, 1985). Parents, relatives and teachers are evasive or reluctant to talk when the topic is raised. There are many reasons why this is the case. For example, it could be a reflection of their own fears about death; a wish to maintain the 'innocence' of young people; a belief that death is essentially unknown and therefore it is unrealistic to try to prepare someone to deal with it; hesitancy because of lack of knowledge of people's life experiences; or a belief that the issue is a personal one and therefore not the concern of the education system.

There is a great deal of personal sensitivity to the topic, sensitivity created by beliefs, people's experiences and the emotions that may be involved in such discussions (Rowling, 1991). This makes it a particularly difficult area in the curriculum.

Most people focus on death as the only loss experience for young people. However, it is a mistake to identify loss exclusively with death. The loss situations that young people can experience, with their accompanying emotional and behavioural responses, are diverse – a change of school or neighbourhood, or migration to a new country; the loss of health through illness or accident; the loss of expectation such as failing to make a team; the death of a beloved pet; the loss of self-esteem through a friend's rejection or a failure in school; and the passage from one life stage to another.

Losses and the resultant grief reaction are involved in all psycho-social transitions (Parkes, 1988).

Developmental, cognitive and psycho-social changes at the time of adolescence put young people particularly at risk of the multiple impacts of loss experiences. Developmentally, emotional reactions are characterized by 'highs' and 'lows' due to changing hormonal levels, and loss experiences can intensify these emotional responses. Additionally, adolescents are at risk because their changing cognitive ability gives them the capacity to re-examine earlier loss experiences.

Psychologically, the developing identity of a young person can be threatened by the death of a parent or parental separation; his or her security is disturbed because the concept of 'the family' changes, the predictability of their world is shattered. Even the first broken love affair can have a major impact on an adolescent's view of him- or herself.

Whilst the effect of death on young people is well documented, there is little evidence, apart from a survey in the United States (Wass, Miller and Thornton, 1990), that talking about death or loss in general is occurring in schools. From a preventive mental health perspective there is evidence of the potential impact of preparation for life transitions that involve loss (Parkes, 1988). In Australia, and in the state of New South Wales in particular, community awareness of loss and grief is high because of a series of community disasters such as bus crashes and natural disasters such as bush fires. Documentary evidence suggests that school systems are also aware of these issues (Heinecke and Spence, 1991; Rowling, 1993). The motivating force for this activity is the need for school communities to be prepared to handle critical incidents (traumatic events) they will almost inevitably face. But LaGrande (1988) suggests that schools can also assist young people cope with loss by normalizing the emotions they experience; educating about grief responses; creating supportive networks; and restoring self-esteem and self-confidence. These areas for intervention can be realized through formal and informal education in schools.

This has occurred in New South Wales where the topic is included in the new curriculum documents for the compulsory Personal Development/ Health Education Syllabus (Board of Studies, 1991) and resource material has been published (Glassock and Rowling, 1992) to support the curriculum. The Australian context is focused towards viewing death as part of loss experiences in general and there is an acceptance of a role for schools in teaching about loss and grief.

In Britain, a survey of the health needs of primary school age children reports the children declaring an interest in the area of loss, but teachers and parents in the same survey did not see it as a priority (Balding and Shelley, 1993). However, in Britain materials have recently been produced for teachers to handle grief and critical incidents (Wagner, 1993; Yule and Gold, 1993).

As indicated previously, from a mental health perspective there is ample justification for consideration of loss and grief, but there is also justification in the aims of schools, most of which would indicate a responsibility of the school to prepare young people for future life experiences. This can occur not only in a preventive way – psycho-education through the curriculum – but also through structured support and guidance when young people experience life events involving loss. The experience of loss as a justification for its inclusion in the curriculum is well established (e.g. Grollman, 1967; Smilansky, 1987; LaGrande, 1988; Wass *et al.*, 1990; Weekes and Johnson, 1992).

The purpose of such curriculum is seen as 'enhancing human development and quality of life' (Weekes and Johnson, 1992, p. 220), hence the title of this chapter.

Various tasks have been identified that grieving people need to achieve for the acceptance of their loss (Worden, 1991; Zisook, 1987). One of these tasks was what Zisook labelled 'normalisation through education' (p. 11), a process that can help grieving people realize that their experiences are a normal part of the grieving process. The school environment, through its curriculum, structures and processes, can contribute to this normalization.

Several researchers in the early 1970s advocated educating young people about death, with broad goals for such education being enunciated by Leviton (1971). This was followed by whole texts that had objectives and suggested age-appropriate teaching strategies (Eddy and Alles, 1983). The basic orientation of these approaches was in exploring affective responses and a cognitive understanding of death. For example, Hopson and Scally (1980) approached grief through an examination of life transitions. More recent curricula have either dealt with divorce and separation in isolation from other loss experiences (Children's Society, 1992) or had a general focus on loss and grief (Plant and Stoate, 1989; Ward and Houghton, 1988).

Current approaches reflect an emphasis on involvement of mental health professionals in schools to cover topics associated with grief. This could be as a result of the lack of teacher training in this area (Smilansky, 1987; Wass *et al.*, 1990), and/or the basis of the identification of the need for interventions, that is, a clinical individual treatment orientation. But leaving the teaching about loss and grief to mental health specialists does not acknowledge the normality of grief. It is seen as something 'outside the normal experience of teachers'.

Despite the need for the teaching of young people in this area, little systematic documentation of the issues involved is available. What follows is a description of research in New South Wales, Australia, that portrays the experiences of teachers and students in teaching and learning about loss and grief.

RESEARCH RESULTS: STUDENTS' AND TEACHERS' EXPERIENCES

The research involved two school case studies of grief over two years of fieldwork. Sites for the case studies were chosen which optimized the potential for explicating the substantive topic of concern – loss and grief. One secondary school was a large multicultural comprehensive high school in the Sydney metropolitan area of New South Wales. There were approximately 120 teaching staff and about 1350 students, 75 per cent of whom came from non-English-speaking backgrounds. The other secondary school was a semi-rural school about 300 kilometres from Sydney. There were about 90 staff and approximately 700 students attending the school, drawn from the town and from the surrounding countryside.

Methods employed in the research were: repeated in-depth interviewing of parents, teachers and students; participant observation in lessons, discussions and meetings; and document analysis. Anonymity and confidentiality were maintained and pseudonyms used throughout the reporting of findings.

At one of my research schools I observed a senior class which talked about grief. This lesson was conducted about 8 weeks before a car accident that involved some of the students. The teacher had forewarned the class of the topic. I had observed several previous lessons so the group were relaxed about my presence. The teacher introduced the lesson by distributing a bulletin from her son's school about the death of one of the school's Year 11 students in a bus accident, a death witnessed by a busload of students. The class was hushed as they read it to themselves. Later, in a small group discussion with me (Louise), students (pseudonyms) described their responses:

Louise   It was hard to believe that given that situation that is what could happen.

Natasha   Not just that, but three-quarters of this school catch buses home. Something could happen just like that! Anybody at this school. No warning. No one tells you, tomorrow your friend is going to die in a bus accident. It brings up a lot of issues.

Franco, Leila, Nina Yeah.

Otto   Knock on wood. (*knocking on the table*)

Louise   Does that make you a bit frightened?

Nina   Yes.

Franco   Yes. Wary of what you do and of others.

Leila   You cross the street and think . . .

Otto   What if I die now . . . ?

Louise   Is that an unusual thing for your age group to think about?

Otto, Franco Yeah.

Natasha   No. It's not unusual, but you are not really talking about it because you have the rest of your life ahead of you, whereas if you get to the end of your life . . .

Leila   Our age group is more interested in the present.

Louise   Some teachers and some parents might say that you shouldn't talk about death, and the class was very quiet after it saw the film. Do you think people were upset by the lesson?

Natasha   No, I just think they were thinking about how they would react.

(group interview, Year 11)

The class discussion challenged these students' views of life; their frameworks for making sense of such experience; life's predictability and their ability to control events. Another student recounted her involvement in the lesson and the disclosure the lesson prompted:

Louise	Have any of you had any experiences where something has happened to you and you haven't talked about it?
(*Pause*)	
Ursula	Yeah, Me. I broke out to Sarah that day, I spoke about it.
Louise	You talked to someone after that lesson?
Ursula	Yeah, Sarah. (*indicating other group member*) I told her everything.
Louise	You hadn't done that before?
Ursula	Not for six-and-a-half years.
Louise	Really! That must have been . . . what was it in the lesson that prompted you . . . ?
Ursula	I don't know. I think I realized that people do care. 'Cause like I had the impression that no one cared. 'Cause at the funeral everyone was there, but two years down the track you don't see these people again. They were hypocrites. I thought 'No one cares I'm not going to talk about it'. I've been holding it in for six-and-half years. Now I've told Sarah. I just told her everything . . . When the teacher said we are going to talk about death I looked at Sarah. I got really scared. I thought I am going to burst in the class. But it was all right. I just burst out and told her everything. It was good to have that lesson. (*laughs*)

(group interview, Year 11)

The students described how they perceived the teacher in these lessons. They said: 'She was sort of nice and calm and she talked about how WE (student's emphasis) felt, not just this is how PEOPLE (student's emphasis) feel.' This strategy of drawing on students' experiences was emphasized by a parent, who was potentially supportive of teaching about loss and grief, depending on the way teachers did it: 'They need to find out from the students, their experiences.' Another student said:

> This is the first time we discussed about death, but everyone was open. It is the kind of lesson where everyone can share their feelings.
>
> (Nina, Year 11)

Whilst the students valued the lesson, they didn't necessarily enjoy it. They experienced fear and anxiety about what could happen in the future. But they still thought it should be discussed. They made comments such as: 'It turned out good. It turned up things I didn't know'; 'I found it interesting to talk about feelings that you had'; 'You have to talk about it, be aware of it. It is not something you can take easily'; 'It gives you ideas about how to explain yourself if you were in that situation, to watch what they are doing.' But it was recognized that if you don't talk about it:

> it is still inside you, if someone else is talking about it, you will just be sitting there hearing what they are saying, you are getting upset inside.
>
> (Ursula, Year 11)

One of the most interesting findings of this research was that, unlike teaching about other sensitive issues such as drugs or sexuality, in teaching about loss and grief teachers used their personal experiences during the lessons in talking to the students. For example, in the second research school, issues of loss and grief were not normally well covered in the curriculum. One of the teachers (Anna) whom I had met many years previously when I had conducted a workshop about coping with grief, wanted to include the topic in the curriculum, starting with the new 25-hour compulsory Personal Development and Health Education course for senior students. Early in the first year of the study, a book I had co-authored on teaching about grief was published. On the first day of the new 25-hour course for senior students in 1992, Anna used some of the ideas from this book. The Year 11 students were divided into small groups of 15 for each of the four days. I participated in Anna's small group as she talked about grief in the last session of the first day. In her group, to exemplify grief reactions, she shared her experience of the death of her 19-year-old brother.

Later I talked with students who had participated in Anna's session on grief. They reacted positively to her personal disclosure. To them it demonstrated that she was 'human', as the following discussion demonstrates:

Tessa　She told us about her brother and that, I was really surprised with that, because I didn't know – the teacher telling us something like that. Sort of shocked me at first, but then I thought 'Oh yeah! She is just trying to be like one of us.' I thought it was really good.

Louise　Was she trying to be like you?

Beth　Becoming human probably.

Louise　Is that unusual for teachers?

Simon　Yes.

Beth　Not Mrs Bailey. She is like that all the time. It is being aware of us. A lot of teachers are not in tune with what the kids are up to.

(group interview, Year 11)

'Being human' was seen by these students as an important quality in teachers. It did not seem to lessen the students' respect for their teacher. The students' experience was that those teachers who were 'human' were more likely to understand them as individuals. However, personal disclosure by teachers does involve risk. This will be discussed later.

Subsequently, in talking with the other teachers involved on that first day, I found that a number of them had also used personal experience to talk about grief. Joy had talked in detail to her group about the death of her baby niece. She recounted to me what she told the students:

What I said to them was how my niece died. I think lots of kids . . . me, not just the kids, have never been through that process. I said 'I don't know about grown ups, but when a little baby dies, there are all these things that I never thought I had to do!' I actually felt it was very difficult to talk. I had to go (*takes a deep breath*) like that, to talk about it. But I continued to talk about it, because it only happened in March and it's really very soon after it. But I thought, not I had to, but I thought that they would gain from it . . . I said, 'Sometimes it's very hard to talk about it and really you might break down and cry' and I said, 'It doesn't matter. It doesn't matter!' So I really got to the point where I thought I was going to break down and cry. But I didn't, tears didn't come to my eyes or anything, but I felt as if I was going to . . . I felt that choking sensation come up and . . . but I didn't. The kids were very interested. I actually told them the nitty-gritty of things. Simple things like – my brother didn't want to buy an urn, so I had to be in charge of buying something to put the baby's ashes in.

Then we had to ask this morbid question, which people don't like asking, 'How much flipping ash does a baby produce?' That sort of thing. Then I got them the urn and my sister-in-law said, 'How do you know that all the ashes can get in there?' and I said, 'Look, Freida, that chap said 1½ mugs.' I had to prove it to her. Those were the sort of things I told the students. I think they were absolutely fascinated . . . They wanted to ask me questions, I think what I said to them was – not shocking, it was shocking to me at the time, but it was so new and foreign. I explained to them how I had to dress the baby and how she became stiff. I think they were so . . . they weren't prepared I suppose in a way for details like that. I actually said to them my feelings as I went through it . . . when I first heard it, I thought she was unconscious, conked out, I said 'That's unconscious!' and then I said, 'Oh dear me!' . . . and my brother said, 'I think it's very important that you come'. Then I heard this voice in the background saying – 'Honey they can't find a heartbeat' – as a whisper in the background. So I sort of – I was in a state of shock and all through, I said to the kids, 'All through going to the hospital I kept on hearing "Honey, they can't hear a heartbeat"', the thought more or less trying to prepare me that she might die, she might die. When I got there I still did not believe that this was all happening and I said to the kids: 'All I could think of was that I am actually in an episode of *Days of Our Lives* and that it is all happening there, but I'm just watching, I'm just watching TV, it's not really happening and it's not reality.' But I said, everything, everything that came was real. But I kept saying, 'No, no it can't be, it can't be!' All this sort of thing and how I felt when she was stiff and I had to really literally bend her legs back to put her nappy on. I said to them, 'It's really jolly hard to do.'

(Joy, Interview 2, 12/92)

Joy said there was silence as she told this story. I too was stunned when I heard it. She thought the quietness meant they were not involved, but the evaluations the students filled in showed that they were totally involved, but not talking. The 'not talking' phenomenon was to be experienced by other teachers. A year later when the course was taught again to a new Year 11, Grant had the same experience. He had not been involved the previous year, but he also spontaneously drew upon his personal experience in his teaching. His group were quiet, but listening intently as he said to them:

'At times during this session I will talk about things that have happened in my life, if you want to ask questions about them, let me finish and then ask them.' That's what I said to the kids. I also said, 'There will be times when I need to talk about that to help you people. If you think I'm forcing something on you let me know please, and stop me.'

(Grant, Interview 5, 9/93)

Grant told them about the sudden death of his best friend's wife and about crying at the funeral. Students listened quietly, but Grant believed they were still involved. I asked what he thought was going through their heads. He replied:

This person's real. (*Pause*) Maybe it is okay to cry, maybe there IS (*Grant's emphasis*) nothing wrong with crying. Here's a person (this is a self-perception of me in this school), here is a person who is seen to be friendly to every child in the school, spilling out a personal experience of himself, telling US (*Grant's emphasis*) he has actually cried, when we have never seen him cry. But telling us of a time when he has. Those sorts of things I think probably went through their head. I think they were, not happy, happy is the wrong word, they had that sense of feeling fine in themselves because this man spoke about something that was really an important event in his life.

(Grant, Interview 5, 9/93)

During a follow-up interview I pressed Grant to explain to me what he meant by 'feeling fine in themselves because this man spoke about something that was really an important event in his life'. His response was an exposition of his philosophy of teaching Personal Development and Health Education – using personal experience; and what he sees as the purposes of that teaching – to open up values debates for students:

Grant   Because I want the kids in this school to know that here is a man who can talk about himself, about his feelings and I want to be the person who can use himself as an example.

Louise   Some people would say that is not what schools are about.

Grant   They might. I believe that I took on that role to use my skills as a human being, my skills as a teacher to do the best job I could. In dealing with things like this I think you can do a lot in opening up your own values and beliefs and use some examples from within your life, because after all that is what we are asking the kids to do a lot of in Personal Development and Health Education. To open up their own values and be able to talk about them. So how can I require that of them if I am not prepared to do the same back?

Louise   It is interesting that you separate out human being and teacher.

Grant   Let me say it another way. I am using my skills as a human being plus my skills as a teacher to put that course together.

(Grant, Interview 6, 12/93)

Another teacher echoed the idea of interaction of the teacher as a person and the process of teaching in the area of grief and other sensitive areas:

There is that personal element because you are talking about people and about the way people change and develop and the way they react to situations, thinking about things on a personal level. These type of areas do that. A lot of the things I have done in grief education and drug and alcohol, it makes you have a step back and think about yourself and your reactions and interactions.

(Gail, Interview 3, 12/92)

But not all teachers felt comfortable with self-disclosure or disclosure by the students. Pam questioned the need for it:

I don't really think it has to be big. I got the impression from some of them that it had to be really delving and have tears and really like an absolving sort of thing. That to me is not really what I wanted and if the kids want to come up later and say something to you, fine. But I think it is more of just a general awareness type of thing and what some of us go through and what type of counselling goes on.

(Pam, Interview 1, 12/92)

Pam was teaching in the first course with Year 11 in 1992. She too had a small group of 15. She said: 'I was on the same level as them. I'd never had anyone really close to me die.' But later she described how she was surprised at the experiences the students had spoken about in the group.

It showed that she was not on the same level as the students, as she had presumed. In her account of her teaching session the students seemed to have avoided personal disclosure about feelings and Pam was uncertain of the need for it, as this exchange indicates:

Pam	It's amazing how many of them have had experiences.
Louise	What sort of experiences?
Pam	Horrific things . . . fishing a head out of a river and three of them, their teacher had a heart attack while teaching them judo.
Louise	Did they talk about it?
Pam	Not a lot. I let them say as much as they wanted. The boy who gave the example (*of the judo teacher*) was talking about his parents separating. He was the only one who identified that as a loss whereas others were thinking of grandma dying and that. But I just let them go, I didn't want to delve, I didn't know actually whether you need to or not, I didn't get deep. I sort of touched on a few different things I suppose and didn't say – now how did you feel? I didn't carry it on too much . . . One girl was a little teary-eyed when we were talking about another girl killed this year. I knew that she had been close to her. I just let them go . . . I was all new to me and I don't know . . . I was a bit worried about it being last session of the day. Reading some of the notes I was getting a bit sad myself about it. To me it was fairly interesting that most of them had had someone fairly close to them die or some pretty horrific things, you know for 16-year-olds . . . We discussed funerals and I could not see anyone withdrawing from it.

Louise   And you had expected that?

Pam   Yes. I guess I imagined them saying: 'What's it got to do with us!' Because at that age I might have been a bit like that.

                                                        (Pam, Interview 1, 12/92)

An overall evaluation was conducted for all the Year 11 groups who participated in the course in 1992. On their evaluation forms they stated that they believed it was valuable to talk about grief.

The following are a representative selection of the range of comments:

I was pleased we talked about a variety of topics especially death as it helped me understand about death and how we can cope with our grief and others' grief.

I was surprised to see how easy it was to talk about things that hurt.

I was surprised that someone else had the same problem as me and made me feel 'normal'.

I was surprised that we did talk about death but it was a good topic, although it isn't a nice thought though.

The last comment highlights the ambivalence echoed by other students: 'They didn't like doing it but felt they needed it.' Being divided into small groups of 15 influenced students' reactions. They reported experiencing trust in this environment and recognized how important trust was to the topics they were discussing:

How we brought all the chairs in and made a smaller circle. I thought that was really good.

                                                        (Tessa)

There was an atmosphere of giving in that group because everyone was sharing and you think 'Hell I'm going to!'

                                                        (Simon)

At least the opportunity was there because right at the beginning they said you can share anything, but at least knowing that you could and there was someone there to listen to you if you needed to, that was good.

                                                        (Beth)

The openness because I don't usually talk to people about my problems. I just felt free to talk about things on the day. I don't normally do that.

                                            (Dot) (group interview 1, Year 11)

Also found to be a valuable teaching strategy was a 'buddy' system, having students talk about the exercises with one other student rather than having a whole-class discussion. This allowed them to participate in the sharing of opinions and experiences with a peer.

The Year 11 students acknowledged the value of the whole Personal Development and Health Education course:

We have to have mechanisms for coping with problems. You have to have

your network of friends to help you with problems, you have to have all
that. It's not going to do you any good if you've got a wonderful mark in
3 Unit Maths if your personal life is totally ruined, because you did not
deal with a problem properly. It's balance.

(Tessa)

So that you are more aware of them, so that you can deal with other
losses, so that you know the process you have gone through. It's important to talk about those sort of things because it makes you not forget,
that is, not brush it aside. Also it stops you from saying 'I won't think
about that' and push it down. The more you push those sort of things
down the harder you find it.

(Beth)

Emotional well-being. Stuff you wouldn't talk to your parents about at
home, like I wouldn't talk to my parents about AIDS probably. It's better
with the teacher and your friends.

(Simon)
(group interview 1, Year 11, 9/92)

Simon made the distinction between talking to his parents 'They always try
to tell me how to feel and I don't like that!' and the discussion in the group:
'People in the group were not trying to tell me how to feel, they were
saying "There are variations in how you feel and it is okay to feel like that."'

Students like Simon valued the openness in discussions with teachers
and recognized that they were different to discussions he might have with
his parents.

Teachers saw that teaching about loss and grief and supporting grieving
adolescents was a natural part of their professional role. Harry explained
this by saying:

I don't see it as something that is beyond what I do as a teacher. I think
it is because so much of what you do in teaching relates to the well-being
of the student . . . So in the context of what I do as a teacher, relating to
the students so that they can feel confident in their learning, requires
understanding of the students and being prepared to accept them as they
are and move on from there. To me the welfare component of what you
do in the school is more important because without getting the support
for the kids right, then you are not going to succeed in terms of your
educational goals.

(Harry, Interview 5, 9/93)

It was through teaching about loss and grief that Harry was able to explain
his philosophy of his teaching life.

CONCLUSIONS

These brief descriptions about the learning experiences and the
teacher/student interactions demonstrate that including loss and grief in
the curriculum can serve both to intervene to support grieving young
people and act in a preventive way, by information exchange and positive
attitude formation for handling experiences. The accounts not only give

insight into teaching in this sensitive area and the students' experiences, but also highlight the use of self-disclosure by teachers as a teaching strategy. But this personal disclosure involved risk. Teacher self-disclosure about other sensitive issues such as sexuality and drugs has moral and legal implications and is usually avoided. But it is different in the area of grief, where the risk to teachers is more likely to involve leaving themselves open to ridicule by students and risking their professional image. Teachers in this study consistently used their personal experience when teaching about grief or counselling grieving students. They felt a personal connection between themselves and their students was important.

Respect was a characteristic of these interactions: the teachers for the students in trusting the students' handling of the personal information; and the students for the teachers in that students saw the teachers' disclosures as evidence of their 'being human'. For students, personal connections with teachers were very important in that they helped to make students feel like individuals rather than just one of many people in a school. The self-disclosure by teachers was seen as natural behaviour. Their day-to-day work is about finding ways to help young people understand academic topics. Teachers in the research schools stated that in their personal development type of lesson they were trying to teach about life, so they naturally went to their own life experiences for examples, to make it concrete.

A possible conflict exists here with existing recommendations in the literature on grief counselling (Worden, 1991). Those in a supporting/counselling role are cautioned about the use of their own experience, so that it is not interpreted as a prescriptive way to grieve and they are not using the situation to work through their own grief. But schools are different environments to the normal counselling situation. Relationships already exist between students and teachers. In schools, young people are continually looking to adults in the environment for models of behaviour. In sharing their experiences the teachers modelled ways of behaving (being open and honest) and attitudes to the expression of feelings (it is all right to cry and talk about feelings). The students also appreciated learning about how other people, particularly their peers, have coped. They reported that it gave them models of ways of behaving.

Teachers were careful not to suggest that their behaviour should be a model for the students, but used their experience as a springboard for the students' own discussions. But there could be risks in this for teachers' well-being. Teachers also need to guard against using the learning environment as a way of working through their own grief, although being able to talk openly about one's loss can be healing. That is, teachers need to consider carefully their readiness, emotionally and content-wise, to teach in this area. From a mental health perspective, for students in this study talking about loss and people's different ways of reacting and coping did provide for them some degree of mastery of these life events. Discussions with peers, hearing about other's experiences in the formal education sessions and considering how they would react provided vicarious experience for them. Additionally, this knowledge enabled them to be supportive to their peers, because they understood their peers' reactions. Despite these positive aspects students were ambivalent about the lessons, not liking them, but accepting their importance in helping them with their current and future life experiences.

In confronting loss experiences, students' view of life – their 'spirituality' (in a broad non-religious sense) – was challenged. Their security was threatened, their control of life shaken and a challenge made to the coherence between their experience and their beliefs. Confronting loss was a stimulus to spiritual development.

The teaching about loss and grief, because of its brevity in the research schools, did not include teaching supportive skills. The value of this aspect of the curriculum, whilst recommended (Glassock and Rowling, 1991), has not been explored.

In conclusion, the link between the importance of education for students' personal and social needs and topics such as loss and grief was very clear in some teachers' minds. It was articulated by their reflections during the research, as their philosophy of education. They also learnt more about their teaching lives. Some students' spiritual beliefs were challenged. They learnt more about themselves and how to cope with future life transitions.

REFERENCES

Balding, J. and Shelley, C. (1993) *Very Young People in 1991–1992. Primary Health-related Behaviour Questionnaire Results*. Exeter: Exeter University Press.

Board of Studies (1991) *Personal Development, Health and Physical Education Years 7–10: Support Document*. North Sydney: New South Wales Board of Studies.

Children's Society (1992) *Divorce and Children*. London: Children's Society.

Dyregrov, A. (1991). *Grief in Children: A Handbook for Adults*. London: Jessica Kingsley.

Eddy, J. M. and Alles, W. F. (1983) *Death Education*. St Louis: C. V. Mosby.

Glassock, G. and Rowling, L. (1992) *Learning to Grieve: Life Skills for Coping with Losses*. Newtown: Millennium Press.

Grollman, E. (1967) *Explaining Death to Children*. Boston: Beacon Press.

Heinecke, R. and Spence, R. (1991) Children and loss: a proactive model for schools. Paper presented at Third International Conference on Grief and Bereavement, Sydney, New South Wales, July.

Hopson, B. and Scally, M. (1980) *Lifeskills Teaching Program*. Leeds: Lifeskills Associates.

LaGrande, L. E. (1988) *Changing Patterns of Human Existence: Assumptions, Beliefs and Coping with the Stress of Change*. Springfield, IL: Charles C. Thomas.

Leviton, D. (1971) The need for education on death and suicide. *Journal of School Health*, **39**, 270–4.

Parkes, C. M. (1988) Bereavement as a psychosocial transition: processes of adaptation to change. *Journal of Social Issues*, **44** (3), 53–65.

Plant, S. and Stoate, P. (1989) *Loss and Change: Resources for Use in Personal and Social Education Programmes*. Exeter: Pergamon Press.

Raphael, B. (1985) *Anatomy of Bereavement*. London: Hutchinson.

Rowling, L. (1991). The health promoting school: a supportive social context for sensitive health issues. In B. Brunn Jensen (ed.), *Action on School Health*. Proceedings of the Satellite Congress, Copenhagen, Denmark, June.

Rowling, L. (1993) Schools and grief: a comparison between New South Wales and the United States. Paper presented at the Biennial Conference of National Association of Loss and Grief. Yeppoon, Queensland, September.

Smilansky, S. (1987) *On Death: Helping Children Understand and Cope*. New York: Peter Lang.

Wagner, P. (1993) *Children and Bereavement, Death and Loss: What Can the School Do?* Coventry: NAPCE Base.

Ward, B. and Houghton, P. (1988) *Good Grief: Talking and Learning about Loss and Death*. London: Jessica Kingsley.

Wass, H. Miller, M.D. and Thornton, G. (1990) Death education: grief/suicide intervention in public schools. *Death Studies*, **14**, 253–68.

Weekes, D. and Johnson, C. (1992) A second decade of high school death education. *Death Studies*, **16**(3), 269–79.

Worden, W. (1991) *Grief Counselling and Grief Therapy*, 2nd edn. New York: Springer.

Yule, W. and Gold, A. (1993) *Wise before the Event: Coping with Crises in Schools*. London: Calouste Gulbenkian Foundation.

Zisook, S. (ed.) (1987) *Biopsychosocial Aspects of Bereavement*. Washington, DC: American Psychiatric Press.

CHAPTER 21

Developing spiritual, moral and social values through a citizenship programme for primary schools

Don Rowe

INTRODUCTION

This chapter will introduce readers to the Citizenship Foundation's Primary Citizenship Project, the materials from which were published under the title *You, Me, Us!* (Rowe and Newton, 1994). The project was made possible by a two-year Home Office grant to develop a pack of materials to support the development of social and moral responsibility within the primary curriculum. The project aimed to explore and develop approaches which could encourage the children to become more aware of the complexities of the moral dimension underlying familiar moral issues such as the making and keeping of rules, being kind or unkind to others, stealing or caring for the environment. In view of the lack of a strong tradition of moral education in English schools, the project set itself the task of developing highly supportive materials which would be appealing to general teachers, engaging for children and, above all, would contribute to the long-term development of confident, competent, morally-aware citizens.

The Citizenship Foundation was founded in 1989 to continue and extend the work of the secondary-focused Law in Education Projects (Rowe and Thorpe, 1989 and 1993). The primary project provided an opportunity to develop a curriculum for younger pupils based on the same key concepts (see below). This can therefore be seen as the culmination of ten years of development work, putting in place a continuous and progressive citizenship programme for all key stages (Rowe, 1992). To some eyes the project might appear to have been more of a short-term response to rapidly increasing government and public anxiety about the civic and moral education of children (epitomized by the huge outpouring of anxiety over the murder of 2-year-old James Bulger by two 10-year-old boys) and the announcement that schools' policies for spiritual, moral, social and cultural development would be subject to OFSTED inspection (OFSTED, 1993).

CITIZENSHIP AND THE DEVELOPMENT OF SPIRITUAL AND MORAL VALUES

Traditionally, education for citizenship (or civic education) was closely identified with teaching about constitutional rights and structures. This was true in the UK, the United States, France and elsewhere in Europe and this model of constitutional civic education is still very influential. It has, however, been criticized by many (Davies, 1993, p. 165) as failing to address the key issue of motivation. Knowledge of the parliamentary processes alone will do nothing to encourage pro-social attitudes or reduce juvenile offending. Citizenship education therefore must adopt a fuller, multi-dimensional model in which knowledge and understanding develop alongside values and attitudes. This was spelt out in the government's own guidelines on citizenship education (NCC, 1990). Citizens are first and foremost moral agents, acting in the public arena according to their own spiritual and moral values, whether these be selfish, altruistic, religious or humanitarian. Thus the Primary Citizenship Project placed importance on helping children see citizenship issues (such as bullying, stealing or making rules) as shot through with interconnected and often conflicting value issues which can be subjected to critical enquiry. One of the project's central aims therefore was to develop these skills of enquiry and encourage a proclivity towards the rational justification of behaviour.

There has, of course, long been uncertainty about how to deal with moral and social values in the classroom. Wilson (1990), for example, has suggested that a number of significant psychological reasons may underlie teachers' reluctance to engage in the kind of education which is based more on reason than authority. He also points out that many conceptual confusions have hindered progress. Confusions also exist over the aims of citizenship education (Rowe, 1994), concerning whose values are to be promoted and what 'good' or desirable citizenship actually amounts to.

All aspects of mature citizenship have their roots in the early development of the child and therefore citizenship education should begin as soon as the child develops its first ideas about how the world works. There is no case for suggesting that citizenship issues do not enter the experience of primary children nor for arguing that they do not naturally reflect on what happens to them as individuals or as members of different communities. The task of the school, therefore, is to engage with and extend this spontaneous reflection as the children become increasingly aware of the complexities of their moral lives.

The project's strong emphasis on the need to develop children's personal skills of thought and analysis should be set in the context of what I would describe as 'democratic dialogue'. Democratic dialogue is essential to the socially-engaged citizen and is characterized by a number of basic assumptions including:

- the existence of a set of core values rooted in notions of respect for persons and freedom of belief;
- the universality of these core values such that no one person or group in the democratic community can claim their rights as *a priori* more

important than anyone else's;
- respect for differences of values, beliefs and insights where these do not impinge on the core values; social and moral values may be based on, or influenced by, underlying spiritual insights concerning, for example, the purpose of human existence or the nature of divine law;
- the understanding that views may be challenged, for example, on grounds of intelligibility, truth and relevance (see Haydon, 1993, p. 18);
- the belief that common solutions are desirable where problems are faced by the community as a whole;
- the view that shared insights and decisions can be broader, more adequate and more caring when these are based on respectful, thoughtful dialogue in which everyone has had a chance to participate.

CONSTRUCTING A CITIZENSHIP CURRICULUM

Many areas of legitimate disagreement are possible within the framework of democratic dialogue and therefore the citizenship curriculum should contribute to pupils' understanding of the relevant contested concepts. In a democracy citizens differ both in their understanding of concepts such as equality and in their beliefs about the social policies which flow from these different interpretations. The project came to the view that the most fundamental of these contested concepts were *justice, rights, responsibilities*, with *power* and *authority*, *rules* and *laws*, *equality* and *diversity*, *freedom* and *constraint*, *individual* and *community* being contingent on the first three. In other words, a citizenship issue is likely to involve questions of fairness, rights or responsibilities and other concepts may well be addressed also. Five units of materials were developed around the themes of *Friendship, Rules, Property and Power, Community and Environment* and *Respecting Differences*, because these themes brought to the fore many issues commonly encountered by the children in their daily lives. Material was developed to enable each theme to be dealt with in both key stages so that the concepts can be introduced early and revisited at a later date at more complex levels. For example, in the environment unit, key stage 1 children consider the value of making useful things out of rubbish, whilst in key stage 2 the much more complex moral obligation of individuals to care for the school environment as a shared resource is considered.

In addressing the question of precisely how teachers should engage children in moral enquiry, the project has drawn on significant recent developments in theory and practice to develop a three-fold pedagogical model, emphasizing the distinctive contributions of (a) moral reasoning, (b) philosophical enquiry and (c) the development of empathy and a sense of community. I would argue that this approach provides the conceptual clarity for teachers to draw on each of these models in turn during each session. This is not to argue that they are exclusive of each other but it is certainly to make the claim that *much can be gained from being aware of the distinct purposes of these three models and adjusting the organization of the learning situation appropriately, to maximize the effectiveness of each.*

Moral reasoning

The primary project recognizes the complex nature of moral reflection. John Wilson (1990) has argued that it can be broken down into different elements including

- being able to draw on concepts such as 'person' and 'justice' and being motivated to act in accordance with them;
- being able to recognize the influence of conscious and unconscious feelings;
- being able to identify relevant facts including knowing how to act in moral contexts;
- being able to bring the preceding elements together in the process of decision-making.

Although Wilson's own position is a good deal more complex than this (many would feel too complex for practical purposes) his analysis is helpful in emphasizing the importance of detailed analysis before coming to any conclusions. However, a significant problem with Wilson's 'lateral' model is that it describes only the mature moral decision-making process and this presents difficulties for teachers working with less than mature reasoners who, for example, have little ability to empathize with others or think in terms of abstract principles. For this reason, the project took the view that the developmental perspective, associated particularly with Kohlberg's moral stage theory, was indispensable (see e.g., Colby and Kohlberg, 1987). Though Kohlberg's own claims for his theory (which indicates a maturational progression towards increasingly abstract and pro-social concerns) have been widely disputed in detail, the evidence for the development of sociomoral awareness amongst children is indisputable.

During the project, teachers trialling the materials regularly observed pupils reasoning in ways qualitatively different from their own. For example, the very familiar stance of children regarding severe punishment as the best way to ensure law-abiding behaviour is an example of early-stage reasoning and is based on the belief that all morality is externally imposed. Teachers frequently found pupils in full agreement about the wrongness of an act such as stealing and were then unsure how to move the discussion forward. The development model provides a way out of this apparent impasse because it highlights the fact that law-abiding (or 'good') behaviour may still be immature, in terms of its egocentricity and lack of concern for others. Consider the reasons against stealing given me by the 10-year-olds in this example:

DR   *Can we think of all the reasons why it might be wrong to steal?*

Pupil   You might get caught and all your friends might tell on you.

Pupil   If you're going to steal and someone sees you, they might tell the police and you'll get into even worse trouble.

Pupil   You won't go to Heaven, you'll go to Hell.

Pupil   It's better not to steal, you'll just get into trouble and it's better not to.

Pupil   You'll get a police record and if you're old enough you'll get put in jail.

DR	*You've given me lots of reasons about why it's better for yourselves but what about the effects on other people?*
Pupil	Well, if one person goes in and steals, the others might think it's cool and they'll go on stealing and then even more people will go stealing.
Pupil	If you're caught stealing and they tell your mum, you might get grounded for two weeks or one.
DR	*What other effect might it have on your mum?*
Pupil	She'll be cross.
Pupil	She might be upset her daughter's turning into a bad person.
Pupil	And she might think she's been a bad mother.
Pupil	She might be upset because when she goes into a shop people might think she's going to steal from them.
Pupil	Her mum might have to pay back some money.
Pupil	Her mum might feel guilty and embarrassed about their son or daughter's going round stealing things.
Pupil	She would be astonished.
DR	*But what about the people you're stealing from? No one has mentioned that. No one has worried about the people who have had something stolen.*
Pupil	If they've trusted you for years, they might be surprised and they might feel shocked.
Pupil	If you go into a shop and steal and tell your friends, they might think it's a good idea and they might go into a shop and the shopkeeper might catch them and he or she gets into lots of trouble and her mum or dad might feel really angry.
Pupil	That happened to me once. I went into a shop with my mate and I was looking at some sweets and bought them and when we got out of the shop, he opened his coat and said, 'Look, I've stolen two Wispas' and I got into a lot of trouble for it.

Notice that the technique of probing the reason for the children's opinions unlocks a whole new range of issues to discuss. Although almost all of the responses in the example had an element of egocentrism, some of the answers displayed greater awareness of others and these can be reinforced by the teacher asking children to consider them further. In this way, the teacher operates at or just beyond the children's developmental level, which research confirms (e.g. Blatt and Kohlberg, 1975) is the most effective way to encourage progress towards maturity. Lickona (1991, p. 246) quotes another study by Colby, Kohlberg, Gibbs and Lieberman comparing different teaching techniques in classes where dilemma discussions had produced varying results. The one technique characteristic of all classes where the children made gains in moral reasoning was the repeated use of the question 'why?'. The method alerts children to the fact that moral reasons which have 'others' or 'the whole group' as their focus of concern must be considered if moral judgements are to be as fair as possible.

The project materials present moral situations where the right course of action will be in dispute and where different levels of analysis are possible. The problem might, for example, demand the consideration of individual rights, the duty to obey laws or rules, the extent of obligations towards others, the intentions of the actors and so on. One of the stories for Key Stage 2 (*Wild Life*, pp. 207–14) focuses on an act of vandalism against a school pond by a boy called Anthony. Anthony is a slow learner who feels alienated from the class and despised by many of the children. In an angry outburst, provoked by a supercilious child, Anthony hits someone and then seriously pollutes the school pond with engine oil, killing two fish. He only realizes the seriousness of what he has done when he is later shown kindness and understanding by one of the girls in the class. In this particular story the demands of justice and care – two different sources of moral motivation – are in conflict and the issues surrounding what should happen to Anthony and who was responsible for his behaviour are enough to provoke thoughtful discussion from adults, let alone children. During the trials of this material, the children in one class were so angry at the way Anthony had been treated that they could not bring themselves to say he had been wrong to pollute the pond. This worried the teacher, who wanted a round condemnation of the sin (though not the sinner), but the children's stance simply showed their lack of maturity in not yet forming a coherent and integrated resolution. The fact that the children were able to empathize with Anthony and consider his intentions helped them get well beyond the lower-stage responses to the situation. The very act of analysing situations from various standpoints contrasts with much of the morally superficial material children encounter, where the message of the story is clear, duty and virtue are always rewarded and people are either wholly good or wholly bad.

Despite the fact that such dilemmas were found challenging, teachers reported that the children relished the opportunity for serious discussion. Over a period of weeks, they showed marked improvements in their ability to listen and respond thoughtfully to each other. Towards the end of the trials, two Year 6 classes were tested for moral reasoning and empathy compared with matched classes which had not been exposed to the materials. Using the *Sociomoral Reflection Measure* (Gibbs et al., 1992), Seery (1994) found in both cases the reasoning of the taught classes was markedly more mature than that of the control groups.

Wilson (1990), in analysing personal moral reflection, demonstrates the vital nature of the social context in which it takes place:

> The child learns to wean himself from the merely autistic [egocentric, isolated] expression of his own feelings, or the equally autistic fear of saying anything at all, and to take part in a kind of public game with rules and procedures of its own. He has to submit himself to criticism, not mind too much about making a fool of himself, attend to the meanings of the words he uses, make some respectable connection between what he feels and what can truthfully or sensibly be said, exercise tact and tolerance towards others, not become too angry, not take criticism personally, stick to the point, face the facts, keep the rules of logic and so forth.

(p. 42)

This passage, in fact, highlights many of the skills, attitudes and values which should be systematically developed within the citizenship community of enquiry. For such trust and confidence to be established, the rules of the community need to be spelt out clearly and reinforced consistently.

Philosophical enquiry

The model of the class as a *community of enquiry* is gaining widespread acceptance and owes its popularity to the work of the philosopher Matthew Lipman (1980) who has pioneered the concept of *Philosophy for Children*. This has great potential for the citizenship curriculum, which is founded, as we have seen, on contested concepts which have exercised philosophers for centuries. For this reason the project suggests that teachers, having examined the moral aspects of a problem, encourage more open-ended philosophical enquiry into those broader spiritual and moral values which underlie much citizenship discourse. This would involve reflecting on questions such as what we mean by 'good' and what it is that makes it good. This approach is very much in line with OFSTED's (1993) criteria for spiritual development defined as reflection on aspects of daily life and the human condition. The concept of the 'community of enquiry', when applied to moral and spiritual values, underlines the importance of mutual support in the moral life, the quest for truth or enlightenment and the need to search for common ground at the same time as respecting differences of value and belief. Lipman's model also recommended itself because of indications that it can be effective in the development of greater tolerance and respect towards others (an essential attribute of the democratic citizen). Lake (1987) experimented with a year group of ten-year-olds, offering one-third the experience of a philosophy session twice a week, whilst the others followed a cognitive skills enhancement course, singly or in groups. One of the striking and unexpected gains made by the philosophy group was a marked reduction in aggressive behaviour compared with that of the other two groups.

Lipman stresses the importance of equality of status for all members of the community of enquiry. Everyone's beliefs and opinions are sought and respected and no one value-system can claim pre-eminence without justification. This approach emphasizes that the children should be asked to raise issues of concern to themselves and not merely respond to the teacher's agenda. During the trials, several teachers expressed surprise that the preoccupations of the children were different from what they imagined them to be. This would not have emerged in heavily teacher-directed lessons.

Lipman advocates the use of narrative to present a wide range of issues to stimulate children's reflective thinking. Narrative is a universal medium for the transmission of spiritual, moral, social and cultural values because of the way in which it embeds abstract concepts in the realities of the human experience. Narrative also has the strength of being able to draw on the affective as well as the cognitive domain (Vitz, 1990), which is an area where Kohlberg's model is weak.

Empathy development

The development of *empathy* is seen to be vital to a holistic approach to moral discourse. Gibbs (1991), drawing on the work of Hoffman, has attempted a valuable integration of the cognitive with the affective within moral discourse. Whilst the perception that something is unjust is a spur to moral action, many would see our basic biological drive towards empathic identification with others as even more influential in pro-social behaviour. Many studies, including that of Seery (1994), show positive correlations between empathy and pro-social behaviour.

The development of citizens who are sensitive to the needs of others is essential to a healthy and cohesive society. As in cognitive awareness, our innate empathic capabilities have to be nurtured. Young children have very little awareness of how other people think or feel. This awareness develops as the child's emotional and intellectual powers grow. The first step is doubtless for the child to recognize his or her own feelings and then to appreciate that other people experience similar emotions such that it becomes possible to say 'I know what that feels like'.

The development of empathy has, perhaps, been thought of as being learned largely through experience and therefore as more appropriately nurtured via the school's ethos of respect and care. However, during the Primary Citizenship Project it became increasingly clear that empathy can develop in response to the feelings and experiences of others and the growing feeling of 'connectedness'. Thus children who are bullies, who steal, tell lies or break promises can be exposed to the feelings of children in the class who have been the objects of such behaviour. The building of a mutually supportive community encourages social bonding and trust, enabling children to recognize and express their feelings. This is especially valuable for those children who are not encouraged to do so at home.

Community building also occurs in the tackling of shared problems as a whole group. Whether this is an outbreak of stealing or an untidy playground, by placing this problem in the hands of the community, the teacher acknowledges that everyone can be part of the solution. This sense of inclusion is central to the development of a sense of social responsibility and offers a balancing experience for many children alienated from school by academic failure and negative labelling. Within the community of the class they are equal members and are embraced as the community shares responsibility and searches for common solutions.

I have written in this chapter of a three-fold pedagogical model and argued that each part integrates well into the other two. For this reason, it has not been found difficult to implement in practice, although in the early stages the trial materials did not spell out the importance of the empathy model. The trials of the project material in over forty schools highlighted weaknesses in the draft materials for both pupils and teachers. In particular, teachers requested more detailed guidance on structuring discussions into small-group and plenary sessions. It is not necessary for every session to be spent in whole-group discussion since such discussions inevitably place less articulate and confident children at a disadvantage. Small-group preparatory exercises can help all children to come back to the whole group with something to say.

I have referred to the positive results of Seery's (1994) study into the moral reasoning of children who had used the project's materials. This research continues but the long-term success of the project's approach will be shown by the willingness of teachers to integrate it into their whole school policies for behaviour and social responsibility. Certainly, our experience has been of a profession willing to engage with issues which are causing increasing concern. As one teacher put it:

> We feel, with regret, that behaviours which were once only observed in secondary education are now becoming more familiar in the primary sector . . . [This is] a difficult, abstract area for the children to feel free to discuss without an initiative being used in the first instance.

REFERENCES

Blatt, M. and Kohlberg, L. (1975) The effects of classroom moral discussion upon children's level of moral judgement. *Journal of Moral Education*, **4**, 129–63.

Colby, A. and Kohlberg, L. (1987) *The Measurement of Moral Judgement* vols 1 and 2. New York: Cambridge University Press.

Davies, I. (1993) Teaching political understanding in secondary schools. *Curriculum*, **14** (3).

Gibbs, J., Basinger, K. and Fuller, D. (1992) *Moral Maturity: Measuring the Development of Sociomoral Reflection*. Hillsdale, NJ: Erlbaum.

Haydon, G. (1993) *Education and the Crisis in Values: Should We Be Philosophical about It?* London: The Tufnell Press.

Lake, M. (1987) 'Thinking skills in the middle school.' Unpublished MPhil. thesis, Cranfield Institute of Technology.

Lickona, T. (1991) *Educating for Character: How Our Schools Can Teach Respect and Responsibility*. New York: Bantam Books.

Lipman, M., Sharp, A. M. and Oscanyan, F. S. (1980) *Philosophy in the Classroom*. Philadelphia: Temple University Press.

National Curriculum Council (1990) *Curriculum Guidance 8: Education for Citizenship*. York: NCC.

OFSTED (1993) (revised May 1994) *Handbook for the Inspection of Schools*. London: HMSO.

Rowe, D. (1992) The citizen as a moral agent: the development of a continuous and progressive conflict-based citizenship curriculum. *Curriculum*, **13** (3), 178–87.

Rowe, D. and Newton, J. (eds) (1994) *You, Me, Us! Social and Moral Responsibility for Primary Schools*. London: The Home Office.

Rowe, D. and Thorpe, T. (eds) (1989) *Understand the Law*, vols 1–4. London: Hodder & Stoughton.

Rowe, D. and Thorpe, T. (eds) (1993) *Living with the Law*, vols 1–3. London: Hodder & Stoughton.

Seery, G. (1994) 'Can virtue be taught?' Unpublished research thesis, Oxford Brookes University.

Vitz, Paul C. (1990) The use of stories in moral development: new psychological reasons for an old education method. *American Psychologist*, **45** (6), 709–20.

Wilson, J. (1990) *A New Introduction to Moral Education*. London: Cassell Education.

CHAPTER 22

Can the denominational sector offer a paradigm in RE?

Bernard Stuart

INTRODUCTION

Any question concerning religious education in schools is linked, to a greater or lesser extent, to a consideration of the 'local' community and the education system to which the schools belong. In this essay I shall refer generally to the denominational sector of education and, in particular, to the denomination of which I have some little knowledge – namely, the Roman Catholic one. I do so in the belief that a group within a system, in this case the educational system, can provide an example for the whole. I also believe that references in this chapter to Roman Catholic and denominational are, in general, interchangeable and of equal application.

THE CONTEXT

Addressing a conference in Cambridge in July 1993, Albert Price, Director of the Catholic Education Service, is reported in a *Universe* article entitled 'Catholic Schools' as having said:

> The partnership of Voluntary schools with the State in the dual system, though at times a troublesome matter, is more than a partnership of convenience – it is a unique arrangement with an enormous but as yet unrealized potential.
>
> *(The Universe*, 25 July 1993)

The dual system involves a unique partnership in education between Church and State. Church schools exist and receive state funding. By paying a substantial part of the costs of providing the schools, church authorities retain a decisive control in the running of the schools but as part of the national system these same schools are responsible to the State for maintaining adequate educational standards.

Price went on to say,

> In the professional sphere the Church school should help to remind the State that it is bound to all citizens by principles of ethical justice when

deciding educational policy and by principles of distributive justice when allocating resources . . . and the companionship of the State should help remind the Church school that the majority of the schools in this country are secular. Secular schools are not an inferior alternative to be rejected by the Church. They are a large and important part of the public service through which God can and does work. They deserve and need the support and concern of the Church.

(The Universe, 25 July 1993)

Nevertheless, the Catholic community is right to have some general expectation of these schools. The expectations should not be exaggerated or unreal, and have something to do with helping to give children a firm grounding in the Catholic faith.

Both religious education and catechesis are concerned with a comprehensive and systematic consideration of the whole mystery of Christ and to explore and be challenged by this mystery is the source of the authentic growth of the child. The Catholic school's religious education programme will therefore include, at the very least, planning for the possibility of catechesis. In other words, it has a part to play in the faith-formation of children and young adults. This has no possibility of success without the active involvement of parents and the caring and welcoming support of the parish community. Therefore, it is important to take seriously the interrelationship of home, parish and school within any wider RE programme.

There are three main grounds for retaining denominational schools and the dual system. These are that

● they provide specific religious instruction;
● they have a distinctive ethos;
● they promote the unity of education.

The religious education offered in Catholic schools is the combined effort of all three, and this demands a whole-school approach. The denominational school, therefore, has a role within the dual system. All schools are public institutions and so are accountable to society for their work. In the case of maintained schools, this means that they are answerable to the LEA and the DFEE. For aided Catholic schools it is more complicated: they are accountable both to these authorities and to the Church; they have a dual accountability. Although religious education in Catholic schools is exempt from the control and inspection of the public authorities, it cannot remain unaffected by the general educational demands made on schools by the State. At the same time, given the principle of dual accountability, it must remain faithful to the valid educational expectations of the Catholic community. It is in holding together these two sets of requirements that religious education in Catholic schools will realize its distinctive potential and display its specific strength.

These comments, while specifically 'Catholic', would appear to be significant for the entire voluntary sector within the educational system.

A CATHOLIC PERSPECTIVE

In their *Low Week Statement of 1989* the Roman Catholic bishops of England and Wales pointed to a whole-school religious approach:

> The whole curriculum and way of life of the Catholic school is designed to enable its pupils to grow in every way to Christian maturity. The Catholicism of the school is more than its religious education programme; its whole curriculum must be rooted in a religious under-standing of life, and its life should be based on the Gospel.
>
> (Bishops of England and Wales, 1989)

In their *Commentary on the Education Reform Bill* the bishops complained that 'the Bill plays down the importance of Religious Education and fails to include Religious Studies in the core and foundation subjects' (Bishops of England and Wales, 1988). The need for a Catholic school to have a religious education programme which is both distinctive and specific is founded on the belief, as the bishops state in another part of their commentary, that

> Religious Education is not one subject among many but the foundation of the whole educational process. The beliefs and values it communi-cates should inspire and unify every aspect of school life. It should provide the content for, and substantially shape, the school curriculum, and offer living experience of the life of faith in its practical expression. Religious Education is not simply a body of knowledge coterminous with Religious Studies, not merely to be 'fitted in' after time and resources have been allocated to the ten Core and Foundation subjects prescribed by the Bill. Rather it stamps the Catholic school in every aspect of its operations with its distinctive Catholic character.
>
> (Bishops of England and Wales, 1988)

Nearer home, Bishop Kelly, in his paper entitled *Catholic Schools*, spells out the need for the whole [voluntary] school to have a shared vision. He states, 'it would be false to the whole truth to say that subjects can be taught in some neutral fashion with formal religious education offered alongside them' (Kelly, 1985).

Even Parliament seemed to say as much in the *1988 Education Act*. Within the subject timetable of the school, religious education was and is to be seen as an important and integral part of the school's 'balanced and broadly based' curriculum which 'promotes the spiritual, moral, cultural, mental and physical development of the pupils . . . and prepares such pupils for the opportunities, responsibilities and experiences of adult life' (DES, 1988).

Around the same time, Pope John Paul II wrote in his 1988 document entitled *The Religious Dimension of Education in a Catholic School* that 'a school has as its purpose the student's integral formation. Religious instruction, therefore, should be integrated into the objectives and criteria which characterize a modern school' (John Paul II, 1988).

Despite the very different sources of these statements, there appears to be agreement that the RE curriculum should be of a piece with the rest of the curriculum, contributing to the overall personal development of the pupils whether or not they have now, or later, a personal commitment to the Catholic faith or, indeed, will have to any particular faith.

SOME PRINCIPLES

Since RE does not rest on any assumptions about the faith of the pupils, it is important that we should be able to explain its contribution to, and justify its status within, the curriculum in non-faith terms.

Any study of religion must involve the pupil in a way that is both interesting and related to the society which he or she may encounter in adult life. The aim, in general, should be for all pupils to come to the possibility of understanding that RE can, as the Southwark Diocesan REPLACE scheme states, 'help them to understand that religion is a phenomenon that is considered by the wider community as important and therefore worthy of respect and tolerance' (Southwark Diocese, 1991, p. 6). In this it would be hoped that the opportunity to study Catholicism would be seen as worthwhile, indeed, as an experience which would help pupils to understand about God and other religious ideas. Such a study would provide a background to school studies in general and be part of a school's total educational offering.

Religious education must pursue specific, identifiable objectives which are both educational and religious. For RE to be educational, it must be faithful to educational principles and especially sensitive to an understanding of how children and young people learn. It must address and inspire the wholeness of the child and encourage him or her to reach out beyond the factual to the reflective and evaluative objectives of RE. It must accept children and young people where they are, in the moment of their experience, integrity, freedom and abilities.

There are, too, sound reasons for religious education to make use of some elements of the National Curriculum's intentions, language and structure. The principle of continuity and progression across the whole curriculum is no less important for religious education. Indeed, the use of what is good in the National Curriculum could allow religious education to be well planned, to relate to the other subjects and indeed to become the paradigm for the whole curriculum.

A National Curriculum Council report states that,

> Nationally, a large proportion of Agreed Syllabuses used in County schools describe two broad areas of attainment in RE. These are that pupils should:
> – understand the teachings and practices of Christianity and other world religions;
> – be encouraged to develop their own beliefs and values.
> (NCC, 1991, p. 12)

It is by maintaining a balance between these two that RE is generally seen as contributing to the spiritual, moral, cultural and intellectual development of pupils. Most proposed attainment targets in RE reflect these two aspects of development.

The contribution of religious education to the curriculum is the development of those areas of knowledge, skills and attitudes which will help the pupils to understand and appreciate the role of religion in life and behaviour, to help them to clarify their own beliefs, values and attitudes so that they may be able eventually both to reach their own personal decision about the place of religion in their lives and to respect different religious commitments in the lives of others.

In a unique manner religious education enables pupils to reflect on their own needs, experiences and questions, and to confront life's most important questions: Who am I? What is life about? Is one way of living better than another? By helping them to explore religious ways of thinking, believing, valuing, choosing and relating, it expands pupils' ways of looking at the world and their own place in it, and provides them with the means of judging among the vast array of conflicting values and attitudes with which the world confronts them. Religious education thus not only contributes to the preparation of pupils for the opportunities, responsibilities and experiences of adult life, it also opens up a possible spiritual frame of reference within which to face them. By providing children with basic knowledge and the necessary skills for understanding, evaluating and explaining religious topics at various levels – imaginatively, emotionally and intellectually – and for assessing the personal and social, ethical and cultural implications of religious belief, religious education offers to children the motivation and the essential tools for determining their own religious position.

Through religious education our pupils should be trained to acquire gradually a more perfect sense of responsibility in the development of their own lives. They should be prepared to take their part in the life of society in order that they might participate fully in the life of that society. Therefore we should develop in our pupils the ability to make sound moral judgements based on a well-informed conscience and to put them into practice with a sense of personal commitment. In so doing, they should come to know and to love God more perfectly.

Here it is useful to note what was said in the 1977 document *The Catholic School* about the special mission of a voluntary school as 'a privileged place in which, through a living encounter with a cultural inheritance, integral formation occurs' (Sacred Congregation, 1977, p. 12).

The importance of religious education with regard to the overall development of pupils was affirmed by the Department of Education and Science in a document entitled *The School Curriculum*. It noted that

the place of Religious Education in the curriculum and its unique statutory position accord with a widely shared view that the subject has a distinct contribution to make to a pupil's school education. It provides an introduction to the religious and spiritual areas of experience and particularly to the Christian tradition which has profoundly affected our culture. It forms part of the curriculum's concern with personal and social values and can help pupils to understand the religious and cultural diversity of contemporary society.

(DES, 1981, Section 1)

Having given some consideration to the 'educational' purpose of RE, it is important now to consider the 'religious' one.

If RE is to be considered religious in the voluntary school setting, it must be about developing knowledge and understanding of God, Jesus and his Church, the central beliefs which Christians hold and the basis for these beliefs. Developing awareness and appreciation of what and why people believe and the impact of such belief on their behaviour lies at the heart of all religious education. In a denominational school, RE should necessarily include the development of positive attitudes towards, and dialogue with, people of other faiths and denominations. In so doing the Catholic school, as any voluntary-aided school, must pay attention to the nature of the school and the intention of the providing body. In short, religious education must be in accordance with the religious beliefs of the community which originally founded the school (this information can be found in the trust deed of each denominational school). This means that as the overall provision of a Catholic school is education seen as a wholesome endeavour, related to a community's vision and way of life, so its religious education content should be especially related to that community's vision and way of life.

For schools (voluntary, controlled or county) which are not rooted in or committed to any specific religious point of view it may be difficult to determine what ought to be the content of religious education, how it should be selected and organized. However, the study of religion encompasses such vast possibilities that selection is imperative. Varying principles of content selection have resulted in a wide-ranging and contrasting collection of RE programmes, projects and syllabuses.

SOME BENCHMARKS

In 1988 Pope John Paul II's guidelines for reflection and renewal were published under the title of *The Religious Dimensions of Education in a Catholic School* (John Paul II, 1988). It is an essential reference document for any serious discussion of how a Catholic school, as a voluntary school, and its religious education are to do two things: first, reflect a distinctive Catholic (denominational) vision, and, secondly, realize its distinctive nature and its specific strength.

The document goes on to present the task of religious education in a Catholic school as trying 'to convey a sense of the nature of Christianity, and of how Christians are trying to live their lives', and by way of example it offers 'an outline for an organic presentation of the Christian event and the Christian message' (John Paul II, 1988).

Three points raised by this document can be highlighted as significant indicators for any programme of RE within a Catholic or any denominational school.

● In the first place, there can be real conflict between breadth of content and depth of learning. Perhaps more important than trying to cover everything, we must ensure that in those topics that are studied, pupils are given the opportunity to recognize how they radiate from or relate back to central beliefs.

● Second, pupils need time and assistance to explore and to discover, to think through a given religious topic, to relate it to the central vision, to search for other connections, to assess its significance for those who believe it, to express and pursue their own questions, to develop their knowledge and understanding.

● The third point is linked to the fact that there are many aspects and implications of religion that pupils will not encounter until after leaving school. It is important to give pupils the techniques of study of religion and religious issues as an essential element of their continuing religious education.

In *The Easter People* the Catholic Bishops say that our expectations of what can be achieved in religious education in school must be 'realistic'. They go on to say that 'prominent among those things which can be expected of a Catholic school are a knowledge and understanding of the content of the faith, the experience of a Christian caring community, and the experience of a living liturgy' (Bishops of England and Wales, 1980). In Catholic schools, therefore, religious education seeks to offer sound knowledge and understanding of the Catholic faith tradition, through exploring its scriptures, history, theology, liturgy, morality and the witness of some of its outstanding members. It seeks to do this in a manner which will reflect the organic nature of Christianity. And it seeks to foster in pupils the ability to continue their own search. The same might be said for any school within the denominational sector of education.

In a Catholic school not all the pupils may be members of the Catholic Church, not all may be Christians. However, no effort should ever be made to impose the Catholic faith, and the religious freedom and personal conscience of individual pupils must always be respected. At the same time, the Catholic school has a right and duty to provide religious education of a nature and content which is explicitly Christian.

Whilst religious education should not rest on any assumptions about the faith of pupils, and certainly should not seek to impose beliefs and practices on them, it does, nonetheless, make a contribution of great significance to the possibility of their growth in faith. If children do not have a sound knowledge of religion, if they have not developed some measure of understanding and the skills to think through religious issues, they will not be in a position to make real personal decisions about their own faith. Here, the school's religious education may offer the knowledge, understanding and ability to think through religious issues that neither the home nor the parish, let alone the wider community, is equipped to offer.

That religious education in a Catholic school has to be in accordance with the trust deed does not mean that there cannot be any place for the study of other faiths. The expectation expressed by the DES in Circular 3/89, 'that all those concerned with religious education should seek to ensure that it promotes respect, understanding and tolerance for all those who adhere to different faiths' (DES, 1989), applies to all.

Children who are living and growing in a multi-faith society need some introduction to understanding religious diversity, to recognizing the faith convictions of others, and to appreciating how these convictions influence their lives. This understanding helps also to broaden awareness of religion as a universal concern and not as a concern simply of Catholic schools. Once again, however, there is a question of breadth of content in relation to depth of learning and acquisition of skills to be considered. Carefully limited selection of content is called for with the aim of promoting not only awareness of and information about other faiths, but a level of understanding that will encourage genuine respect and real tolerance for what is different yet important in the lives of others.

The case for the multi-faith dimension rests on four considerations described by Watson:

> The first is that in many schools in Britain today there are children whose home backgrounds reflect a multi-faith presence in our society . . . Second, Religious Education has a most important role to play in promoting an international and world-wide consciousness . . . Third, if taught well the study of world religions can be fascinating, challenging, demanding and illuminating . . . Fourth, the teaching of world religions can help to prevent any feeling of attempted indoctrination in Religious Education.
>
> (Watson, 1987, pp. 144–5)

I do not believe that any RE teacher would quarrel seriously with this list. It makes clear that some genuine multi-faith approach is a possibility in any denominational school. In this matter our common needs and concerns appear to far outweigh any fears and differences. Christianity (a faith) is a vast, exciting, kaleidoscopic and colourful multi-ethnic faith. It may well be the case that, if our commitment to Christianity (a faith) is to be seen as of educational value, it will have to be expressed in a context of an ecumenical or a multi-faith programme.

Nearer home there are some points in the Salford Diocese's recently published *Guidelines for Religious Education*. While this document does not give a great place to a discussion of the multi-faith issue for Catholic schools, it does provide one potentially useful insight which, if developed, might usefully contribute to current and future thinking.

This document states:

> that the teaching of Christianity from a faith perspective, besides promoting the religious and spiritual growth of pupils, will also provide the best framework within which to examine the relationship between all Christians and to foster dialogue between Christianity and other faiths. By enabling pupils to learn and appreciate how beliefs affect people in their lives, Religious Education will make a vital contribution to the understanding and mutual respect, toleration and co-operation upon which such dialogue rests. This in turn makes possible the search for truth with which all religions are ultimately concerned.
>
> (Salford Diocesan RE Centre, 1991, p. 5)

At this point we need to consider another related issue. It is a perfectly acceptable approach in RE to present its purpose as that of conveying understanding about religion rather than religions. As Cox notes in *Problems and Possibilities of Religious Education* (Cox, 1983), 'instead of looking at it as a mound of facts to be systematically transmitted,

perhaps it should be regarded as a quarrying ground from which to excavate a sufficient number of examples to illustrate the principles involved
in understanding'. However, can this purpose be achieved with one
religion or tradition forming the content of the programme used in a
school?

Perhaps it would be good to examine one further idea. It is put forward
by Küng and Tracy in the introduction to *Paradigm Change in Theology*.
They conclude,

> precisely because we are committed to the one true religion, we can risk
> conversing with them [all possible confessions and denominations and
> religions] in a process which, the longer it lasts, the deeper and more
> extensive it becomes.
>
> (Küng and Tracy, 1989, Introduction)

For, as they say elsewhere, 'in relation to this ultimate and absolute reality
of God – which Arabs call Allah, which Jews and Indians decline to name
but worship none the less – even the true religion is relative' (Küng and
Tracy, 1989, Introduction). However, any inter-religious dialogue may be a
difficult area to embark on in a Catholic or any denominational context.
Some people are convinced that the lines have been drawn once and for all.
Any attempt to revise them or to transcend them would be considered
either the height of stupidity or fraud.

Küng found this true with the response to his book, *Christianity and
the World Religions* (Küng, 1981). However, even the Vatican Council in
its *Declaration on the Relation of the Church to Non-Christian
Religions* declared that 'the Catholic Church rejects nothing of what is
true and holy in other religions' (Vatican Council, 1965). This was made
more 'real' in the 1980s and after, when the Pope attended prayer-meetings
in Assisi with leaders and representatives of other faiths.

In a denominational school the RE programme has to ensure two
things:

- the specific religious instruction and formation of children;
- the maintenance of a distinctive ethos and atmosphere of the school.

All of this has to be achieved in a school which will most probably contain
pupils who deny allegiance to any faith at all, others who are quite lost in a
confusing/conflicting world, as well as some who display a personal faith
commitment.

SOME CONCLUSIONS

At this time within the field of religious education (but not exclusively so!),
we seem to find ourselves in the midst of curriculum innovation. In this the
denominational school is required to pay heed to the twin demands of
Church and State, the former presented by local, national and international
authorities; the latter in the form of National Criteria and guidelines. Beyond
all of this, too, the particular needs and circumstances of pupils in an individual school have to be taken into account. In a denominational school this
should provide a valid aim for the religious education programme.

In a setting of freedom the denominational school RE programme should be called upon to do three things:

- First, it should help each pupil to acknowledge *each* person's dignity and purpose in the community of which they are a member (be that at a local, national, or international level).
- Second, it should prepare each pupil, *openly* and *honestly*, to respond to life's challenges and his or her search for God.
- Third, it should strive to present to each pupil the possibility and importance of both *respect* for other faiths, and the acceptance of good *wherever* it may be found.

Within such a school the RE Department has a particular responsibility to build upon the religious understanding that pupils bring to the school, in order to help them to leave school with an appreciation of the relevance of religion. To this end, programmes of study should be balanced, challenging, informative, interesting and fully supportive of the denominational and educational aims of the school.

In the denominational school the RE Department and its programme are not left alone to meet extraordinary demands. It is part of the interrelationship of home, parish and school which makes genuine efforts to help children grow in faith. In fact, the whole enterprise rests on three principles:

- parents are the most important educators in faith for their children;
- growing into faith involves growing into a community of faith;
- the specific contribution of a denominational school to the religious development of its pupils should be proper to a school.

While the religious education in Catholic schools is exempt from the control and inspection of the public authorities, it cannot remain unaffected by the general educational demands made on schools by the State. At the same time, given the principle of dual accountability, it must remain faithful to the valid educational expectations of the Catholic community. In holding together all of these requirements, I believe, religious education in Catholic schools will realize its distinctive nature and its specific strength.

When all of this has been said, it seems both right and proper for denominational schools to do more than simply follow the RE pattern laid down for maintained schools. Indeed, it is not too difficult to imagine a time, in the not too distant future, when it will be the case that denominational schools will provide maintained and controlled schools with a model or paradigm for a programme of religious education.

REFERENCES

Bishops of England and Wales (1980) *The Easter People*. Slough: St Paul.
Bishops of England and Wales (1988) *Commentary on the Education Reform Bill*. London: Catholic Information Services.
Bishops of England and Wales (1989) *Low Week Statement*. London: Catholic Information Services.
Cox, E. (1983) *Problems and Possibilities for Religious Education*. London: Hodder & Stoughton.

Department of Education and Science (1981) *The School Curriculum*. London: HMSO.
Department of Education and Science (1988) *The Education Act*. London: HMSO.
Department of Education and Science (1989) *Religious Education and Collective Worship*. Circular 3/89. London: HMSO.
Kelly, P. (1985) *Catholic Schools*. Salford: Diocese of Salford Trustees.
Küng, H. (1988) *Christianity and the World Religions*, London: Collins.
Küng, H. and Tracy, D. (1989) *Paradigm Change in Theology*. Edinburgh: T. & T. Clark.
National Curriculum Council (1991) *Religious Education: A Local Curriculum Framework*. York: NCC.
Pope John Paul II (1988) *Religious Dimension of Education in a Catholic School*. Rome: Catholic Information Office.
Price, A. (1993) Quoted in article, 'Catholic schools'. *The Universe*, 25 July.
Sacred Congregation for Catholic Education (1977) *The Catholic School*. London: Catholic Truth Society.
Salford Diocese Religious Education Centre (1991) *Guidelines for Religious Education*. Salford: Salford Diocese Trustees.
Southwark Diocese (1991) *The REPLACE Scheme for Religious Education*. London: Church of England Board of Education.
Vatican Council (1965) *Declaration on the Relation of the Church to Non-Christian Religions*. Dublin: Dominican Publications.
Watson, B. (1987) *Education and Belief*. Oxford: Blackwell.

CHAPTER 23

School education and the spiritual development of adolescents: an Australian perspective

Marisa Crawford and Graham Rossiter

INTRODUCTION

An education review in an Australian newspaper commented on recent developments in British education under the headline 'Teachers told to be moral guardians: juvenile crime levels push for moral values . . . a new crusade for spirituality and moral values in the classroom' (Oswald, 1993, p. 43). Even after discounting the predilection of the press for eye-catching headlines, one still finds in the article evidence that with both educators and the wider community there remains widespread ambiguity about the role of schools in promoting the moral and spiritual development of students.

Too great a public expectation is placed on schools to solve social problems and account for young people's personal growth. This obscures the real possibilities and limitations of schooling in promoting personal change.

Increasingly the words 'spiritual growth' and 'spirituality' are being used with reference to education. Comparable with the situation in the United Kingdom, the Common and Agreed National Goals for Schooling in Australia include 'self-esteem, attitudes, values, and judgment in matters of morality, ethics and social justice' (Finn Committee, 1991, p. 11). Similarly, one government aims document stipulated that 'The moral, ethical and spiritual development of students is a fundamental goal of education', and that teachers were to 'inculcate in their students positive values and a capacity for moral and ethical judgment' (Metherell, 1990, p. 65). However, no matter how well these aims are accepted, there is still considerable disagreement about what this actually means in everyday classroom practice (Crawford and Rossiter, 1993).

If efforts to promote personal/spiritual development in the classroom are to be appropriate and effective, and if teachers are to avoid reinforcing unrealistic community expectations, then there is a need to clarify and articulate the ways these aims are translated into practice. The particular perspective we take on this problem draws on experience in religious education. What has been learned from this controversial area of curriculum is relevant to broader questions about the way education has the potential to bring about personal change. Specifically, our concern here is the relationship between schooling and the spirituality of adolescents (aged 13 to 18 years).

DEFINING SPIRITUALITY

Spirituality, like identity, always appears to be an important concept when education and personal development are being considered. However, it is notoriously difficult to define. For the purposes of this discussion we need to avoid:

- Defining spirituality more or less exclusively in formal religious terms. This tends to alienate those who have a spirituality that is not associated with religion. Also, it does not take into account the way many of today's young people form a secular spirituality that relates to religious traditions in different ways from those often presumed by religious people. Similarly, it tends to neglect the spiritual significance and potential for human fulfilment in contemporary non-religious movements.
- Defining spirituality with the exclusion of any reference to religion. This ignores the long-term focus on spiritual issues that has been important for religions; it can neglect the significance of religious heritage as a component of culture and the place of contemporary religious movements.
- Defining spirituality so broadly that all aspects of life are regarded as spiritual. This makes anything and everything relevant to education for spirituality and curriculum implications become vague and impractical.

We define spirituality to embrace the ways in which people look for and perceive meaning, purpose and values as well as other personal aspects like beauty, appreciation of nature, fulfilment, happiness and community. Spirituality often, but not always, revolves around belief in God and the practice of religion. It includes abiding dispositions towards life and patterns of behaviour that are influenced by spiritual and/or religious beliefs. While spirituality may be regarded as the reflective and active expressions of religious beliefs, it is not limited to a necessary association with organized religion. It has to do with what people call the 'beneath the surface' or the 'more than you see' dimension to life: the meaning and value that lie beneath externals and perceptions.

Whatever the stance that educators may take regarding the place of religion in their own spirituality, we consider that they will misunderstand the spirituality of many young people if they make the concepts 'spiritual' and 'religious' identical. Similarly, we argue that some clarification of the relationships between youth spirituality and religion is important background for exploring how education might cater for spiritual development – in both county and religious schools.

RELIGION AND THE 'SECULAR' SPIRITUALITY OF YOUTH

In a text on modern European thought, Franklin Boumer (1977, p. 439) wrote about the process of secularization in a chapter entitled, 'The Eclipse of God'. He began with these words from Dietrich Bonhoeffer:

> The secular movement which I think had begun in the 13th century has in our time reached a certain completion. People have learnt to cope with all the questions of importance without recourse to God as a working hypothesis. In questions concerning science, art and even ethics this has become an understood thing which one scarcely dares to tilt at anymore.
>
> (Bonhoeffer, 1966, pp. 194f.)

This draws attention to a process with a long history that now has a contemporary prominence and universality in Western countries. While not neglecting those who are religious and who are active members of a parish (or synagogue, mosque, etc.), we are interested in the education of the adolescents who do not draw much spiritually from their own religious tradition. Their school education should still foster the development of spirituality whether or not they are associated with any organized religion.

As regards religion and spirituality, today's young people tend to be different from older generations in the following ways:

● they are at a high-water mark of secularization;
● they tend to forge meaning and purpose in ways that are different from those used by older generations; the focus of their spirituality is different;
● they relate to traditions and traditional religion in different ways;
● they have a different approach to understanding and forming identity and religious identity in particular.

While young people share the same source culture as adults, they have grown up taking for granted, and not knowing anything different from, particular elements like television and rapid social change – elements which the older generations have accommodated. They see people thinking about life and forming values more from their own initiative, with less dependence on traditional religious guidance. This has more to do with their experience of organized religion than with a fundamental belief in God. For many adolescents in industrialized, urbanized countries, religions and Christian denominations no longer speak with a voice they wish to hear, or a voice that is believable. If they have concerns about the environment, human rights, personal relationships and sexuality, there are organizations in society, unaffiliated with religion, that seem to have a more authoritative and legitimate voice. Young people have nominated associations like Amnesty International and Greenpeace as action groups with which they have more affinity than with church groups involved in similar work. Even when they recognize the contribution of church-related organizations to social causes, their perception is that these groups are not typical.

A high proportion of young people do not see religion, including their own particular tradition, as likely to have a prominent place in the way they work out their values and purpose in life. It can be said that this is not a new phenomenon, because the description fits many nominally religious adults. However, today's youth, as well as inheriting a tradition of secularization, are subject from birth to an electronically conditioned, global village culture that colours their view of religion itself and offers alternative sources of meaning and values.

Young people do not start life with a relatively static cultural baseline; for them, the constant as regards education, lifestyle, employment, fashion and entertainment is *change* itself. In fact, change may have become more of a natural ingredient in the formation of personal identity. Hence, the same cultural realities can be experienced differently by the older and younger generations. There results different perceptions, understandings and values, and this in turn influences the way young people respond to the efforts of adults to hand on a religious tradition, identity and spirituality. But the very idea of 'handing on' has become problematic. In response to adult concerns to foster a particular denominational Christian identity through religious education, young people may not so much question the appropriateness of methods and content, but will wonder why there is any need to be concerned about a religious identity at all.

This type of response gives an impression of apathy and lack of interest in religion, but the situation is more complex. It is often an indication of a detached, almost clinical anthropological interest in what they perceive as outmoded elements in the belief structure of an older generation – quaint or antiquarian, with little relevance for them or for today's society. They may see what their own religious tradition is offering as just one of a number of potential spiritual contributions from different religious and non-religious sources.

Relativism

A sense of relativism is strong in adolescents. Many see no problem in trying out different churches and religions to see what they are like and if they meet felt needs. People today are conscious that their society includes a type of religious/spiritual supermarket. Many adolescents are interested in buying, but they are discriminating; they feel that the product needs to be relevant and give them some sense of purpose and direction.

Theologian Gregory Baum (1987) considered that the relativism dominating Western culture is rooted in the market economy. Everything, including human relations and happiness, seems to have a price. Even sex, religion and personal values seem to have become marketable commodities.

One response of parents and educators is to try to shield young people from these comparisons and relativism by opposing the study of world religions in religious education. However, any such shielding at school is likely to be ineffective if students still have access to transport, cities, television, radio, newspapers and magazines, and to their own friends. The classroom should be one place where it might be expected that students look at different religions to become better informed.

The privatization of beliefs

One of the corollaries of secularization is the privatization of beliefs. As the social prominence of religions in pluralist societies decreases, so the tendency to regard religion as a matter of private beliefs increases. This is one way in which religion can be domesticated and its capacity for social action and justice limited. Religion can be treated as a matter of private, personal opinion, where it may offer personal meaning and motivation without getting in the way of business and life in general.

As noted in an earlier research study of the beliefs of British youth:

> Freedom and individualism are values that strongly influence the pattern of beliefs of young people. A consequence is the 'privatisation' of belief. This trend is part of a general acceptance of the atomisation of our culture. A person's life seems to be increasingly split up between various parts . . .There was a time when the Church claimed to be the unifying influence standing over everything else that happened in life. Now it is seen as one among many institutions competing for attention.
>
> (Hare *et al.*, 1977, p. 19)

Privatization of beliefs also diminishes the importance of the communal expression of faith in local church communities. Some consider that one of the psychological ills of contemporary societies is the alienation of individuals from shared belief systems. While not devaluing the need for a personalized faith, it may be expecting too much of individuals to construct meaning for life in isolation without reference to a community that can support and nourish personal beliefs and values.

Religion as an option

Young people can comfortably dissociate their search for a spirituality from the need to belong to any religion. They tend to locate *formal religion* in one corner of their lives and their *search for a spirituality* in another. But they do not see 'real' religion (that is, a personalized belief system) as divorced from life; any secular/religious dichotomy tends to have little meaning for them.

They know they have a real option as to whether their search for meaning will involve remaining in active contact with organized structures in their own religious tradition. It is also significant that they can do this without feeling any guilt at giving up their religion (older people who have given up their faith often have lingering guilt feelings).

It is foreseeable that many young people will develop a spirituality that is more *individualistic, eclectic* and *personal* than communal in its expression. This does not mean that they no longer need any link with organized religion or other reference group. But it suggests that in our type of society, most of the young people who seek religious affiliation will look for a community that supports spirituality that is personal and eclectic and which focuses on both local and world issues.

The spiritual life of children

Robert Coles (1992, p. 278) reported on thirty years of work interviewing children about their spirituality. He suggests that for children, spiritual/

religious issues do not surface initially as religious questions *per se*, but in the form of questions about life's meaning: questions asked at even an early age about death and the importance of life on earth, about animals and plants and the natural world. It is mainly in the context of their family that these beliefs are formed. However, he considers that schools have an influential role in helping young children get into some perspective their relationships with parents and siblings as well as with the wider natural world of animals, pets, etc.

A spiritual profile of today's young people

We conclude this section with a summary of some aspects of the spirituality of adolescents. While these generalizations do not apply to all young people, they provide a composite picture that can be a useful guide for educators.

When looking at these general characteristics, we do not imply that the search for a conspicuous spiritual dimension to life is uppermost in the minds of many young people. It is not. The major part of their psychological and emotional energy is taken up with surviving the perils of adolescence and negotiating the tasks of school and the potential employment that (they hope) lies beyond it. They will be more concerned with what has an immediate bearing on their well-being: their friendships, entertainment, films, television, music, sport, etc.

So, in areas of curriculum where educators try to get young people to examine spiritual and religious questions – as in religious education, ethics, personal development, etc. – the teachers need to understand that they will bring to the study complex, eclectic patterns of belief that they have acquired through particular life experience. It is here that educators need to be aware of the many influences that colour young people's spiritual sensitivity.

Teachers need to be realistic about the extent to which students will respond. Similarly, teachers should not underestimate the capacity of students to consider spirituality seriously. With approaches and content that are sensitive to the needs and interests of youth it should still be possible to plan an education for spirituality that is relevant and useful.

Ten prominent elements in the spirituality of young people

- *Ideals.* As regards the direction of their living, young people look for guidance in clear statements of ideas and ideals about life and its management.
- *Varied sources of spirituality.* In forming beliefs and values, they draw from various sources: family, friends, personal mentors, their own religion, other religions, secular movements. Their ideas and ideals can be modelled on those of prominent people, heroes/heroines and pop stars. They can absorb ways of valuing and thinking about life from magazines, film, television and music. Their spirituality will be eclectic.
- If interested in religion, they would like it to be *personalized*, and not too prescriptive in the areas of beliefs and morality. They may want to explore this personalized religion within a community of worshippers.

It is not inconsistent for them to want to dismiss particular beliefs, dogmas and regulations of their religion, while at the same time wanting to be part of a community.

- Young people *tend not to see any so-called division between the secular and the religious*. They see a spiritual dimension woven through life.
- *Inspiration from secular sources*. Rather than join religious groups, they may become involved in some form of social comment or activity concerned with issues in the environment, prison reform, Amnesty International, employment, international relations, etc. – all the issues that are related to improvement of the quality of life. There are, however, a significant number of young people who do want to be part of a religious group; at universities, those in the religious groups tend to have a conservative theological outlook and are active in evangelizing activities.
- *Social morality*. The concerns of young people about values have been exacerbated by what has happened in Australia and other countries during the 'greedy' 1980s. They are conscious of the negative effects of what they see as irresponsible economic activity on the part of the corporate 'high-fliers'.
- *Questioning the myths of economic rationalism*. Young people are increasingly questioning the economic values and principles that inform many aspects of politics and culture. They are calling into question whether economic progress – presuming there must be economic growth and so on – is really necessary for meaningful and happy human lives, and they are conscious of the damage this causes to the economically marginalized.
- *Pressures of recession and uncertainty about employment*. There is more questioning and agitation about values in times of social stress, such as the present economic recession where there is uncertainty about future employment and future education. By contrast, in the 1960s there seemed to be a more naïve view that individuals could take time off to work out ideas on what society should be like and that these could naturally flow into action. Present difficulties tend to make people more cynical and realistic about what can be done to bring about constructive change.
- *Questioning authority*. There is a greater tendency to challenge authorities directly. Young people see others from all walks of life being critical of current situations, and more ready to confront the *status quo*.
- *Anxiety about a violent society*. They are more conscious of the violence in society that apparently increases during difficult economic times. They are concerned about the complex of escalating unrest; increasing repression; heavier police presence; more racism – especially with reference to blacks; tighter immigration controls; more people in prison; more sophisticated surveillance; harsher hostility to intellectual critics and activists; more ready acceptance of authoritarian regimes.

A SCHOOL CURRICULUM TO PROMOTE SPIRITUAL DEVELOPMENT

What follows does not claim to be a comprehensive account of all that might be hoped for as regards the school's role in fostering the development of pupils' spirituality. Our interest is in the way ordinary classroom studies can be relevant to spirituality. We refer initially to principles that influence the personal dimension of classroom learning.

Complexity of 'personal' learning in the classroom

Personal learning, that is, a change in values, attitudes, beliefs, emotions, aesthetic sensitivity, etc., is a very complex internal process that is not fully open to scrutiny. Because of this complexity, there is a natural degree of uncertainty in discerning the relationship between teaching interventions and personal learning. It is more obscure and unpredictable than the links between educational interventions and cognitive learning/skills. This is not to suggest that teachers cannot or should not educate for personal learning. Teachers can *hope* to catalyse personal learning; they should not be unrealistic about what might be achieved, recognizing that the classroom does not have any monopoly on personal learning.

Potential of the classroom for appropriate personal and spiritual experiences

As a public forum with respect for the freedom and privacy of individuals, the classroom has a naturally limited capacity for personal/spiritual experiences, and thus limited scope for personal/spiritual experiences intended to be educative. Within these limits, personal, spiritual and emotional experiences may be planned to promote learning. For example, planned experiences designed to generate emotion need to be judged in advance as to their educational appropriateness and likely responses. This does not mean exclusion of spontaneous emotional experiences and expressions that are a natural feature of the life and work of human groups and which have educational value in themselves. Care about limits and precautions should not inhibit but promote attempts to foster personal learning. Research suggests that key personal/spiritual experiences are not likely to be common in classrooms.

In addition to classroom learning from immediate personal or spiritual experiences, there is also the possibility of personal learning in an indirect way; that is, through analysis and evaluation of non-classroom experience – one's own, that of others, the collective experience of society, potential future experience, etc. This is explained in more detail in the final principle below.

Ethical teaching procedures

What is done in the classroom to promote personal learning needs to conform to high professional ethical standards on the part of teachers. Not all interventions that might promote personal learning would be ethically acceptable: e.g., extremely emotional experiences or pressure on an unwilling student to reveal personal thoughts or feelings. Whatever might stray into emotional manipulation is inappropriate.

Personal learning through reflection and study

There is a dominant motif, or natural contextual emphasis, to classroom learning and it is *cognitive*: schooling is especially about learning how to think, how to become literate and articulate. This view postulates that in the classroom (and not as in other contexts more suitable for personal learning) most personal learning comes through reflecting on experience and on how to get the most from experience. The use of the term cognitive as contrasted with personal (or affective) should not create an artificial dichotomy, because both aspects are invariably linked in any learning. However, this distinction remains useful for identifying the learning emphasis in a classroom at any particular time. We are not advocating an overly rationalist style of education; but we propose that where the overall classroom learning emphasis is on reflecting/thinking and not on feelings/emotions, then this provides the most appropriate classroom context for emotional and spiritual experiences, and for getting those experiences into some sort of perspective. At times, use of the words 'cognitive emphasis' seems to antagonize some educators who identify with a holistic approach; they then dismiss the argument without fully understanding it. We are very pro-holism. But we are also critical of a vagueness that does not seem to acknowledge the complexity of personal learning in the classroom or its natural limits, a vagueness in talk about affective learning in the classroom, as if this could be turned on and off like a switch at the discretion of the teacher, and of too great a reliance on interpersonal processes and discussion as if these have a monopoly on personal learning.

We affirm the appropriateness and educational value of experiential learning in the classroom. The special attention we give to the conditions for personal learning in the classroom should not be read as reservation about its appropriateness or value, but rather as some ground rules for making it appropriate, ethical, relevant and effective.

APPROACHES TO PERSONAL LEARNING IN THE SCHOOL CURRICULUM

In the light of these principles we refer to three classroom approaches that we think should be considered when planning a curriculum that includes the aim of promoting spiritual development. They relate specifically to the fourth principle, 'Personal learning through reflection and study'. They do not exhaust the possibilities for personal learning in the classroom; they focus mainly on studying personal subject matter.

● *Direct study of personal/spiritual subject matter.* There is a need for a learning area (or subjects) that look *directly* and specifically at questions of human meaning, purpose and value – subjects like philosophy, ethics, religion, personal development. Such studies should have a philosophical centrality in the curriculum. They also give students the opportunity to evaluate their education, to put it into some perspective, to see how it relates to the rest of their lives. However, such subjects are not automatically 'personal' (there is no scope here to explore this issue in detail).

- *'Indirect' study of personal/social issues.* It would be artificial and inappropriate to try to limit the study of personal/spiritual issues to particular subjects like those noted above. In addition, there is a need to examine such issues when and where they arise in the curriculum; they need to be addressed in ways that are informative and empowering for students without subverting the standard aims for the host subject. If these issues are ignored at the time, there could be a subtle suggestion that the curriculum is not sufficiently concerned with young people's spiritual development.

- *A personal spiritual dimension to all curriculum learning areas.* All learning areas should be able to help students learn general skills that will contribute in some way to their personal growth: for example, skills of analysis, evaluation, interpretation, appraisal of arguments, etc. In addition, each learning area should be able to articulate a distinctive contribution that it can make to the personal integration of students' school learning.

Below we elaborate on these strategies.

The need for a philosophically central area in the curriculum that provides for a study of values and questions of meaning

A common community response to worrying social problems is to propose the introduction of a relevant school course (e.g. AIDS, sex education, protective behaviour, driver education, etc.). While not discounting the value of such courses, educators need to avoid the mentality of naïve structuralism that often drives such developments: that is, thinking that the added subject will automatically alleviate the problem, like an educational prophylactic, without looking realistically at how the classroom interventions are supposed to influence students personally.

The schools' role, as part of the wider community's attempts to address social problems, is related to what schools do best – helping students to be well-informed and to learn how to think about the issues. Of fundamental importance, then, is the need for an established, credible subject area that can serve as a natural forum for studying such matters. But it should not be just a social problems subject; it needs to be part of a wider, positive study of philosophy of life and of the answers to human questions that religion, philosophers, psychologists, etc. have offered.

Subjects that include elements of religion, philosophy, ethics and personal development could provide students with the opportunity to study questions of meaning and value with the same rigour as is expected in traditional subjects. Such studies provide for some correction to any trend in the curriculum which glorifies the market-oriented subjects or ignores values education.

Educators cannot presume that questions of value and meaning will be adequately explored within a general curriculum that does not include a specific study of these issues. While it will always be important to try to address moral and spiritual issues in all subjects, this is not a desirable alternative to a subject area where these issues are the main focus of study. School education needs both strategies.

In addition, a values-centred subject provides a place where the purpose and value of students' education itself can be examined and debated; it is in a pivotal position in the curriculum where students can try to evaluate and integrate into their lives their diverse school experiences and learnings.

Educators will argue that offering such a subject is no simple solution to the problem of devising a holistic curriculum. We agree. But it is a good beginning. The idea is not new. There are already subjects like this in place in schools: personal development, religion, living skills, etc. However, no matter how prominent they appear in the school's prospectus or mission statement, they are more like 'fringe dwellers' than central subjects in the curriculum; they are stressful for teachers, who often perceive them as educational 'health hazards'. Questions are often raised about their effectiveness and their poor image in the eyes of students, parents and school staff. The experience of those who teach them suggests that their educational potential is often subverted by school structures and by what we call the 'psychology of the learning environment'.

Certain subjects are seen by students as having high status and importance in the curriculum. Even if they do not like studying them, most students pay at least some attention to what is being taught and in general try to understand the basics, just on the off chance that it may come in handy for a job.

Also, when subjects are fully accredited (and examinable either by continuous or summative assessment) and when they count towards university entrance, students are more inclined to perceive these subjects as important and correspondingly they are more ready to work at them. Students' attitudes to subjects become problematic when they do not have 'credibility' and 'mark status'. The point is well illustrated by the history of subjects like non-elective art and music, personal development and religion. This same problem has also been one of the major hurdles to be overcome in developing more equitable curricula in the post-compulsory years where the bias has traditionally been in favour of university-oriented students.

If school structures and community opinion are not supportive of the purposes and value of personal subjects, then they will subvert their value in the curriculum. Hence, to make the study of religion, ethics, philosophy and personal development a valuable and effective exercise in the school, it needs to have well-defined and highly visible support structures to help show its value to students. We are not suggesting that the values related subjects will only be acceptable when and if they are fully accredited, or that accreditation will solve most if not all the problems. However, any attempt to implement such studies that does not take into account the psychology of the classroom learning environment runs the risk of being quickly marginalized. This is not a statement of unquestioned support for the system of examination- or assessment-geared learning. But it is an acknowledgment of the realities within schools and community that have the potential to undermine any programme that does not keep these issues in mind and does not attempt to address them.

Indirect study of personal/social issues

While the above strategy proposes a central place in the curriculum where questions of values and meaning are the formal content for study, it would be too narrow to try to channel all reference to values/spiritual issues exclusively into such subjects – as if they could adequately handle the school's role in values education and in promoting spirituality. To do this would be to distort values/spiritual education considerably. The companion strategy – scope for addressing relevant moral/spiritual issues in all subjects – is also needed.

This possibility is usually threatening to teachers, at least initially. They may feel that values education is trying to take over their subject. What is needed is flexibility to acknowledge and explore briefly the moral/spiritual issues that arise naturally within the subject in question without compromising the integrity of the subject matter. For example, in drama and literature, questions of conscience and ethics can be identified, articulated and discussed to some extent without turning the study into a morality lesson – or worse, into a sermon! As school subjects are becoming more issue-oriented, it is now becoming easier to identify particular issues that are to be addressed directly, rather than just when and if they happen to be raised in students' questions; examples here would be environmental and bioethical problems in the study of science. It is possible for subject departments to include the study of relevant issues.

A personal/spiritual dimension to all curriculum learning areas (the dimensions of meaning, value and purpose in the general curriculum)

We propose a third strategy in which *all* subjects can make a distinctive contribution to values education and to the personal/spiritual development of students.

In a student-centred curriculum, each subject/learning area needs to show how it contributes in both general and distinctive ways to the personal development of students (Castles and Rossiter, 1983). One aspect involves alerting students to the *meaning* of their learning.

This can be approached in two ways:

- Showing *how the subject contributes to general skills for personal/spiritual development.* For example, collecting and analysing data; identifying and evaluating arguments, and learning how to articulate an informed point of view with logic and with supporting evidence; empathizing with the situation and point of view of others; identifying moral and political issues; differentiating emotional and reasoned responses to an issue; identifying conflict and its sources, with reflection on possibilities for non-violent conflict resolution; speculating on short-term and long-term human consequences of particular actions; reflecting on implications for quality of life and respect for the environment; showing how events in the past can help illuminate and interpret what is happening at present (to name some of the general personal skills that schooling can help promote).
- Showing *how learning from this subject contributes in a* distinctive *way to students' understanding of life*. This learning has a spiritual

or 'purpose' dimension in the way it adds to the range of an individual's access to physical and cultural inheritance. It has some ultimate value and meaning in equipping students to respond to life. For example, learning a foreign language enhances the capacity to enter into another culture and literature.

Every now and again teachers should attempt to alert students to the long-term meaning of their current learning, even if this seems to fall on uninterested ears. Whether they agree with it or not at this stage, it is important for students to know that the teacher has reasons why this study is valuable for their personal development.

CONCLUSION

The idea of educating the whole person is behind the growing concern to expand the school curriculum to include areas for study that have previously existed on the margins of school life, even though they are said to be of vital importance for young people – areas like personal development, philosophy, ethics and religion. In addition, holistic education proposes that all subjects have a role in helping young people develop morally and spiritually.

We are at a critical point as regards the future of this personal development thrust in education in Australia and other Western countries. If it is to develop and take a central place in schooling in the decades to come, then it needs a clarification of both theory and practice that makes it more coherent, more practical and more self-evidently valuable for the practitioners and the consumers.

In determining how it addresses the aim of fostering young people's spirituality, the school must filter the demands made on it by the community, selecting what can be covered appropriately and realistically within its educational framework. We have tried to stress the aspects of appropriateness and realism because we consider that the pressures of unrealistic expectations for personal change and naïvety about the potential effectiveness of classroom materials and methods have hampered the clarification of the school's role in the personal, moral and spiritual development of pupils.

Given that the history of universal education over the last century has shown it to be so successful (especially in what it set out to do in developing knowledge and skills), it is not surprising that people have high hopes that schools can be equally successful in promoting personal and spiritual development and in addressing social problems. During this period many desirable social changes have occurred – one of the most influential factors must be judged to be universal education. Hence it is not unreasonable that many educators are, as Postman and Weingartner described (1969, p. 12), 'simple, romantic people who risk contributing to the mental-health problem by maintaining a [stubborn] belief in the improvability of the human condition through education'.

Postman and Weingartner hastened to add that they were not so simple and romantic as to think that all personal/social problems are susceptible to solutions through any means including education. We would agree. Still we maintain that education through schooling has limited but significant potential for promoting personal and spiritual development in young people; and we see it as very important to continue with efforts to clarify how this contribution is spelled out in classroom teaching practice.

REFERENCES

Baum, G. (1987) Pluralism and religious identity. Keynote address, annual conference of the Religious Education Association of the United States and Canada, Chicago.

Boumer, F. L. (1977) *Modern European Thought: Continuity and Change in Ideas, 1600–1950*. New York: Macmillan.

Bonhoeffer, D. (1966) *Letters and Papers from Prison*. E. Bethge (ed.). New York: Macmillan.

Castles, G. M. and Rossiter, G. M. (eds) (1983) *Curriculum Theory and Religious Education*. Sydney: Australian Association for Religious Education.

Coles, R. (1992) *The Spiritual Life of Children*. London: HarperCollins.

Crawford, M. L. and Rossiter, G. M. (1993) The future of holistic education: the recession we had to have? *Curriculum Perspectives*, **13** (1), 37–46.

Crawford, M. L. and Rossiter, G. M. (1988) *Missionaries to a Teenage Culture: Religious Education in a Time of Rapid Change*. Sydney: Christian Brothers Province Resource Group.

Finn Committee (1991) *Review of Young People's Participation in Postcompulsory Education and Training*. Canberra: Department of Employment, Education and Training.

Hare Duke, M. and Whitton, W. (1977) *A Kind of Believing?* London: General Synod Board of Education.

Metherell, T. (1990) *Excellence and Equity: New South Wales Curriculum Reform*. Sydney: NSW Ministry of Education and Youth Affairs.

Oswald, L. (1993) Teachers told to be moral guardians: juvenile crime levels prompt push for moral values. Education Review, *The Weekend Australian*, 24 April.

Postman, N. and Weingartner, C. (1969) *Teaching as a Subversive Activity*. Ringwood: Penguin.

CHAPTER 24

The spirit of education: a model for the twenty-first century

Roger Prentice

RENEWING EDUCATION AS REFOCUSING ON THE DEVELOPMENT OF THE HUMAN SPIRIT: EDUCATION OF THE WHOLE PERSON

Introduction

Major changes, paradigm shifts, have been described in various social movements in the twentieth century; including the women's movement, health and the environmental movement (Capra, 1982). Education remains resolutely conservative. If education is a prime means for social development, then minds that are set in their ways, some of which seem medieval, must change to a mode that will enable humanity to come of age. The shift is seen here as being toward greater concern for the whole person and for the development of the human spirit, with less concern for the mechanistic, the material and the fragmentary.

Pastoral care and concern for the personal and social education of pupils, like education generally, is inevitably shaped by the *beliefs* and *decisions* of the teacher, by the perspective he or she holds about what it is to be human and what learning and teaching is or could be. By 'the teacher' I mean *all* teachers, since the whole child is present in all lessons, in all subjects, even if major areas of being and consciousness, such as the affective self, are not called upon. In this sense all teachers are teachers of PSE and therefore are concerned with the ethical, the moral and spiritual. These 'subjects', dimensions of the human spirit, are therefore potentialities in all lessons. This is so simply by virtue of the individual and social selves of the participant human beings, who are being human, and are *in the process of becoming more fully (or less fully) human*. A shift to deepen and widen concern for the human is necessary because the pupils of today will shape the characteristics of the global society in which we will all live out tomorrow's world. That world can be characterized by an even greater selfishness than at present or by an effective concern for the whole of humankind.

In this chapter I present a holistic perspective, a model that I have developed for myself as a teacher and researcher, using a spiritual and moral foundation. I argue for construing education as an activity that draws upon the spirit of teachers, and parents, for the nurture of pupils as whole human beings. This 'spirit used for the nurture of spirit' is not seen as a religious activity. It is seen as a human-centred activity as expressed in the aesthetic, the ethical, the intellectual and the social. It is such activities that together make up the means for the development of the human spirit, so I argue that to be fully *human is* to be spiritual. What we need is open dialogue to (re)discover the language of the spirit independent of, but without rejecting, the religious.

Belatedly the UK government's National Curriculum has parcelled together the 'Spiritual, Moral, Social and Cultural' ('SMSC') as an after-thought, a sort of mopping-up operation after the really important subjects that will make us materially stronger. No doubt in many cases SMSC will be bolted on to the curriculum as a new label for PSE. From the emergence of SMSC are we to conclude that there are no moral issues in geography, no spiritual content in English, no intellectual process in PE? The argument of this paper is that SMSC should be the centre of all that is done and that it should be the heart of all subjects. Where there is good teaching SMSC matters are probably at its heart, or are at least contextually implied. What we need is greater consciousness of the central and universal concerns of those issues that fall within SMSC so that our education system generates human-centred continuous development.

SPIRITUALIZATION AND THE WHOLE 'LEARNING SELF'

Spiritualization is seen here as the process whereby teachers and pupils employ and develop unique combinations of positive qualities from within all the domains of being human. Whilst emphasizing the singleness of consciousness, I choose to map the intrapersonal and interpersonal matrix of the whole 'learning self' within nine domains. Intrapersonally there are the domains of

1. potential/the subconscious self/the self as a mysterious entity
2. belief and values
3. the self as a personal history, with a particular degree of self-under-standing
4. the volitional self
5. the affective self
6. the aesthetical self
7. the cognitive self

Interpersonally, there are the domains of

8. behaviour, action and social interaction
9. the social and cultural self, including the self as citizen expressed through economic and political roles

Any model using such a set of domains is, of course, open to debate. For example, should values be viewed separately from beliefs? Is every domain a product, an admixture of all of the others? etc. However, this is the model with which I work. These nine domains are seen as constituting the human soul or mind. Each demonstrates capabilities and qualities, e.g. the ability to make a fine distinction intellectually, the ability to overcome selfishness spiritually, the ability to persist volitionally, the ability to make people laugh socially, etc. Together they constitute the human spirit. Together they are the soul or mind's emanating energy or spirit: the whole person, the inner world and the social self. Each of us is unique through our particular admixture of qualities. Consciousness of these nine domains and their interconnections in the interplay of the human spirit of his or her pupils with his or her own spirit is what is involved as the teacher shapes the flow of a lesson through a continuum of micro-decisions. Awareness and skilled responsiveness to these nine domains in the pupils, and in his or her self, is what makes the teacher a holistic educator and it is to this consciousness that education should, so I argue, turn its attention. The domains provide the means for generating questions or new viewpoints, to spur new understanding and expanded consciousness both for the teacher's self-understanding and for understanding of his or her class or individual pupils.

In presenting a view that is holistic I am arguing for education that is human-centred. This is to urge that all aspects of the educational process, and the systems that support it, be designed to cultivate the human spirit to the highest level, as *the primary concern*, not as an afterthought following skills with which to compete economically. I argue that education should be human-centred and holistic not only as a way of engaging the moral and spiritual more universally but also as a way of focusing more energy on working with the human spirit *as a whole*, and focusing less energy on information that comes from specialization. This pedagogical refocusing on the whole of the human spirit and a withdrawal from the fragmentizing effects of over-specialization is the central argument in the holistic approach. This is not to argue against the possible usefulness of further specialized information from e.g. psychology or sociology. It is to argue, however, that the quality of learning is governed by the overall consciousness of the teacher and the ecology within her or his class. Teaching is a process characterized by a continuum of 'micro-decisions' that the teacher makes, within what can amount to more than a thousand human interactions in a single school day. The professional and personal development of teachers is therefore seen as development and employment of that consciousness and decision-making for (a) creating (b) managing and (c) reflecting on, learning environments. With such a view comes the assertion that we need to focus more on the forest and less on the trees.

Having argued for spiritually-founded education as the process, content and product of the human spirit, as opposed to allegiance to a religion, it is not my intention to reject the religious; my argument is humanistic, not Humanist. In fact I would argue that, approached without prejudice, the writings of the world's great religions are treasure troves of understanding for human education as a whole. Given that religious differences are a cause of disunity, perhaps we can, through research into inclusive models, learn to celebrate our diversity more positively.

RESEARCHING PRACTICE AND PRACTISING RESEARCH

The holistic model presented here is my way of trying to make one or two aspects of my vision of twenty-first century education work for me, on a day-to-day basis. It involves trying to research practice and practise research. Such an approach concerns our asking, as Jean McNiff (1993) says in her wonderful book about action research, *Teaching as Learning*, 'How do I live more fully my values in my practice?'

As with Cunningham (1988, p. 167), I try to research through a combination of collaboration, dialogue, experience, action research, reading and what he calls contextual locating. By contextual locating he means feeding into and feeding off the whole context within which one operates. He says,

> I see interactive holistic research as an omni-focused activity. By this I mean that one keeps a focus on the person (as researcher); the problems to be addressed; other persons; and the context of the research (social, cultural etc.) I want to avoid simplistic notions of 'person-centred' or 'problem-centred' as they are *all* at the centre. In taking this stance I relate my research principles to the connectedness and ecology of Taoist philosophy.
>
> (Cunningham, 1988, p. 167)

Regarding 'the person as researcher', in this case the teacher as researcher, I am also attracted by the notion of heuristic research. *The Concise Oxford Dictionary* defines heuristic as:

> serving to discover; proceeding by trial and error; *heuristic method*: system of education under which the pupil is trained to find out things for himself.

Moustakis (1990, p. 38) wanted a research method that would meaningfully encompass those processes that he considered essential in investigation of human experience. For him 'heuristic research' refers to discovering or finding the nature and meaning of experience.

> In heuristic methodology one seeks to obtain qualitative depictions that are at the heart and depths of a person's experience – depictions of situations, events, conversations, relationships, feelings, thoughts, values and beliefs.
>
> Moustakis, 1990, p. 38)

Heuristic method is seen as engendering growth in self-awareness and self-knowledge consonant with understanding the phenomenon with increasing depth.

Moustakis says that for his version of heuristic method he gathered a range of recent investigations, personal notes, spontaneous self-reflective writings, reviewed heuristic literature and re-examined his seminar outlines. He also, he says, returned to lyric poetry, autobiography and biography.

> I engaged in an immersion process, open and receptive to the nature of discovery, welcoming alternating rhythms of concentrated focus and

inventive distraction. I searched within my knowledge and experience for deepened and extended awareness that would further illuminate structures and essences of heuristic discovery. I found particular meaning in studies that exemplified the heuristic paradigm and provided practical methods and procedures for its operational effectiveness in investigating human experience.

(Moustakis, 1990, p. 10)

The final notion, knowledge of the heart, I have added to my model of holistic research and it is drawn from Baha'i Writings, the Baha'i faith being the youngest of the world religions, dating from the middle of the last century. Described in my own words this notion states that meditation is to converse with one's own spirit and that the heart is the seat of revelation. From this I understand that knowledge is created in the centre of our consciousness, the centre of our spirituality, through dialogue with our 'Higher Self' without necessarily making what we would normally think of as intellectual labour.

It is clear that there is overlap between this Baha'i-derived notion and the definition of heuristic research by Moustakis. Moustakis seeks 'qualitative depictions that are at the heart and depths of a person's experience' and that is what I understand we receive through meditation – with two provisos. The first is that the knowledge or understanding that we draw from meditation requires that we have in place the willingness to doubt our understanding, and that we test it against the best sets of standards that we can discover. Willingness to do this and the ability to see straight are dependent on spiritual qualities being in place, e.g. humility, truthfulness, honesty. Interestingly, the Baha'i Writings place justice very highly, not just as a process in judicial life but as a prerequisite in the inner life for possessing true knowledge, for seeing straight and for possessing what I understand Abraham Maslow to mean by 'self-actualized' being. Here is the particular sacred writing I have in mind, by Baha'u'llah, founder of the Baha'i faith, which expresses this:

O SON OF SPIRIT!
The best beloved of all things in My sight is Justice; turn not away therefrom if thou desirest Me, and neglect it not that I may confide in thee. By its aid thou shalt see with thine own eyes and not through the eyes of others, and shalt know of thine own knowledge and not through the knowledge of thy neighbour. Ponder this in thy heart; how it behoveth thee to be. Verily justice is My gift to thee and the sign of My loving-kindness. Set it then before thine eyes.

(Baha'u'llah, 1932, p. 5)

Another perspective, that of collective social responsibility, is seen in the well-known statement by Martin Luther King Jr, 'Injustice anywhere is a threat to justice everywhere.'

In a juxtaposing of such perspectives as these we can see one of the central tasks of education, namely to start seeking the effect and importance of spirituality on all aspects of learning and teaching. Such a challenging task is also part of my suggested holistic research model, namely the conscious application of spiritual qualities to the task of under-standing and carrying out research and teaching.

There is one further point that I suspect some of those who are believers would want to add and that is that the heart as the seat of revelation is the gateway between us and the Holy Spirit or between us and souls who have passed on, who want us to understand certain things. The alternative view of what happens when we derive new knowledge, is that such new know-ledge is either tacit knowledge made explicit or a new combination of elements that 'drops into place' by a more than rational creative process. In this the mind works on a problem below the level of reflective thought. Perhaps all these are explanations of the same reality.

Taking together the notions of *collaboration, dialogue, experience, action research, reading, contextual locating, writing and publishing, meditation* (as conversing with one's spirit) and the *application of spiri-tual principles*, we seek, as Moustakis has said, to gain 'qualitative depictions that are at the heart and depths of a person's experience' and 'deepened and extended awareness that would further illuminate structures and essences'.

I have come, then, to see researching practice and practising research as *multi-faceted dialogue*, in which the children I teach speak as much as the academics I read, in which I converse with my own spirit as well as having dialogue with colleagues, in which classes as 'communities of inquiry' mirror inner dialogue of meditation and reflection. The whole I would describe as *holistic research*. It sets an impossibly high standard but the idea is to aim for the stars even if we have to live with terrestrial imperfections. As a method it aims to maintain and extend consciousness, to create knowledge from the whole person including social contexts and certainly not just from cognition. Altogether the purpose is to nurture the development of authentic personhood, including the ethical, the aesthetical and the intellectual, within community.

The final point I want to make before turning to examine several key principles and purposes in holistic modelling is that the components of the holistic research method are also in many ways goals in teaching, goals across researching teaching and teaching research. They are also goals for nurturing the development of the whole child. In such teaching the teacher has permanently to be engaged in his or her quest for whole development, drawing on his or her own potentialities, experience and sources of in-spiration from all of the nine domains. This 'drawing on the spiritual' means the method is also the content and the aim. It is the process *and* the product.

SOME PRINCIPLES AND PURPOSES FOR SPIRITUALIZING AND MAKING HOLISTIC OUR MODELS OF EDUCATION

Spiritual and moral contexts for holistic education modelling

If we want to unify what has been fragmentary, the 'cement' for the 'bricks' might as well be made up from what distinguishes the human from the animal, that is the spiritual, including such central concerns as the aesthetic, the ethical and the intellectual. We need a pedagogy of the human spirit in which consciousness of the spiritual and of the whole person is omnipresent.

Practically, my approach to modelling the holistic is spiritually and morally based for two reasons.

- Unless classrooms, schools, communities, and society as a whole, can integrate all that they do within a sincere, effective spiritual and moral framework, there will be no future worth having. For many colleagues this spiritual focusing will have to be via a 'non-specific faith' model since their own positions are those of humanist, agnostic or atheist. There is much to learn from good religious schools, including from the Catholic sector (see Lesko, 1988), which could be utilized by non-denominational schools that are seeking to enhance their spiritual or holistic nature via an inclusive non-specific faith model. For example: the type and frequency and quality of messages of an ethical nature that are communicated from the school as an institution to the pupil body; the type and frequency of praise and positive valuing of pupils; the frequency and type of messages that emphasize the community and corporate responsibility as well as individual worth. On the other hand the model needs to be workable for those of a religious persuasion. The need for an effective spiritually based holistic approach is vital, so I would argue, within the family and within the community and its institutions.
- Second I believe that to be human *is* to be spiritual, that is to say, there is within each of us, unless we are brutalized, a desire to manifest a range of qualities and capabilities more fully. This desire to become our fullest selves is there just as much as the constancy of the mountain, or the 'desire' of the rose to bloom in perfection or of the horse to run and express its 'horseness'. Not blunting sensibilities, not closing minds, not helping the cancers of cynicism and apathy – all these seem to be getting harder at the end of the twentieth century as childhood seems to 'die' earlier and earlier. Yet they remain as important as ever and point up the need for a new approach.

In public statements about teaching, especially by members of the government, the public is insufficiently reminded that teachers can only work with what parents provide – the important work is done by the time the child starts school, all of the major formation of intellect, behaviour, attitudes. Similarly no mention is made of the massive rise in child poverty or poverty generally, or the health of the poor or the diet of the poor. The physical, spiritual, moral and intellectual grow together in a single reality with the first prerequisite being unconditional love as part of effective parenting, particularly in the first 5 years. The school, inevitably, is as much in the business of transforming as forming and, in the worst cases, of simply containing the effects of bad parenting. Full recognition is still required for the critical nature of the first 5 years. This is more than the much-needed provision of nursery-school places. It includes all possible means for educating and supporting parents in managing the first and most critical stage, in being the child's first educators. A new spiritual approach is therefore required with schools in partnership with community and with parents. It needs to be a popular and multi-agency approach.

Developing new forms of group process as ways to support human-centred education

Today, it is sometimes said, people visit and worship in shopping malls as the cathedrals of the late twentieth century. Not long after I first heard this quip I was in the County Mall in Crawley, and I was astonished to realize how cathedral-like the interior is. However, I see the dominance of contemporary materialism not as the success of manufacturers or of retailing nor because of some intrinsic failure of today's citizens but because of unsatisfactory or narrow forms of spirituality.

Almost all the forms of major religion fail to maintain the universal love, the wide embrace, that was the chief characteristic of their founders. There are, of course, notable exceptions. Harmonizing diversity is essential. Pope John Paul II (1979) talked of the 'many reflections of the one truth . . . attesting that though the routes taken may be different, there is but a single goal . . . a quest of God . . . and the full meaning of human life.' Some would argue that rock music has brought the world together, albeit superficially, far more than all the religions put together. Perhaps the materialistic is reassuring when we can see some 'men of the cloth' and politicians speaking with forked tongues. Rejection of the corrupt is understandable but unfortunately (to change the metaphor) the baby can go with the bathwater. When we reject the spiritual as well as debased religion we lose our selves.

Combined with the forms of spirituality, and the lack of the application of spiritual principles, is the problem of the cultural dominance of misleading myths such as the one which says that if I follow specialization undeviatingly I will know more and develop more. 'Progress' equals 'knowing more and more about less and less'. Such ideas, such myths, seem to hold our view of reality itself in their grip and paralyse consideration of alternatives. Scientism holds the sway that corrupt religion once held.

There are other key challenges that point up principles. Clearly such issues as those surrounding justice in relation to resources and development, and security and stability, are vital parts of the overall challenge facing humankind, as are issues to do with the inequality of women and men, international communication, access to education, the need for proper global federation supported by a world legislature and police force, etc. However, at the heart of the great complex of problems are the spiritual principles that individuals uphold or fail to uphold and it is in this arena that education can act most effectively. Justice, for example, as we have argued, is a way of seeing the world, of living our lives as individuals; it is not only a process effected by courts.

In addition to the question of how well individuals live out principles there is the great challenge of how *individual* rights, freedoms, responsibilities and development are related most effectively to *group* rights, responsibilities, freedoms and development. A key notion is 'harmony in diversity'. We have grown very skilled at asserting the importance of the interests of the diverse, e.g. through self-help and pressure groups. Some now think this has gone too far and refer to it as 'rightsism'. Relatively little time, money or human genius, however, has been applied to ways, means and forms of harmonizing diversity.

I want to mention two movements that have developed considerable experience in this key task of learning how to harmonize the diverse. The first is the Baha'i faith, a religion whose history of one and a half centuries, lived much of the time under the severest of persecution, stands unparalleled as a long-term social experiment in harmonizing the diverse peoples of the world. The second is a programme developed over the last twenty years by Professor Matthew Lipman called the *Philosophy for Children* programme (PFC). PFC is virtually a complete form of education and as such fulfils many of the criteria of a holistic education programme; for example, the affective self as well as the thinking self and its work on concept development underpins all subjects. However, its importance here, like the social system of the Baha'is which is centred around the process of consultation, lies in the insights, inspiration and skills it provides about harmonizing diversity through its discussion process.

Philosophy for Children is taught within the idea of 'communities of inquiry'. In the case of the PFC programme I think that it should more accurately be called, albeit clumsily, PFCCCCC, or PF5C, Philosophy for Caring, Critical, Creative Citizenship in Community. The point being made here is that, although its application to adult use is less developed than that with children, it has enormous potential. It is consonant with the educational and social process developed by Paulo Freire, the two educators having communicated. PFC is now virtually global, in that many countries are starting to use the programme and there is now a world organization.

There is also the great range of work done on negotiating skills within industry and the work of such researcher-writers as Edward de Bono. However, any such system can be lifeless unless the people using it draw inspiration to nurture their desire to act in fully human or spiritual ways, i.e. to apply higher-order values as principles to live by even though to do so costs us discomfort or real pain. Such inspiration can be found in religious faith and more eclectically from a wide range of inspiring individuals.

Given the range of problems confronting us, the world community can make any of several choices. We could choose a recently revealed religion that has the solutions to the range of problems, practical and spiritual, with which we are beset. The Baha'i faith would make the claim to be that religion. Many Christians and other religions would say that their essential teachings, properly applied, could solve the problems. Another alternative is to support the inter-faith process. However, this can be grudging tolerance if the position I uphold in this chapter is absent. That position is recognition that we have to work with the spiritual because that is human nature in its developed form. This care for the full development of humanity and of each human being is something we must uphold together. This model of 'the spiritual and the full human expression being the same reality' is, I believe, the way forward at least for the immediate future. This requires, of course, widespread acceptance of such a humanistic model, with a transcendent support for the spiritual being seen as more important than any particular faith's belief system, at least in non-denominational schools. No doubt many would say that this is pie in the sky. However, the 1990s so far have, in the UK, shown some reason for hope in the range of conferences held concerning moral and spiritual education. Although these might be said to have arisen because of the requirement in recent Education Acts to provide for the 'Spiritual, Moral, Social and Cultural' in all schools, I feel the conferences showed that there is considerable grass-roots interest in renewing education, and the spiritual within education. Whether this activity marks anything like the beginning of a new era remains to be seen.

We have to work in groups because that is an inescapable reality. However, the application of spiritual principles within groups requires that the individuals seek to make those principles part of their behaviour, part of their nature. For the present time we need to concentrate on creating a coherent practical model based on a view of human spirituality that transcends particular faith-stances. For this we need underpinning philosophy and ways and means developed together in praxis. These I see as the most important steps in making education holistic and spiritually and morally based.

Working both as a community and as individuals is a prerequisite for contributing toward harmony in diversity. If we are to avoid the full horrors of social breakdown that some countries are experiencing, the development of our schools also needs to be in partnership with parents and communities. Given the background against which current education operates, it is vital to debate how far holding a holistic view and using a general holistic model can benefit our understanding and work as teachers.

Reasserting our humanity is not primarily about the invention of new methods or content

The issue that contemporary crises present us with, in education and society generally, is not primarily the need for a replacement of 'fragmentary education methods' with 'holistic education methods' or the generation of new content. It is primarily the need *to raise, or reassert, our consciousness as to the full nature of that with which we deal*; i.e. the humanness of our students, ourselves and the communities of which we are part. My personal metaphor concerning content and process here involves a sheet of paper, a magnet and iron filings. Drawing the magnet under the paper causes the iron filings to arrange themselves into 'harmonic' patterns. My point is that we do not need new, additional iron filings so much as a recharge of the harmonizing influence, a reassertion of what it means to be fully human in relation to the information and skills in the various subjects. Of course generic forms of religion can contribute powerful positive influences to such a recharging.

This reassertion and re-examination of our humanity should combine teacher education and curriculum and school development so that they become a whole devoted to human development in its fullest sense. Whilst I believe that the results could amount to a radical improvement, the process of change described here is less an elimination and reversal than a compensation and re-balancing. The questions this poses include: 'How can the good and the beautiful counterbalance being clever and technical?' 'How can individual and community development interests be combined?' 'What does a holistic perspective have to offer that produces positive results?' 'Above all, how can the fragmented be harmonized within a whole?' To answer vital questions such as these we need more research and development of radical alternatives than currently take place in the UK.

Spiritualization as the 'glue' of holistic education

Raising consciousness about a full vision of human nature (including the restorative, reclaiming and re-balancing process) I see as synonymous with spiritualization. Spiritualization is the development of higher-order qualities and values in a person. We develop these qualities through their *application* to the problems we face. The notion of 'spiritual' that I use here refers to a wide range of qualities observable in a person's character and behaviour, such as love, justice, kindness, wisdom. Spiritualization is the process of developing such qualities through interaction with others in solving problems. The self and its unique admixture of qualities emerge through the dialectical. Teaching, from this spiritual holistic perspective, is primarily the rearrangement and recontextualization of activities to maximize the nurture of such qualities. Humanist colleagues may well see such qualities as being life-enhancing values. Believers will see such qualities as the names and attributes of God.

Of course we are not intrinsically good or bad. We all learn to reflect, through our interactions with our environments, the negative side of those qualities as well as the positive. Indeed personality can be viewed as the particular admixture of qualities, the positives being development and the negatives lack of development. Each individual can be seen, at each moment, to be on the journey of life. Both negative and positive mark us as human since consciousness, and therefore development, rests upon an infinitude of opposites. The negative is absolutely necessary for appreciation of the positive. These opposites seem to be what Jarvis (1992) calls paradoxes. Duality and seeing beyond duality of course have deep roots in religion, not least in Buddhism.

I am aware that some will want to say that spirituality as the development of higher-order qualities and values is no different to moral development. Others will say we need to include experience of transcendence, aesthetic experience and so on. I agree. The point is that the spiritual includes the moral rather than the other way around. However, these aspects of human experience are of limited value if they do not help us become more just or compassionate or loving. Mark Halstead (1992) has given us a model for use in schools which he divides into (1) looking inwards; personal identity and individual development (developing a sense of self and identity within a group, personality and behaviour, educating the emotions, developing qualities of character, developing the conscience and the will) and (2) looking outwards; some spiritual responses to life creativity, contemplation, commitment, quest. Children should, says Halstead, 'be encouraged to consider each of these as significant dimensions of what it is to be human, and to explore the resonances, if any, with their own lives.' Such a model is very helpful in support of my argument that just as recognition of common humanity is what should unite people so also should the human condition and the human spirit be what unites the educational curriculum and process.

My chief reason for staying focused on the development of qualities and values, such as justice and compassion and respect, is the widespread inability to separate concern for the spiritual from the particular belief structure of a particular faith. In such a state of being a rose ceases to be the expression of roseness and becomes a Baptist rose or a Methodist rose or a Catholic rose or a Baha'i rose. Where inter-faith work is truly success- ful, it is not through grudging toleration but through working toward commonly held goals such as justice and respect. When that happens beliefs become the servants supporting the spiritual or moral principle, not vice versa.

Spiritualization as the process for twenty-first-century education

Spiritualization as the development and application of higher-order values, such as fairness, compassion and respect, is not a luxury, but is a pre- requisite for all other forms of progress. Such a process of spiritualizing the whole of education is vital for the twenty-first century. Indeed, in my personal vision the successful application of such principles will come to exemplify the change not just from one century to another but from one mode of being to another. The heart of this is to find ways and means for schools to support the development of pupils, staff, the school as an insti- tution and the community as a meaningful co-owned whole. Like all other attempts at creating holistic modelling this requires a mindshift, not a nod in the right direction, a new paradigm, not just the stirring up of present practice. Of course it is essential that such ways and means accept individ- ual variations of belief whilst maintaining holistic, moral and spiritually based contexts. As we find, adopt or develop elements of such a process in current practice and theory, we shall start to create education as it needs to be, in order to create a future worth having for all. The general framework here is offered as the core to a set of ways and means to enable such inte- gration.

Such a reordering through the application of spiritual principles requires that we see all aspects of learning within a school, and within the levels of community from family to humankind as a whole, as having both a *primary specific purpose* and a *secondary or wider purpose*. This is more than the hidden curriculum or pastoral care systems, it is continually to ask how each bit of the work of the school advances its general aims toward the fullest possible development of children and staff and, ideally, community. For example, a lesson might have a primary purpose of raising understanding and use of alliteration and onomatopoeia as literary devices, but its more general purpose might be to lead to a fuller expression of care for self and others or to underpin the pupil's sense of place in the physical universe. It is an overall consciousness and understanding of the wider purposes that we need to develop and articulate further.

In its community outreach the school can support the life of families through providing for the learning and leisure needs of its members as well as help in parenting and child development, but the parents need to co-own the process of classifying the wider purposes.

The shift to wider human goals is part of a raised consciousness that must reside primarily in teachers and how they work and develop. Above all there is the need of time and support in this process, from parents, politicians and administrators. Such a consciousness fully brought to bear I would call the humanization of education. It has been said of the humanities that their central concern is to serve as custodians of the human image. This can be more accurately stated in this way: the fullest realization of the humanity of those who learn and those who teach is *the* central concern of education, and central to that is being faithful custodians of the human image. That image is defined by qualities that are eternal verities but the image is also constantly reformed as those truths are applied to the needs of each age.

PRINCIPLES IN PRACTICE

The teaching–learning–teaching cycle is dependent on what the children teach us as teachers (and as parents), including what they show us about their needs. My task as the teacher I see as creating spaces for consciousness to expand or affirm itself. I say affirm because the children I teach seem to know so much at the spiritual/moral/philosophical level. Much of the time they astonish themselves, as well as me, by what they articulate, given the 'structured spaces'. Creating these spaces, e.g. in the flow of a lesson or in developing a unit of work, there is employed one of the chief skills of the teacher: the structuring of the ecology of learning opportunities. In a discussion it is (as it were) 'on the hoof'. In writing a unit of work the structuring can be more reflective (but it always gets modified 'on the hoof'!).

With Lipman I believe that children have an appetite and a need for the abstract. With Lipman I believe that children need opportunities to experience and participate in higher-order thinking. I have earlier argued that higher-order values, or spiritual principles, should underpin children's learning opportunities. I want therefore, via the 'Squantoo' lessons outlined below, to comment briefly on three concerns when teaching: *the abstract, higher-order thinking* and *higher-order principles*. The three are of course interwoven through the consciousness that the pupils and I have as a group, and that each of us has as an individual. As the teacher I have the responsibility to decide to what, as a group, we shall turn our attention. However, I seek ways and means to increase the extent to which the children take that responsibility and correspondingly decrease the extent to which I exercise that responsibility, especially as the children mature. As a teacher I can support the creation of spaces for consciousness to expand by the attention-switching decisions I make in the flow of the lesson. This teacher 'attention-switching' reflects what we do in consciousness generally; i.e. we continuously switch our attention from one point of focus to another. Becoming professionally conscious of our continuum of decisions could also be compared to the work of a news editor who decides what parts of film footage to use and how much and in what order.

I turn now to two particular lessons with a class of 9-year-olds. I have for some time been concerned with whether there are key concepts, or clusters of concepts, that ought definitely to be periodically in every child's school experience: for example, sets of concepts involved in analogical or metaphorical thinking. The alternative point of view is to say that the mind is an entity, the admixture of concepts, viewpoints, feelings, life-experience, etc. is such a complex unity that it is more important to focus on the *type of experiences* in which development, given genetic make-up and social history, can take place, rather than worrying about specific 'content'. It seems clear that certain *types* of thinking are essential, e.g. children who finish school with little or no command of analogical or metaphorical thinking would seem to have been sold short. Even more broadly, it is clear that there is a need for mixes of creative, critical and caring thinking. But what about concepts or clusters of concepts? Are some of them major keys to opening up the mind? The point about the child having some engagement with certain sets of concepts at fairly regular intervals rests upon the argument that concept development is gradual and progressive (though often in spurts) and teaching consequently needs to be recursive. Lipman and colleagues, for example, have, in their massive teachers' files developed to accompany the stories in the original Philosophy for Children programme, listed and sequenced concepts along with what they call Leading Ideas. The files are of monumental proportions in that they can contain in excess of two hundred Leading Ideas, each with many exercises, in a single teachers' file. Many concepts are revisited or reworked in the successive stories that provide the text for the philosophizing. Of course concepts and a Leading Idea are not the same thing; each Leading Idea is explored through a number of concepts.

Although this is not the place to go deeply into the analysis of a full range of practical examples that illuminate the issues I have touched upon, I want to share just this one piece from my own teaching, which I think of as *The Meaning of Squantoo*. I wanted to find a way into giving year 5 children a 'bite' at the ideas around 'Meaning'. I had in mind the various relationships that meaning has with language, the fact that meaning is not an accumulation of individual word definitions, the fact that meaning is subjective, the fact that meaning can shift, that it can be elusive, etc. I was not clear what children of this age knew or what they were capable of or what might interest them. I wanted to find out. Here are condensed notes based on two Year 5 lessons.

I decided to start by presenting a mixed-up sentence: 'ears large elephants have All'. Before I had finished writing the words on the board and before I had said what I was wanting them to do, or answer, or discuss, hands went up, 'I know the answer!' (The *answer!*) There followed vigorous discussion. I asked *where* the meaning was. Quite often children were only able to hear that question as, 'What is the meaning of . . .' or 'In which word/s does the meaning particularly lie? This last became very clear in an alternative sentence that I suggested, 'Roses are beautiful.' Hands went up to argue that the meaning lay primarily in 'beautiful' or 'roses' or even in 'are'. No suggestions yet that it lay in particular personal meaning-making or in social contexts (*though come to think of it I will ask them/other children to imagine in how many different contexts that statement, 'Roses are beautiful', might have different meanings – e.g. between lovers, flower show competitors, husband who has forgotten his wedding anniversary, etc. This has also given me an idea for drama, i.e. give children a line and ask them to improvise a play which ends with the line, 'Roses are beautiful,' or whatever sentence is chosen*). No suggestions that it depends on the individual's experience. Try not to prompt at this stage. We also considered whether 'Roses are squantoo' (*I made up the word there and then*) was a sentence.

I had decided to invent a word and the one that came out was 'squantoo'. Massive energy by the children went into arguing the possibility that it was in a dictionary somewhere, or in a foreign language. One boy said that since every minute (second?) seven people are born and two die there was a high chance somewhere that someone had just named their baby boy or girl Squantoo! We also discussed how 'squantoo' could come to mean beautiful, i.e. words could have substituted or coded meaning, etc.

The following week I had planned something different that I wanted to try but I had forgotten that I had asked them to think about the issues from the first 'squantoo' week. They were straight into the discussion again – I had no chance, and didn't want one! Consequently it went something like this.

Arguments that 'squantoo' wasn't a word.
More arguments that it was in a dictionary – one boy had walked around with a dictionary for some time after the first week. Someone had decided that it meant short and fat (and in doing so resembled the Ugly Sister who considered chopping bits off to make the article fit – since this pupil was thinking of 'squat' and conveniently, the 'n' had been changed to a 't' and the 'too' had been lost altogether!).
More arguments that it might be in a foreign language – these arguments to defeat my claim that I had simply invented the word in the previous lesson.

Then – 'It's not a word because you made it up.'
'A squantoo is like the film *Gremlins*. You had *Gremlins I* and *Gremlins II* so there's a Squan II and there must have been a Squan I!' (*spontaneous applause from the class for this girl's ingenious reading*)

I ask, 'If squantoo isn't a word then what is it?'
'A bit of rubbish at the top of your head.'
'OK, what else might it be said to be?'
This is when I get zapped.

Robert, 'I don't think it's a word until you give it a meaning.' (Pow!)
'So if I give it a meaning, then it will become a word?'
'Yes.'
'Right. At 12.25 I will announce the meaning of squantoo.' (about 8 minutes to go)
I hadn't reckoned on the continuing high energy of the discussion, so when inevitably I heard a voice say, 'It's 12.25,' I said, 'I need more time.' (*booing and jeering*)

There followed a rare moment of inspiration.
'OK, so Robert says that a word is not a word until we give it meaning, right?'
'Yes.'
'Right, well, the meaning of squantoo, as a noun, is "that thing which when you add meaning to it becomes a word"!' (*That was help from 'above'.*)

Certain individuals, including Robert, then tried to move the goalposts or legislate retrospectively, 'It's not in the dictionary so even if you have given it a meaning it's not a word.' I protested, and pretended that I was much upset that having delivered according to the criteria they had set out I was now being subjected to new rules. (In PFC rarely would discussion be seen as combative but this time I childishly was pleased that I had won! I defeated the brilliant young Robert and his few, but vocal, like-minded peers by calling for a vote.) 'Hands up those who think that now we have given squantoo a meaning it is now a word.' Two-thirds majority – wahooey (now what does that mean?).
More discussion.
Then the girl who gave us Squan II said, 'I think squantoo is now a word. It's like a baby. When it's in its mother's womb it's not really a person. When it's born we give it a name and then it's a real person. Giving meaning to squantoo is like that, now it's a real word.' Immediate calls from some quarters to challenge the notion that a baby is not fully a person until it's named. Ask class to leave that aside for another day. Bell. Larger than usual group of individuals crowd round wanting to make final points. Try to deal with them appropriately. Retire to staffroom in exhilarated knackerdom.

My conclusion about the pair of lessons was that it is useful to work with the leading idea of 'meaning' in Year 5! Clearly many of the children did have a rich and intense experience of abstract thinking and utilized what Lipman would regard as higher-order thinking skills. Many quieter children, who often listen but take little part, did contribute. It was certainly *spirited*, if not *spiritual* in any narrower sense. However, most if not all of the benefits of the lesson could underpin spiritual and moral concerns, e.g. the ability to make distinctions, listening to each other, wondering, examining meaning and significance, etc. It was serious fun. I now have the makings of a module of work with this age group. For the children it was, I believe, a good learning experience. For me it was dialogue of a high order.

The children taught me, and helped me teach myself, a great deal. It was 'dangerous' teaching in the sense that when I started I did not know exactly the content, the process or the goals, only that I wanted to find an appropriate way to bite at the cherry called 'meaning'. If I were to continue to teach these children I would choose once a year to, recursively, give them a bite at the same 'cherry' of meaning-making, since it is so central to human education.

Such lessons have sent me, recursively, back and forth between various aspects of theory and practice. This kind of teaching is what I mean by researching teaching and teaching research. If a country wants an outstanding education system then such teaching–researching–teaching should be the norm, not the exception. It is the educational equivalent of Continuous Development in industry. However, it needs counterbalancing with the best of the past, the eternal verities.

Teaching is such a high-pressure process that most teachers, most of the time, have little time for reflection. However, given that rapid change is the only certainty, and assuming the need to stay with eternal verities and the humanizing process, it is vital that teachers become committed to research in their initial education and then have opportunities, including sabbatical terms, to recursively develop the dynamics of their theory–practice. Implicit here of course is a paradigm shift from training as 'command over existing information and aping of existing skills' to 'a pattern characterized by the continual, recursive, process of being and becoming an educator who teaches and develops, self and others, through multi-layered dialogue and "dialectical creativity"'.

There is no space here to analyse fully everything that went on in those two lessons. However, I do want to indicate the kind of methods and analysis that I see as appropriate, given the general theory of my holistic–spiritual–consciousness approach.

At its simplest the teaching–research–teaching process requires (a) experience in which data is received or collected, (b) ways to analyse, as stimulus to reflection and (c) ways to reform or develop teaching consequent to reflection. For me this third part is done as a teacher of English but could equally be from within the professional knowledge of a primary school teacher or a teacher of geography or biology, etc. The teacher who chooses or is enabled to be reflective, has in every lesson a vast stream of data projected at him or her. With the 'squantoo lessons' I made notes during and after the lessons. I also video lessons. The need is to develop instruments and processes that can aid in the reflective process. This analysis as the first stage of reflection aims to raise questions, see possible connections, articulate decision-making processes, build confidence, extend creative possibilities, make clear good practice, enrich the dialogic and the dialectic, etc. Strengthening the dialogic and dialectic makes knowledge more the product of the whole self instead of the movement of information, i.e. it makes the learning more holistic. The nine-domain model of the self provides us with a matrix for generating questions for reflection. (See Table 24.1.)

We can ask nine questions based on the domains themselves: 'In this interaction/lesson/course what are the implications, for pupil and/or

	1 potential/subconscious/the self as a mysterious entity	2 belief and values	3 the self as a personal history, with degree of self-understanding	4 the volitional self	5 the affective self	6 the aesthetical self	7 the cognitive self	8 behaviour, action and social interaction	9 the social and cultural self, inc. citizen expressed through economic and political
1	potential/subconscious/the self as a mysterious entity								
2	belief and values								
3	the self as a personal history, with degree of self-understanding								
4	the volitional self								
5	the affective self								
6	the aesthetical self								
7	the cognitive self								
8	behaviour, action and social interaction								
9	the social and cultural self, inc. citizen expressed through economic and political								

Table 24.1 Matrix for generating questions for reflective teaching based on nine-domain holistic model of the learning self (see pages 320–1).

teacher, of *the unknown self; the self of values and beliefs; the personal history; volition; the affective self; the aesthetical self; cognition; the behavioural self; the social–cultural, the political–economic self?*'

These obviously are the nine basic questions. But we can then start generating questions that combine the domains: *affective–cognitive, values–behavioural, social–affective,* etc. Ask new questions and we learn new things.

Questions using the matrix can apply to the class, individual pupils and/or the teacher. Or the teacher could think of him- or herself on the x-axis and the pupils on the y-axis. This is not the place to try to develop an exhaustive list of questions. Indeed, I think that each piece of analysis–reflection should use instruments like the matrix to generate context-specific questions. Ideally the analysis–reflection should also include dialogue, e.g. with a study-buddy or co-researcher. The questioning and self-questioning stimulate reflection, reflection explores or extends consciousness, extended consciousness is used in creating and managing learning episodes. Personal Construct Psychology techniques might also prove useful.

However, before, during and after asking specific questions we should focus on questions of the whole flow of spirit. Did the lesson/class/individuals/own contribution ring true? Did the spirit flow – was it a high-energy lesson? Did I see/sense high-level engagement? Did faces shine? Were problems posed? Did dialogue take place? What kinds of feedback did the pupils produce? What do we feel intuitively?

Clearly such a matrix approach is itself highly cognitive, left-brain and masculine. What if we used painting, meditation, chanting, deep relaxation, etc. more widely to reveal understanding and generate creativity?

Many of the questions that can be generated from the matrix point up the need for areas of research, e.g. 'In what ways did/do affective influences impact on the learning process?' 'How does strengthening the cognitive affect the volitional?' 'How can we develop and learn from intuition?' 'In what ways can we combine the critical and the creative?' 'Does it make sense with key stage 3 children to make the aesthetic dialectic?' 'How do teachers construct and deconstruct the flow of the learning process and their decision-making within that process?' etc.

CONCLUSION

Economic success is not the determinant of the quality of our lives and ought not therefore be the central determinant in how we construe education. The quality of our futures depends on how positively human we can be. The (re)humanization of education requires that we seek to nurture the whole of the self. The 'Spiritual, Moral, Social and Cultural' need together to be the central concern and not low-status nor bolt-on afterthoughts.

Human-centred, holistic education requires:

- A shift from a materialistic to an inclusive spiritual notion of what it is to be human and what it is to educate or be educated;
- A new human-centred pedagogy based on dialogical, dialectical process that allows 'reciprocal consciousness raising' approaches to

teaching and learning and to researching and teaching. I have sketched a view of such a pedagogy here. To flesh this out we need to gather new, or appropriate, holistic views of
- educational philosophy, including purpose and society's needs
- teacher development
- classroom management and teacher–pupil–curriculum relationships
- the nature of knowledge and the curriculum
- school management
- school–wider community relationships
- school design and architecture
- Wide commitment and resource provision – from parents, communities, institutions, politicians – for making education part of the process of spiritualizing society, i.e. shifting the overall dynamic from materialism and greed to community and concern for others.

In such a transformation is both future vision and the basics back to which we should go!

Practically, the purpose of such consciousness raising will both require, and contribute to, the creation of *new mindsets and new contexts* within which pupils and teachers carry out those activities we call education. Teachers alone will never achieve such a change. Parents, politicians, religious leaders need to support, and on occasions initiate, such change at all levels of education. 'Context' refers to the parts that precede or follow a passage and fix its meaning or surrounding conditions. The term is appropriate here because we are looking at new emphases, new meanings, new aspects to value – as a result of a holistic and spiritual perspective. Doing and theorizing are reciprocally vital; researching practice and practising research need to be the norm, not the exception. Central to the process is focusing on the connectedness of teaching and its relatedness to the inner life of pupils and teachers – i.e. effective concern with pupil and teacher development as whole human beings.

How teachers approach (or more correctly, are allowed to approach) three questions will govern the whole process of spiritualizing education. Those questions, implicit throughout this chapter, are:

- What is it to be human?
- What is the nature of knowledge when viewed holistically?
- What kinds of teaching and learning promote development of the whole person?

One way to create the new contexts is to explore the relationships of the nine domains within the singleness of consciousness. This is a paradox, of course. We have to move out of the whole to the part in order to gain a fuller sense of the whole. The vital point is to not move to the part and then *stay* with the part. Much writing within the UK National Curriculum seems unable to recognize the complex, and ultimately mysterious, reality of whole human beings. The domains and their interrelatedness can be used for analysing teaching episodes and for various levels of dialogue. Herein lies much work for the future! Everything I have written here calls for a new human-centred pedagogy focused on teacher-researchers raising consciousness, i.e. developing the whole mind in reciprocal relationship with pupils.

My argument has been for utilizing a holistic education framework, a generalized model that can be used for teacher education and for curriculum and school development. Included in the view I have taken is restoration not just of concern with values but of philosophy. Education is starting to urge the essentiality of meaning-making. Philosophy, perhaps excluding the more sterile twentieth-century forms, is not only the theory of meaning-making but is the most central of human activities. In the restoration of philosophy comes the restoration of education as a human-centred activity, since as a 'subject', a process, it corresponds to the whole of human consciousness. Here when I speak of philosophy I am thinking particularly of programmes like Matthew Lipman's Philosophy for Children. Of course the first thing that is necessary is that some teachers, colleges or schools must want to take on, or further develop, the responsibility of thinking and acting holistically, spiritually and ethically.

If education does affect the decisions citizens make, then the kind of mindshift and re-contextualizing of education that I have sketched must take place before 'destruction (so) sickens' that we can no longer become more positively human. Hope lies, along with the rest, in the human spirit. It lies in its ability to rise to new challenges and at the same time to rediscover those eternal verities that lie in the human heart, and indeed at the heart of the great world religions. Chief among these eternal truths is radiant love for humanity, recognition of its oneness, cherishing of its diversity and, most important, commitment to living 'justice' as a guiding principle, not simply a right to be demanded.

In rising to the new challenges and in reapplying ancient truths, we can create for all the planet's children a future worth living in the wholeness of their humanity.

REFERENCES

Abdu'l-Baha (1994) *Love: Jewels from the Words of Abdu'l-Baha*.
    Oakham: Baha'i Publishing Trust.
Baha'u'llah (1932) *The Hidden Words*. London: Baha'i Publishing Trust.
Capra, F. (1982) *The Turning Point: Science, Society and the Rising
    Culture*. London: Fontana.
Christian, J. L. (1994) *Philosophy: An Introduction to the Art of
    Wondering*. New York: Harcourt Brace.
Cunningham, I. (1988) In P. Reason (ed.), *Interactive Holistic Research:
    Researching Self Managed Learning in Human Inquiry in Action*.
    London: Sage.
Jarvis, P. (1992) *Paradoxes of Learning*. San Francisco: Jossey Bass.
Halstead, M. (1992) *Times Educational Supplement*, 18 December.
Lipman, M. (1991) *Thinking in Education*. Cambridge: Cambridge
    University Press.
McNiff, J. (1993) *Teaching as Learning*. London: Routledge.
Moustakis, C. (1990) *Heuristic Research: Design, Methodology, and
    Applications*. London: Sage.

Conclusion

CHAPTER 25

By no means the last word!

Ron Best

In this short conclusion I shall attempt to draw together what I see as the most important themes running through this book. These are themes which need to be considered by anyone wishing to adopt a whole-school, whole-person approach to the provision of education, and who is anxious to give due regard to moral and spiritual development in so doing.

This book is by no means the last word on the nature of spirituality and spiritual development, or on their significance for the education of the whole child. It should be clear enough from the chapters in this volume that these questions lend themselves to programmatic definitions for the purposes of analysis, reflection and the development of practical strategies rather than to ultimate statements of universal meaning.

That such things should be cut and dried is, in any case, contrary to my concept of what it is to be human in the context of society. We live our lives within a field of tension, contradiction and dilemma (Winter, 1982). The motors of human development and social progress are to be found in the oppositions which, dialectically, move us forward. The release of tensions, the transcendence of contradictions and the resolution of dilemmas (for better or worse) confront us with new challenges. We may strive towards consensus, hunger for agreement and co-operation, look for unity of purpose and common understanding, but our attempts are unendingly beset with oppositions.

That said, one theme which certainly runs through every chapter in this book is *the nature of spirituality and spiritual development*. The opposition here is between (on the one hand) the idea of spirituality as a dimension to our existence which is qualitatively different and categorically distinct from our everyday experience as thinking, feeling, social beings, and (on the other) the spiritual as an integral quality of experience which in all other respects is to be understood rationally or scientifically.

Here our contributors are definitely divided. For some (e.g. White and Lealman), spiritual experience is typified by the sort of wonderment which we associate with small children confronted by the enormity of the cosmos, or by adults suddenly entranced by a sunset or the delicate beauty of a tiny flower or a baby's fingers. Such experiences (it seems) speak to us of dimensions of existence which transcend the 'normal' world of daily life, of things with which we have somehow lost touch, that cry out to be explored. One place to start investigating such an issue is with the children themselves: what is the nature of their spiritual experience and how do they make sense of it? (Erricker and Erricker; McCreery). For others (e.g. Lambourn) it is not at all clear that such talk gets us very far at all, or that there is a leap of logic between our inability, with the current state of knowledge, to explain all such experiences and the creation of a separate category (the 'spiritual') to describe or account for them through rational thought and empirical evidence.

There is some justice in the argument that our desire to 'explain everything away' may rob us of an important (non-rational) dimension to our lives. I am in agreement with those who see the Enlightenment as having a variety of effects: excising dogma, but also remodelling – and perhaps diminishing – our capacity for *feeling*. As Heron (1992) has argued, we do not so much think that we exist as *feel* that we exist, that we have a particular identity, that we share a particular destiny with the world of which we are part. In this regard, the popular Christian apologist C. S. Lewis may have gone too far in urging those who sought his spiritual guidance 'not to try to feel too much' when at prayer or worship (Lewis, 1988).

It is right, therefore, that this book should be primarily an intellectual endeavour. In the search for understanding of spiritual development through education, we needs must go beyond faith and dogma. Such weighty matters require critical analysis, reflection and debate. Most of the chapters in this book are, in one way or another, concerned with seeking rational grounds for what we identify as spirituality, and therefore for any curricular programme we may construct for its development. In an age when theory is too often derided by those in power (e.g. see Prime Minister John Major's comments on teacher training in Chitty and Simon, 1993, p. 144), it is all the more important that such a quest be undertaken, especially in an aspect of human development which is traditionally accepted as to do with *faith* rather than rational thought or scientific evidence. Both philosophy and the sciences (Mott-Thornton; Wright; Nye) have something to offer the debate.

The spiritual is conventionally thought of as to do with *religion*. Some contributors have approached spirituality from positions of personal faith, or from the convictions of those committed to education within church schools (e.g., Warner; Stuart). Here, *spiritual leadership* is seen as crucial. Others (e.g., Newby, White) argue for a concept of spirituality and spiritual maturity which is universal and not premised upon theism, and there are some clear warnings of the dangers of indoctrination (e.g., Rose). Whatever the denomination of the school, most children will encounter teachers (and peers) who represent a range and variety of religious conviction, and none, and for the staff of any school some accommodation to this plurality will be necessary. As White's chapter points out, there are many people in society who are all too willing to use difference as a lever to separate and oppose, rather than seeking a common ground and a mutual respect and tolerance. One issue for schools is how to *reconcile different faith positions in order to adopt a planned, rational and effective whole-school policy on spiritual development.*

A further theme is that of the *problematic relationship between wholes and parts*. For those who adopt a broad concept of education as the intentional development of the whole person, a view embraced especially by those teachers concerned with pastoral care and personal-social education, a great deal hangs on two questions: first, what we mean by *the person*; and second, what we see as the *constituent parts* of the whole person. The first question is addressed directly by some contributors (see especially Ungoed-Thomas). As for the second, for all the contributors education is as much about personal, social and moral development as it is about the nurturing of intellect, although it is arguable that the concept of the 'whole person' as an accretion or amalgam of 'parts' is fundamentally flawed. In much the same way as the division of the child into the 'cared for' and the 'learner' – the 'pastoral/academic split' (Best and Ribbins, 1983) – such a conception does violence to the essential *indivisibility* of the person.

Be that as it may, the 1988 Education Act requires a balanced and broadly-based curriculum which should

(a) promote the spiritual, moral cultural and physical development of pupils at school and of society; and

(b) prepare such pupils for the opportunities, responsibilities and experiences of adult life.

(DES, 1989, p. 7)

This requirement is not, by and large, reflected in the National Curriculum requirements themselves or in the timetable of the average school. Of course, much may be achieved through the ethos and 'hidden curriculum' of the institution, and there are some important pointers in this book to how this might be less left to chance.

An important aspect of personhood is the social context within which, alone, it can develop. The fully-developed person is inconceivable other than within the framework of social relationships through which empathy, respect for persons and a sense of common destiny may grow. Humankind is, after all, social. But society is not enough. As the 'founding fathers' of sociology realized, something is lost with the decline of 'mechanical solidarity' (as Durkheim called it), and its replacement with the functional but depersonalized relationships of the 'organic solidarity' of modern, industrial societies. No amount of functional interdependence can be a substitute for the genuine sharing of values, ideals and beliefs and an awareness of one's common destiny and collective identity.

Durkheim used the concept of the '*conscience collective*' to encapsulate this common world-view, but we may wonder whether 'collective spirit' might not have been a better formulation. For schools, the challenge is to develop a curriculum based in a concept of spirituality which gives due regard to the communal basis of personal development, and the importance of citizenship for the individual as a member of both the school community and society at large.

This is something which, ultimately, requires vision and purpose on a grand scale. Only holistic approaches which adopt a position from which to think in terms of the whole child, whole person, whole curriculum, whole school, whole society and whole world are likely to encompass the spiritual development of the individual. It was the hallmark of the 'great educators' – Froebel, Rousseau, Pestalozzi – and, to a lesser extent, their successors – John Holt, A. S. Neill – that they were not afraid to adopt such a stance. For most of us, such a task is too great, but we may make our modest contributions by trying not to lose sight of the 'big picture' while we focus upon one or other detail (Prentice). It is the poverty of so much of contemporary policy-making, constrained as it is by a preoccupation with 'efficiency', 'performance indicators', 'league tables' and the other trappings of the market mentality, that such thinking is stunted and actively discouraged.

Those who have written the articles which make up this book have made a valuable contribution to a much freer and much less blinkered consideration of the nature and purpose of holistic education. We should be grateful to them all.

REFERENCES

Best, R. and Ribbins, P. (1983) Rethinking the pastoral-academic split. *Pastoral Care in Education*, **1** (1).

DES (1989) *The Education Reform Act 1988: The School Curriculum and Assessment*. London: HMSO.

Heron, J. (1992) *Feeling and Personhood: Psychology in Another Key*. London: Sage.

Lewis, C. S. (1988) *Letters*. London: Fount/HarperCollins.

Winter, R. (1982) 'Dilemma analysis': a contribution to methodology for action research. *Cambridge Journal of Education*, **12** (3).

Name index

Subject index